From the Mind
and Heart of
Phil Campagnoli

ALSO BY ANTHONY SHADID

Legacy of the Prophet

NIGHT DRAWS NEAR

NIGHT

IRAQ'S PEOPLE IN THE

DRAWS

SHADOW OF AMERICA'S WAR

NEAR

ANTHONY SHADID

HENRY HOLT AND COMPANY ■ NEW YORK

Henry Holt and Company, LLC
Publishers since 1866
175 Fifth Avenue
New York, New York 10010
www.henryholt.com

Henry Holt® and ® are registered trademarks of
Henry Holt and Company, LLC.

Distributed in Canada by H. B. Fenn and Company Ltd.

Library of Congress Cataloging-in-Publication Data
Shadid, Anthony.
    Night draws near : Iraq's people in the shadow of America's war /
Anthony Shadid. — 1st ed.
            p.   cm.
    Includes bibliographical references and index.
    ISBN-13: 978-0-8050-7602-8
    ISBN-10: 0-8050-7602-6
    1. Iraq War, 2003 — Press coverage — United States.   I. Title.
    DS79.76.S52   2005
    956.7044'31 — dc22   2005040348

Henry Holt books are available for special promotions and
premiums. For details contact: Director, Special Markets.

First Edition 2005

Designed by Kelly S. Too

Printed in the United States of America
10 9 8 7 6 5 4 3

To Greg and Laila, Memories and Hopes

And this illustrious city, although she still remains the capital of the Abbasid Caliphate, and center of allegiance to the imams of Quraish, yet her outward lineaments have departed and nothing remains of her but the name. By comparison with her former state, before the assault of misfortunes upon her and the fixing of the eyes of calamities in her direction, she is as the vanishing trace of an encampment or the image of the departing dream-visitant. There is no beauty in her that arrests the eye, or summons the busy passer-by to forget his business and to gaze — except the Tigris.

—IBN JUBAYR,

TWELFTH-CENTURY ARAB TRAVELER

CONTENTS

Author's Note   xiii

Prologue   1

I. BEFORE

1. The City of Peace   13

2. Tabaghdada   33

II. THE AMERICAN INVASION

3. What's Written on Your Forehead   51

4. Like a Flower   73

5. A Dark, Dark Tunnel   83

6. A Daughter's Diary   97

7. For You, Iraq   110

III. AFTERMATH

8. Dry Bread with Tea   129

9. The Blood of Sadr   156

IV. THE OCCUPATION

10. A Very, Very, Very, Very, Bad Neighborhood   197

11. The Mud Gets Wetter   219

12. If You Want a Gazelle, Take a Rabbit   245

V. THE INSURGENCY

13. A Bad Muslim 279

14. Baghdad Is Your City 316

15. Oil and Punks 332

16. Myths of Resistance 350

Epilogue 391

Selected Bibliography 399

Acknowledgments 403

Index 407

AUTHOR'S NOTE

Journalism is imperfect. The more we know as reporters, the more complicated the story becomes and, by the nature of our profession, the less equipped we are to write about it with the justice and rigor it deserves. *Night Draws Near* is no exception. This book's account of the years I was in Iraq as a reporter are a first glance at those sweeping events. Some parts of the account may suffer from a lack of perspective and distance, and the years ahead may prove some interpretations wrong. I can make no claim to being comprehensive, either. Crucial parts of those years—the debates among American officials, the experience of the Kurds in northern Iraq, and the encounters of the U.S. military in Baghdad and elsewhere—are dealt with only cursorily.

Night Draws Near relies overwhelmingly on the reporting that I conducted during my visits to Iraq. The first was in November and December 1998, when I traveled there as a reporter for the Associated Press. I returned to Baghdad in October 2002 with the *Boston Globe*. My longest stint was with the *Washington Post*, which sent me to Iraq in March 2003, weeks before U.S. troops invaded the country. I stayed through the war and its aftermath before leaving in June 2004 to write this book.

At times in the book, particularly in the later chapters, I have borrowed from reporting by my outstanding colleagues at the *Post*, namely Ariana Eun-jung Cha, Rajiv Chandrasekaran, Thomas E. Ricks, and Karl Vick. Through-out, I have relied on the assistance and insights of the Iraqi staff at the Baghdad bureau, particularly Khaled Al-Saffar, Omar Fekeiki, Naseer Nouri, Bassam Sebti, and, of course, Nasir Mehdawi.

In the book's first section, the historical passages rely on accounts men-tioned in the bibliography. Of particular use was Richard Coke's *Baghdad: The City of Peace.* In the book's last two sections, I drew liberally from the statements, leaflets, and posters that proliferated in the wake of Saddam Hus-sein's fall. For biographical information on Grand Ayatollah Ali Sistani, I am indebted to the material provided by the Imam Ali Foundation in London. During much of my time, the office of Muqtada Sadr was generous in pro-viding access to its followers as well as background on the workings of the seminary in Najaf. Those interviews were also essential in reconstructing the life of the elder Sadr.

Throughout the book, especially for discussions of religion, I have relied on earlier years of reporting in the Middle East, particularly Egypt, Lebanon, Palestine, Iran, and Turkey. Some passages of *Night Draws Near* draw on my earlier book, *Legacy of the Prophet*, which explored the intersection of politi-cal Islam and democracy.

Finally, a note on Arabic. As I mentioned in *Legacy of the Prophet*, translit-erating Arabic into English is typically a messy business. This book does noth-ing to make it less so. In most cases, I have spelled names as they were given to me by the person interviewed or as they appear in common usage. It is the style of the *Post* to drop articles from proper names; for the sake of clarity, I have often followed that usage. In translating from Arabic, I have tried to stay as faithful as I can to the original words, while still conveying the meaning in a way understandable to a reader of English.

NIGHT DRAWS NEAR

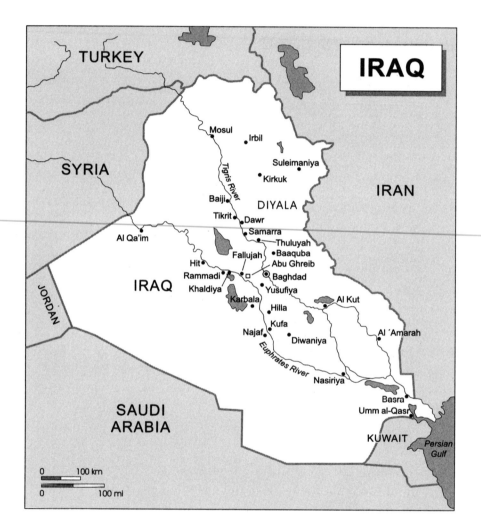

IRAQ

TURKEY

SYRIA

IRAN

Mosul
• Irbil
Suleimaniya
• Kirkuk
Baiji
Tigris River
DIYALA
Tikrit
Dawr
Samarra
Al Qa'im
Thuluyah
Fallujah
Baaquba
Hit
Abu Ghreib
Rammadi
Baghdad
IRAQ
Khaldiya
Yusufiya
JORDAN
Karbala
Al Kut
Hilla
Kufa
Najaf
Al 'Amarah
Diwaniya

Euphrates River

Nasiriya

Basra
Umm al-Qasr

SAUDI
ARABIA

KUWAIT

Persian
Gulf

0   100 km

0   100 mi

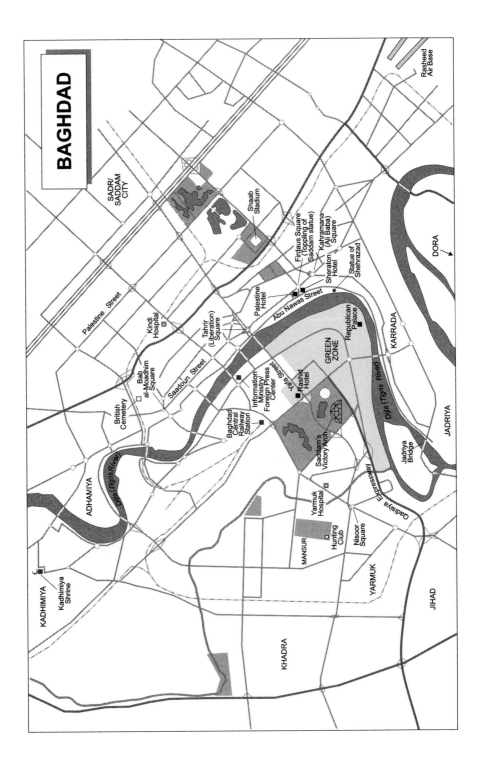

BAGHDAD

SADR/
SADDAM
CITY

Shaab
Stadium

Firdaus Square
(Toppling of
Saddam Statue)

Kahramana
(Ali Baba)
Square

Sheraton
Hotel

Statue of
Shehrazad

Palestine
Hotel

Abu Nawas Street

Republican
Palace

GREEN
ZONE

KARRADA

DORA

Palestine Street

Kindi
Hospital

Tahrir
(Liberation)
Square

Rashid
Hotel

14th Street

Dijla (Tigris River)

JADRIYA

British
Cemetery

Bab
al-Moadhim
Square

Saadoun Street

Information
Ministry/
Foreign Press
Center

Jadriya
Bridge

Baghdad
Central
Railway
Station

Saddam's
Victory Arch

Yarmuk
Hospital

Qadisiya Expressway

Dijla (Tigris River)

ADHAMIYA

MANSUR

Hunting
Club

Nisoor
Square

YARMUK

KADHIMIYA

Kadhimiya
Shrine

KHADRA

JIHAD

Rasheed
Air Base

PROLOGUE

In the United States during the autumn of 2002, the drums of war were thunderous. The long-anticipated invasion of Iraq seemed imminent. The Arab world was outraged, seething with a sense of injustice and frustrated by its leaders' inability to prevent more bloodshed. In Baghdad, Saddam Hussein's government, fearing the consequences of the coming attack, tried vainly to rally the country's grim, long-disillusioned citizens for yet another confrontation. The amnesty decree, issued on the afternoon of October 20, 2002, was the most spectacular and unexpected of these attempts.

The communiqué was brief: in a handful of words, it declared a "full, complete and final" amnesty for Iraq's tens of thousands—perhaps hundreds of thousands—of prison inmates, many of whom were innocent victims of Saddam's cruelty. The decree was read on radio and television; hour after hour, the bulletin was repeated and across the nation listeners were shocked, even astonished, by its contents. The voice that delivered the news, emotionless and monotone, belonged to Information Minister Mohammed Saeed al-Sahhaf, but the words, utterly unanticipated, had come from Saddam Hussein himself. In a country shaped by his brutality and caprice, disfigured by dictatorship and decades of war, his was the only voice that mattered.

I had come to Iraq to witness the latest referendum on Saddam's rule, a meaningless charade perpetuated by his government every seven years. Even by the Middle East's ludicrous standards of balloting, this election was a particularly memorable farce. According to official results announced soon after, every eligible Iraqi participated, and every single one had voted for Saddam.

The amnesty was framed as an official gesture of thanks for the unanimity of this referendum, a self-proclaimed act of generosity by Saddam. From pickpockets and smugglers to long-persecuted political prisoners and murderers, nearly all the country's incarcerated were released. In a surreal moment that confirmed his bizarre unpredictability, Saddam had transformed his constellation of slaughterhouses, bestowing a strange and dangerous freedom.

In the cathartic scenes that followed—moments unparalleled in Iraq's history, perhaps in any history—the hidden complexity of a country we had known only by its surface played out before us. The powerful forces we saw fermenting beneath the veneer of absolutism would reappear, five months later, during the aftermath of the American invasion and Saddam's fall.

Prisons emptied in hours, forshadowing the later turmoil and madness unleashed in the country by the war. As always in Iraq, the array of sentiments was overwhelming, sometimes conflicting—suffering, and relief; freedom, and regret; liberation, and shame over what had been allowed to occur.

Within an hour of the decree, as word feverishly raced along the country's well-trodden paths of rumors and whispers, thousands and thousands had arrived by car, foot, and truck at Abu Ghreib, Iraq's largest prison, which sprawls over a parched, low-lying stretch of scrubland near the Euphrates River. The approach of the many who gathered here and at other facilities was, in itself, an act of liberation, a march on the very walls of fear that Saddam had built for decades.

Previously viewed by few beyond guards and inmates, the notorious Abu Ghreib was the worst of Saddam's hellholes, a place whose very name spoke to the horrors of his ubiquitous terror (and, later, to America's own capricious abuse of power). Abu Ghreib was more than a symbol. It was fear made manifest; during the years of Saddam's reign, no story to come from its cells was too far-fetched. Prisoners were barbecued alive. Some dangled from meat hooks; some were strapped to ceiling fans. Some were forced to pull out the whiskers of each other's beards. Inmates' corpses were left to rot in a summer sun. It didn't matter whether these stories were true. They were believed, passed around the country with a devotion that bordered on religious submission.

But after the decree, fear, for a moment, subsided. Crowds looking for family members or old friends surged past the straggling eucalyptus and palm trees toward the prison's towering cinder-block walls. They overwhelmed the beleaguered guards, then stampeded through hulking iron gate after hulking iron gate into the prison courtyard, a dusty expanse bordered by a forty-foot-long wall, two stories high, of fetid garbage. A scalding sun, its heat putrefying, deepened the stench.

"They live here. Like rats," Asad Zaidan, a thirty-two-year-old doctor, said as he waited for his father, who he said had been jailed for twelve years for importing unauthorized medical equipment. He pointed to the trash and grimaced at the odor.

"Do you see my tears?" Dr. Zaidan asked.

I fumbled for a response, then resorted to questions to bridge an awkward moment. My presence—I was, of course, a foreigner, a journalist, someone not to be trusted—made others around the doctor uncomfortable. One cousin, his jaw clenched, whispered to him, "Say you are very thankful for Saddam Hussein." But Dr. Zaidan, a tall, fair-haired man, still young but carrying himself with the dignity of age, would have none of it. "I thought I might die before I saw this moment," he told me.

We followed the crowds forcing their way through each gate, deeper and deeper inside the prison. Heading the other way were newly freed prisoners. After the amnesty was announced, Iraqi officials at the prison, as bewildered as we were, had told us that five hundred inmates would be released every hour. But as word of freedom spread, a stampede erupted inside the cell-block walls, and the prisoners surged out. So violent was the crush that some were trampled to death at the very moment of their liberation.

Those who emerged alive before us wept, danced, or staggered, literally, into the unfamiliar world. Some carted out televisions, mattresses, and blankets. Others dragged iron trunks along the pavement. They hurried as fast as they could. These were unpredictable times, and to everyone, the event felt more like a prison break than a planned release. In waiting buses, prisoners blew kisses and threw their hands upward in gestures to heaven. I remember the words of one especially jubilant inmate. "Sheer joy. That's all I feel. Sheer joy," said Mohammed Kadhim Aboud, a forty-five-year-old father of three who had been jailed a year for stealing. "I'll join my family. I'll see my kids. I'll talk all night." He smiled, then added, "When the party finishes, I'll sleep."

Before us, other prisoners performed as they thought necessary: "With our spirit, with our blood, we will sacrifice for you, Saddam," some cried as they thanked God and the dictator in the same breath. "Yes, yes, to the leader, Saddam," shouted others.

Yet the silence of many—Dr. Zaidan among them—was far more eloquent. As we stood together, the doctor did little to acknowledge my presence. When he did, it was usually a nod. "What do you expect me to say?" his expression appeared to suggest. The people could not talk freely, so why the charade of questions, he seemed to inquire. At one moment, though, the calculus of sanctioned and unsanctioned speech finally collapsed in the chaos of the day, and the soft-spoken doctor was overwhelmed. His anger welled up. "You see what we suffer," he blurted out, clenching his jaw against the torrent.

Volleys of celebratory gunfire echoed through the din of celebration, with young men playing drums, blowing trumpets, and waving their shirts underneath the ubiquitous portraits of Saddam. Impromptu markets grew up, as they do wherever crowds gather. "A hundred dinars!" vendors shouted. Below them in soiled Styrofoam coolers were green, orange, pink, and yellow ice pops, creating parasols of color, ever more vivid against the black gowns of elderly Shiite Muslim women swaying to the frenetic beat of drums. Shared taxis shouted out their destinations. "Karbala! Najaf! Hilla!"—cities battered by Saddam's repression, in war-scarred southern Iraq, scenes of perpetual discontent and occasional unrest.

As night fell, traffic was jammed for miles along the main road. And then, no less quickly, jubilation turned to grief, and grief turned to anguish. Fathers, mothers, brothers, sisters, and cousins searched in vain in the darkness for relatives they had expected to be among the freed. They called out names, but often the entreaties were futile. Many of the missing were, despite the families' desperate hope, long dead. Some searchers held handwritten signs in the streaming headlights of cars. There were moments of recognition, the names legible in the random flashes of light, the sloping cursive of desperate Arabic momentarily decipherable. But then the names would fade back into the enveloping dark, returning to anonymity and the long curse of the dictator's wrath. As I left Abu Ghreib that night, hitching a ride to Baghdad, so many names passed before the windshield of the car in which I traveled that I soon lost count.

In Iraq, only Saddam could bring down what he had built with a few lines of text read on radio and television. But as the events at Abu Ghreib unfolded, it became clear that Saddam's diktat had given rise to an element of subversion; for the first time, people were standing up, demanding to know what had happened to their unaccounted-for sons, husbands, and family members. The combustible ambiguities of Iraq—the ancient pride, the desire for justice, the resilience—were emerging from beneath the fear, conformity, and silence after so many years.

Two days after the jail release, more surprising rebellion burst forth in a crowded parking lot outside the drab Information Ministry, along one of Baghdad's busiest streets.

"I don't know where he is," one elderly woman wailed to me, her hands flailing. "I don't know whether he is alive, I don't know whether he is dead."

I never learned her name, or whom she had lost. Nor did I see her again. But dressed in her black *abaya*, her mere presence here endangering her life, she revealed the depth of anger lurking beneath what had for so long been controlled. How many Iraqis bore such emotions behind their careful countenances? I wondered.

Dozens of protesters—women in black, young men in street clothes—gathered at the ministry's bunkerlike building near the Tigris, demanding to know why their relatives had not been among those freed on the day of liberation. It was a show of strength. It was a demand for accountability. Some of their relatives might have been among those whose names I had seen written on placards outside Abu Ghreib; most, if not all, had probably been executed.

The protesters had used the cover of a pro-Saddam rally to approach the building. They held up a banner declaring, "Yes, yes to the leader Saddam Hussein." Others chanted, "With our soul, with our blood, we sacrifice for you, Saddam." But then, in whispers whose volume escalated over minutes, they insisted on information about their missing relatives. The women approached journalists, begging them to help. In anguish, they repeated, "We don't know where they are. We don't know." Some of the women volunteered the names of their relatives, their ages, and when they last saw them—great acts of courage in Saddam's Iraq.

Secret police, some armed, fanned through the masses to disperse the people. After a handful of men and women forced their way into the Foreign Press Center, shots were fired into the air, scattering the protesters.

But two hours later, the determined people returned. Their usual fear had been shattered by the circumstances. For the first time in years, words were spoken in public that rang with truth. One man pleaded to an official that he had not seen his brother since 1980. The official replied that the delay was just "procedures," that he would still be set free. "No, everybody is gone," the man answered, shaking his head defiantly. "It's *not* procedures, there are no more procedures. We want information." The dam had broken.

In time, the crowd broke up. I walked down the street, trying to catch up with two women. The conversation was brief, as I expected it would be, and I was afraid of attracting attention, so I didn't take notes. Speaking hurriedly, one woman told me that her son had been arrested two years previous, the other woman's son in 1991, the time of the Gulf War. "We've looked around," one of the women said to me, as I scanned the street. "But he's nowhere." Moments later, a red sedan pulled up at the corner. The driver shouted, "Get in! Get in!" And they were gone. I lingered at the curb, scared and excited. This was something none of the journalists in Iraq had seen before. What was playing out in Baghdad's streets was political, moving, and filled with an unpredictability that was both menacing and exhilarating.

That same night, I saw my friend Wamidh Nadhme, a political science professor who was one of the few those days in Baghdad who dared to speak his mind. Like many in the anxious and confused city, he was stunned by the open public outcry. Often, Wamidh had mentioned, as did others in the city, particularly those from an earlier generation, that Saddam's terror had succeeded in depoliticizing the country. Raised in a climate of intense partisanship, he saw this as one of the dictator's most far-reaching and destructive legacies.

But the day's events had defied that diagnosis: there was life underneath what Saddam had wrought. Wamidh was invigorated, full of pride. Saddam had not destroyed his citizens' spirit, their basic expectation of political fairness. Wamidh spoke of justice, honor, and courage, qualities that meant much to him and, historically, to all Iraqis. To him, they were elements of politics as well as of principle, and that day they had motivated Iraqis, or at least some of them, to reclaim some sense of power over their own fates.

"I was surprised, utterly taken by surprise," he said. "We have never heard of such a thing. The most you could do if you had a friend or relative in prison was to ask someone who had contact with security about him and about his arrest. But if you made a fuss, you might be persecuted. If you talked to foreigners, they could charge you with spying.

"I have never heard of it," he kept repeating, shaking his head at the idea of the women's protests. A veteran of interrogation, he could usually hide his emotions, but not on this day. He paused for a minute, as if calculating the cost of his words, but the day's events propelled him forward, a little recklessly. "Once people dare to speak their minds," he told me, "more people will be encouraged to show their different views."

WAMIDH HAD DESCRIBED WHAT LAY AHEAD FOR HIS COUNTRY AS IT BRACED FOR its turbulent passage from dictatorship to invasion to a tyrant's fall to an aftermath that no one was (or is) quite sure how to describe. The tumultous scene at Abu Ghreib and the rebellions in the wake of the amnesty decree foreshadowed that passage. They suggested a more nuanced vision of Iraq than had previously been available. The powerful emotions, along with the resilience and determination of the people, were revelatory. In the wake of what was, essentially, a bizarre propaganda exercise gone awry, we finally had a glimpse, fleeting as it was, of the country's complex reality that had, for so long, been hidden from our view. Soon enough, the people would surge forth again, taking their country in unforeseen directions.

Repression determined much of what happened in Iraq before the war. But the nearly absolute emphasis on the all-encompassing tyranny blinded many Americans to everything else that was there. Time and again, we envisioned, or were given, a simple, two-dimensional portrait of a country, waiting for aid and dreaming of freedom as it suffered under the unrelenting terror of a dictator. Iraq, we were told by our leaders in Washington and others, was trapped in a relationship of submission and victimization; its people were voiceless, deprived of the power to determine their own destiny. Once the dictator was removed, by force if need be, Iraq would be free, a tabula rasa on which to build a new and different state.

If we can change Iraq, George W. Bush and his determined lieutenants maintained, we can change the Arab world, so precariously adrift after decades of broken promises of progress and prosperity. This rhetoric—idealistic to Western ears, reminiscent of century-old colonialism to a Third World audience—envisioned the dawn of a democratic and just Middle East, guided by a benevolent United States. For the Americans, aroused by fears of terrorism, Baghdad, the capital of the Arab world's potentially most powerful state, was the obvious choice for a place to begin a wave of democratic reform. This rationale for invasion ran at least as deep as the illusory warnings about weapons of mass destruction or the rhetoric emphasizing the tyranny of Saddam. Iraq was an instrument of change for the United States, a lever to pull, the first Middle Eastern domino to fall.

But on the day of the amnesty at Abu Ghreib, I got a glimpse of tensions entrenched over decades, even centuries, by deep-seated grievances and the narrative of a complicated history. At that point, I started to realize how little any of us—journalists, policy makers, citizens—really understood about Iraq. Proud but humbled, rebellious but humiliated, the country was never simply a black-and-white photograph of dictatorship and repression. It was a time-worn sculpture, born of a distant past and weathered by more recent, wrenching events. And its people were more than victims.

To start to understand Iraq one must the consider the legacy of Baghdad's medieval glory—a burst of brilliance followed by a long autumn of decline—along with the nation's wounds inflicted in more modern times: the war with Iran from 1980 to 1988, one of history's most savage conflicts; the decadelong period of international sanctions imposed after Iraq invaded Kuwait in 1990; Saddam's brutal rule. When the United States arrived, its soldiers, diplomats, and aid workers marched into an antique land built on layer upon layer of history, a terrain littered with wars, marked by scars, seething with grievances and ambitions. Willingly or not, they added their own chapter to this chronicle. The Americans came as liberators and became occupiers; but, most important, they served as a catalyst for consequences they never foresaw.

The U.S. experience in Iraq was a microcosm of America's broader struggle with the Arab world, a generational battle that has spun around axes of religion, culture, and identity, waged by two cultures so estranged that they cannot occupy the same place. Iraq was an unwilling participant, drafted into a fight that it did not solicit. The Americans brought a revolution without ambition and an upheaval without design. "Liberation" was the U.S. mantra, reiterated at every occasion. Iraqis hailed their new freedom, but quickly found themselves grappling with forces that had long remained subterranean. Even the Iraqis themselves did not always comprehend these phenomena— the revival of ancient religious rituals, repressed for decades but still resonant to many of the country's Shiite Muslim majority; the awakening of militant Islam, imported from other parts of the Arab world and tailored to fit the resistance to the Americans by a disenfranchised Sunni Muslim minority; the lurch toward civil war among Iraq's ethnicities and sects; and stubborn, resilient attempts to defy that fratricide through a surprising, and surprisingly durable, nationalism. Those consequences of the invasion would, as the months passed, shape the country that the United States had inherited. These surprising ramifications affected the lives of the Iraqi people in ways that were never anticipated. Despite the promise of the American occupation, the new dawn never really arrived. The fall of Saddam marked not a finale, but rather the beginning of an era that was neither war nor peace. The period was a hiatus, a still indeterminate setting for those incomplete arcs of religious revival, resistance, and questions of identity.

The war and the occupation that followed, a turbulent passage of two long years, were the crucible for the birth of a different country.

THE MIDDLE EAST, A REGION BOUND BY LANGUAGE AND FRUSTRATION, HAS always meant a great deal to me, by reason of birth and by virtue of experience. My grandparents, known to me mostly through stories, immigrated from Lebanon, from an Orthodox Christian family in a town called Marjayun that was then part of Syria. I was born in Oklahoma, but most of my career has unfolded in the Arab world. In many ways, the Middle East is home; over time, I embraced my Arab roots and learned the language. To this day, in the simplest of ways, I enjoy life there. I am drawn by the civilized propriety of the Middle East. Call the tradition hospitality or respect, generosity or decency, but the small, easy-to-ignore gestures add texture and create familiarity. No one enters any room, anywhere in the Arab world, without being greeted. It never happens.

I always feel more Arab in America, more American in the Arab world. The hyphenated complexities of being Lebanese-American or Arab-American create a confusing feeling of being in between, a self-conscious awareness complicated further by our troubled times. I find it almost impossible to bring coherence to the contradictions of my own heritage, an identity far less complicated and ambivalent than that of most Iraqis.

Iraq is variegated, contradictory, endlessly confusing. Over the years its people have watched as others have sought to define them, creating images to be displayed beyond its borders. In the end, Iraq has always seemed to mock these efforts. Our televisable notions never captured the haunting, ambivalent, and bitter complexity of even one conversation, during war or in its shadow.

There is a word in Arabic that I have heard uttered over and over in the city: *ghamidh*, meaning "mysterious" or "ambiguous." If Baghdad's soul is loss, its mood always seemed to be *ghamidh*. Through that word, I began, at first in a woefully superficial way, to understand the panorama of attitudes that is Baghdad. Communicating that shifting truth has been a challenge. The best journalism embraces nuance and celebrates it. War, however, leaves little room for subtleties. How does a journalist convey the ferocity of violence without losing meaning in a mind-numbing array of adjectives? How does one cover war from a professional distance when, as someone reporting from a city under siege, one has no distance? Perhaps we simply surrender to the ambiguities and embrace what is *ghamidh*. Perhaps we simply tell stories.

PART ONE

BEFORE

1

THE CITY OF PEACE

Baghdad is a city of lives interrupted, its history a story of loss, waiting, and resilience. In the days before the American invasion in March 2003, this capital scarred by war after war felt torn, aggrieved, and filled with longing for the greatness it once possessed and has never forgotten.

As we drove beneath a cloudless sky, the familiar voice of Abdel-Halim Hafez, one of Egypt's legendary singers, rose from the car's tinny speakers. Karim, my driver and friend, maneuvered his white Chevrolet along the avenues, as the city wavered between the anxious wait for American bombs and the fear of what Saddam would do to defend himself once they arrived. Knots of Baath Party militiamen manned sandbag emplacements, their nervous eyes shadowed by their berets or camouflage helmets or kaffiyehs of checkered reds and blacks. They stood in relief against the barricaded dun-colored utilitarian buildings constructed during the three decades of Saddam's rule. Nearby, the Tigris River meandered, its muddy waters encircling overgrown reeds that had never grown so high in gracious times. Along its banks were mosques with their hourglass domes of turquoise and gold, bricks in shades of blue, tiles with calligraphic contours of black and white. The colors of the city were softened by the afternoon sun into the hues of an antique Persian carpet.

Through the car window, we could hear the call to prayer dividing the day, embracing the summons from other minarets and soothing the neighborhoods. Staccato bursts of horns—the refrain of Arab cities—enlivened subdued streets, accompanied by the clatter of battered wooden carts pulled by weary horses, two men atop each. Behind them were loads of *anabib*, the kerosene cylinders used in the stoves of Baghdadi kitchens. Some were blue, some yellow, some rusted into a monochromatic brown. The drivers banged screwdrivers on the cylinders to announce their arrival, as they have done for decades. Karim and I were headed for the Hawar Art Gallery, but on the way we meandered a bit.

I wanted to take a last, long look at Baghdad before the bombing began. We drove down colonnaded Rashid Street, a once grand boulevard named for the capital's most illustrious ruler. It was now collapsed, colored in the grays of poverty, its arches sagging and its shutters hanging at the slack angles of neglect. We passed a bust of Baghdad's founder, Abu Jaafar al-Mansur, in a dreary square of the neighborhood that takes his name. Its pedestal of tan brick was crumbled, its blue tiles fallen amid the plastic bags and cigarettes that littered the circle. The founder's eyes glowered beneath his turban, staring out over a jumble of garages, a gas station, shops, and cars with cracked windshields.

Haggard already, the capital was immersed in uncertainty, awaiting another battle. Iraq had been waging wars for a generation, usually at Saddam's instigation. There was shame, in many quarters, over what had been done to Kuwait and Iran in Saddam's name. Iraq felt weary as the Americans prepared to invade; all the fighting over all the years had taken away much of the nation's generosity and dignity and left brutality.

I had returned to Baghdad on March 11, 2003, five months after the opening of Abu Ghreib and just days before the bombing began. My previous itinerary had carried me through the bleak, post–9/11 Middle East. The American response to the destruction of that day—the martial rhetoric of the Bush administration, the dispatch of the U.S. military to Afghanistan, and the detention of prisoners at the military base in Guantánamo Bay—had evoked Arab anger as the lopsided conflict between Israel and the Palestinians accelerated further. Anyone who defied the Americans was admired. Osama bin

Laden, whose venomous ideology actually alienates the vast majority of Arabs, had become an unlikely folk hero.

In Jordan and in Egypt, emotions were heating up, but Arab leaders had already thrown in the diplomatic towel. "To say that we can put off the war would be fooling ourselves," said Hosni Mubarak, the president of Egypt, a figure who then seemed as modest in ambition as his predecessors were larger than life. As he and his fellow leaders capitulated, their people grew angrier. At protests across the Middle East, nervously tolerated by the governments, chants denounced "American terrorism" in the same breath as "Israeli aggression." At some demonstrations, Iraqi flags went up with Palestinian flags, as the two battlegrounds became conflated in Arab eyes. I remember the chants. "Wake up, Arabs, save your Palestinian and Iraqi brothers!" Or, more to the point, "There is no god but God and America is the enemy of God!" And then, an appeal that was at once clichéd and resonant, earnest and hollow: *"Biruh, bidam, nafdeek, ya Baghdad,"* marchers chanted outside Cairo University. "With our soul, with our blood, we sacrifice for you, Baghdad."

Time and again, I am struck by how seldom I hear the word *hurriya,* "freedom," in conversations about politics in the Arab world. It does appear, but often in translations or in self-conscious comparisons to the West, where the word is omnipresent. Much more common among Arabs is the word *adil,* "justice," a concept that frames attitudes from Israel to Iraq. For those who feel they are always on the losing end, the idea of justice may assume supreme importance.

And justice, it seemed to many in the Middle East, was no longer being served by the Americans; this feeling was becoming more and more enflamed, even in places where U.S. citizens had once been welcomed. Well-to-do Jordanians spurned invitations to dinners attended by Americans. Cairo taxi drivers occasionally declined to pick up foreigners in expatriate enclaves. Americans would still be greeted when they entered a room, but they were no longer always offered the almost requisite coffee or tea. Among Egypt's wealthier residents—a group long disposed favorably toward America— there was a resurgence of piety that some saw as a repudiation of the West and a visceral reclamation of Arab identity. Devotion had become a statement as political as it was religious.

And then there was Shaaban Abdel-Rahim, a former laundryman and part-time wedding singer in Egypt catapulted to fame all around the region in 2001 by his song "I Hate Israel." Now he came out with another manifesto, "The Attack on Iraq," a blend of anger, fear, and humor, wrapped up in the staccato vernacular of Cairo's streets. It became an overnight pop sensation in Egypt, Lebanon, Jordan, and elsewhere. Hour after hour it played. Bootleg tapes poured into the market. The hit blared from taxis careening through downtown streets. Lines were quoted from memory.

Enough!
Chechnya! Afghanistan! Palestine! Southern Lebanon! The Golan Heights!
And now Iraq, too? And now Iraq, too?
It's too much for people! Shame on you!
Enough! Enough! Enough!

Against the cacophony of the Arab world, Baghdad seemed quiet, so hushed that it felt a little unreal. As America framed the war one way, the Arab world another, Iraq simply seemed to be trying to come to grips with its arrival.

There were hints of preparations, but the sense of crisis seemed strangely routine. Checkpoints set up on the modern, German-engineered highways were manned by torpid soldiers. Long lines formed outside some bakeries and gas stations. For the most part, though, the city went about its business as usual. Workers methodically splashed cement on brick, building a long-planned addition to the Information Ministry. A worker wielded a buffer, slowly shining the granite highlights of the ministry's walls and windows. There was little anger; most fervency was manufactured, the tired climax of farcical, government-organized protests. Few were sincere in their defense of Saddam, who was loathed. Few objected to his demise; many hoped for it. But the feeling most prevalent was subdued anxiety. People were preparing—for war, so unpredictable, and for what they anticipated would be a long and bloody aftermath.

LATE IN THE AFTERNOON I ARRIVED AT THE HAWAR ART GALLERY, A BUCOLIC outpost of whitewashed stucco walls and a gate painted in a Mediterranean blue along a quiet street shaded by trees. A cool, gentle breeze blew off the Tigris River nearby, drifting over the stone patio as the artists gathered here paused to appreciate the fleeting tranquillity. Maher Samarai, speaking with the exuberance of a performer and the reflectiveness of an artist, pondered Baghdad on the eve of its reckoning. He was an Iraqi, he said; the city was his capital. He was a resident, he continued; it was his soul. He was a ceramicist; it was the inspiration of his work. And then, suddenly, the gravity of the situation hit him, and his confident smile faded. As his city stood on the verge of war, he stared out at a towering palm tree that leaned over the gallery, waiting in silence before he could continue.

"For a week, I can't sleep. Really," Maher confessed, finally speaking again as he methodically thumbed his string of blue worry beads. "I worry about the bridges, the homes, the beautiful buildings, our artistic scene that we built after 1991 that is going to be smashed. A lot of artists have left for cities outside Baghdad, and there is no guarantee we will gather again." His friends nodded in agreement, and Maher stopped once more, savoring the fleeting moment of nostalgia. "Our art is like a white dove, and the B-52s are about to come to make it black," he said. "I hate the color black."

I mentioned a line from George W. Bush's speech a day earlier; on March 17, 2003, the president had declared to Iraqis: "The day of your liberation is near." Maher, sipping sweet lemon tea, smirked again. He was garrulous, fifty years old, a father of three, his hair gray but still lush. His mustache was trimmed, carefully. "They're going to burn the forest to kill the fox," he said smiling. "That's my idea."

There's a line from history that nearly everyone in Baghdad remembers: "Our armies do not come into your cities and lands as conquerors or enemies, but as liberators." The speaker was Major General Sir Stanley Maude, the British commander who in 1917 entered the capital to end Ottoman rule. (He died in Iraq eight months later of cholera and was buried in Baghdad.) Although Iraqis tend to forget his name and often reduce his remark to a simpler phrase—"We came as liberators, not as conquerors"—the idea has proved memorable. So has the aftermath, a legacy that Iraqis ruefully note. The British remained in Iraq and in control of its oil for decades. "Exactly the same sentence," Maher said to me, his voice rising as he compared Maude's words to Bush's. "It's a flashback to when Iraqis were still without shoes, without clothes, and the oil went directly to other people's pockets. You can't trust the Westerners."

As the afternoon wore on, cigarettes burning idly and dark tea sweetened amply, the bravado became apparent that is so much a part of Iraqi national character. There was talk of the surging Tigris and its ferocity. For Egypt, with its reputation for humor and revelry, the Nile was its good fortune. The river brought life when the waters surged over the banks, leaving millennia of rich silt that enabled people to impose a verdant farmland on the desert. The Tigris—reckless, unpredictable, and given to temper—destroyed when it flooded. It left hard personalities in its wake, they told me, and it delivered Iraqis their well-deserved reputation for toughness.

Yet beneath the artists' moments of swagger was fear for Baghdad's fate— fear of the destruction of an American-led attack, of the lawlessness and looting that almost everyone expected, of the destiny of the capital. A friend of Maher's, a woman artist sitting nearby, set down a clip for an AK-47 rifle on the table in front of him, then left the gallery without saying a word. "I borrowed the gun from a friend of mine," he said, in answer to his friends' stares. "I worry about thieves. I just bought a new car and a new computer and they're expensive. If I have to fight for my house, I will."

As the hours passed, the painters, sculptors, and ceramists at the gallery indulged in *hanin*—nostalgia—as they gazed out at the city's concrete overpasses and martial boulevards, past Saddam City, the teeming Shiite Muslim slum. They spoke of the past, invoking the names of history, the names of memory: the caliph Haroun al-Rashid, the poet Mutanabi, and the tenth-century philosopher al-Hallaj, whose ecstatic utterances of divine love were not always well received. ("I am the truth," al-Hallaj once said, a pledge to God read as blasphemy that got him dismembered and his body burned.) Baghdad, to the artists on the eve of war, retained the greatness of those names. It still rivaled Damascus and Cairo, as it had when it was truly the seat of the Arab world.

ROME CAN STILL SEE ITS PAST, THE MAGNIFICENCE OF ITS ANCIENT EMPIRE gracing the modern cityscape. Paris and London, storied cities reinventing themselves as they age across centuries, live in their histories, which surround them. Baghdad, its ancient grandeur utterly destroyed, cannot see its past, its glory. It can only remember. Baghdad's is a culture of memory; the city draws strength and pride from the myths to which it continually returns. But the curse of recalling is the reminder of what has been lost.

All cities are shrouded in legend, some fabulous, others more pedestrian. The tales of the founding of Baghdad in the eighth century revolve around the conqueror Abu Jaafar Mansur, second caliph of the Abbasid Empire. The Christian monks who served him lunch at their monastery not far from the future Baghdad told him of a prophecy that a great city would be founded nearby by someone with the name Miqlas. "By God, I am that man!" one historian quoted Mansur as shouting. The caliph insisted that he, as a boy, had been nicknamed Miqlas.

After spending the "sweetest, most gentle night on earth" at the site, he awoke to see its perfection. Here, the Tigris River watered lush fields, and canals stitched the rich countryside. Along with the nearby Euphrates, the Tigris promised revenues for Mansur's empire, which already stretched from North Africa to Central Asia. In 762, Mansur himself laid the first bricks for his capital, inaugurating a project that took four more years to complete, a truly imperial undertaking. Craftsmen, architects, and laborers were drafted from across the empire; 100,000 were always on hand.

Towns in Iraq were stripped of material. From famous ruins in ancient Babylon and the Persian city of Ctesiphon came quotas of bricks. Wasit, to the south, surrendered five wrought-iron gates that, according to tradition, were built by demons under the sway of King Solomon. Kufa gave another gate, as did the city's imperial predecessor, Damascus. They would all adorn the fabled Round City, a perfectly circular capital that served as Mansur's residence and the nexus of his Islamic empire. It was protected by brick walls, insulated by a deep moat, and fortified by an inner wall ninety feet high. Roads radiated from the four gates: the Khorasan Gate opened to the frontier of China, others to Mecca and its pilgrims, west to Damascus, and south to Basra.

Arising from the palace, known as the Golden Gate, was the fabled green dome, visible from the river to the city's outskirts. The figure of a warrior horseman stood atop it—a fitting symbol of an empire that came together and was preserved by Mansur's sword. Medinat al-Salam, Mansur called his capital. The City of Peace.

The founder lived for thirteen years here, passing away in 775 on the road

to Mecca. According to his orders, one hundred graves were to be dug to confuse his enemies. His death preceded his city's glory: Baghdad would soon
spread far beyond the shadow of Mansur's green dome, growing to ten times
the size of Constantinople, one of its few imperial peers. Based on the number of its bathhouses, some estimates claimed that 1.5 million people lived in
the city, with at least 2 million in its heyday. Another estimate, not altogether
sober, boasted of 96 million residents.

Perhaps the number was no more than 300,000, but no city in Europe could
claim a fraction of that population or match Baghdad's array of hospitals, places
of worship, museums, libraries, law schools, racetracks, zoos, public baths, or
asylums for the insane. In the words of one contemporary historian, "I have
seen the great cities . . . but I have never seen a city of greater height, more perfect circularity, more endowed with superior merits or possessions, more spacious gates . . . than Zawra, that is to say the city of Abu Jaafar al-Mansur." To
him, the city was faultless: "It is as though it is poured into a mold and cast."

Not a trace of Mansur's original city remains; of medieval Baghdad, there
is a crumbling minaret here, a collapsed wall on the old city's outskirts, but
no more. What makes the city's memory tangible is its reputation. Its cultural legacy was indisputably one of the great flowerings of human achieve-
ment in history. In the West, the names of the geniuses behind the city's
golden age mean little, but in Baghdad, in the Arab world, the names of those
times remain heroic, even fabled. Their mere mention evokes two centuries
of intellectual splendor, drenched in confidence. The ancients studied in
places like Bayt al-Hikma, the House of Wisdom, founded by al-Ma'mun, the
great-grandson of Baghdad's builder. Not a simple library, it was a true mar-
ketplace of ideas, a pristine place of scholarship whose translators of Plato,
Aristotle, Hippocrates, Galen, Euclid, and Ptolemy created an intellectual
heritage that was not Islamic but universal. That it was written in Arabic was
incidental. As one modern historian put it, "Baghdad became the intellectual
battlefield upon which Roman law, Greek medicine and philosophy, Indian
mysticism, Persian subtlety and the Semitic genius for religion could meet on
common ground."

In Baghdad, *hanin* crosses eras. There's the *hanin* of history, and there's the
hanin of memory. In the narratives of *hanin* of memory now familiar in Bagh-

dad, the 1970s rival the era of the Abbasids as a time to recall with longing. Five-star hotels had begun to open, and restaurants did brisk business in a city that celebrated its libertine nightlife. Baghdad, in the eyes of many of its residents, was no different from any other Oz-like capital on the Persian Gulf, endowed with limitless oil and springing brashly from the desert with little logic; only this Oz had far more history than most. The newly resurgent Baghdad, modern and vital, drew Arab writers fleeing the anarchy of Lebanon's civil war. Egyptian intellectuals still recall the free plane tickets and ample Johnnie Walker Black that awaited them on sponsored trips to the Iraqi capital. The ferment of those years gave rise to the saying that "Cairo writes, Beirut publishes, and Baghdad reads."

Viewed through the lens of the wars that followed, the 1970s in the city have taken on a somewhat illusory glow of heroic progress and material comfort. Yet the economic gains at the time were real, and Iraq's living conditions neared those in Europe's more modest countries. Income from oil—Iraq has the world's second-largest reserves—skyrocketed. In 1968, oil revenues totaled $476 million. By 1980, they had reached $26 billion. That newfound wealth radiated Iraqi culture, influence, and power across the region. Baghdad rippled with optimism and confidence, and the country prospered. Food was subsidized, wages were hiked, and land was redistributed.

Money poured into health, housing, and education. Massive campaigns were launched to eradicate illiteracy. Free education, from kindergarten to university, was bestowed by law. Women's rights—from equal pay to an at least formal ban on discrimination– were ratified in Iraq's legal code. While crushing economic and social disparities persisted—and political repression deepened, especially against Shiite religious activists—most see the 1970s as a comparative golden age.

I MET NAHAD SHUKUR AT HIS GUN SHOP IN THE WORKING-CLASS NEIGHBORHOOD of Bayaa, a few days before the American bombing began. He welcomed me with bravado, and with a crash, as he slammed down a plastic bag stuffed with rounds for a Kalashnikov rifle. He listed his inventory of bullets, pointing to a row of eight bags behind the counter and ticking off his stock. "When customers come, we're ready, whatever they want," he told me. "The way things are, we don't even have time to count. Business is a thousand times better than before!"

In the days before the bombing, Baghdad's residents emptied gun-store shelves of weapons, restocked on ammunition whose price went up fourfold, and brought for repairs everything from World War I–vintage rifles to the latest in double-barreled Czech shotguns. As inventory dwindled, shotguns sold at $100 to $1,200—this in a country where newly graduated doctors made $5 a month. Pistols were going for $50 and up, $700 for a Browning. Each bag of fifty Kalashnikov bullets at Nahad's store cost about $6. Hundreds of customers had come in the past few days. "Every day we get closer to war, we sell more," Nahad told me, as we shared a glass of sweet lemon tea. "It's nonstop all day. Families are buying guns like they are stockpiling food and water."

Nahad and his customers spoke darkly about the anarchy they believed inevitable. As it did for many in the city, the prospect of the chaos that would follow the war colored their fears about the American attack. Faith in their fellow Iraqis was scarce for those people who were blunt, as blunt as they could be in Saddam's Baghdad, about that: they saw days of bloodletting, score-settling, and lawlessness in the near future as their brutalized society came to grips with itself.

As we talked, Nahad became increasingly serious; he seemed to be trying to warn me of my own peril. Many in the city with the means to do it plotted their escape. "As for the rest, we're sleeping with our guns under our pillows," Nahad said, to concede something more sincere. "We won't fall asleep without them there." He saw my quizzical look and explained, "It's something we've inherited from the past."

IF BAGHDAD'S MEDIEVAL HISTORY HAUNTS THE CITY, ITS MODERN CONFLICTS have cursed it as vehemently, molding the country that the United States would find after the invasion. Saddam seized power in a bloody putsch in 1979, and three times during his reign, Iraq and its twenty-five million people found themselves in devastating conflicts, often as a result of their ruler's catastrophic blunders and miscalculations. None was more ruinous than the war with neighboring Iran, which began in 1980 and continued for eight bitter and devastating years. The country still suffers from those wounds. The conflict inflicted the horrors of modern combat—from World War I–style trench warfare to the casual deployment of chemical weapons—on an entire generation. When the fighting ground reluctantly to a halt in 1988, many in Baghdad, with only a hint of exaggeration, said the city they knew as children would never return. So began the curse so many in Baghdad suspect has befallen their city.

The country that American forces took over in 2003 was still reeling from the war's toll. In terms of carnage, the Iranian conflict was to Iraq what World War I was to Europe; in terms of spiritual trauma, it was Iraq's Vietnam. More than a million Iraqi men bore arms, and 600,000 others served in militias: that is, a tenth of Iraq's population became soldiers. So militarized, many of them were schooled in violence, which they would turn to again when trouble came their way.

Saddam called the Iranian war the Second Qadisiya, recalling the battle fought in A.D. 637, when outnumbered Arabs vanquished a far larger Persian force of the Sassanid Empire on the plains of Mesopotamia. The Arab victory made imminent the Persian Empire's fall, and the date marks one of the opening chapters in a conquest among the most sweeping in world history. Saddam's war fell far short.

It began as a gamble, reckless even by his standards. In a style that, along with his predilection for brutality, will serve as his epitaph, Saddam sent half his army across the Iranian border in September 1980. As always, the arithmetic was personal: Saddam felt threatened. He feared that tremors from Iran's religious upheaval in 1979 would threaten his government, which was awash in real and imaginary plots. He felt humiliated by concessions that, a few years earlier, Iran had forced upon him over a border dispute along a southern waterway. He felt like flexing his muscles; he got eight years of incessant war.

When it was all over, a quarter of a million Iraqis were dead (a good portion of them Iraqi Kurds killed by their own government, which viewed them as fifth columnists). Twice that number were wounded, and tens of thousands more were left captive in Iran, some remaining there a decade after the war. Beyond Saddam's own survival, none of his aims were achieved. The nine-hundred-mile border between the two countries remained the same. Iran's Islamic revolution, while twisted and exhausted, wound up further entrenched: plots, real and otherwise, were still being hatched against Saddam and his

Baath Party after the final battles. Iraq's economy was wrecked, and the country landed deep in debt, a situation that led to another war: the 1990 invasion of Kuwait.

For many Iraqis, the years of battle with Iran represent great suffering without a real purpose. People will often shrug when asked what it was about. More than a trillion dollars was spent. The modernization of the 1970s was undone. A generation was disfigured. Some consider those broken soldiers, even those who returned, a lost generation forfeited to Saddam's delusions.

When I hear someone speak of Iraq's lost generation, I often think back to a dank Baghdad workshop perched in a wasteland of grease, stagnant water, and carcasses of cars. The stench of gasoline had settled over everything like a mist. Hammers banged on steel to their own cadence, and saws squealed through metal. Kadhim Fadhil, his gestures feeble, spoke timidly, as Iraqis usually did to foreigners during the reign of Saddam. He rarely raised his eyes to mine, and this seemed more dreary than impolite. "I think life for me is like a cigarette," he said. "It has burned away."

It was November 1998, and the setting was Baghdad's Victorious Garage in the poor neighborhood of Sleikh. A former prisoner of war, forgotten during most of the 1990s, Kadhim had been freed by Iran only months before, as part of a prisoner exchange that sent 5,584 Iraqis home. Despite his so-called freedom, his life was shattered.

He sat wearily near a pile of blackened rags, empty oil cans, and cigarette cartons. For sixteen years, from 1982 to 1998, he had withered away in a prison camp, growing accustomed to dead cockroaches in his rice, occasional beatings, and, in moments of grace, apples or oranges that usually arrived once a year during Ramadan. As the seasons elapsed and his life passed, he waited. In winter, the concrete walls of his cell were like a freezer, absorbing cold. In the boiling summer, they felt like the walls of hell.

At forty-three, his once-black hair gone gray, Kadhim had returned home to find that in his absence, Baghdad had been devastated by more conflict, dictatorial whim, and devastating sanctions, imposed by the U.N. Security Council after Saddam's foray into Kuwait. Kadhim, aged far more than his years indicated, could no longer work at the garage where he was employed before the war. His legs and hands were crippled by rheumatism. The pain in his stomach from what he called nerves was perpetual. He often mumbled;

even when he didn't, his words came out slowly, tentatively. His gestures were weak, each movement testing his strength.

The government payment he had received on his return—150,000 dinars, or about $88—had quickly run out. His back pay from the army (138,000 dinars, about $81, the salary he would have received over sixteen years had he not spent the time as a prisoner) would, at current market prices, have bought about forty chickens, or 1,380 eggs. It wasn't enough for a bus ticket or a government travel permit out of the country. It would have taken nearly seven times as much to buy the cheapest twenty-year-old Russian-made car. A house? He shook his head dismissively. His frustrations? "I could tell you enough to fill up your notebook."

Outside, the sun had washed the landscape of color, leaving a pallid sheen behind. After our chat, Kadhim brought in Abbas Ahmed Salah, another former prisoner. Captured at nineteen, thirty-year-old Salah had been released seven months earlier, in April, in the same exchange as Kadhim. Like nearly all Iraqis, the men were circumspect in what they would say to reporters, but suggested—through the hints that often stood for declarations in those days—that their bitterness came from being betrayed by their government. They had given their lives to the war with Iran, to pointless battles, to years in prison camps, to sacrifice without promise. All the while they had hoped to return to the Iraq they remembered before they left when the country was flourishing.

"I thought I would return to a modern city. The bridges, the buildings, and the hospitals, I thought there would be more. I thought that the people would be better off," Abbas told me. "But everyone is weary." The yellow paint was peeling off the walls of the Victorious Garage. The room was lit by two candles—power had been cut, and would remain off for a then unheard-of six hours. I asked him what he was doing for work. "Nothing," he answered glumly.

There used to be a slogan scrawled on the walls of neighborhoods throughout Baghdad: "The Baath, fifty years of jihad to achieve the goals of the nation." It seemed so ludicrous when I thought of it that day. Across the Arab world, jihad—an almost revered concept of empowerment—had become the tiresome cliché of hackneyed sermons and political hectoring. "The nation" referred to in the slogan was Saddam's fantasy of a community among Kurds, Sunni Arabs, and Shiite Arabs that had never really existed in Iraq's history. Even the Baath Party's name seemed ridiculous. "Baath" means "renaissance" in Arabic, but by the time Kadhim and Abbas were freed in 1998, Saddam was holding court atop the wreckage in a junkyard of broken promises.

LIKE THE HAUNTING PHOTOS OF SEBASTIÃO SALGADO, IMAGES OF THE CARNAGE of the Iran-Iraq war remain indelible in Iraq. A line from a colleague's interview with a general in the Iraqi army, proud but sober, precisely evoked the waste of life: "Soldiers lying like matches on the ground," he recalled. An anecdote from the war-scarred Fao Peninsula along the Persian Gulf recalled hypodermic needles littering a desolate, sandy spit of land, the record of a futile attempt by Iranian soldiers to stave off convulsions and death from chemical weapons fired by the Iraqi military. Both sides, of course, committed sins. Iranian commanders hung keys around the necks of Iranian children, some as young as nine, and sent them to detonate mines. The children were told that their martyrdom would unlock the doors to paradise.

"This was the end. You know when they write 'The End' after a movie? It was the end. That's it. *The end.*" I vividly remember Dr. Shahla Kadhim Atraqji saying this to me about the war with Iran. She was a thirty-eight-year-old doctor who had helped me understand what Saddam had done to her country. "Sometimes, my loneliness is killing me," she once said, almost casually. "But I won't be a follower to a man who enslaves me. No, never." She was beautiful, with the features of her father, from Basra, visible in her dark complexion and liquid eyes. Her brown skin almost glowed. Her tan jacket, black shirt, and black pants were distinctly modern, as was her choice to remain unveiled in a society that, for a decade, had been growing inexorably more conservative. She spoke her mind, adamantly, and she had a grim take on her country and city.

We were sitting at the Hunting Club, a relatively inconspicuous locale in the neighborhood of Mansur, sipping hot tea at a white plastic table in a sprawling courtyard ringed by beds of pink and red roses and manicured shrubs. Sidewalks of tan brick passed under palm trees just starting to bear fruit. In the air was the faint scent of bitter oranges on *naranj* trees. From nearby speakers came the sugar-coated voice of Nancy Ajram, one of Lebanon's latest pop sensations. The setting, I thought, was far more pleasant than the conversation. "War is war," she told me simply. "It destroys everything."

The history of the war with Iran has yet to be written, but Shahla has her memories. One, particularly, haunts her. It was the summer of 1983, nearly three years after the fighting had begun. She was in high school, but classes had been dismissed. Shops and government offices were closed. Crowds headed into the streets for the spectacle of war, as hundreds of Iranian prisoners were paraded in pickup trucks through the city. Guns to their heads, they were like ancient booty, an Assyrian relief celebrating a now-forgotten victory. The mob snarled, spat, and threw rocks, shoes, and invective. The Baghdad that Shahla loved was fading before her eyes.

"It was a disaster," she told me. "It was inhuman. I remember it very well. The poor guys. Their fathers, their mothers. Why would he" — Saddam — "do this to them?" she asked. "We were standing in the street. We were obligated to go out. In all the streets, on both sides." She drank her tea, letting the memory, still vivid, pass before her eyes. "All this changed people. When a child saw this, he didn't understand. How they were treated, how they were insulted." She went on. "Day and night, everything changed."

Baghdad was becoming sick. To plead for rules in the savagery of war may be risible, but Saddam's Qadasiya was a conflict without evidence of human civility. As Iranian defenses reeled in the war's early months, soldiers ransacked and pillaged, stole and looted in Iran's cities, setting an example that would in time haunt their own country. Khorramshahr, an Iranian border town occupied early on, was emptied. As the war progressed, in rampages time and again blessed by Saddam, the Iraqi army picked clean Kurdish villages in the killing fields of the north.

Shahla's brother-in-law was a soldier. He had witnessed these things. "The men changed," she told me. "We saw them."

The rules of Iraq's countryside are brutal. They have been for centuries, their traditions imported from an inhospitable desert. After Baghdad's fall in 1258, ferocious and unforgiving bands of marauders almost extinguished civilization in Mesopotamia, abetted by the wars that washed across what became a no-man's-land. Survival required hardness. In Iraq's countryside, in places like Fallujah, Thuluyah, and Tikrit, there have always been such hard men; Saddam himself was raised near Tikrit. During the war with Iran, the culture of the *rif*, the countryside, came to dominate the entire country; its rules were imposed everywhere. Already renowned for their severity, Iraq's people became even harder.

"When they see their colleagues dead in front of them, it changes their heart. Their hearts stiffen," Shahla said of the soldiers. "Their feelings change. War makes people change. Really. The killing, blood, it makes people different. It changes their psychology." Her words slowed. "The war gives them an excuse to do anything."

Hers was a culture where it was not uncommon for men of a certain age to bear scars, to walk without legs, to shrug without arms. Hundreds, sometimes thousands of casualties poured in every month; their arrivals prompted the unfurling of black banners of mourning. Saddam lavished money on his officers (those he trusted). Soldiers were given priority in buying houses and cars. To families who lost their sons, he gave ten thousand Iraqi dinars and a car. Others received a plot of land and an interest-free loan to build a house.

"He changed the people," Shahla repeated once more. "Some people didn't care if they lost their sons in the war. Life was expensive, and people needed money." Her usual cheerfulness had left her. "It took a lot of people, the Iranian war." Her words tumbled out slowly. "It was a long war," she said.

Akhlaq is a refrain of Islamists; the word is often translated as "morals" or "morality" in English, and it is the lens through which the Islamists see society. (At heart, they are social reformers, and their rectitude is part of their appeal.) But the word can have a more textured meaning. "Character" is perhaps a better translation. And in Baghdad, *akhlaq* is often used to describe Saddam's dictatorship and his wars; people speak of what he did to *akhlaq* during the war and afterward.

Videos danced across the nearby television screen in the Hunting Club's courtyard. The music—the percussion-driven, intoxicating refrains of Arabic pop—reminded Shahla of Iraq's most popular modern singer, Kadhim al-Saher, whose song "After Love" she recalled. A story of an affair, its meaning resonated with her at another level.

Love is dead, feeling is dead, and the light that shows us the way is dead.
The humanity is dead inside us. It is dead. It is dead.

The day you traveled, and I said farewell to you,
Tears lined my cheeks. But the day you returned, I welcomed you with coolness.

Where are my tears, where are they?
Where are your tears?

"We feel that we've changed inside," she told me. "That makes us feel sorry. All of us. We say, 'Do you remember when it was like this and this and this?'"

It was as if Iraq had been eroded, not by a force of nature but by a willful, methodical wearing away at what had been accomplished in the 1970s and before. For the generation that came of age during the war with Iran, the cost was especially great, the toll especially exacting.

"You know," Emad Zeinal told me, lighting a cigarette, "each night, you dreamed of the miracle that would come and take you away. *Ten years!* Not a day, not a month, not a year! You had to postpone all your dreams. I like life. I like sports, arts, poetry, music, whatever, all these things. So, when some situation prevents all this, creates a block between you and life, it becomes something hard to accept. It's something hard to tolerate. *Saabat al-tahamul.* There is no color in your life, in military life. You can't feel the colors. There's just one color, everything is khaki. This color. It's a metaphor."

A little more than a week after the war with Iran began on October 1, 1980, Emad, who grew up in Basra, entered the army. He was twenty-five, not young for a soldier, but he had lost his student exemption after completing his degree from Basra University in marine resources. Until 1984, he was a commando in the 444th Brigade, 21st Division. Then he was deployed to a tank unit, where he was a communications officer in a Chinese-built T-55, a cramped 1960s-era model known for its endurance. Throughout the war he was stationed in rugged northern Iraq, as far from home and family as they could send him.

"I have a request," Emad remembered saying in 1984 when he was homesick. "I have to be in Basra, to fight the enemy in Basra." His superior was stunned. Basra? he asked incredulously. It was as if a German soldier in World War II—and a not very enthusiastic soldier—had asked to go to Stalingrad in winter. The officer said it was the first time anyone had asked to go to Basra. "No problem," he told Emad, smiling and shaking his head. "You can go to Basra." Two days later, he received his papers. He had been sent farther north instead.

Nothing in the war really made sense to Emad, who saw only farce. No one actually wanted to fight. No one except the Iranian volunteers, fired by religious faith, with the keys to paradise around their necks. They turned out to be little more than human sandbags. Their commanders, perhaps believers too, told them that Najaf and Karbala—the most sacred Shiite cities in

Iraq—were just fifty kilometers beyond the front. Often the volunteers were no more than children and, Emad said, all he and his fellow soldiers could do was shoot them.

One Iraqi general recalled: "We sometimes had a small bottle that we used to bury with them. We would put the name or something in the bottle and bury it next to the body. But with all the torn body parts, often it was hard to gather them." The general shrugged. "And it's so hard—the body, the heat, the corpses." He offered the usual verdict: "This is war."

Emad recalled the proverbs from that war. One he liked to quote often: "Anything short of death is acceptable." He borrowed another one from Egypt. It was a play on the phrase "God have mercy on him," always said when the names of the dead are mentioned. "A thousand times a coward, but not once, 'God have mercy on you.'" Every time Emad said it, he smiled. He turned more serious in telling me about what he and others called the soldier's friend, *sadeq al-jundi*. It was an antipersonnel mine: soldiers used it to blow off their feet so they could return home alive. The mine was a little bigger than a grenade, and some men would simply step on it.

Others, as Emad put it, "were more creative." Before they stepped on the mine, they might throw a sandbag over their feet to shield the rest of their bodies from the blast. If the men were lucky, the explosions would sever only the fronts of the feet, or the heels. Sometimes they weren't lucky. The blasts would often shatter the lull before dawn. The men's screams would follow, interrupting the call to prayer. For the less religious, still sleeping, the screams would wake them up.

"The night was the most difficult time. They would spend the night thinking about their friends, their lover, their families. They would reach the decision by morning," Emad recalled. He spoke with awareness. Time and again, the thought had played out inside Emad's own head. Night after night. "You would hear the scream. Whenever you heard the scream, you knew what happened. You're lucky. *Niyalak.* You're going home. Go, go and enjoy your life!" Emad thought for a moment. "You have to be brave to do something like that."

There was Lieutenant Jalal, his tank commander, another "fucking coward," Emad said. One night, Jalal asked to speak to Emad. He had a plan. The next day, he would give Emad his pistol. (Not a Kalashnikov. That would do too much damage.) When the battle erupted, Emad would shoot Lieutenant Jalal in the leg as they rode in the T-55 tank.

"Are you able to do that?" he asked Emad.

"I said, 'Why not? Whatever you order.'"

The next day, there was no fighting, and Emad started rethinking his promise. What if there was an investigation? What if he was caught? But Jalal was anxious, telling Emad that come the next day, even if there was no fighting, he should shoot him.

"I said, 'Okay, okay. I will shoot you just to get this over with.'"

The next morning, fighting erupted. Jalal gave him the pistol. For a moment, Emad hesitated. That was all it took. A bullet fired by the Iranians struck Lieutenant Jalal.

"He shouted at me, 'Fuck you! Damn you, Emad! I've been shot.'" Jalal thought he was dying. "'You son of a bitch, if you'd shot me, you would have saved me.'"

But the shot had only grazed his head. There was plenty of blood, but no serious wound. "I started joking with him, 'No, it's nothing. God helped you. It's a sign. He gave you his gift.'"

Lieutenant Jalal got two months off and a medal for bravery.

"That fucking officer," Emad said.

The surreal moments lingered with Emad, and he began to recount anecdote after anecdote. He recalled the fighting near the eastern Iraqi city of Kut, toward the end of the war. At night, Emad said, he had left the tent to urinate. Groping in the dark, he felt the coarse fabric of a uniform and turned on his flashlight to reveal the corpse of an Iraqi soldier. His skin was black, flaking; he was a victim of chemical weapons, probably mustard gas. The gas may have been his own army's, blown by an unfortunate wind. "I was pissing on a martyr," Emad said. His voice showed no emotion, and I wondered whether the irony was intentional. "It could have been me."

"It's the most foolish job you'll have—to fight for the sake of another person," he said to me. "It's not your war. It's not your people's war."

The longer Emad talked, the more reflective he grew.

"Some people believe it was a curse," he said a few minutes later. He looked out the window of the car we were riding in, past the desolate, sun-baked scenes of southern Iraq so familiar to him, scarred by war and Saddam's whims.

I waited for him to go on, and he said nothing. "What was a curse?" I asked, finally.

"What happened to Iraq," he said softly. "What we did to the Kuwaitis. Some people think it's because of all the miserable things that we did."

He shrugged his shoulders.

Emad was released from the army in February 1990, after nearly ten years of service. He had entered as a twenty-five-year-old. He had missed the childhood of his two sons. He had lost the ties of intimacy with his family. He had forgotten his friends. A year later, a call went out on Iraqi state radio. It was January 17, 1991. Iraq was again at war—this time with the United States. All people born in 1955, the radio bulletin instructed, should report to their unit.

Emad was born in 1955.

"Fuck them," he said.

And he deserted.

2

TABAGHDADA

Saddam was a rough-hewn peasant, but his pretenses produced in him an obsession with history—his reading of history—and his place in it. His selective recall created an in-between of reality and delusion, a fantastic terrain that indelibly colored Iraq. For speeches, he borrowed episodes from the greatest Mesopotamian kings, imposing irrelevant contexts. Among his favorites was Nebuchadnezzar, the Babylonian who occupied Jerusalem and destroyed the Jewish temple in 587 B.C. In the Abbasid caliphs, whose greatest legacy was a culture of ideas, Hussein saw an era of martial glory and imperial ambition. Unabashedly he claimed the mantles of Mansur, Baghdad's founder, and his illustrious grandson Harun al-Rashid. Saddam craved the swagger of the old heroes. In Baghdad's early days, Harun al-Rashid deployed an army of 135,000 after sending a message to Nicephorus I of Constantinople. It read: "From Haroun, commander of the faithful, to Nicephorus, the Roman dog. I have read your letter, you son of a heathen mother. You will see and not hear my reply." The language recalls Saddam's.

Saddam had pretentions to glory; his was the politics of deformed grandeur. And for three decades, he dragged his country through the sewer in delusional attempts to impose a legacy. The efforts would have been pathetic if not for the horrific toll they inflicted. He transformed parts of the society in his image; he altered the shape of the capital with a coarsely martial style that helped conceal the fact that he had created a utilitarian city shorn of history.

In a capital inundated with monuments to the dead in war, the Victory Arch was possibly the most distinguishing aspect of Saddam's vision of Baghdad— this for its vulgarity alone. Conceived in 1985, the arch of crossed swords celebrated an Iraqi victory at a time when Iran was winning the war. At each end, springing from the ground and weighing twenty tons each, were a colossal arm and fist—as the story goes, molded from Saddam's own and enlarged forty times. The fists clutched curved blades that spanned the sprawling parade route, and were designed with intentional medieval imagery. They are said to be replicas of the swords of Saad Ibn Abi Waqqas, the Arab general who defeated the Persians in the seventh century. Each required twenty-four tons of metal, recast from the guns of dead Iraqi soldiers. From the arch's wrists dangled vast metal nets bulging with (real) captured and often bullet-riddled helmets of Iranian soldiers. In all, there were five thousand, spilling onto the ground and cascading down the road. According to one account, the original plans called for actual Iranian skulls.

Another monument was built over the capital's Bilat al-Shuhada primary school to commemorate thirty-four children who were killed when an Iranian missile struck on October 13, 1987. It was, of course, a shrine to Saddam. There was the grim metal and stone monument, picturing infant angels grasping the Iraqi flag. There were the standard paintings and drawings of Saddam inside the schoolrooms and along the corridors, which were inscribed with banal slogans and rhetoric. I once saw children there, lined up and shouting "With our soul, with our blood, we'll sacrifice for you, Saddam!" Waving Iraqi flags, they wore the sand colors of desert camouflage. Baath Party members watched, their very presence striking terror in the pupils' teachers. The teachers screamed at the children, almost frantic. "Yes, yes, to the leader Saddam Hussein!" The children shouted back, at the tops of their voices. And on it went, pointlessly, orders given, orders received.

ACROSS BAGHDAD IN THE DAYS BEFORE THE INVASION, THE ICONOGRAPHY OF Saddam remained ubiquitous. One image, on posters, pictures, even statues, featured him firing a rifle into the air. On display at the gun shops all around the city, it gave us Saddam in his best Godfather pose. The other image, also ubiquitous, portrayed the leader as a devout Muslim, praying in uniform, in beret, with a pistol holstered to his side. There he was, everywhere, submitting to God, sending up his prayers.

A few days before the U.S. bombing began, I saw that picture hanging at the entrance of one of Baghdad's grandest shrines, along with other images— Saddam reading the Quran, Saddam waving before an Iraqi flag, Saddam in various poses of supplication. On the edge of Baghdad, not far from the Tigris, the Kadhimiya shrine is the resting place of two of Shiite Islam's holiest saints—Imam Musa Kadhim and Imam Mohammed Taqi Jawad, who died in the ninth century—and its history is as blood-soaked as the record of the man on its walls. Flames consumed its teakwood domes in 1051 as Baghdad was racked by sectarian fratricide whose roots are long forgotten. The shrine was destroyed two hundred years later in one of the city's many conquests. Its present incarnation—twin domes and four minarets, a foundation of Persian-inspired ornament—dates to the sixteenth century and the start of a succession of Turkish-Persian wars over Baghdad and its hinterland.

Yet the shrine of Imam Kadhim remains a tranquil place, as though perched above the turmoil that surrounds it. Light is rarely graceful in Baghdad; it has little patience. But at the shrine, around the domes of gleaming gold, the light restrains itself, bathing the flowered tiles of blue and green. The light accents the grace of Arabic calligraphy, dancing in its yellows, whites, and blacks. It dazzles in the huge mirrors that arch over the entrance, and it warms the white marble floor, shuffled over by the bare feet of worshippers.

The courtyard is a contemplative place, usually filled with families strolling, children playing with the pigeons who flock for seed, pilgrims speaking in respectful whispers and rolling their worry beads. This is a destination for the devout, as they seek healing and invoke the intercession of the two saints for the forgiveness of sins. Here, pilgrims, their numbers always seeming to grow, seek the fulfillment of their needs. On the eve of war, only days away, the shrine was crowded.

Like so much else in Baghdad, the phenomenon of religion in Iraqi life has been little understood. In the 1970s, Saddam's Baath Party largely kept faith out of political life: the veil was an uncommon sight, bars flourished in freewheeling neighborhoods, and the government propagated a secular Arab identity that, in its most benevolent reading, would arch over the country to unite its tapestry of faith and ethnicity. That era was short-lived. As the state became Saddam, the party his instrument, his men flailed about in a quest for elusive legitimacy. Their speeches, symbols, and slogans appropriated Islam for a language. Saddam claimed descent from the prophet Mohammed's family. He poured religious rhetoric into his speeches. Despite its meager resources and the remarkable repression meted out to organized religious opposition, his government began building two of the world's largest mosques in Baghdad and, in a move that disgusted more devout Shiites, lavished patronage on Shiite shrines (the same shrines he had badly damaged in crushing a revolt after the 1991 Gulf War).

Did the campaign inspire or reflect the growing religiosity of Baghdad? It was difficult to say. But in the wake of the succession of tragedies that had befallen the city, many of its people, buffeted by weariness and hopelessness, desperate for respite from the misery of wars and sanctions, had turned to faith. A majority of women donned the veil. In a televised meeting of the Federation of Iraqi Women, a group that was once a symbol of the rights the secular Baath Party bestowed on women, virtually all of the members were covered. The influence of the clergy—as intermediaries, as figures of authority—grew markedly in the 1990s. Sermon leaders said that the number of worshippers had doubled over the past five years. At the Imam Kadhim shrine, as many as 50,000 pilgrims came on a typical day before the war, up from 15,000, perhaps 20,000, a decade before.

"They are waiting for the mercy of God," one pilgrim, Mazin Abdel-Hussein, told me, as my government minder stood nearby, bored and staring into the distance. Mazin looked out at the gaggle of families, many of them sharing food brought in plastic bags and tea kept warm in plastic thermoses or battered tin kettles, as they seized a moment of solitude on the shrine's sprawling stone floor. "Most people feel that life is difficult. They come here to make it easier," he said. He was forty-two years old. He carried his small boy in one hand; with the other, he gestured gracefully. "They wish for God to provide for better conditions—for their families, for their houses, and for their way of life."

God, before the bombs fell, was tangible. His will was solace, his presence unquestioned. Everything else was *ghamidh*, ambiguous.

▪ ▪ ▪

RECOLLECTIONS OF THE 1991 GULF WAR INFORMED THE EXPECTATIONS MANY
Iraqis had for the approaching invasion. Although the Gulf War lacked the
brutally epic narrative of the war with Iran, the resulting damage remains
awesome. The most spectacular was done by the forty-three days of air strikes
that preceded the American-led ground attack to drive Iraqi forces out of
Kuwait. In the bombardment of more than seven hundred sites in Iraq, U.S.
forces targeted leadership facilities, weapons plants, air defense, military
forces, and communications networks. The choice of these targets was justi-
fiable; their losses would incapacitate the Iraqi army, recognized as an aggres-
sor by the United Nations. But the bombs, their targets multiplying at a
dizzying pace as the war progressed, also wrecked bridges, railroads, oil
refineries, and electrical plants.

A report made after the war by a public health team from Harvard University noted that of Iraq's 320 generating plants, thirteen were damaged or
destroyed in the first days of bombing. By the war's end, only two were still
functioning, generating 4 percent of Iraq's prewar output. That left many
Iraqis without power for weeks, and without clean water and sewerage for far
longer. With devastating speed, the crisis unleashed epidemics of typhoid
and cholera. (Iraqis recalled vividly how the government got electricity up
and running, at least partially, within two months. The contrast with the U.S.
occupation in 2003 was a sharp one.)

The U.N. sanctions, which banned air travel to and from Iraq and barred
exports from Iraq's oil reserves, worsened the people's nightmare, although
American officials in Baghdad and elsewhere were always loath to mention
the sanctions' devastating impact on innocent citizens. As long as they
live, many Iraqis and others around the Arab world will recall the words of
Clinton's secretary of state, Madeleine Albright, who, when asked about the
horrible human toll of the sanctions, refused to back down. Was the price
worth it? she was asked. "Yes, I think the price is worth it," she answered.

By the time of the U.S. invasion, nearly thirteen years after sanctions were
imposed, incomes had dropped to one-fifth of prewar levels, infant mortality
had doubled, and only a minority of Iraqis had access to clean water. One-
third of six-year-olds had dropped out of school. The adult literacy rate fell

from nearly 90 percent during the war with Iran to 57 percent a decade after it was over. The United Nations said half of all sewage treatment plants were inoperable and another fourth were polluting the already fragile environment. In all, 500,000 tons of raw sewage were spilling into the Tigris, the Euphrates, their canals, and other waterways each day. Growing numbers of Iraqis were showing symptoms of severe protein deficiency usually only seen in famines. The record at that time amounted to what the United Nations called "a semi-starvation diet for years."

Victims of that diet were among the clientele of Dr. Adel Ghaffour, whom I met one evening before the war at his clinic on Saadoun Street. The patients seemed largely poor; theirs were the weathered, masculine features of country women. Nearly all wore the *abaya*, the black, shapeless, flowing gown of the more traditional.

Adel greeted me with a stethoscope around his neck, wearing a white short-sleeved shirt and a tie. His first words: "We see our patients dying before our eyes."

Adel, who spoke with authority, but avoided pedantry, saw himself as a bridge between worlds—Eastern and Western, Christian and Muslim, Iraqi and American. Born and raised in Iraq, he had been influenced by the United States, where he had spent ten years. In 1963, he began his residency in internal medicine in Cleveland, where he met his wife, Gayle Brozina. They married in 1966, then left for Miami, Florida. Three years later, they returned to the Midwest and he taught at Ohio State University for two and a half years. In 1972, they moved to Baghdad, where they raised three children. When I met Adel, he had a faculty job at the University of Baghdad, still the most prestigious in Iraq. Like other doctors, he conducted his clinic during off hours.

Sadly, he remembered his impressions upon returning to his country in 1972: "If it is like this now, we'll look like Chicago in five years," he recalled thinking. "I wish you came to Iraq in the 1970s, before the war," he said, his voice heavy. "You could see that in a few years we were ready to leave the developing world."

We sat for a moment in silence, and then he continued. "It really is a human tragedy," Adel said. "I doubt in history a nation has suffered like Iraq. For no good reason."

We talked on in his clinic. Clearly, he had little anger toward the United States. In fact, I suspect he considered himself an Iraqi-American. "I love that country," Adel told me. "If there is a paradise, it is there." Speaking of his time in the United States, he got excited. "It's so easy to make friends. . . . I can go anywhere and make friends in half an hour." Like others in Baghdad, he insisted that of the Arabs, the Iraqis were the most similar to the Americans—in the way they worked, the way they lived, the way they enjoyed themselves. "When I was there, I never felt a stranger," he said.

His affection didn't extend to U.S. foreign policy, though. Adel, like nearly all Arabs, blamed the United States for its unswerving support for Israel, a stance that defied logic to most in the region. The support was so unrelenting, so unqualified that Adel, like many here, relied upon complicated conspiracies to explain it. He was baffled, too, by what he saw as an American obsession with Iraq. Adel had no love for his government—he had pointedly refused to join the Baath Party—but in his view, his country was pathetic, not a threat to a superpower. The American focus on it was bewildering.

"What is Iraq?" Adel asked in disbelief. He threw his hands up. "This is crazy! The United States is so powerful. It should respect itself. It should use its power wisely. What is Iraq to the United States? Who is it going to fight? We're not Russia or China. We're a small country."

He thought for a moment, then recalled a story from his days in Cleveland, before the 1967 Arab-Israeli war that redrew the map of the Middle East, before OPEC was a household name, before Iran's Islamic revolution in 1979 and Saddam's seizure of power that same year. In that simpler time, Adel told a colleague in Cleveland, a doctor, that he was from Iraq. "Iran?" the doctor asked him. No, Iraq, Adel said, and he proceeded to draw a verbal map: "Well, to the south of Turkey, to the north of Arabia, to the west of Iran." The doctor still looked puzzled. Finally, Adel said to him, "Mesopotamia."

DISAPPOINTMENT BECOMES DESPAIR IN THIS CITY OF OLD GLORIES WHEN THE present fails to measure up to a past that now can only be imagined. When memories, sometimes illusory, fill the void, reality looks all the less bearable. It is an endless circle: *Baghdad deserves better.* The refrain is often heard in the city. There's a word in Arabic that now seems to exist only to taunt, to bring sadness over what has been lost. *Tabaghdada*, a verb, is taken from the city's name, and it means "to swagger" or "to show off." It is rarely used today, the capital's grim reality relegating it to occasions for melancholy.

Mohammed Ghani, one of Iraq's best-known sculptors, often brought up this word; it was like an artifact he kept returning to. "The Iraqis are proud," Ghani would tell me, with a hint of rare enthusiasm. Putting his finger theatrically on his nose, he would push it up. "Their nose is like this!"

In 1998, when I first met Ghani, I noticed the way his exuberance and dramatic flair could turn swiftly to nostalgia, yearning, *hanin*. The precipitator was usually a memory of Baghdad before the sanctions of the 1990s and before the war with Iran. He would bring up the 1970s, that breath of respite, and his eyes would again flicker. "It used to be much, much cleaner than now," he would say as, with his hands, he imitated the flies that he said had descended on Baghdad. "Not thousands! Not millions! Billions of flies!" His expression softened: "It was not like this before."

Pollution, Ghani told me, had also grown worse, fed by decades-old cars belching their exhaust, black smoke chugging from buses. His hands waved in circles, imitating the billowing clouds that he imagined. The air was thick, he complained, poisonous. It dulled life. He described it as though it were a metaphor; perhaps it was. Pollution—sometimes visible, sometimes not— had enveloped the city. And that was just the beginning of the changes, the decline.

Baghdad, he often complained, was isolated. "No one comes here," he told me. "They've all stopped coming."

Isolation plays a wicked game with pride. The ostracism it brings is distressing, particularly to those accustomed to society and its civilities. As Ghani pointed out, few people came to Baghdad during the terrible years of the U.N. sanctions. Few left, either. By 1998, Iraqi businessmen were permitted to travel only to Syria, and even that border had only recently opened. Saudi Arabia and Kuwait, still seething over the 1990 invasion, rarely, if ever, granted visas. Iran was pretty much off-limits. The Turkish border was beyond the government's control. For those who hoped to travel, that left Amman, Jordan, a destination once an hour or so away by plane but that now required ten hours of driving across the desert. There was one other way out: a ferry from the port of Umm al-Qasr went once a week to the Persian Gulf city of

Dubai, but it took thirty-two hours and cost $330 for a round-trip, 115 times the monthly salary of a bureaucrat.

Iraq was a nation under house arrest as the world around it hurtled forward. By 1998, almost embarrassed by their backwardness, professors would ask me about the Internet, amazed and bewildered. (When the Internet did finally make its way to Iraq, in 2002, a typical annual subscription of $250 was far beyond the means of most.) Satellite television, then creating a revolution in the Arab world with racy entertainment from Lebanon and provocative news from stations like Al-Jazeera in the Gulf, was banned in Iraq. (A truncated state-run version arrived before the U.S. invasion.) Cell phones didn't exist, though a few enterprising and appearance-conscious businessmen toted around hulking handpieces with long aerials that could pick up calls from a landline a few kilometers away.

Each time I saw him, Ghani would lament how hard it was to fall behind the rest of the world. "Iraqi artists were always on the move, always out to see what was new," he said. "No one visits us anymore and no country gives us visas to visit them. Nowhere."

Long past were the exhibitions and lectures he once gave in Europe and America. He complained that he could no longer find or afford the bronze, teak, or mahogany to sculpt his works. Wire for welding was scarce. Paint was too expensive. "I go around Baghdad and people know to look for old pieces of wood for me," he told me. "I work with that." He stopped for a moment and shook his head. "This is art. We are not soldiers. Why do they treat us like everything is forbidden? Everything. *Nothing* is allowed."

The next words he spoke were a refrain in those days. "This is *Baghdad*," he would say, as if disbelieving. Often, his tone was dead, or anguished.

In the self-confident societies that define the West, technology is elective. Isolation is imbued with romance. In many Arab countries, and perhaps in other regions of the Third World, progress—driven by technology and a notion of modernity—is the long-wished-for antidote to centuries of weakness. While religious activists may differ on the degree of Westernization they deem acceptable, almost all agree that without progress Middle Easterners will be sentenced to backwardness, condemned to manipulation and exploitation by outsiders. In essence, without progress, there will be an endless replay of the last century or two.

This sentiment grew deeper over the 1990s, exaggerated by Iraq's taste of something better in the 1970s. Iraqis compared their nation not to fellow Arab countries like Egypt (proud and populous but impoverished), but to the glittering emirates of the Gulf, whose oil wealth had transformed their cities into country clubs for their tiny populations.

"We are so far away from modernity. New things, we don't know them," Ghani told me. "We are living as the rest of the world lived fifteen years ago. When you see the world, you become very sad with how we live. Iraq is a rich country, living as a poor country. It is not a desert—camels and tents. It is a civilization. The saddest thing is that rich people have become poor people."

"What is your ambition?" I asked, and Ghani did not need to think. The answer shot out. It was the same answer that the former prisoners of war had given me:

"To live like other people," he said.

During the years that I had known him, I always admired Ghani's eclectic collection of art. On one wall, on a day I visited before the war began, there was a sculpture of Christ, bound for a Catholic church in Baghdad. On another was a sculpture I had seen before, of Bahraini women with fish in baskets on their heads. Against the wall were plaster representations of scantily clad women. In limestone, a Kurdish prince was propped up, his face still undone. Nearby was a miniature of the flying carpet, a model for a sculpture in a downtown square. Bunches of dates, in shades of brown, hung a little out of place from the two-story ceiling.

During one of my visits to Ghani's studio in the days before the war, the sculptor's thoughts turned to the turmoil ahead, and he began talking again. Not to me, necessarily. Baghdad deserves better, he said. Baghdad is Baghdad, the city of the Abbasids. "This country is full of civilization—inside. What do they want to destroy?" He stopped for a moment. "Baghdad," he said slowly, drawing out the last syllable of the city's name, like a lamentation, "is the heart of Arab civilization. Baghdad was the capital of religion and power. It was the capital of Arabs, the golden age of Islam. Arab poetry was Iraqi poetry." He paused again, then went on. "Baghdad was the capital of the world. Inside the hearts, inside the minds, Baghdad is still Baghdad."

Some Iraqis foresaw the American invasion as a liberation. But there were many who understood the latent passions it would ignite. "I know the character of Iraq," Ghani told me. "It doesn't accept foreigners."

Ghani understood the power of the Americans, and he understood the psychology of Saddam. He and his city were in between, and he feared a calamity as they collided. The anticipation, the momentum it built, was terrifying. "As I hear, as I read, as I see," he said, shaking his head, "it will be terrible, a disaster." He stared at me, silent.

"We'll bend but we are not broken," he finally went on. "They can bend us but they cannot break us. We are like palm trees. The wind will bend them but it never breaks them. We live. This is the Iraqi character. We cannot be broken."

But, as our conversation went on, I realized he was telling me that something had already begun to break. In Ghani's lifetime, Baghdad's population had grown from one million to five million. Its morals had changed, as had its etiquette. Overrun and disfigured, it was no longer the city he had known. Fighting had brutalized it. Soldiers came back from the war with Iran jobless. The culture of the gun and its unsubtle logic had come to dominate. Conflict, miserable in its duration, had destroyed the middle class, leaving only the rich and the poor. Vulgarity, he said: that was what he saw in Saddam's city—"people throwing dinars at belly dancers."

Having spoken too bleakly for too long, Ghani caught himself. He looked at me, and his smile returned, as did his exuberance. Don't worry, he said, reassuring himself. All of this horror will pass. Baghdad deserves better. Then he spoke a line I had heard him utter before.

"What is ten years in the history of Iraq? It will come back," he said. "The character of Iraqis is good, simple, and proud. We will return. I think so. This period will pass and we will return back."

Those days in Baghdad before the war felt like choppy, run-together scenes from a movie trailer, Saddam's visage in the background, colored by apprehension and anticipation. At one hotel, young men at an Internet café gathered for group pictures, farewell photos, their arms slung around one another, their grins suggesting that their lives together had been good while they lasted. Taped Xs went up on the windows of hotels and homes. Some windows still bore tape from previous wars.

Workers methodically emptied 1970s-era ministries of documents and equipment, piling pushcarts with video monitors, computer hard drives, keyboards, and a less modern assortment of chipped desks, rickety chairs, and battered filing cabinets. Sandbags were piled waist-high at traffic intersections and outside ministries and government offices. Many were staffed by the less professional and visibly unenthusiastic part-time militiamen of the Baath Party.

As I was leaving the Internet center at the small, family-owned Hamra Hotel, where I was staying, a young woman who worked there came up to me. She was sweet, her face innocent. Visibly shaken, her uncertainty imbued with dread, she blurted out, "We are so scared." We had spoken before, usually no more than a simple exchange of greetings, but at this moment, no words came to me. I was not a journalist at the moment and no question was appropriate. All I could think of was a cliché in Arabic. "*Shiddi halik*," I said. Stay strong. It sounded trite. It seemed to confuse her.

"We've been through fourteen years," she said. At that, she started to cry.

WAMIDH NADHME WAS A BURLY ACADEMIC, SIXTY-TWO YEARS OF AGE. WITH short-cropped gray hair and a cough from a lifelong cigarette habit, he was a presence. He kept a stately house along the muddy Tigris River, a tranquil spot overlooking a stretch of the waterway that bent sharply, with a reedy island in the middle. Unkempt but picturesque, the banks of the river were lined with stone and shaded by palm trees. From Wamidh's patio, there were few visible hints of Baghdad—a dome here, a minaret there, among the green fronds. Often I would hear the call to prayer tumble down the river. The melancholy of the call's strains floated through the valley and along the quarters spilling out along its banks. Sometimes the cacophony of many muezzins suddenly glided into a moment of elegance. Grace begets grace. Wamidh remarked to me, "I wish I could devote more time to the pleasures of life than indulging in the miseries of life."

Miseries? I asked. "Politics," he said.

On the eve of war, Wamidh shed no tears and exhibited no fear of the bombs to come. And like so many, the professor stressed the fact that his country had been cut off from the rest of the world. His textbooks were outdated. The economy preoccupied him: after twenty-eight years as a professor, he was earning, he complained, less than when he was appointed to Baghdad University in 1975. He feared for the future, for students whose education he still deemed important. "There is a sense with them that there is no future," he said. "Even if we got a degree, what can we do with it? Somebody selling spare parts or cigarettes has a better job than a political scientist."

I had met Wamidh in 2002. He was a forthright voice in those tense, uneasy days after the 9/11 attacks, someone who tried to speak with complete honesty despite what consequences this might have in a police state. With an ever-present Dunhill cigarette, pulled from the distinctive red-and-gold pack, he would slowly field questions, reasoning out his every response, surrounded by his French-style furniture, worn Persian carpet, and framed piece of papyrus from Egypt, where he had spent time in exile. Around the room there were also telltale signs of his politics—a profile on a gold background of former Egyptian president Gamal Abdel Nasser, an icon of Arab nationalism, and photos of Wamidh's father and grandfather wearing the suits and ties of those with secular outlooks.

Saddam's regime, he declared, was "utterly unpopular. At a certain point in history, people get fed up with repression." He lamented the barbarism (his word) of "Arab regimes," one of his rare code terms for the Iraqi government. And he lamented what he called Iraq's wars for "dignity, pride, and conceit."

I didn't have the courage to ask him in those days how he could speak in such a fashion, but it stunned me. No one but Wamidh ever spoke like that during Saddam's reign. Who would dare? For Wamidh, though, life's miseries dictated candor. They made it possible. His was a political life.

The son of a government official and member of parliament, Wamidh had been drawn to politics young, tempted by communism and nationalism. In 1956, at age fifteen, he joined the party that would one day become Saddam's, the Baath Party, which had been founded in the early 1940s in Damascus by two Syrian schoolteachers. The party was radical, secular, and modernizing, and its platform stood on twin pillars. One was pan-Arabism (aimed at creating a united Arab state that would dispense with the arbitrary borders drawn by Western colonial powers). The other was socialism, which some saw as a way to redistribute the oil wealth then transforming the Middle East. Both programs appealed to the young Wamidh.

In 1959, during a time of revolution after the Hashemite monarchy fell to

General Abdel-Karim Qassem (a popular but authoritarian military strongman), Wamidh went underground and then to Egypt to avoid arrest. He was still a teenager then. Qassem had little tolerance for the Baathists, and ferocious crackdowns were not uncommon. But from the vantage of Egypt, Wamidh began to grow disillusioned with his party.

In 1961, he decided to leave it. Two years later, on trumped-up charges of plotting to overthrow the new Baathist government, which had toppled Qassem, Wamidh, who had returned to Iraq, was tortured so badly by his former colleagues that, on his release, he began carrying a gun. He decided he would not be taken alive again, and again he went underground, into exile in Cairo. That was 1963. He was not yet twenty-three years old.

Some years before that, Wamidh had made an acquaintance who perhaps inspired his predilection for risk. In October 1959, a group of young Baathist activists—among them Saddam Hussein—had ambushed the car of General Qassem, then still in power. They shot him at close range on Rashid Street, then Baghdad's main commercial thoroughfare. Qassem escaped death, but the attempt served as a defining myth for the career of Saddam, who became a wanted man sentenced to death in absentia. He was said to have dug a bullet out of his leg with a knife, swum across the Tigris, and escaped on horseback through the Syrian Desert, avoiding military patrols in hot pursuit. In time, he and others managed to make it to the relative safety of neighboring Syria, where they were hailed as heroes.

Wamidh had a role in the myth-making. During his first period of exile in Egypt, Wamidh—then still officially a member of the Baath Party—had received orders to escort seven visitors on their way from Damascus. Saddam was among them. Wamidh had met their bus coming from the airport and brought Saddam and another conspirator to his modest apartment, which he shared with three Bahrainis as poor as himself. Quiet and quick to smile, Saddam was wearing a suit.

"He wasn't arrogant," Wamidh recalled. "I was told that he was a thug or a man of violence, but in Cairo, he wasn't. I never saw him or remember him shouting or hitting. He was always calm and polite. He was dignified. . . . He used to drink alcohol, but in a very moderate way. I never saw him drunk at all. His social relations, I think he had some." Wamidh smiled. "You know, Cairo for us was an open society, like someone moving from Basra to Paris."

Saddam stayed just three nights at Wamidh's home. But he and Wamidh kept up their acquaintance in Cairo, where Saddam had his tonsils removed at Kasr al-Aini hospital in 1960. Wamidh thought it proper to pay a visit. He was the only visitor, and he stayed until Saddam awoke from the anesthesia. Saddam apparently remembered the gesture. In a conversation many years later with one of Wamidh's colleagues, a bodyguard for Saddam would later quote his boss as saying, "I had an operation in Cairo and when I opened my eyes, I saw Wamidh sitting beside me."

"It was really accidental," Wamidh said, over a lunch of traditional dishes— *kebab, maqluba, kibbe,* and *fatush.* "I usually don't like waking up early in the morning. But I thought, you know, he's by himself, so I went to the hospital. Perhaps this is one of the reasons why Saddam did not cut off my head. I think, somehow, he had good memories of me. "

Like so many Baghdadis, Wamidh was trying, in vain, to make sense of the cacophony that surrounded him in those months before the U.S. attack.

"I won't hide my feelings—the American invasion has nothing to do with democracy and human rights. It is basically an angry response to the events of September 11, an angry response to the survival of Saddam Hussein, and it has something to do with oil interests in the area." He talked about the 1990 invasion of Kuwait and suggested that the U.S.-led attack in that instance might have been justified. But what about more than a decade of sanctions? And now another war? "It will bring more destruction, more civil war, and a nationalist war against American intervention in the internal affairs of Iraqis.

"Even if the Americans are capable of overthrowing the regime, they will face more and more resistance from factions and groups who are not necessarily pro-regime or armed by the regime," Wamidh told me as he endured the curse of waiting, the confusion, the dread over the conflict he saw clearly approaching. "This is not politics." He shook his head. "This is a circus."

PART TWO

THE AMERICAN INVASION

3

WHAT'S WRITTEN ON
YOUR FOREHEAD

At 5:34 A.M., on Thursday, March 20, 2003, the United States began a war of its own choosing, buoyed by grand ambition and perhaps folly. At that moment, its power unparalleled, the American military began its long march toward Saddam Hussein's citadel of Baghdad, across the valleys of the Tigris and Euphrates Rivers and past the cities of Ur and Babylon. Its aim was to conquer and then remake an ancient land in its own brash, confident image. Its expressed intention was to spread democracy throughout the Middle East. It offered the catchwords it used reflexively—liberation and freedom—to a country whose own values it did not understand.

It unleashed its war, in Baghdad, with the equivalent of a murmur. Operation Iraqi Freedom's official commencement on that clear, early morning was an unsuccessful attempt to kill Saddam. Forty cruise missiles were fired from six U.S. warships in the Persian Gulf and precision-guided bombs were dropped on a bunker in Baghdad where U.S. intelligence believed Saddam was hiding. As he would repeatedly, Saddam survived, though the attack surprised the defenders of his capital. A minute passed before air-raid sirens began to wail, and more time still before the staccato answer of antiaircraft fire. For the next hour, long pauses were interrupted by red-and-white tracer bullets racing across the sky, which was given a gray cast by hints of an approaching dawn.

Nearly three hours after the missiles struck, the leader appeared. Wearing a green military uniform and the owlish reading glasses he rarely used in public, Saddam called on Iraqis to resist. Reading gravely from a stenographer's pad, his face drawn, he denounced the U.S. president as "the little Bush" and proclaimed that "Iraq will be victorious and our nation and humanity will triumph." He punctuated his words with an invocation: "God is greatest!"

Baghdad seemed more ghost town than garrison. Instead of the massive air assault that many expected, the opening volley produced a brief and almost modest tremor on the southern outskirts. The heart of the city was left unscathed. Stray dogs wandered downtown streets and the occasional taxi sped along Abu Nawas Street on the banks of the Tigris past Mohammed Ghani's sculpture of a flying carpet. The soft murmur of the call to prayer drifted across the city, drowning out the air-raid sirens that lingered plaintively even after the firing. In the early hours, the capital remained lit up—its bridges, its downtown, even the riverine palace of Saddam bathed in lights. At Firdaus Square, where the arm of a towering statue of Saddam pointed down a largely empty Saadoun Street, a handful of cars and buses circled unhurriedly.

Elsewhere in the country, the war had already begun to rage. U.S. and British troops had barreled across Iraq's southern border, and American airpower began to dismantle the country's air-defense system. Oil fields near Basra, in southern Iraq, fell, as did the nearby Fao Peninsula, the graveyard of so many thousands of soldiers in the 1980–88 war with Iran. But for the most part, the city was spared, even if its citizens were frightened. For Baghdad and its people, the real war would not begin until a day later, on Friday, March 21, with the arrival of the so-called campaign of shock and awe that the American military had promised for weeks.

On that night, at 8:09 P.M., the air-raid sirens sounded once again, puncturing a muted, nighttime sky. Minutes passed with Baghdad waiting; and then a sledgehammer broke the silence. With method and fury, the rumbles of modern war shook the city. Wave after wave of explosions rolled down the Tigris valley, their bursts of light illuminating the weary capital. Antiaircraft guns sent volleys into the air, and red tracer rounds arced across the cloudless horizon—the vain acts of an already humbled defender awaiting his inevitable fate.

Emergency vehicles wailed through the roads, still lit by the ghostly yellow of streetlights yet lifeless but for the dogs. Fires raged, smothering the city in an acrid haze. For twenty minutes that night, explosions—deafening thunder matched by gusts of wind they unleashed—detonated every few seconds. A lull followed, then another round. The cadence, at once ordered and chaotic, continued as the evening drew toward midnight. Under a full moon, the shimmer of raging fires reflected in the river's placid waters.

Baghdad's residents, whose memories of the destruction from the 1991 Gulf War remained vivid, were terrified. In the three-hour blitz, at times bringing a new blast every ten seconds, Saddam's garrisons and the symbols of his three-decade rule were shattered by an assault of 320 cruise missiles. A narrative told so often in the city's history had begun again: the City of Peace awaited its conqueror.

At dawn on March 22, with Baghdadis desperate for sleep, buildings in the Republican Palace complex were still smoldering. The turquoise-domed palace, transformed under Saddam into a marbled and mirrored tribute to himself, was left standing. (After the war, it would become the headquarters of the occupation.) Across the city, institutions of control and fear, some emptied and abandoned in the days before the war, were devastated.

At least five missiles had struck the headquarters of Special Security, a fearsome domestic-intelligence agency housed in a ten-story, pyramid-shaped building ugly even by Saddam's garish standards. The Salam Palace, a gaudy fortress built on the site of the Republican Guard headquarters that was destroyed in the 1991 Gulf War, was left with a gaping hole in its cream-colored dome. Four busts of Saddam, dressed in the helmet of a medieval Arab warrior, gazed on the destruction.

In the wealthy neighborhood of Mansur, the headquarters of Internal Security, a building so feared that Iraqis were reluctant to mention its name, was gutted. The fortlike complex was wrecked by a flurry of at least eight missiles, although its imposing, intimidating gate of concrete and steel remained standing. The nine-story Baghdad Security Headquarters, near the landmark Rashid Hotel, was left with slabs of concrete dangling precariously from its highest reaches. In Karrada, a neighborhood along a sharp bend in the Tigris, a sprawling crater scarred the right side of the General Security Headquarters and concrete spilled out over the road. Across town, thunderous blasts virtually wiped out the air force command center in Mansur. Its four floors were pan-caked, spewing metal and brick into the street. Iraqi soldiers walked gingerly around the rubble, looking dazed.

Baghdad, exhausted, was perched between what it was and what it would be.

BY THE WAR'S THIRD DAY, OFFICIAL BAGHDAD HAD FINALLY SET ASIDE ITS NON-chalance. Heavily armed militiamen of Saddam's Baath Party, a motley mix of men in berets and kaffiyehs, fanned out across the city, manning sand-bagged positions and keeping nervous watch. Some looked tough, rocket-propelled grenade launchers on their shoulders; others were bored-looking middle-aged men whose paunches stretched their green fatigues. Blue-uniformed police at intersections wore helmets and took up assault rifles, and small knots of soldiers wandered the city.

There was little bombast in the streets, though. When the first, brief air strikes had ended, residents cautiously left their barricaded homes. They had stockpiled food and now they began evolving a routine of life under siege. Even after the barrage of March 21, that same routine resumed. It would per-sist, in varying degrees of unease, through assorted episodes of carnage, until the war's end.

Scenes from normal life persisted: young boys, their bodies dark and thin, swam in the muddy Tigris, while fishermen led their boats along the clumps of green reeds rising from the banks. Trucks still picked up trash, and the double-decker, London-style public buses, painted in red, methodically plied their routes. Yet anxiety seemed to color everything: the time ahead was inscrutable. In neighborhoods such as Karrada and Arasat, stores were emptied of their high-priced consumer items—computers, big-screen televisions, air condi-tioners, stereos. In poor markets, stragglers hurried to purchase plastic jerry cans for fuel and the last supplies of food. Markets did brisk business, selling out their stocks of bottled water and of flour, cucumbers, beans, eggs, squash, and bags of rice. Potatoes, a staple in war because of their long shelf life, swung dramatically in price, a barometer of the mood at any one hour in the city. Lines of cars snaked out of gas stations, which hiked fuel prices to one dollar a liter from the usual two cents.

The telephone lines were still working, and after just a few tries, I reached Omar Saadedin, whom I had first met in October 2002 when he worked as a press officer with the United Nations. From our first few words, I had liked him. The son of Faruq Ahmed Saadeddin—a scholarly-looking former diplomat—Omar had studied in the United States, a stint that did nothing to temper his anger about U.S. policy. He was gentle, warm, and engaging, never afraid to (carefully) criticize his own government, though he considered himself a patriot.

My call found him at home, about a half-hour drive from the Palestine Hotel, where I was staying, past groves of date palms, concrete tract housing, and the sprawl of food-processing plants, ice makers, and cement factories. It was the morning after the first barrage, and I asked him how he was. "It's kind of normal," he said, somewhat resigned. He and his family had managed to buy groceries and they still had plenty of fuel, even finding time to fill up his 1990 BMW. "Last night was a little rough, but life goes on." As usual, he kept up a brave face, even if his voice suggested fatigue. "To tell you the truth, I was neither shocked nor awed." The conversation was short, but he invited me to join his family for lunch soon. With his country at war, and my country waging it, I thought it was an amazing gesture of hospitality.

Riad Abdel-Rahman, another Baghdadi whom I met in those early days, had seized on the lull in the bombing to stock his house. He had gathered fuel, eggs, cheese, bread, and meat. He bought four steel tanks, filling them with water—a precaution, he said, after the experience of 1991, when many residents were forced to haul water from the Tigris, which was flooded with tons of raw sewage. Riad also took his lumbering 1988 Cadillac Eldorado for an oil change, then filled it with overpriced fuel before visiting the popular Shurja market, where he picked up eight chickens. By afternoon, he declared his work done and, with his friend Ahmed Omar, plopped himself down at Sa'ee Restaurant.

His opening words were bravado: "Before the strike, I was worried about Iraq. I didn't sleep, but now I feel comfortable again," Riad said, squinting as he looked out at the handful of customers casually eating chicken *shawarma* sandwiches. Down a nearby street, a family strolled, savoring the cool, sunny day. Children played soccer in a dirt field, just feet from a row of pickups equipped with antiaircraft guns. At a neighborhood café, elderly men in kaffiyehs checkered in black and white drank piquant lemon tea and played fiercely competitive backgammon on battered boards. Riad's own children—a nine-year-old boy and two girls, ages four and two—were at home, school having been canceled before the war began.

Dragging on a cigarette and sipping tea, Riad first predicted a quick victory for Iraq. Then he seemed to catch himself, appreciating what had happened. Perhaps realizing he could give voice to his unease, he approached a new candor. He was worried, he admitted, that a far bleaker future might await his country; this was a sentiment that seemed common. If chaos ensued, he would take his family to Diyala, the neighboring province to the east. He insisted that taking Baghdad by force would be bloody, and did not question that the city would be defended. He seemed to speak sincerely, even fearfully, more worried about his own government's potential for ferocity than the Americans'. His face serious, he warned: "You should get out of here and escape."

WAITING WAS PERHAPS THE MOST ANXIOUS OF PASTIMES IN THE WAR'S EARLY days. There were the inevitable waits for more bombing, waits for what many in Baghdad feared their government would unleash, waits for the Americans to arrive. For Karima Salman, a stout matriarch with eight children, there was another kind of waiting: a mother's hope for news, and her dread of it.

Karima lived in a three-room apartment in the working-class district of Karrada, overlooking a sagging brick sidewalk and entered through a dented, rusted steel gate. Discarded furniture was stacked in the hallway, and wires hung from the ceiling. Her flimsy wood door was symbolic rather than secure and, as always, it was cracked open.

Inside her home, lit by a setting sun, Karima and her five daughters sat on old mattresses scattered over the tile floor. Cockroaches had made the place a playground. Fissures in the walls had been sloppily patched with plaster; deep, open cracks ran along the floor. Most of the interior doors were missing their handles. In one corner stood a battered refrigerator.

Staring down on the family was a portrait of the prophet Mohammed's grandson Hussein, the most beloved saint of Shiite Muslims. Outnumbered, betrayed, and deprived of water, Hussein and his family and followers were killed in a battle in A.D. 680 close to the present-day city of Karbala, near the

Euphrates River in southern Iraq. He was decapitated and his head was carried away on a stake. For Karima, as for all devout Shiites, his death evokes emotions comparable to the sentiments inspired by the crucifixion of Jesus. Hussein's martyrdom is an emblem of solace and suffering. The latter has shaded Karima's life, an existence defined by a deeply religious idiom.

The room that evening was quiet. The women were alone. Karima's son Ali had left to fight in the war, and they were waiting—for what all this would bring, and for Ali to return. "God willing, the war won't last long," Karima told me. Her daughters were quiet, as their mother spoke. "I wish it hadn't lasted one day."

Karima's ample body was draped in a black *abaya*. Her raven hair was covered by a black veil, framing eyes that always seemed sorrowful. She looked older than her thirty-five years but was still beautiful. Her daughters, hovering near her, treated her with respect, even adoration.

Amal was the most vivacious of them. She would turn fourteen that week, on March 23. Still awkward at times, she would put her face in her hands, her shoulders hunched. Her adolescent giggle concealed her remarkable intelligence and curious mind. Sometimes, she spoke defiantly, parroting the hollow slogans of her crumbling state.

Next to her sat the twins, who were almost identical. Eleven years old, the girls were lean, even gaunt, their faces somewhat boyish. Hibba wore a *hijab* over her hair, while Duaa had braided hers. Not yet burdened by tradition that soon would force them to keep a distance from men, they were friendly, even effervescent, eager to show off their Quranic recitation, chants for Saddam, and snippets of elementary school English.

Zainab, the beautiful fifteen-year-old, wore her black hair pulled back. She was the quietest of the girls, more reticent than awkward. In moments of conversation or argument, she deferred to her sisters, often looking down to the ground or busying herself with chores in the apartment. She seemed content to stay mostly silent.

Fatima, at sixteen the oldest daughter, had left school two years earlier so that she could help Karima raise the children. In the brief time since then, her literacy had faded, as had some of her confidence. A striking woman, she had dark, almond-shaped eyes and full lips, accentuated by the black scarf she tied tightly around her head. As I sat with Karima, Fatima entered the kitchen, leaving the rickety door, painted in yellow, barely ajar. Minutes later, she emerged with tiny white cups of Arabic coffee on a battered tin tray, brewed in a brass kettle over a stove fired by kerosene. Water came from a faucet in the courtyard outside.

Karima had left her village and married at twelve. Her crippled husband, wounded six times in Iraq's wars with Iran and the United States, died during the holy month of Ramadan in 1996 when the brakes of his car failed. Years ago, she had lost her job as a maid, when the Lebanese doctor she worked for returned to his country. Before the war, she had sold gum from a canvas mat in the street. A few months earlier, in January 2003, she had been evicted from the only home her children had ever known, a cinder-block garage near the Dar Hotel. Through the years, the family had gradually transformed the place, pirating running water and electricity. After being forced out, they found this apartment, whose rent, depending on the exchange rate, was about eighteen dollars a month, a sum the family could not afford. One of war's few blessings, Karima said with irony, was that she doubted the landlord would try to kick them out immediately.

The family's little money went for food, but war inflation tested their budget. A tray of twenty-four eggs had nearly tripled in price, rising from 50 cents to $1.40. A kilogram of potatoes jumped in cost more than three times in a week. The price of tomatoes quadrupled and then some. Bakeries closed, and bread was scarce. On the war's first day, they visited the market, but found nothing they could afford.

Many of Karima's friends and relatives—those with enough money—had already fled the city, leaving her family even more isolated. Her sister-in-law had put her children in a car bound for Syria, Iraq's neighbor to the west, leaving everything else behind. Karima said she felt lonely with everyone missing. Sometimes she began to cry.

"We're just sitting here. We're so weary. Whoever could leave has left. Whoever couldn't just sits in their homes," Karima said, looking to the floor. In her voice was the hopelessness that forced so many in the once-proud city to put their faith and future in God's hands. "We only have God," she told me. "Thanks be to him."

Prompted by my silence, the clumsy, awkward moments of an interview, she began to tell me the story of her twenty-one-year-old son, Ali, who had

had been at home on leave from the military, working as a plumber, when the war started. At nightfall on the day bombs first crashed on Baghdad, she helped him pack his bags. Powerless, her destiny in the hands of God, she then took him to the city bus station and sent him off to man an antiaircraft battery in the north. Their final conversation was metered by the rhythm of Arabic, a language that leaves little room for awkwardness. Every sentiment has an expression, every situation has a phrase, as did their farewell.

"There is no god but God," she told her son at their parting: the first phrase of the *shahada*, the central creed of Islam. As he bought a thirty-cent ticket and boarded a red bus bound for the northern city of Mosul, her son completed the couplet. "Muhammad is the messenger of God," he said. More phrases poured out, the prayers of farewell. "God be with you," Karima recalled saying. "God protect you." Those words were their last.

As she sat with me, tears ran down her fleshy cheeks. Moments passed, and she vainly brushed at her tears with her worn hands. Lines furrowed her face like scars.

"A mother's heart rests on her son's heart," she said, her home still lit by the setting sun. "Every hour, I cry for him. We don't know what will happen. We don't know when it will happen," Karima said, her voice slowed by sleeplessness. "There's no life, there's no death. Only tension."

The curse of waiting, and the dread of what lay ahead, filtering across a city at war. Those were the sentiments I felt mingling in Baghdad that night. To Karima, the war that had begun was a play; on its grand stage, people were mere actors. "Life's not good, it's not bad," she told me, as we sipped the bitter coffee. "It's just a play."

WEEKS BEFORE THE WAR STARTED, I HAD PROMISED MYSELF THAT I WOULD stay in Baghdad through the conflict, whatever the circumstances. In hindsight, there was perhaps an element of ambition there; it is sometimes difficult for a journalist to desert a story of such proportions. I didn't want the Pentagon to write this war like a screenplay, with expert scene-setting, and the temptation, irresistible in conflict, to manipulate reality. The project to embed reporters with U.S. troops as those soldiers prosecuted the war offered a perspective otherwise unavailable, but embedding wasn't nearly enough. We had to have

eyes and ears in Baghdad, among the people whose lives were being transformed by our leaders' decisions.

I can't say I wasn't scared, but by the war's first week, the fear had evaporated. There was simply too much else to think about. I asked my colleague
Hamza Hendawi, one of the best journalists in the Middle East, whether he
was afraid to stay in Baghdad. His answer always made sense to me: "Was I
scared? If you gave me time to think, I would have been terrified."

Hamza and I shared a room, 622, in the sixteen-story Palestine Hotel.
Built in the mid-1980s as Le Meridien Palestine, it was once a fashionable,
luxurious building, gracing the banks of the Tigris along fabled Abu Nawas
Street; now little allure remained. A relic of the era of its construction, its
decor was washed in dreary browns and oranges, and the wallpaper was peeling. Like much of Baghdad, the hotel was frozen in the 1970s. But it had
been worn down, inevitably, by more than a decade of American sanctions.

We had prepared ourselves, as much as possible, with dozens of bottles of
water and canned food. Our diet rarely ventured beyond tuna, an Egyptian
brand of somewhat bland beans known as *ful*, and a particularly loathsome
canned cheese. Small generators, gasoline, and car batteries stood on the porch
outside our room, to charge computers and satellite phones in the event of
a blackout. Underneath the desks, we kept cheap white candles, fragile kerosene lanterns, and flashlights; in the closet was a very appreciated bottle of
Glenfiddich. On the first night of the bombing, we wore our clunky blue flak
jackets and black helmets to bed. After the bombs detonated, sending a smell
of burning fuel that we mistook for chemical weapons, we ran for our protec-
tive suits, in duffel bags along the wall. As I pulled the mask out of the black bag,
I realized I had no idea how to put it on. By the time I got it out of the clear
plastic wrapper, laboriously connecting the few parts there were, I would
have been dead.

At the start of the war, I was already close friends with Hamza, a tall, well-
built Egyptian who had been my colleague at the AP bureau in Cairo. But
the duress of war almost unraveled our friendship. We fought over the petti-
est things: his deadlines were earlier; I kept him up at night with mine. It
wasn't long before my pack-a-day smoking bothered him—not the smoke
itself, but rather my tendency to exhale loudly. Hamza deemed it "too artistic." Tempers flared, though we didn't have time to stay angry.

Early in the war, the cast of government officials inside the Palestine Hotel changed markedly. The Ministry of Information types were still there, but a new contingent of probably one hundred had arrived. These men were Mukhabarat, the dreaded intelligence agents of Saddam's tyranny, and their faces were hard. I have often wondered why, in places like Iraq, men such as these are always so identifiable, and I think Hamza pinned it down: he once remarked that it was their lives that made them unmistakable. After a man sees so much bloodshed, oversees so much torture, inflicts so much pain—orphaning children, widowing women—the fear he instills begins to mark his face. Men with this unmistakable look came to our door one night to seize Hamza's satellite phone, which we used to communicate with our offices and file our stories. Officially, satellite phones were to be used only at the Information Ministry, but our minders seemed to be looking the other way. You never knew, though. At first, not wanting to press our luck, we hid the phone in the closet, under clothes, after filing our stories. Soon after the war started, with a little more confidence, we moved the antenna to the balcony, concealing it behind cartons of bottled water. That was where the Mukhabarat spotted it. They came once, a little after nightfall, checking things out. Ultimately, they said nothing. When they returned, Hamza realized we were in trouble. Neither of us knew what they would do. Hamza answered the door and, with a smile, simply crossed his hands in front of himself. *Arrest me*—that was his gesture, and it was an attempt at levity. The men were expressionless, humorless. (They left us alone, but took the phone, which Hamza managed to get back a couple of days later. Mine was still at the Information Ministry. All in all, we got off light.)

A HOWLING WIND MUFFLED THE CHORUS OF BOMBS ON BAGHDAD'S BELEA-guered outskirts. It was the sixth day of war, with the bombing following a persistent rhythm, when a savage, relentless storm blanketed the capital with desert sand and cast over it a translucent, otherworldly glow. The storms that visited Baghdad through that first week of the invasion were so fierce they seemed harbingers of disaster. Scraps of paper, plastic bags, and tattered cardboard were hurled across deserted streets. Traffic lights, still working, and palm trees, still standing, swayed under the force of the wind. A lonely soldier hunkered near his house along the Tigris River, a black scarf draped over his head like a veil. The sandstorm was foreboding, ominous, and, in Imad Mohammed's eyes, a portent of divine will. "The storm is from God," my new acquaintance said, looking out his trembling window.

Again and again in Baghdad's history, the weather has seemed to signal cataclysm: floods have unleashed the Tigris over and over, generation after generation; in 1074, a storm shattered medieval dams and dykes, sending black water coursing through Baghdad's bazaars and streets and cascading into the crumbling grandeur of the Round City; in 941, the famous green dome built by Baghdad's founder, Mansur, was destroyed by a single bolt of lightning after standing for 180 years.

Centuries later, in 1258, when the Mongols sacked Baghdad, rain poured, submerging shops and houses. When the armies arrived—200,000 infantry and horsemen—lightning raged over the city, igniting fires. An earthquake followed. Writers tried to outdo one another in describing the carnage of Baghdad's fall. One account recalls two Mongol soldiers killing a passerby, opening his torso, and filling it with their treasure. In another street, a soldier killed forty babies—a gesture seen as humane since their parents were already dead.

The code of the Mongols, the *Yasa*, prohibited the spilling on the ground of royal blood. So the caliph, Mustasim, who had foolishly rejected surrender, was rolled up in carpets and trampled to death by horses. The dikes and canals that delivered water to Baghdad's hinterland, an irrigation system built across millennia, were wrecked so systematically that they have yet to recover nearly eight centuries later. According to legend, the waters of the Tigris River ran red one day, black another. The red came from the blood of the tens of thousands, perhaps hundreds of thousands massacred by the ferocious horsemen of Genghis Khan's grandson. The black came from the ink of countless books from libraries and universities.

The fourteenth-century historian Ibn Kathir wrote about the fall of Baghdad as though he himself had endured it: "They came down upon the city and killed all they could, men, women, and children, the old, the middle-aged, and the young. Many of the people went into wells, latrines, and sewers and hid there for many days without emerging. Most of the people gathered in the caravanserais and locked themselves in. The Mongols opened the gates by either breaking or burning them. When they entered, the people in them fled upstairs and Mongols killed them on the roofs until blood poured from the gutters in the streets."

A huge fire followed the massacres, laying waste to the city. On its outskirts, Baghdad's treasure was piled "like mountains" around the tent of the conqueror. The carnage did not end for a week. By then, five hundred years of rule by the family that had founded Baghdad, the city of peace, had come to an end, and a civilization that dreamed of eternity had vanished. Baghdad had become a memory that the Americans, like so many others before them, would struggle to understand.

The storms of 2003 followed a feeble attempt by the government to conceal Baghdad from air strikes by digging deep trenches and burning oil in them through the city. The billowing black smoke cast an acrid haze across the capital, blotting out the sun. So dense was the cover that, even in midday, cars almost collided on a Baghdad overpass, but it did little to deflect the bombing: the thunder of hundreds of air strikes rolled over the city day and night. Meanwhile 100,000 U.S. troops, while harassed by sometimes suicidal paramilitaries, marched along the valleys of the Tigris and Euphrates in southern Iraq toward the capital.

The fires and, even more, the storms abruptly ended the city's determined attempts to reclaim ordinary existence. Aside from a handful of working-class cafés, shops were again shuttered and streets deserted as the sky went from blinding yellow at dawn to blood red in the afternoon. A dusklike brown was followed by a surreal, eerie orange that shepherded Baghdad into the evening. At the city's bus station, winds coated cars, taxis, and buses with a veneer of dust, as drivers cried out their destinations: "Tikrit!" "Baiji!" "Mosul!" From time to time, usually at random, mosque loudspeakers blared: "God is greatest, God is greatest! Thanks be to God!"

The winds slammed sheets of corrugated tin siding against roofs, and with Sisyphean determination, workers vainly tried to mop up the dust that kept blowing inside. Vegetable stands flung up the rare array of colors, their cucumbers, oranges, beans, onions, and eggplants challenging the hegemony of brown. In the streets, weary residents—still conditioned to be cautious about what they said publicly—spoke of divine intervention and God's determination to help Iraq. But beneath the surface one sensed other impulses at work: fear and the urge for flight, fatalism and bravado, grief and dread.

Imad Mohammed, whom I encountered early on, was hunkered down with his wife and their two sons, Fadhil and Abbas. Politics was still a forbidden subject, and I didn't push, but the storm seemed to make Imad, who ran a video store, reflective. At times, as the wind gathered strength, he marveled at its force. "The only times I saw a storm like this was in the American movie *Twister* and in the words of the holy Quran," the forty-year-old man told me, as we sat in overstuffed leather couches and sipped orange sodas.

Like other Iraqis, he boasted of his thirty days' worth of provisions—water, kerosene for cooking, frozen meat and staples like rice—to get him through a war that many thought might last weeks, perhaps months. Before his family, he declared himself fearless, his fate in God's hands. "What God wishes for us, we will see," he said. But when his sons left the room, their faces pale with fear, he turned more thoughtful. "I can't show my fear in front of my children," he said softly, with a hint of guilt. "If I'm afraid, they'll become afraid." He paused for a moment, then went on. "Life's not comfortable," he said, recalling the twenty missiles that had struck nearby the night before, their shock waves rolling through his one-story house. "You sit in your house, and there's bombing. It might hit innocent homes by mistake. How do you feel? You can't trust a missile. You can't trust a pilot. This is my country, this is my city, and I'm scared."

Imad Mohammed never seemed all that angry at the United States, and he never mentioned Saddam. Yet there was still a sense of pride, wrapped up, I thought, in his country's deeply held traditions of honor and dignity. Iraq, he acknowledged, was a Third World country, and the United States was a superpower. A fight against it might amount to suicide. But dignity remained of paramount importance; for him it was the good fight, whatever the odds. "We can't give up our country for free," he said, shaking his head, "without resistance." He let his words linger. Silence followed

By that evening, the sandstorm gave way to rain. Drops of mud fell on the city, clearing the sky for the last light of dusk. But the winds soon returned, with even more force than before, driving the last cars off the road and shaking houses like a persistent bombing. Like others, Imad thought of what he called an ordinary life. The phrase was heard often in conversations in Baghdad these days.

■ ■ ■

MY MEETING WITH IMAD WAS MADE POSSIBLE—AS WERE SO MANY OTHER meetings during the war—by a man in his mid-thirties named Nasir Mehdawi, my official government escort. In reporters' parlance, he was my minder. And, over the weeks of war, he proved to be the worst minder ever employed by the Iraqi government. There was simply no competition. Through those days of reporting, shadowed as they were by paranoia, he came to be the greatest asset I had. He never forced me to play by the rules.

Tall and handsome, with the mustache obligatory in Baghdad, Nasir hailed from a somewhat prominent, ethnically mixed Iraqi family. His mother, Sabriya, was Kurdish; his father, Akram, was a Shiite Arab and, until the 1970s, a well-known activist in the Communist Party. His father's brother, Colonel Fadhil Abbas Mehdawi, was even better known. Under Abdel-Karim Qassem, the popular but authoritarian general who had seized power from the monarchy in 1958, his uncle became the head of the People's Court set up to try members of the ancien regime. He had a bullying style not unfamiliar in his nephew. Nasir liked to tell the story of how his uncle, facing the firing squad after a coup in 1963, spat on his executioners before they shot him, General Qassem, and others at the national television headquarters. (The footage, televised repeatedly, of their bullet-riddled, mutilated corpses remains a vivid memory for a certain Iraqi generation.)

Nasir's career was more humble. A graduate of Baghdad University, where he studied English literature, he eventually joined the Tourism Board, rising at a young age to become foreign relations manager. During his ascent, he began to master the Iraqi style of bureaucratic infighting—swagger around those below you, suffer those above you, and, if that all fails, try to bluff your opponents by threatening their contacts with your contacts. In those days, getting things done often meant frightening your counterpart—a style of social interaction that Nasir, in time, managed to dilute but never to abandon.

A few weeks before the war, Nasir took a leave from that job and was transferred to the Information Ministry, which was in need of English-speaking help to cope with the deluge of foreign journalists. He seemed to enjoy the switch. Surrounded by hard-drinking reporters, he could socialize into the early mornings. (My favorite line from Nasir: "I'm a drunkard but I still have faith in God.") With a certain relentlessness, he brushed up on the vulgarities he'd picked up from Hollywood and that seemed to introduce his every sentence. (Half of the people we met were "fucking assholes"; the other half were "army deserters.") Working with me, he seemed to relish the risks that came with testing a government's suffocating restrictions, risks few of his colleagues would take; almost immediately, he seemed to enjoy the status that came with working for a foreign organization, even a newspaper like mine.

On several occasions, Nasir looked the other way as I visited contacts—a clear contravention of the ministry's orders that minders stay with reporters at all times. I always had a plausible denial for Nasir—that I was going to lunch, that I was going to check up on a friend, that I had errands to run. None were all that convincing, but with a shrug, Nasir let them go. I had the sense that he felt the less he knew, the better. We both understood the danger of this and I suspect that strengthened our friendship. "I'll be in prison," Nasir would say virtually every morning, occasionally flashing a subversive grin. "I'll be in prison tomorrow." After a particularly arduous day—the label "arduous" fit most days during the war—he would threaten to quit. I would cajole him, shamelessly beg him, then ask him to wait a couple more days and decide for sure. Invariably, he would, starting the whole routine over again soon after.

I still wonder why Nasir did what he did for me during the invasion. No doubt, there was a current of opportunism in his cooperation. Like many others in the city, he could read the writing on the wall, even before the war started. Once while we were walking together through the neighborhood of Kadhimiya in Baghdad, next to the majestic Shiite Muslim shrine's ornate tiles, he openly predicted the government's collapse, a downfall he later said he foresaw as early as 2002. "Nobody here likes this guy," he told me. The identity of the guy was obvious.

But opportunism only went so far. There was a war on and, like everyone else, Nasir was lonely and craved camaraderie. Like his city, he had suffered too much loss. In 1991, he had lost one of his two closest friends, Ahmed Bayati, who was killed with his uncle when a train collided with their car. Two weeks later, his other best friend, Hassan Fleih, was killed in another car accident as he returned home on military leave. Nasir's mother died two months later of throat cancer, a death that still haunts him. Soon after, his father kicked him out of his house, the culmination of a fight over his father's second wife, whom Nasir detested, and they soon stopped talking. Over the next few years, he wandered from house to house, provided shelter through the obligation of relatives and the goodwill of friends.

When I met him, Nasir was married, as was I. But in those days of war, Nasir, the driver Karim, and I basically turned to one another. We relied on one another, as friends and as colleagues. Together, we covered the inevitable migration from the city as its inhabitants, bracing for a climactic battle between an omnipotent America and a mercurial Saddam, began to flee their homes for the countryside.

On the road to Diyala, the exodus had begun before dawn, when U.S. troops broke through Iraqi defenses near the Shiite holy cities of Najaf and Karbala. Into rickety flatbed trucks, battered orange-and-white taxis charging sixteen times their usual fare, beat-up Volkswagens, and minibuses plastered with signs that read "God is greatest," people piled the artifacts of broken lives. There were colorful mattresses and coarse blankets, pots and pans. There were bulging suitcases and black-and-white televisions. Sacks of flour, jerry cans filled with gas, and ovens for baking bread were perched precariously in trunks. Most abundant were the long gazes out windows, as the thousands leaving Baghdad regarded their uncertain city. They looked past a picture of President Saddam Hussein in black beret on the neighborhood Baath Party building, past cream-colored Iraqi tanks parked on the city's outskirts, past the heaped-up wreckage of the bombing and past Mufid Jabouri, who watched the exodus as he smoked a water pipe on the curb, a few feet from a pool of sewage.

"The world is filled with war," the seventy-year-old said to me, surveying the scene above his thick-rimmed black glasses. "The war is here."

Given the emotions that visited wartime Baghdad—the bravado of a resilient people; worry over a bloody battle; fear of God, inspired by the weather—flight might have ultimately been inevitable, yet it wasn't the first response of Baghdadis, nor was it the only one. But, in time, as the bombing dragged on and rumors spread hotly, desperate, unsettled scenes began to recur across the capital. The reports passed along were at least as credible as those on the radio, where Iraqi government statements bordered on lunacy and the American military tried its hand at disinformation. The morning we drove to the city's outskirts, it seemed many Baghdadis had finally had enough.

Long before dawn, the procession had snarled the main road out of Baghdad to northern Iraq, with bumper-to-bumper traffic stretching up to five miles. The scenes reminded me of *The Grapes of Wrath*. Most people were headed to Diyala, a relatively tranquil province of farms irrigated by a river that shares its name and renowned for its groves of oranges. Many said they would find houses or hotels or share space with relatives already there. How long before their return was a question no one was able to answer.

"When it's calm, we'll come back," Osama Jassim told me. He and his three brothers had put their families in a flatbed truck piled with bags of flour, rough wool blankets, mattresses, and an ancient radio. Their faces were drawn. Osama spoke hurriedly, sounding forlorn. "Maybe tomorrow, maybe a week, maybe a month," he said when I asked him when he expected to go home. "It all depends on God."

His clan's departure, decided that morning, had cost their life's savings. They had paid fifteen dollars for the car, the equivalent of about three months' salary for a government employee. Rent for a house in the town of Khalas, north of Baghdad, would run eighty dollars, ten times what it cost before the war. As Osama saw it, he had little choice. There was no water, and electricity had been stolen away by a blackout. His three children—ages two, three, and four—were afraid and, standing away from his wife, he acknowledged the toll taken by a bombing campaign that showed no signs of ending. "War is death," the thirty-three-year-old told me.

As he spoke, two Iraqi tanks rumbled by. Along the street were patrolling soldiers and knots of people waiting for rides, sitting astride their televisions and carpets on sidewalks soaked in sun. A chaotic line snaked around a gas station, where cars, vans, and trucks filled up for a drive of one or two hours. Sweat pouring down their foreheads on this first sweltering day of the spring, several men pushed a broken-down red truck carrying eight women in black abayas; traffic moved in lurches on the four-lane road. In the tumult along the street, some spoke of helplessness, a resonant theme in Baghdad's latest chapter. Others spoke of God and complying with his will. Many shared the rumors that raced through the capital that morning, which gained credibility with every retelling.

As we sat and talked, Osama insisted that President Bush had warned Baghdad's residents to leave within forty-eight hours. Afterward, the city would be devastated. I told him that this wasn't the case; he looked back at me in disbelief. Others debated how close the American troops had come—to the village of Yusufiya, in the south; on the road to more distant Karbala; to Radwaniya, on the edge of Baghdad; near Saddam International Airport. Rumors were repeated, their spread mirroring the palpable rise in panic. Anxiety seemed to come from every direction that day, in markets and in traffic jams, wherever people were concentrated. Usually, it showed itself in no more than overheard snippets, phrases, even a grimace or a frown. As Nasir and I walked along the street, seeking anonymity, we had to avoid Baath Party cadres spaced along the road, themselves anxious. Each conversation could last no longer than a couple of minutes.

I flagged down Raed Kadhim, who had packed his family of ten in a minibus, its windows bulging with bedding and blankets. On the floor stood rice, flour, oil, and tea, what the family had left from government rations. They were headed to their relatives in Diyala. "There's a rumor that the Americans are coming to Baghdad," he told me, "and the women and children are scared." That rumor, I said, was probably true. As he spoke, his veiled mother in the front seat, Um Abbas, grew angry. They were late, she yelled, as the traffic crawled forward. "Hurry! Hurry!" He got in the car, leaving his home behind. For how long he didn't know; that depended on God. But it was time to go.

He looked out the window at me and said good-bye.

"God save you!" he shouted.

THOSE WHO CHOSE TO STAY PUT GRAPPLED WITH PERHAPS THE MOST PAINFUL condition of war: isolation. Remaining was also a flight of sorts. Unlike the pilgrimage to safety that I saw on the road to Diyala, the isolation was, in a way, an inward journey, a descent into greater insecurity and deeper fear.

One day, at about the same time as the exodus, Nasir, Karim, and I arrived at the Baghdad office of the International Committee of the Red Cross, which was pandemonium. Some people clambered on flower pots. Others pushed impatiently against a steel door guarding the entrance, girded with a metal fence. Into the air, residents thrust tattered business cards, yellowed scraps of paper, and pieces of newspaper, all bearing phone numbers outside

Iraq. Since the early morning, they had laid siege to the small, sandbagged compound. In a city with few working phone lines, they had heard rumors—true, as it turned out—that residents could make a call for free anywhere in the world. They had three minutes to sum up to their friends and relatives their lives during war.

"Every family has someone worrying about them," Laith Hazem told me as we stood outside. A forty-one-year-old electrical engineer, he was waiting to call his brother, Luai, in Stockholm, Sweden. "They worry about their lives, they worry about the danger they face." On a sun-drenched day, a respite from the storms, he stood on the sidewalk, waiting a few hours with dozens of others to make the call. Antiaircraft fire and the air strikes they failed to prevent thundered within a mile of the compound. The land war was still a ways from Baghdad. But it didn't matter. Days ran together; the threat seemed indiscriminate. With practiced understatement, not unfamiliar in Baghdad, he shrugged. "War is very dangerous," he said.

The ravages of war advanced methodically. Ambulances careened through the streets with sirens blaring. Some hospitals, though not all, overflowed with hundreds of wounded, both civilians and soldiers along the line of fire. Through the day, the deafening sounds of battle built to a crescendo, then relented. For many residents, the isolation of their beleaguered city and the dread that isolation feeds were the most unsettling aspects of the experience, recalling more than two decades spent withering under sanctions, dictatorship, and other wars.

The streets were always deserted by nightfall. Phone lines began to fail after a few days of U.S. air strikes. (Most calls on Baghdad's phones were answered with a recording: "All circuits are busy at this time. Please try again later.") The government warned of severe penalties for Iraqis found with satellite phones, which became one of the few ways to call abroad. The blackout, whose cause remained a mystery inside Baghdad during the war, left vast swaths of the city without water, sewerage, or electricity. In many ways, the darkness made the city lonelier.

Some residents hauled blankets, mattresses, and suitcases from the southern outskirts—the gateway for U.S. troops—to neighborhoods closer to the heart of the city in a search for safety. Many were without cars. A few braved the fighting to walk the streets, crowded with soldiers, militiamen, and civilians clad in green ammunition belts and carrying rocket-propelled grenades, rifles, and heavy machine guns. Others waited in their homes, shrouded in darkness, hoping to hear word about relatives perhaps just miles away.

At the Red Cross office, one satellite phone was available for calls; some people had arrived as early as ten A.M., waiting to make a call five hours later. As shelling approached, people hurried for cover under the building's concrete entrance, near two generators that powered the office. Others milled in front of the building. A few asked me if they could borrow my pen to fill out a brief application.

Laith, the electrical engineer, waited his turn. At the start of the war, he had spoken to his brother once, often twice a day. They had last talked eight days before. Laith said he was cut off even from his friends inside Baghdad and, like others, he tried to sort through the torrents of gossip to glean the truth. Weighing heavily on him this morning was a rumor he heard that two friends in the southern neighborhood of Dora—Hussein Ali and Faris Abdel-Raziq—had been wounded in the bombing. He had no way to find out. "You're cut off from everyone around you," he told me. "It's not easy. It's not easy not being able to communicate."

Finally, tiring of waiting, he turned to me for help. In my notebook, he wrote down his brother's number—0046739944423—the handwriting hesitant. "Tell him everything is okay," he instructed me. "Tell him his mother and father are fine. Tell him hello. Tell him not to worry about us."

That night, I did.

AROUND THAT TIME, I VISITED WAMIDH NADHME AND HIS FAMILY IN THE NEIGHborhood of Adhamiya. On one of the fiercer days of bombing, eleven cruise missiles had crashed into the military intelligence headquarters, across the Tigris from where they lived. The blasts had shattered the windows of their home and the Nadhmes had spent the day of my visit cleaning up the mess. "People don't think the Americans intentionally hit civilians," Wamidh told me, "but we were saying last night that a one-millimeter mistake would end up with a missile landing in our house."

He was resilient, but astonished at the disconnection between the Iraqi government and events on the ground. "For the president to speak about victory," he lamented, his voice trailing off. "The United States is a *super-power.*" He spoke of promises of democracy and his belief that a war would deny the possibility. "I never thought the Americans could bring it by tanks," he said.

Then he lamented the tragedy of Baghdad: "The last four centuries were hell," he said, his voice grim. "Despotic, tyrannical, bloody regimes and most of them were foreign. Muslims, all right, but Turks, Persians, and Ottomans."

But what next, I asked him. "I have no idea what will happen," he said. "I can't even think of scenarios."

4

LIKE A FLOWER

On a cold concrete slab, a mosque caretaker washed the body of fourteen-year-old Arkan Daif for the last time. With a cotton swab dipped in water, he gingerly ran his hand across the boy's olive corpse, dead for three hours but still glowing with life. He blotted the rose-red shrapnel wounds on the soft skin of Arkan's right arm and right ankle with the poise of practice. Then the caretaker scrubbed the boy's face, scabbed with blood left by a cavity torn in the back of his skull that revealed his brain.

The sounds of war around them, the boy's relatives and neighbors had gathered in the sanctity of the Imam Ali Mosque, near Arkan's home. They stood somber, waiting to bury a boy who, in the words of his father, was "like a flower." In phrases of faith, reassuring in their familiarity, some quietly invoked God. In words inflamed by war, others searched for the reason for the boy's death. Through the rituals of burial, the mourners tried, futilely, to escape the questions that had enveloped so many lives in fear and uncertainty. "What's the sin of the children?" asked Haider Kadhim, the caretaker. "What have they done?"

During those days of war in Baghdad, there was often a sense of the apocalypse that the weather had seemed to foreshadow. When death came, I heard anger, grief, and always the feeling of powerlessness, the horror of being caught in the middle. This was not a war of their making, many would say, yet they suffered for it. In some of those moments, the emotions were so intense they ripped away decades of stifling repression. At times of suffering, people talked in ways they perhaps never had.

Rituals of death were enacted quietly in homes and mosques while chaos raged outside. Arkan Daif was buried according to custom. The Muslim funeral rite was sadly routine in Iraq, but equally dignified and unhurried whenever it was performed. During the bombing, in times so precarious, such traditions began to assume new meaning; they were constants, filling time, busying and distracting relatives when their grief was greatest. At once formal and intimate, like the Arabic language, the rituals brought consolation and solace as the world outside grew ever more threatening and unpredictable.

In the propaganda battle it clumsily waged, the Iraqi government, again and again, escorted journalists to hospitals and devastated homes. The tours, little more than the marketing of wartime tragedy, were macabre. Yet aside from some neighbors and his family, there were no witnesses to Arkan's death or burial; the boy's funeral, under a sky cast in melancholy gray, went unnoticed by the government. We learned about it by chance when we asked for directions at a nearby street corner. When we arrived, the residents of the Shiite Muslim neighborhood of Rahmaniya were laying Arkan and two cousins to rest in the solitude of their dirt-poor warren on the city limits.

The boys were killed at eleven A.M. on March 30. As another relative recalled, "the sky exploded" as Arkan dug a three-foot-deep trench in front of the family's two-room concrete shack. He was attempting to create a bomb shelter and was working with cousins, sixteen-year-old Sabah Hassan and fourteen-year-old Jalal Talib. White-hot shrapnel cut down all three. Beside them, seven other boys lay bleeding in a street choked with the stench of sewage. A white car was sprayed with fragments, its tires sliced flat. The windows along what maps designated as Street No. 60 were shattered.

The explosion left no crater; the residents of Rahmaniya, a name drawn from the Arabic word for mercy, struggled to pinpoint the source of the destruction. Many insisted they saw an airplane. Some suggested that antiaircraft fire had detonated a cruise missile in the air. Others thought that rounds from Iraqi antiaircraft guns might have fallen back to earth and onto their homes in deadly coincidence. Often there was anger, grief turned aggressive. Without war, some insisted, the boys would still be alive.

"It's an unjust war," said Imad Hussein, a driver and the uncle of one of the dead boys. "They have no right to make war against us." He pointed toward his family's huts, too rickety to withstand blast tremors. "Look at our homes," he said. "We have no shelter."

At the mosque, hours after the blast, the young, burly Haider Kadhim and another caretaker prepared Arkan's body for burial—before sundown, as is Islamic custom. Bathed in the soft glow of turquoise-blue tiles, the room was hushed, as the caretakers finished washing his frail corpse. Arkan rested on his back, naked except for a cloth that covered him from the navel to the knee.

The minutes passed, and Haider and his assistant, Mohammed Jabr, wrapped the boy's head, his stare still fixed, with red-and-yellow plastic, tying it with a string around its neck. They rolled the corpse in plastic sheeting, fastening it with four pieces of white gauze—one at each end, one around Arkan's knees, and one around his chest. Haider worked delicately, turning the body to the side and swathing it tightly in a sheet, securing it with four more pieces of gauze. The sheet was white, the preferred color. The boy's wounds were hidden.

Under their breaths, the men in the room muttered prayers, breaking the suffocating silence. They then moved toward the concrete slab and hoisted the limp body into a wooden coffin. Haider looked up and pointed to other men standing along the wall. He motioned for them to bring the coffin's cover.

"It's very difficult," he said, as the men closed it.

TWO DAYS EARLIER, AT NIGHT ON MARCH 28, HAIDER KADHIM HAD GONE TO another mosque, Imam Moussa Kadhim, to help bury dozens killed when a blast ripped through a teeming market in the nearby Shiite neighborhood of Shuala, a working-class swath of low-slung houses on Baghdad's northern outskirts. On the day of Arkan's funeral, the memories still haunted Haider. (No one saw those scenes just once; inside the witnesses' heads, the violence took place over and over. This is what they often told me.)

The blast in Shuala—the bloodiest single episode in Baghdad during the war—had struck when the market of vegetable stalls, grocers, handymen, and barbers was at its most crowded. On Friday, the Muslim Sabbath, it was teeming with shoppers, despite the war. As in Arkan's neighborhood of Rahmaniya, stories conflicted about what had caused the blast. Iraqi antiaircraft fire may have been responsible in Shuala. But some residents insisted they heard a plane overhead, and one said he saw the orange glow of the engines.

It really didn't matter; the result was the same. When the explosive landed, the people heard no blast and saw no fire; there was only a shower of razor-sharp shrapnel that shattered glass and sliced through flesh. A pregnant moment of silence followed. For an instant, there was quiet, the hush of devastation.

Then the place erupted. Men, women, and children staggered in every direction, stumbling over a tableau of bleeding bodies and limbs. Children cried for their parents. Mothers and fathers shouted the names of their children, lost in a market that had become, in the flash of war, a cauldron of human wreckage. Dozens were killed; neither Haider nor anyone else knew how many for sure. The government said fifty-eight; residents said fifty, maybe; a nearby hospital said at least thirty.

In the streets, one resident said he saw the decapitated head of thirty-three-year-old Hassan Jabr on the sidewalk. Another said he saw the severed legs of fifty-six-year-old Sayyid Hassoun Musawi, tossed in improbable directions. One passerby recalled a five-year-old child with half his face blown off. In the aftermath, a rickety red Volkswagen sat parked along the sidewalk, its windows shattered and its doors sprayed with shrapnel. Corrugated tin, wires, and insulation hung from its roof like vines from a tree. At the entrance of a shuttered shop, a pair of worn sandals sat undisturbed, a stream of blood and water dribbling across their soles.

That night, television cameras cast an eerie luminescence, glowing through the cloak of darkness. The crater left by the blast was barely visible. Ringed by asphalt rubble that was easy to overlook, it was the size of a coffee table—about four feet across, two feet deep. On any other day, it would have melted into Baghdad's ragged, weary landscape.

"What's our sin? What's our sin?" one resident shouted. "The whole world cries when it sees this."

At the dilapidated, overflowing hospital, men stood in the hallway, sobbing, embracing one another. Women ran down the hallways, screaming the names of relatives. Ahmed Sufian, tired and overwhelmed, discarded the detached demeanor of a physician. He spoke of a young child, still breathing but with his intestines pouring out a wound in his abdomen, and he became angry. "Our floors are covered with blood, the walls are splashed with blood. We ask why, why, why?" Ahmed's words raced his emotions. "They came to free us? This is freedom? We have done nothing."

In the neighborhood's dreary, dirty streets, men began carrying to the mosque wood coffins, draped hastily in tattered blankets. "There is no god but God," they murmured, as women in black *abayas* huddled in wailing knots of grief, their silhouettes caught in headlights.

Haider remembered all this. In desperation, he tried to keep pace with the bodies that seemed to come one after the other to the Imam Moussa Kadhim Mosque, a small building of corrugated tin roofs and concrete walls.

Hastily built wood coffins were piled on the floor. Watching over the mourners was a portrait of Imam Hussein, who in popular iconography is a handsome man with liquid eyes shaped like almonds, his beard groomed, his unbound turban perched loosely on his head. Below the portrait at the mosque, in graceful calligraphy, Hussein's name was written in white, each letter in Arabic dripping with stylized blood to represent his seventh-century martyrdom.

Haider recalled the severed hands and heads that passed before Hussein's portrait that night at the mosque. He recalled bodies with gaping holes in their chests, their torsos torn open and mutilated. Thirty, he said, maybe more, laid out in a sanctuary lit by three chandeliers. "It was awful and ugly," he said, grimacing at the memories. "It was the first time I had ever seen anything like that."

AS HAIDER RECALLED THE CARNAGE IN SHUALA, THE MEN SET ARKAN'S COFFIN on the stone floor of an open-air courtyard, in a humble mosque still under construction. They gathered for the *salaat al-janaazah*, the funeral prayer. By tradition, it is conducted by the congregation together. In two rows, they lined up behind the boy's corpse, their shoes removed before them. Their lips moved in prayers practiced thousands of times. "God is greatest," the men repeated, their palms facing upward in supplication, birds warbling beyond the walls. Again. "God is greatest."

In the background, men talked of war. The stories that day described carnage unleashed on a convoy taking the body of an eighty-year-old woman to be buried in the southern city of Najaf.

For Shiites, Najaf is among the most sacred cities, housing the tomb of Ali, the son-in-law and cousin of the prophet Mohammed. (Shiites believe that Ali was the prophet's rightful heir.) By tradition, in 661 the dying Ali asked his followers, in a whisper, to place his body on a camel and bury him wherever it first knelt; Najaf was the site. It remains a place of pilgrimage for millions, and devout Shiites will spend their life's savings for the blessing of being buried in the Valley of Peace, home to vast cemeteries that gird the city. The road there, plied by pilgrims, is one of the most traveled in Iraq.

Aida Afus never made it to Najaf. The men at the Imam Ali mosque said U.S. forces attacked three cars, one a gray minibus carrying the old woman's body in a wood coffin, as they made their way to Najaf after dawn. Her corpse, they said, was never found. It was another ignominy visited on the city, the boy's neighbors and relatives said. It was another of war's verdicts, delivered without appeal.

"What God brings we accept," one of the men muttered.

FATALISM IS A SENTIMENT PERHAPS OVERATTRIBUTED TO THE ARAB WORLD. IT is there, but rather than resignation to fate, it often seems more a reconcilement to injustice, an admission of powerlessness in the face of God's will. It is a far less passive stance than it might seem: to accept is one thing; to agree is another.

In the most terrible periods of bombing during the war, fatalism and acceptance were powerful sentiments, tools used by the people to come to terms with tragedy. Few understood the war, though, or why they had been chosen for this pain.

"We get hurt. We are the simple people who get hurt. The government doesn't get hurt, but we end up getting hurt." These words were spoken by Hussein Abdel-Kadhim, a thirty-five-year-old father of two as he stood in his gutted apartment, on the second floor of a building wrecked by one of two precision-guided U.S. bombs that fell in another predominantly Shiite, work-ing-class neighborhood called Shaab. This bombing occurred the same week as the attack in Shuala, which it rivaled in destructiveness. (These were the two worst incidents of civilian deaths in Baghdad during the invasion.) The bombs fell on March 26 at 11:30 A.M., an hour when Shaab's streets, even in war, were crowded with mechanics, vendors of auto parts, customers at elec-trical appliance stores, and families sitting down to a late breakfast after a jar-ring night of explosions.

Residents said they had heard the murmur of a bomber seconds before the first blast struck. It was followed, in moments, by a second explosion across the street. Together, the bombs devastated a hundred-yard swath of shops, homes, and a restaurant; the result looked like a hurricane's aftermath. Shards of cor-rugated tin dangled from roofs like chimes, colliding on the winds of another savage sandstorm. Doors were torn from their hinges, and shattered pipes poured sewage into the streets. The charred carcasses of cars sat smoldering, hurled onto the sidewalk.

So many people seemed to be in a daze that day, under the stormy, for-bidding sky. Amid the wreckage in Shaab, one man watched helplessly as his friend lay on the ground, legs torn off as he repaired his car in the street. The man ultimately survived. Across the street the severed hand of a seventeen-year-old boy was tossed gracelessly in a pool of blood and mud. He died.

As expected, there were the obligatory shouts of fealty to Saddam from the people who poured into the muddy streets of Shaab. They said what they thought they were supposed to say, what they thought they still had to say. But in those bleak few hours, most striking was the range of sentiments and emo-tions. Not everyone blamed the United States. Even in front of Nasir, Hussein complained bitterly to me that the Iraqi military had trucked missiles and other weapons to a grass-and-mud clearing at the neighborhood's edge. Down the road were at least four antiaircraft guns. The government, he was con-vinced, had made targets of its own people.

Hussein said he blamed "both sides" for the destruction that blew out his doors and sent shattered glass cascading through his apartment. His refriger-ator and television rested against the pockmarked wall, tossed across the room by the force of the blast. Flying debris had hurt his mother, father, brother, and sister, all of whom lived in a cramped apartment of two rooms. Shock waves had hurled cars and people several feet. The government "is responsi-ble for the people," Hussein told me. "They should take care of the people." He shook his head. "Civilians live here," he said.

I wasn't sure what to say to him. Finally, I asked what he would do. His look was matter-of-fact, his answer imbued with fatalism. "What can I do?" he asked. "The building is gone. I have to leave." He went silent for a moment. "We're all tired," he said. "We need a safe place."

WITH THE PRAYERS FINISHED IN ARKAN'S NEIGHBORHOOD OF RAHMANIYA, THE men hoisted the young boy's coffin over their heads and bore it through the mosque's gray steel gates into the desolate, dirt streets awash in trash. Some were barefoot; others wore sandals. Bombing on the horizon provided a refrain, a minatory drumbeat that quickened their tempo and gave strength to their voices. They crossed the street, past concrete and brick hovels, the Shiite flags of solid black, green, red, and white flying overhead. Their faces were hard.

Near Arkan's house, they were met by women in black *abayas* who wailed and screamed, waving their hands and shaking their heads. The cries drowned out the chants as the coffin went indoors. The discord of despair poured out of the home, its windows shattered by the blast that had killed the boy. "My son! My son!" his mother cried out. "Where are you now? I want to see your face!"

The men in Arkan's family embraced, sobbing uncontrollably on one another's shoulders. Others cried into their own hands. From within the house, a drumbeat sounded, as women methodically beat their chests in grief. "This is a poor neighborhood. We're poor. We can't go anywhere else. What is the fault of the families here? Where's the humanity?" asked a neigh-bor. "I swear to God, we're scared."

Some of Arkan's neighbors and relatives were convinced the Americans were intent on vengeance for the setbacks they believed U.S. forces were suf-fering in Basra and other southern Iraqi cities. Others, in moments of striking candor, pleaded for the United States and Britain to wage war against their government, but spare the people. "If they want to liberate people, they can kick out the government, not kill innocent civilians," one relative said. "The innocent civilians are not in business with the government. We're living in our houses."

▪ ▪ ▪

IN RAHMANIYA, SHUALA, AND SHAAB, PERHAPS IT WAS AN ACKNOWLEDGMENT OF war's senselessness that lay behind people's fatalism; where was the logic otherwise? Dictatorship, in its own twisted way, was understandable; repression was universal. War is so random, so arbitrary.

Take the story of the Khalil family who were eating a simple breakfast, later than usual. A cascade of bombs the night before had left them sleepless. When a lull came, at noon, they sat down, picking anxiously at boiled eggs, tomatoes, and bread. Nine-year-old Shahida told stories, and her twelve-year-old brother, Ahmed, laughed. Those older, with harrowing memories of bombings in the 1991 Gulf War, sat uneasily, their silence filled with worry.

Then a whisper sounded, ever so slight. In seconds, their house was shattered, wrecked, they said, by a cruise missile. The mother and her daughter-in-law were killed. Shahida, Ahmed, and another son, Ali, were wounded.

In a warren of narrow alleys, sited uncomfortably beside a trench of burning oil that cloaked the neighborhood in a blinding, black haze, the blast had destroyed at least three houses and blown out the windows of others in an arc around its target. Cream-colored brick and cinder blocks were strewn across the muddy street. Rubble poured forth from a crater that left the homes looking like an archaeological dig. Nearby rested the detritus of lives—a mattress spring, a brown scarf, a green plastic bowl. At the sounds of the blast and the smell of smoke, neighbors had rushed into the house, pushing away furniture and throwing aside rubble to find those buried. A baby's cry could be heard in the distance. Five minutes later, sirens announced the arrival of ambulances, which took the four dead and twenty-seven wounded to Noaman Hospital.

Hours afterward, weary and angry, Aqeel, at twenty-seven the oldest son, looked out at his bandaged siblings lying disoriented in their hospital beds. His wife's body was in the morgue. Relatives ran into the ward, their eyes red. "There are no soldiers in my home, there's no gun in my home!" Aqeel shouted. He started sobbing, and his voice cracked. "How can God accept this?"

Before him, the head of fourteen-year-old Ali was wrapped in a bandage. He stared blankly at the ceiling. His sister, Shahida, lay motionless. Her fingernails were painted in sparkles and ringed by dried blood. The face of his brother Ahmed was still bloodied. A bandage sat like a helmet on his fore-head. "We believe in God, we trust in God. What can we do?" Ahmed said softly, curled in a fetal position on his side. "I'm safe and alive. That's most important."

Dr. Abdullah Abed, out of earshot of Ahmed, shook his head. "He doesn't know that his mother has died," he whispered.

BEFORE DUSK, ARKAN'S COFFIN WAS CARRIED FROM HIS HOUSE IN RAHMANIYA and set on the back of a white pickup truck, headed for the cemetery through a street still littered with debris and plaster. Neighbors, already cleaning up the wreckage, had filled a bucket with shattered glass. A fading sun had tempered the destruction.

As the truck drove away, kicking up clouds of dirt, some of the neighbors and relatives shouted, "God be with you." Other men waved, a gesture whose casualness suggested the strength of their faith that they would eventually be reunited with Arkan.

Mohsin Hattab, the boy's thirty-two-year-old uncle, looked on at the departing coffin. His eyes were red, his shoulders sagged, and his face was drawn.

"He has returned to God," he said softly. "It's God's wish."

5

A DARK, DARK TUNNEL

A wail, fearsome and full of melancholy, sailed across the late-morning sky of Baghdad, piercing the walls of Faruq Ahmed Saadeddin's middle-class home in the neighborhood of Jihad. His wife, Mona, hushed, as did their adult children. The family had been kept awake night after night by air strikes, but they were still alert and listening attentively. Mona, her face lined with fear and pain, shook her head and said what everyone else already knew.

"Siren," she whispered.

At that, her daughter, Yasmine, jumped up and threw open the door, so that the shock waves from the bombing would not rip it from its hinges. She ran for the windows next, fearful the coming blasts would shatter them. The son, my friend Omar, sprinted outside, where he checked for low-flying cruise missiles.

"It's terrible," Mona said, as the minutes passed. "We really suffer, and I don't know why we should live like this."

Yasmine, the quietest in the family, sat down next to Mona on a couch against the wall, under portraits of their forebears in the Ottoman uniforms and British suits of a century ago. "I get so scared, I shake," she said, her eyes fixed in an unfocused stare. "I'm afraid the house is going to collapse on my head."

Omar's wife, Nadeen, joined the conversation. Her words were gloomy, much like the overcast day. "We're in a dark, dark tunnel, and we don't see the light at the end of it," she said. Mona and Yasmine shook their heads in agreement. Faruq and Omar sat stoically.

The two-story house had been prepared for the war, which was still in its first week. Furniture was moved away from the windows. Sofas and tables were cloaked in white dust cloths to protect them from flying glass and debris. Two rifles and bags of ammunition were propped against the wall in the living room, as much for the aftermath as for the war itself. Faruq's family, like most Baghdadis, knew the war was only the beginning.

Baghdad is a city that takes pride in its toughness. There was hardly a man in the capital's streets who would admit to fear. Faruq heard the anxieties of his family, then, with a confident air, listed the challenges Baghdadis had endured: two wars, repeated U.S. air strikes, sanctions.

"We have eleven thousand years of history," he said, a phrase quoted often in Baghdad. "I know it sounds facetious, but it gives you resilience."

Omar, brash and thirty-two years old, nodded. "The bark is worse than the bite."

THE MORNING AFTER THE MARCH 21 BARRAGE, OMAR HAD INVITED ME TO lunch with his family. We had agreed on a date, and when that morning arrived, I gave Nasir a lame excuse that he took in stride. Omar picked me up in his BMW a little before noon. Hoping that no one saw me leaving, I got in the car. Under a sky stirred by war, we headed past checkpoints and sandbagged positions in the direction of the airport, onto the largely deserted highway, and then to his family's home.

Bombing or not, lunch at his home started on time, soon after the air-raid siren had stopped. It was a gesture of defiance.

The family had moved their dining table into a crowded room with fewer windows than the dining room. At the head was Faruq, sixty-five, an urbane former diplomat from the northern city of Mosul. He had served in embassies in Iran, Japan (where Omar was born), China (where Yasmine was born), and, in his longest stint, the United States. (Faruq had received his bachelor of arts in international relations from the University of Arizona in 1964.) He was a dignified man, a defiant nationalist, with a sharp mind and a willingness to expound on any subject. His heavy-framed glasses suggested scholarliness, and his personality was forceful. His wife, Mona, ten years younger, was quieter, more reserved, and visibly shaken by the war, as was his daughter, Yasmine, in her twenties. Omar was with his wife, Nadeen, a friendly woman, engaging and self-confident, who had been born in Baghdad but raised in London. Married in 2001, she was enduring war for the first time.

There was a lavish meal of traditional Iraqi dishes—spicy pickled mango, *kibbe*, *kufta*, chicken cooked with rice, peanuts, and raisins, and the thin bread called *raqqaq*. But the Saadeddins gazed out their window at a sky shrouded in the billowing black smoke meant to conceal targets from U.S. strikes. In vain, they hoped the smoke would limit the air assault. They had already had enough, they said.

The worst, so far, had been the March 21 bombing, when U.S. and British forces hurled 320 Tomahawk cruise missiles at Baghdad. Ten had landed near their home, shattering the window in the front of the house. The shock waves were so intense that they had thrown open the refrigerator door and tossed its drawers on the kitchen floor. "They were powerful, really powerful," Mona said of the blasts. "They came one after another."

For a novice there were questions. How do you interpret an air-raid siren? Short bursts of sound meant the attack had begun, came the reply; a continuous wail meant it was over. The Saadeddins mentioned an antiaircraft gun nearby, which fired as much as sixteen hours a day, almost assuredly in vain. It rattled the house, sometimes throwing open the front door, but did little to American armaments. The family found themselves sleeping in daylight, when the bombing was often less fierce.

Over lunch, they became reflective. They had anxious friends who had fled to neighboring Syria two months earlier, only to run out of money before the war started. (They were forced to return to Baghdad.) Others headed north to Faruq's hometown of Mosul, to weather the war with relatives. The Saadeddins had decided to stay put. "The best place is here," Faruq volunteered.

But even he admitted that remaining was a struggle. A pregnant friend of Nadeen's was supposed to have a Cesarean section within ten days. But her doctor had vanished, and hospital after hospital overwhelmed with the wounded had refused to admit her. Another friend, seven months pregnant, had begun taking Valium. A neighbor said she stuffed cotton in the ears of her two young children every night. She fretted about finding diapers and milk. "She's in a complete panic," Nadeen said. "Everything is turned around." Nadeen had yet to leave the house since the bombing had begun, and the isolation had started to become claustrophobic.

"It's your first war," Omar said to her.

The words struck me. At first, they sounded blustery, even acerbic. But Omar was trying to reassure her. It seemed he was telling her that she would, in time, get used to living this way. The days ahead would be easier.

For weeks, Nadeen had helped put the house in order. She and Omar hauled a mattress downstairs, setting up their bedroom in the dining room. The windows throughout the house were X'd over with tape. (Mona noted that her grandfather had left tape on his windows for ten years after an earlier war.) The family had laid in supplies for a siege. Two tanks were filled with kerosene for cooking in case electricity was cut. Mona filled every pan, kettle, and thermos with water, spreading them across the kitchen floor, in case the pumps stopped working, as they had during the 1991 Gulf War. Bags and bags of flour, sugar, rice, beans, powdered milk, biscuits, jam, cheese, macaroni, wheat, rice, and cereal were stored in what used to be the dining room. Against the living room wall were two Kalashnikovs and fifteen clips of ammunition. Two tanks of water stood in the garden, enclosed by a chest-high steel fence; three others stood on the roof, already filled.

"These will last three months," Omar said, surveying the supplies.

Nadeen interrupted. One month, she said, no more. "The men in our family have very big appetites," she joked.

Over lunch, Faruq and his family spoke about politics; at times brashly, they discussed what was usually whispered. Faruq had left the Baath Party in 1968, a move he did not regret but that he believed had prevented his rise to ambassador. He was a critic of Saddam, whom he called rash. "Iraq is ready for change," he said. "The people want it, they want more freedom."

In those moments of frankness, fleeting as they were, the intricacies of Iraq's politics became more understandable and Omar and Faruq came to embody broader assumptions at work in their embattled country. Each represented viewpoints that would greet U.S. soldiers on their imminent entry into Baghdad.

Omar was younger and, as one might expect, more reflexive, his words bitter and somewhat strident. To him, American promises of liberation were no more than rhetorical flourishes to a policy bent on domination, and furthering U.S. and Israeli interests in the Middle East. With decades of politics behind him, Faruq was more tempered. He was no less skeptical, no less suspicious, but he saw the shades of the moment before him. Iraq was changing, and Faruq was already struggling to see the direction it would take.

But the men converged in their denunciations of the invasion. Perhaps more than any other Arab citizens, Iraqis are instilled with traditions of pride, honor, and dignity. To Faruq and Omar, the assault was an insult. It was not Saddam under attack, but Iraq, and they insisted that pride and patriotism prevented them from putting their destiny in the hands of another country. "We complain about things, but complaining doesn't mean cooperating with foreign governments," Faruq said, as if stating a self-evident truth. "When somebody comes to attack Iraq, we stand up for Iraq. That doesn't mean we love Saddam Hussein, but there are priorities."

In the background was Fox News, its jingoistic broadcasts draped in the U.S. flag, boosting "Operation Iraqi Freedom." Omar said his family liked to watch it, wanting to see, as he put it, what Americans were really thinking. In the context of the conversation, with war just outside the windows, the lust for war in the broadcasts was disorienting.

"Either you're with us or you're with Saddam Hussein," Faruq complained, parroting Bush. "You have a problem," he said, addressing the American administration, "you don't understand."

"I don't even care about the leadership," Nadeen added. "But someone wants to take away what is yours. What gives them the right to change something that's not theirs in the first place? I don't like your house, so I'm going to bomb it and you can rebuild it again the way I want it, with your money? I feel like it's an insult, really. What they're doing to us, they deserve to have done to them . . . their families, their children."

Gathered around the table, the family members nodded their heads.

"There are rumblings," Faruq added, as the conversation went on. "But these rumblings don't mean 'Come, America, we'll throw flowers at you.'"

▪ ▪ ▪

FARUQ'S FAMILY WAS ARAB AND SUNNI MUSLIM. SUNNI ARABS ARE ONE OF THE country's three dominant groups, and for much of Iraq's history, they have had the power of the state, in various incarnations, in their hands. They constitute probably a fifth of Iraq's population of twenty-five million, but precise percentages are fiercely disputed because the country has not had a credible census. Roughly equal in number are the Kurds, an ethnic group concentrated in the north. Since Iraq's independence, the Kurds have fought in varying degrees of intensity for autonomy or independence. Under Saddam, they weathered repression sometimes described as genocidal.

The most numerous of Iraq's three main groups are the Shiite Muslims, concentrated in the poorer, underdeveloped south. Like the Sunnis, they are mostly Arab, but for most of Iraq's history, they have been on the outside looking in. Like the Kurds under Saddam, they endured unrelenting repression for thirty-five years of Baathist rule. Iraq also has a handful of small ethnic and religious minorities: Turkomans, Yazidis, Christians, and Sabaeans.

The distinctions among Sunni, Shiite, and Kurd often mean less in Iraq than they do in the West, where they can serve as facile shorthand and thus understate the byzantine complexity of the country's demographics. Tribes, sometimes including both Sunnis and Shiites, still play a powerful, even resurgent role in Iraq. Most Kurds are Sunni, but some count themselves Shiites. Among the Shiites themselves, there are gradations in identity: between the secular and the religious; across a loose caste system built around descendants of the prophet Mohammed's family; between the modern educated and those still molded by the durable but traditional scholastic institutions of the clergy based in Najaf and, to a lesser extent, Karbala and Baghdad.

There is no less diversity among Sunnis. For centuries, Sunni Arabs as a group ruled Iraq; particularly powerful were the elite in the capital. Blessed by wealth, education, and the favoritism of overlords, they were the administrators and officers under the Ottoman Empire, then—in large part through inertia— the favorites of the British, who arrived after World War I. The elite Sunnis, however, were not those members of the sect on whom Saddam actually relied.

Saddam's upbringing in the countryside singularly shaped his dictatorship. To build his version of the Baath Party, he broke the power of the Sunni elite. Ever suspicious, he relied instead on the ranks of disenfranchised Sunnis like himself, the neglected from towns such as Tikrit, Samarra, and Thuluyah and the rural regions around them, men imbued with fierce, often unforgiving traditions. Their loyalty was commanded by patronage; he played to their chauvinism and their prejudices against the Shiites. That alliance lasted for years, though in time he winnowed down the ranks of those he favored to his family. Still, it was generally conceded in Baghdad at this time that the Sunnis, defined broadly, had most to lose in postwar Iraq.

Faruq and his family did not often speak in sectarian terms. Like many in Baghdad, they shied away from the old classifications; asking a question about someone's identity was often seen as ill-mannered. Omar made one of the few mentions of sectarian matters that day, remarking that some of his Shiite friends disagreed with him over the consequences of the U.S. attack. If Saddam stayed in power, they told him, their situation would remain the same; if he was overthrown, they would be done with him, finally.

At present, though, survival was the more pressing issue. By late afternoon, as we sat in the living room after lunch, the thunder of bombing broke again across the horizon. Fox News reported that B-52s had departed their base for Iraq, and the family members guessed at how long it would take the planes to arrive over Baghdad.

They were jittery, flinching at the slightest sounds. "That's wind, that's wind," Faruq said, when the door slammed shut. When Omar got up, his chair banging the wall, the mother jumped. "What was that?" she said.

"It was me," Omar answered.

A few minutes later, he did it again.

"Quit doing that," Mona commanded. "I'm so scared," she said, "every little noise."

Outside, the sounds of life reverberated off the street. A rickety cart passed the house, its driver clanging a piece of metal to signal his arrival. He had come to empty trash and refill kerosene tanks. The ritual was familiar, and as it passed, the routine it evoked seemed to anger Omar.

"I should be able to live like other people are living," he said glumly. "I shouldn't fear bombs falling on my head, I shouldn't be hearing sirens. Why should I have to live like this? Why should this be normal?"

Everyone looked at the floor. No one said a word.

▪ ▪ ▪

YASMINE MUSA—YASMINE IS A COMMON NAME AMONG IRAQI WOMEN—WAS staying with her husband, two sons, and daughter in the wealthy, commercially vibrant neighborhood of Arasat during the war. A petite, beautiful woman with deep, dark eyes, she was the oldest child of a compassionate Shiite Muslim psychiatrist.

Yasmine Musa had chosen to document her experience of the American invasion. In letters to her friends, she created a personal chronicle of the siege. Often, before electricity was cut, she sent the letters by e-mail. Afterward, she kept them on her computer, powered by a generator.

While less outwardly political than Faruq and Omar, Yasmine Musa was no less concerned about the fate of her country. In principle, she was as angry about the American invasion as she was about Saddam, whom she reviled.

Her family had already relocated from the neighborhood of Jadriya in the days before the fighting erupted. Now, they debated whether to stay in this house or move to another, safer home. "We do what we think is safe, then we leave the rest in the hands of the Almighty," she wrote.

Her first letter spoke to an anxiety that was often voiced, the fear that this conflict would be a repeat of the 1991 Gulf War, when bombing of more than seven hundred sites knocked out bridges, railroads, oil refineries, and, most disastrously, electricity. Memories of those hardships were seared into the capital's collective conscience. The Pentagon's warnings of a bombing that would elicit "shock and awe" terrified the population.

"Do you think they will be as brutal as they were in 1991?" Yasmine asked in the letter. "I recall Bush Senior reportedly alleging that he had nothing against the Iraqi people, only to discover after the first hours of dawn that we were cut off from electricity, water, and means of communication even though the war was barely a few hours old. It seems that these were among his main targets and the people hated him for this. Do you think Bush Junior is a copy?" She ended the letter with a plea. "I am so scared. I could die from fear over losing a beloved one. God, please do not let that happen."

Perhaps the most terrifying sensations of life in a city under siege are the sounds of the bombers. In a siege, one's hearing becomes exquisitely sensitive. Much of the time, one waits for the faint sound, the whisper that signals the plane's arrival. The entire body listens. Every muscle tightens, and one stops breathing. Time slows in the interim.

Those waits terrified Yasmine, testing her as a Baghdadi and as a mother.

"Do those people up there have the faintest idea what is happening down here when they unload?" she wrote. "During a close air raid, my daughter asked me, 'Why are they doing this?' To remove the evil Saddam, I answered. 'Wouldn't a bullet in the head do?' she wearily responded. At times like this, one develops a sense of selfishness. When we hear the fighter coming, we hold our breath and our hearts pound as if they are to jump out. Then as soon as we hear the explosion, no matter how close, we launch a sigh of relief. Afterward, one starts to calculate whether it's dropped on a loved one."

"For three consecutive nights in a row, we haven't had a wink of sleep," Yasmine wrote to another friend. "I doubt any special effects in the most thrilling American movie have half the effect these terrible machines hanging high up there have on us down here. May they see days bleaker than the nights they are putting us through. I wonder how they will justify it afterward. Do you think they will try?

"Last night my youngest said, 'Mama, I don't want the night to come. I wish we could skip it. I am starting to hate it.' In the name of God, what should I say to him?" she asked.

She ended the letter with a plea: "Pray for us, for we need every prayer."

As with many of Baghdad's wealthier and more educated citizens, sectarian differences meant relatively little in Yasmine's circles. Although she was a Shiite, her husband was a Sunni, and she was, in a way, a child of the 1970s. Smart and motivated, she earned a degree from Baghdad University in 1979, then found work as a civil engineer at the Baghdad International Airport (soon renamed after Saddam).

Yasmine once told me that, when she graduated, she was filled with hope. Her husband was an architect. Their families were well-to-do, and a then resurgent Iraq had the ambitions of a modern country. Even schoolteachers, Yasmine remembered, were taking their vacations abroad. "We presumed we had it all, a very promising future ahead of us," she said. The only inconvenience, she remembered, was her husband's compulsory military duty. "It was no big deal anyway, just a few months left to finish his army service. That won't do anybody any harm."

Those few months turned into seven years when Saddam invaded Iran. Yasmine's husband was sent from front to front; she and her relatives would try to match his movements with reports on where the greatest carnage was. One of her memories from that time remains especially painful. On a day near the start of the war, she entered the house of her husband's parents, only to hear someone crying.

"I was then five months pregnant. Without asking, I immediately assumed that something had happened to my husband. I stepped into my car and drove aimlessly in the streets for two hours, thinking, 'I'm a twenty-two-year-old widow and single mother.'"

It turned out it was her sister-in-law's husband who was wounded, but Yasmine lost the baby, a miscarriage she blamed on the stress of war.

To a far greater degree than Faruq and Omar, Yasmine despised Saddam; for more than three decades her family had "refused to ride the Baathist wave." They had no party affiliation and, no matter how troubled the times, tried their best to maintain what they saw as their "morals, decency, and integrity." When many others in Iraq were fleeing, they stayed in the country. That record—a decision not to leave—shaped their antipathy, shared by many, toward Iraqi exiles who on their return expected to play a decisive role in whatever emerged from the American invasion.

She was skeptical of the United States, even confused by it. She spoke of the support of the Reagan administration for Saddam's government in the war with Iran in the 1980s, of the sanctions, of the perception—not uncommon in Iraq—that Saddam had remained in power as long as he did with Washington's blessing. She recalled, in vivid detail, the visit in December 1983 to Baghdad by Donald Rumsfeld, then a special envoy of Reagan's, and the pictures of him, in suit and tie, shaking hands with Saddam, dressed in an olive-green military uniform. (According to a January 1984 U.S. State Department memo, Foreign Minister Tariq Aziz was said to have pronounced the Iraqi leadership "extremely pleased" with Rumsfeld's visit. Aziz praised Rumsfeld as a person and noted that he was "a good listener.") Why the support? she asked. Why didn't the United States do anything to stop years of breathtaking abuses? Why didn't American officials see Saddam for what he was years earlier?

Yasmine looked at war through that lens of circumspection. She looked ahead with the same wariness. "On the first day of war, I was worried more about the aftermath than the war itself," she said. Her words would echo in her own ears.

YASMINE'S FATHER, FUAD MUSA MOHAMMED, LIVED IN MANSUR. HIS SON, FIRAS, an acquaintance, had reached me on my satellite phone at the Palestine Hotel and asked that I check on his father, who was staying at the family's home in Mansur.

The drive there was difficult and the house took quite a while to find. Baghdad's red double-decker public buses were still running—a sign of surreal normalcy—but Mansur, long the toniest of the city's neighborhoods, felt like a clenched fist. Soldiers toted heavy machine guns or slung rocket-propelled grenade launchers over their shoulders. Handfuls of militiamen—poorly trained, many in civilian clothes with green ammunition belts slung over their chests—paced the sidewalks or crouched behind sandbags. Some wore helmets; others wore checkered scarves.

Fuad sat alone in the living room, having sent his wife, Suad, to stay with her brother in Beirut, a fairly easy drive from Baghdad. Artillery thundered in the distance, its regularity making it somewhat less threatening. Planes swept overhead—each run making for that familiar suspense—and occasional bursts of gunfire echoed through the maze of largely abandoned streets outside his home. The shooting, in particular, made me edgy, but Fuad didn't seem to be concerned at all. Like Faruq, the diplomat, Fuad was imbued with that trait of trying to instill confidence even when it wasn't warranted.

Bald and with a thin white mustache, lean but not frail, Fuad was light-hearted. Ebullient but proud, he had a compassion that, perhaps, was abetted by the psychiatric training he had completed in Britain in the 1960s. Unlike Faruq or Omar, he was optimistic, as few people were openly those days. Even in the darkest, longest days of the war, with the battery-powered radio his only companion, he was filled with resilience, an indomitable sense of self that had left him his integrity under Saddam.

"Everybody has run away," the doctor said, his voice seeming louder against the emptiness of his immaculate two-story house, where he and his family had lived since 1973. "Everybody has run away from Baghdad."

Fuad looked out the window, which like most glass in Baghdad was covered by tape. There was little respite from the war that day—neither in Mansur nor the rest of Baghdad. "All the time, boom, boom, boom," he said, in a tone of patient observation.

Unsolicited, his grievances poured out, as if the moment and the isolation had made bold talk more permissible. He despised the government, he said, and didn't understand why Saddam would not step down, "for the sake of his people and the sake of his country." A Shiite Muslim, Fuad listed the crimes of his government—exiling tens of thousands of his fellow Shiites to Iran, its brutal rule, eight years of war, and, of course, the invasion of Kuwait. Iraq's resources and wealth had been squandered, he said, and its people deprived, spiritually and materially. With a sense of nostalgia, he recalled what he made forty years ago as a doctor: eighty dinars a month, the equivalent of $350. Today, he told me, doctors' salaries were no more than a few dollars a month. His own pension, after a thirty-two-year career, was about ten dollars every three months, and he was among the better off. And now, with a long life behind him, he had to brace for a battle over Baghdad that many, in private moments, believed was suicidal, orchestrated by Saddam's vanity.

"We hate this person," Fuad said matter-of-factly. "We want him off us. He's not only a dictator, but he's given nothing to the people." He stopped for a moment, glancing at the pictures of his children and his grandchildren lining the wall, then repeated himself and shook his head. "They hate him. Even the soldiers, they hate him. We've had enough. Really, we've had enough."

Fuad talked of the Iraqi leader from the perspective of a psychiatrist born in Baghdad. His themes were familiar to me: Saddam was not from the capital but the countryside, he said, and he grew up in poverty. He never really completed his education. He had no father to speak of; his mother, a rough-hewn woman, was stern and unforgiving. "It wasn't healthy," Fuad said, his tone almost sympathetic. Almost. "He was deprived of affection. That is how he governed."

The doctor realized what he was saying and didn't seem to care. The government at the time was still full of preposterous bravado: that week, the information minister had said that Iraqi officials were still deliberating what religious rites they should guarantee for the corpses of U.S. and British soldiers and whether they should be buried in mass pits or individual graves. But

Baghdad was already in the throes of change. The doctor knew it, and there was a hint of satisfaction in his voice.

"He's finished," he predicted.

Fuad sat in the dark; it was early afternoon. A few days before, at eight P.M., as a beleaguered capital settled into an unsettled routine of bombing and the invasion moved past what no one yet knew was its midway point, electricity had been cut. In an instant, Baghdad had flickered into a blinding black. Darkness quenched city lights that, days into the war, had still shimmered on the Tigris and evoked an elusive serenity. Gone were the street lamps that cast a glow on palm trees and on the wrecked presidential palaces along the river's banks. Gone were the lights that, shining from windows, softened the scars across a withering city. Oases of lights powered by generators continued to dot a handful of hotels and the homes of the wealthy. But within minutes, Baghdad's streets emptied and an eerie quiet descended on the city. The capital was largely lifeless, save for the pinpoints of solitary car lights, redolent of ships gliding along a sea.

The war, some felt, could be divided into before the blackout and after; electricity—something taken for granted in the West—became one of the most enduring narratives of the occupation. Militiamen clad in green khaki and carrying Kalashnikovs still patrolled the streets, but the remarkable resilience the city had demonstrated in the face of adversity, with shops open, markets crowded, and street sweepers plying the roads, seemed drained, at least for now. The capital, perched on a precarious edge of the unknown, reverted to the ghost-town state of the war's early days.

No one knew the cause of the blackout, and no one would know it for weeks. U.S. military officials based in the Persian Gulf state of Qatar said that American planes and missiles had not targeted the electrical grid. That neither Iraqi radio nor television mentioned the outage was unsurprising, given their almost blanket programming of patriotic music, nationalist speeches, and odes to Saddam. (In the end, well after the war, Iraqi and U.S. engineers speculated that fighting near the airport might have cut high-voltage lines that circled Baghdad, sending surges along the grid and forcing plants to shut down.)

Fuad's living room lay in a premature dusk, as the sun reflected softly off the tan tile floors. Half-burned candles were scattered about. He offered a soft drink and apologized for the lack of ice.

Fuad was the kind of Iraqi the United States had hoped to encounter once in Baghdad. But as much as he anticipated Saddam's fall, even longed for it, he shared some of his daughter's worries. He predicted that Baghdad would wait to assess American intentions, but that the opportunity to demonstrate these would be perilously brief.

He shook his head. "If they say, 'Okay, this is your country, we can give you all that you need, and then we'll leave,' that would be great. But when you hear that American generals are coming to govern Iraq and that it will last one year, two years, three years, six months, this view, when you explain it to simple people, the majority, that will be very difficult. They can't digest it."

After an especially loud blast, one that made me start, Fuad stopped for a moment, then went on, his speech slowing. His words were grim, even as he was exuberant.

"They'll say, 'Who's better, Saddam or the Americans?'" he said, nodding, his dark eyes opening wider. "At least Saddam's from the country, and they're from the outside. I may understand it," he added, "but the majority won't."

"If they're honest from the start, it will be different," he said. "But if the military comes here for one year, just guess what will happen."

In a softer voice, Fuad suggested Saddam might even find a way to survive, somehow. He asked me for news, trying to sort out the contradictions he heard on Iraqi radio and the Arabic-language broadcasts of Radio Monte Carlo and the British Broadcasting Corporation. In days that dragged on, he said, he had little to do but listen alone to the radio and wait.

Nasir and Karim were due to pick me up soon, so Fuad and I walked through his front door, guarded by a gate of latticed steel, and wandered into his garden, a lovely, serene setting of date palms and orange and tangerine trees. We stood in the manicured grass, chatting while we awaited Karim. Fuad spoke of Iraqi tangerines, the particularly sweet taste of the variety grown in Baghdad. Despite his soothing conversation, though, he seemed anxious, like everyone. Nasir and Karim ended up being an hour late, having gone to check on their families. As Fuad and I stood listening to the thud of bombs, I conjured up an image of someone from the Baath Party militia having seen me enter Fuad's gate. What if they decided to pay the older man a visit? I tried to act casual and relaxed.

"Time is slow," Fuad said, aware of my unease, "very, very slow."

6

A DAUGHTER'S DIARY

The day her son Ali had boarded the bus for the war, Karima Salman, the mother of eight, had returned home, tears running down her veiled face.

"I don't know his news," she said, a few days later in her cramped apartment. "He has no phone. I can't talk to him." Her voice dropped to a whisper. "This war is such a loss," she said. "Iraq suffers. It always suffers."

Now, as the war raged on, Karima was gathered with her young daughters, all of them reluctant to leave the relative safety of their apartment, which was off a busy four-lane street, just around the corner from a clothing store and across the way from a stall selling postcards and posters of well-groomed Arab pop stars (Nancy Ajram, Asala, and Kadhim al-Saher) and their scantily clad Western counterparts (Shakira, Jennifer Lopez, and Britney Spears). Morning and evening, they shared sweet tea with neighbors, who in turn shared feverishly traded rumors.

At night, at the top of each hour, they tried to pick up Arabic-language broadcasts of France's Radio Monte Carlo, to hear what they considered unbiased reports on the war—the mere mention of southern Iraqi towns and cities like Umm al-Qasr, Nasiriya, Basra, and Najaf bringing fear to those whose relatives were soldiers or residents there. In silence, they scoured the broadcasts for any detail on fighting in Mosul, about 225 miles north of

Baghdad and the closest city to Ali's antiaircraft battery. His mother said he had hesitated only briefly to rejoin his unit.

"He wasn't scared," Fatima said proudly.

Karima shot her oldest daughter a look of disapproval. "Of course, he was scared," she snapped. "He's anxious. And we're anxious for him. But God is present."

The girls, until then giggling, turned quiet as Karima admitted she had eaten rarely and slept little since Ali boarded the bus for Mosul. "This war has no meaning," she declared. "The boys in their twenties, the boys who will have families. They have to fight. Why do they have to enter the battles? Why do they have to face death?" She shook her head, helpless.

Karima rarely mentioned her second-oldest son, eighteen-year-old Mohammed, stockier and surlier than Ali, who was, according to the girls, a bit of a neer-do-well. Sentenced to prison for stealing a car after a night of drinking Shehrazad beer, he served only five months and had been released in October 2002 during the amnesty ordered by Saddam. He had then joined a motley unit of more than a dozen militiamen patrolling Baghdad's streets. In street clothes and carrying a Kalashnikov, they said, he looked after an anti-aircraft gun parked in front of a school. According to the girls, he was looking for a fight.

At times, Karima's smiling daughters broke into a reflexive chant in support of Saddam, reverting to slogans they had often heard. "God protect Saddam," one of the twins would begin. Then the others would join in. They seemed to be repeating, out of fear or habit, what they had always been forced to say and believe.

Like many girls her age, fourteen-year-old Amal was a member of the Baath Party youth group. She said what was expected in public, and she used the only language she knew. "If you were sitting in your house and somebody attacked you, would you accept that?" she asked me. "We won't accept somebody coming into our country. We'll defend our country, and we'll defend our home.

"If a foreigner wants to enter Baghdad in peace, we will welcome him like a brother," she went on. "If a foreigner wants to enter as an enemy, every family will go out and confront them, even with stones. If they don't throw rocks, then they'll throw dirt. Not only the Iraqi army will fight, but the families, the children, even the elderly will."

Karima looked on, a little blankly. Her words were softer, perhaps wearier. "Nobody hates the Americans," she said, sitting cross-legged on the mattress, a tiny cup of coffee beside her. "The opposite. We want peace, and we want stability, between us and them. They have mothers, they have families. We're all born the same."

BEFORE THE WAR BEGAN, AMAL HAD STARTED A DIARY, WHICH SHE TUCKED IN A drawer in the family's apartment. Its passages are a tale of war seen through the gradually opening eyes of a bright but isolated girl. In daily entries—some chronological, others reflective—she narrated her family's experiences in her besieged capital and tried to bring some sense to her world.

The diary's binding was soon broken, and its tattered cover held together by newspaper. The words were scribbled in the handwriting of a child, the sloping script of Amal's not-yet-confident Arabic. Often, she wrote while lying on the floor, her dark, braided hair falling across her back as she hunched over the paper, her head a breath away from the words she wrote. Her work was illuminated by flickering lights or—during the frequent blackouts that soon became permanent—by a paraffin lamp or a cheap candle pouring out black smoke. Her message was not political; during the war, she wrote Saddam's name not once. Rather, she wrote to calm herself, to record what felt like the end of the world. She started simply, with a customary religious invocation:

"In the name of God, the merciful, the compassionate . . .

"My name is Amal. I have a happy family made up of nine persons: three brothers, who are Ali, a soldier in Mosul; Mohammed, an engraver; and Mahmoud, a student. There are five sisters: Fatima, who helps my mother at home; Zainab; Amal; and my twin sisters, Duaa and Hibba. I am very proud of my mother because she is a great person, who works to bring us food because my father died when we were young."

With her family, Amal wrote, she was waiting for what the invasion would bring. "War will be torture," she wrote in the first entry. "You can see sadness in the eyes of children, and fear. My mother is crying, afraid for us. War separates people, the people we love, and we are worried about the war and the destruction that comes with it."

Only in the most cursory fashion had Amal been molded by politics, although like everyone in her generation, she had grown up subject to the relentless indoctrination of the Baath Party. She was too young to remember the previous conflict, the 1991 Gulf War. America she knew only through official portraits.

She had been drawn into the preparations that absorbed all Baghdadis before the bombing. Prices had skyrocketed and families with no money, like Karima's, braced for the fighting but found themselves unable to stockpile supplies. Most shops closed, and streets were deserted by nightfall. Some of their neighbors left the apartment building, seeking safety in the countryside.

"We are supplying ourselves with water, and are scared that the water and electricity will be cut off. Duaa and Hibba are praying to God all the time, to avert war. Fatima feels hopeful that war will not occur. At 8:30, my mom baked a lot of bread for us, so that we will not be short during the war because bakeries will be closed. We keep asking why is there war in the world? Why?

"Praise to God for everything," she went on, "but I wish there wouldn't be a war."

Gradually, as the invasion neared, all the pieces of Amal's ordinary life fell away, one by one. She went to school with her sister Zainab to find only a handful of girls there. So they turned around and went home. Hibba and Duaa, always enthusiastic about their studies, were the only ones in their class.

Her life reeling, Karima wept repeatedly, sometimes uncontrollably. Often, at the sight of her tears, her daughters cried, too. They looked to her for strength, and her weakness terrified them. Duaa and Hibba would read the Quran for solace. Amal would stay hunched over her diary, recording the scene.

"Eyes are crying for everything precious," she wrote in one passage.

At four A.M., in the dark, electricity in their apartment interrupted yet again by a periodic cut, they had heard the war's arrival, with the attack on Saddam's bunker.

"Please, God, save us. Our hearts are full of fright," Amal wrote.

Her thoughts turned to Ali. "Please, God," she wrote simply, "protect my brother."

FAITH FOR KARIMA AND HER FAMILY WAS NOT A MATTER OF RELIGIOUS ZEALOTRY. It was not even piety, really. It gave their lives cadence. Like the Muslim call to prayer, uttered from minarets five times daily beginning at dawn, religion ordered the day. It spoke with clarity, offered simplicity, and served as a familiar refuge in troubled times. Interspersed in Amal's diary are scenes of her neighbors reading the Quran, its passages usually committed to memory. The twins often recited prayers—little more than pleas for the fighting to stop—and similar invocations could be heard throughout the building.

"Oh God, the one and only," Amal remembered one neighbor saying.

"Oh God, oh Mohammed!" shouted another.

"Oh God, protect me!" yelled one woman.

God shadowed their lives. "Dear God, give us peace and safety": in the intimate pages of her diary, Amal wrote this phrase often.

On television, throughout the war, Karima's family and the rest of Baghdad were subjected to a slew of patriotic songs, footage of goose-stepping Iraqi soldiers, and images of Saddam firing into the air. Although the Americans continued their methodical march to the capital and U.S. airpower met no resistance there, the propaganda continued. Yet in Amal's diary, fervor was in short supply. People traded rumors, often wild speculations, really, that terrified Karima's family. "Our neighbor . . . came over," Amal wrote. "He said they bombed the Civil Defense Command, only about twenty minutes from us. They bombed again at 10:45 and again and again. I turned on the radio. Reports said America bombed two main palaces on the Tigris at 10:50. I sat in the corridor of the apartment building with Um Haider and Um Saif, and we talked about the war. Then at 11:10, the raid ended and my mother said, 'Thank God.' Um Haider said, 'Only ten minutes and they will come to bomb us again.'"

In the war's early days, life was power cuts, air-raid sirens, blasts that shook the shoddily built building, and fear. "I am sitting in the corridor in front of the apartment, beside my mother," wrote Amal on one of the worst nights of bombing. "Explosions are becoming stronger and stronger, and in the eyes of Iraqi families, you can see terror and fright."

The narration picks up later, the writing less shaky. "We don't know when Bush's storm will rise again. . . . We had supper at 10:10, and at 10:15 the siren went off again, signaling the end of the raid. We went back to the apartment. Oh, the fear, the waiting and the anxiety in men, children, and women. Children's hearts are filled with fear and pain from war. . . . What fault did they commit, crying and growing up carrying the pains of war?"

Through Amal's eyes, it is possible to see that familiar veneer of Iraqi bravado melting away.

"At 7:50 P.M., the wind was very strong. The main door of the building is closing and opening with big noise because of the wind," she wrote on March 25, a week into the war. "At 9:10, there was an air-raid siren and the wind is still blowing very strong. Now at 10:10, another siren to mark the end of the raid. But is it really the end of the raid? Or what? At 10:55, another one. Why didn't they give us time to rest? Only 45 minutes?"

As the days passed, Karima's family asked again and again when the bombing would end and when it would begin again. Nights were sleepless, and as the war dragged on, the air-raid sirens became more disorienting. Had that siren signaled the end or the beginning of an attack? It was hard to keep track. Outside, sandstorms cloaked the sun in hues of red, brown, and sickly yellow. "The weather is like heaven's anger on the land and the people," Amal wrote. "I looked through the window but found no one there. The skies are dark, dark, and we don't know what's going to happen to us. As I write, tears are running from my eyes."

AFTER THE FIRST WEEK OF WAR, WITH LIFE'S ARITHMETIC STILL BEING RECAL-culated, Karima's family tried to reclaim at least moments of their life as it had been. Neighbors again paid visits, gathering on the floor to chat. It was reported on March 28, Amal wrote, that telephone exchanges had been bombed. On March 30, one of the city's bridges was also hit. Rumors about other targets circulated furiously: people mentioned the sprawling military base known as Rashid Camp; the utility station in Dora; Saddam International Airport on Baghdad's outskirts. Occasionally, after cleaning the apartment, Karima's family would hurry up to the roof to shake out the carpets. One day, they visited peace activists staying at the Fanar Hotel.

During the worst attacks, fearful that an especially close explosion might bring their building down, Karima's family would hurry from their mattress in the corridor and down the trash-strewn stairwell. They waited by the gate, near rust-colored pools of water leaking from the corroded pipes. Soon, as the bombing developed a rhythm, the children ventured into the streets, hoping to escape the solitude and suffocating confines of the apartment's three rooms. But then the bombs would come again.

"The American started bombing at 1:20," Amal wrote in one entry. "The children were playing outside, but when the bombing began, they ran inside, calling my mother's name, with fear in their eyes. Mother said, 'Don't be afraid'; then they quieted down and gathered in one room. Hibba, Duaa, and Mahmoud pleaded to God that there would be no war. Then we went to the roof—me, Zainab, and our friend Emad—to wash the carpet. We saw three planes, the skies covered by black smoke, and we got scared again."

By the beginning of April, Amal had grown almost accustomed to the patterns of war. In two weeks, bombing had become ordinary, while the air raids destroyed presidential palaces, the Information Ministry, military barracks, television transmitters, telephone exchanges, and other communications facilities.

Wednesday, April 2, 2003

At 9:35 in the morning, we woke up to hard, heavy bombing, which went on till 9:48. God protect us. At 10:15, the bombing ended, but electricity went out at 10:20. At 1:30 in the afternoon, there was heavy bombing. It went on and was coming closer. Electricity came back at 3:10, and at 3:30, the bombing stopped. At 5:23, a plane flew over the building, while the bombing was going on. At 7:00, the bombing ended, but at 8:20, a very violent explosion shook the building while I, Duaa, and Hibba were sitting with Saif. Mother, Fatima, Mohamed, Zainab, and Mahmoud had gone to visit her friend because she was ill. They were scared and terrified because the bombing was very violent. At 9:50, the bombing ended, but at 10:35, two missiles flew close to the building; then, at 11:10, another violent explosion shook the building. Very, very heavy bombing. God protect me. At 3:00 at night electricity went out, then came back at 5:03.

IN HER DIARY, AMAL NEVER SPOKE OF THE WAR IN POLITICAL TERMS. THERE WAS only a young girl who did not understand why people were dying. Death in itself was wrong, whoever the victim; angry, she could see no justification.

"Fatima was crying," Amal wrote of her sister, after they had watched scenes on Iraqi television of American prisoners of war and at least four U.S. soldiers killed on March 23 near the southern town of Nasiriya. Burned and bloodied, some of the bodies were partially undressed. Some of the faces of those alive were taut with fear.

"Why?" she wrote, her questions followed in rapid fire. "What's the fault of those soldiers who were killed? What's the fault of the families of the dead, or their mothers, who must be crying over their sons? Why is this war happening?"

Amal, her family's hardship aside, had never seen images of war. She had never thought about its arbitrary and unappealable verdicts. As she wrote at night, the electricity intermittent, she endeavored to make sense of things. She struggled to grasp the images she saw—American and British soldiers binding the hands of Iraqis in the south, brick and concrete homes destroyed, hospitals crammed with the statistics of war:

"I saw on TV the injured in the south. I saw dead children, one without a hand, it was cut off. They were five or six years old, and the young men were aged sixteen or seventeen, injured in their legs. How were they at fault? Why is there fighting? Oh God, have mercy on our dead," she wrote on April 1. "At 11:30, on al-Alam [a station run by Iran and broadcast locally] I saw a very sad picture, extremely sad, that of a dead infant. How are the infants at fault, and the women who died? Is this just? Where is justice, where are human rights, where are the Arabs, the Muslims, the Christians? Where is mercy? . . . I don't know how to describe my feelings, grief over those dying."

Amal's diary, in its own way, marked the onset of her coming-of-age. In its pages, she began pushing herself to make sense of her world. She asked questions she had never before asked, and she refused to accept any explanation—American promises and her own government's declarations both seemed empty—for the conflict that had engulfed her life.

BAGHDAD'S FRAGILE, JURY-RIGGED ELECTRICAL NETWORK WAS NO MATCH FOR war's rigors and it gave out daily. For hours at a time, Karima's home would be thrown into darkness. Sometimes, the family would pull out the lamps and candles, casting the apartment in a soft glow. Time and again, power would eventually return, a semblance of the ordinary.

On April 3, though, the lights stayed out as the war built toward its climax. "We are in darkness, the lights are out, and we can't see anything, not even the stairs outside the door. No one can see because of the darkness," Amal wrote. "Oh God, light Iraq with your magnificent light."

The next day, the faucets in the kitchen and bathroom splashed water for a few moments. A cough followed, then a wheeze, before the pipes finally fell silent.

"We don't know what to do," Amal said in an entry that day. "We went looking for water and found all the taps were dry. Oh God, why this torture? Mother went to make some bread at 3:30 and said, 'God, even the water is off. What do they want?'"

The blackout signaled a new chapter in a war that would prove surprisingly brief, at least for the Iraqis, who had expected (and feared) so much more from Saddam. Now there was more than just bombing to contend with. In the last week of the official war, a foreign army laid siege to Baghdad for the first time since World War II. The battle was brief, but at times ferocious. It brought pandemonium and panic, chaos and uncertainty. Often, it was bloody. Karima's family, in their seclusion, tried to appreciate its progress through sounds, glances, fleeting words on the radio. Neighbors popped their heads through the apartment's battered wood door, speculating to anyone who would listen on how far the Americans soldiers had advanced—the airport, the Rashid camp, their own neighborhood of Karrada. Abu Saif predicted soldiers would begin parachuting into the city. As American troops hurtled across southern Iraq and approached Baghdad's outskirts, the explosions became fiercer. One neighbor suggested the loudest blasts were cluster bombs. "We didn't know what that meant," Amal wrote.

On April 5, the Americans broke through Baghdad's defenses for the first time. The probing foray by thirty Abrams tanks and Bradley Fighting Vehicles was brief but devastating. The wreckage still smoldered long after the attack: burned-out tanks and charred troop carriers were strewn along the Baghdad thoroughfare known as the Qadisiya Expressway. Overturned antiaircraft guns and the twisted carcass of a motorcycle lay abandoned before the landmark Um Taboul mosque. Tank treads plowed across street medians, strewn with charred debris and broken glass, and a lamppost lay mangled across an incinerated pickup. A chunk was blown out of a bridge on the road to Saddam International Airport. In front of Yarmuk Hospital sat a wrecked orange-and-white taxi, its windows shattered and blood smeared across the driver's door. A dog lay lifeless near a curb, where an olive tree was split in half, its gray leaves littered around it.

For Amal, a city that faced war from the air now took on the posture of a capital positioned for battle. The numbers of Baath Party militiamen dramatically multiplied, outnumbering residents in the streets of much of Baghdad. Along with police, they manned checkpoints on the edge of a city that looked more and more deserted. Under bridges gathered groups of Fedayeen Saddam, a poorly trained but particularly zealous paramilitary force supposedly devoted to the Iraqi leader with suicidal commitment. Most of them donned their distinctive black uniforms, but a few chose white gowns with red-and-white kaffiyehs or white turbans. They mingled with groups of soldiers underneath the canopy of palm trees, some lugging mortars, antiaircraft guns, heavy machine guns, rocket-propelled grenade launchers, and rifles. Joining their ranks were men in civilian clothes carrying guns; some of these appeared to be, at most, in their mid-teens.

In the city's center, soldiers dug new trenches along roads that led from the south, where the Americans were approaching; tanks were parked at each entrance to the intersections in the heart of the city, like Nisoor Square. Under a bridge near the Baghdad Central Railway Station, soldiers erected chest-high dirt barriers, with police and Baath Party militiamen directing traffic to alternative routes to downtown Baghdad.

Some in the city chose not to wait for what many expected would be a climactic battle. They joined the tens of thousands of residents already clogging roads out of town. The signs of departure were everywhere. Near Karima's apartment, lines snaked around gas stations, longer than at any time since the war's eve. Whole blocks on the city's southern outskirts were deserted, some houses abandoned and others seized by the army and Republican Guard troops preparing for street-to-street battles.

The final days of Baghdad's war were the bloodiest, as U.S. troops advanced on the city's suburbs. As is their practice, they deployed overwhelming force, often blurring the line between civilian and military vehicles in the streets. Hospitals overflowed with wounded, and emergency rooms were suffused with hordes of flies and the stench of blood, dirt, and disinfectant. Anesthesia ran short and generators struggled with mixed success to fill the void left by a blackout. At one hospital, refrigerators in the morgue were breaking down, leaving corpses stacked on top of one another to rot in a warming sun.

"We heard the sound of gunfire, very close to the building," Amal wrote. "Um Mohamed came and said the Americans are landing in Baghdad."

By April 7, just two days after the U.S. military's first raid into the capital, American soldiers had pushed into the city's very heart, capturing the Republican Palace. The battle was not yet over, but the official seat of Saddam's government was in American hands. It would later serve as the headquarters of the American occupation. Through a morning of cacophony, tank rounds and machine-gun fire thundered from the palace grounds, which straddled the west bank of the Tigris River. Smoke from burning equipment shrouded the valley, and a dust storm descended across the city in the early afternoon, casting a pallid glow.

Gaggles of soldiers still patrolled some streets. With rifles and grenades, they stood in eclectic bunches, wearing green khakis, desert camouflage, or combinations of these. Remnants of the vaunted Republican Guard lingered. In places, civilians, some with green ammunition belts strapped across their chests, mixed with militiamen or darted around the city in pickups caked in mud as camouflage.

But streets that so quickly had assumed the visage of battle just as quickly lost the determination to fight. The fear that enforced discipline began to fade as the government's end neared. Many roads began to empty, even of Baath Party militiamen; the silence that ensued was interrupted only by gunfire and the wail of ambulance sirens and fire trucks. The sandbagged positions that dotted the city's bridges and intersections were deserted, leaving the slogan "Victory or martyrdom" emblazoned across their front alone in irony. Soldiers at the Republican Palace bolted once the fighting began, and more than a few dove into the Tigris and tried to swim away.

As American forces moved across Baghdad at will, the city's landmarks—the storied Rashid Hotel, the Information Ministry, and the presidential palaces—became shooting galleries. The Baghdad clock tower was destroyed. Across the city, the scars of war were fresh: the charred shell of a police car, light poles bent over palm trees coated in dust, a blue-and-white traffic post on Mansur Street turned into a pile of baseball-sized concrete rubble. Highway signs that once directed cars to Abu Ghreib in the west and Mosul in the north, where Ali was stationed, were crumpled along the median. Even before it fell, Baghdad began to look conquered.

"Planes flew over our building," Amal wrote on April 7. "Each time, we repeated, 'God is greatest! God is greatest!' . . . We feel scared and tense. It is dark, smoke filling the skies and rising up. God have mercy on us."

Baghdad residents now acknowledged publicly that it was almost a certainty U.S. forces would soon hold the city. Saddam's fortunes were collapsing. Among the people, certain sentiments seemed to rush to the surface: anticipation of change; pronounced resentment of a government that some saw as suicidal, some as cowardly. There was great ambivalence over the prospect of an occupation. Yet many spoke less about the political future and more about being caught in the junction of war and its aftermath. Many shopowners hastily laid brick across their windows and doors, leaving their businesses to fate.

Inside Karima's home, the urban battle only sowed confusion. The family listened to the BBC, which reported the fall of the Republican Palace to U.S. troops. Then they heard Iraqi radio, whose announcers pleaded with Iraqis to fight U.S. forces: "Rise up against oppression and tyranny. Draw the swords of righteousness in the face of falsehood." Government communiqués insisted that Iraqis join any military unit they could find, even as those units disintegrated before the American onslaught.

"What's going to happen now?" Amal wrote. "We don't know."

The next day, on April 8, the only government Karima's daughters had known began to recede inexorably across the longtime bastion of its power. There were scattered scenes of a functioning bureaucracy, most notably the buses that still, spectacularly, ran their routes, even during the most pitched fighting on the capital's streets. But more common were signs of a city crumbling. Fetid trash piled up on sidewalks and the only open shops displayed generators and suitcases on the sidewalk, poignant markers of blackout and an at times frenzied exodus.

Against the backdrop of artillery, tank shells, and small-arms fire, miles of cars moved bumper to bumper along the snarled highway to the north. Much of the traffic traveled past a banner fluttering outside the al-Nida Mosque: "Iraq will remain steadfast, victorious, and lofty under the leadership of the leader, his excellency President Saddam Hussein." U.S. jets flew low over the city, their sonic booms echoing across the horizon as they banked, swerved, and dove with not an antiaircraft gun in Baghdad to answer them. For the first time since the war started, Iraqi television went off the air and stayed off. Gone was the diet of Hussein footage, patriotic music, and nationalist poetry. In a rapidly disintegrating police state, the police were nowhere to be seen.

For Amal, the change was disorienting and bewildering. Seeking cover in their homes, no one—not her mother, not neighbors, not her friends—knew what the precise situation in the city was. A climax was approaching, but what did it mean?

"We don't know what's going on," she wrote. "Maybe it's a big catastrophe. At 11:30, the building was shaking, and it almost collapsed. You can't imagine the fear and panic. We thought these were our last moments alive, that we were about to die. But God saved us. We implore him every day. Praise and thanks to God."

A lull followed, creating a rare moment of silence. "Every time there is quiet I feel more afraid," she wrote in the same passage. "After the quiet ends, we don't know what will happen."

The hours that ensued were replete with scenes she had never encountered: Abu Saif, a neighbor, told them of burned corpses he saw littering the bridge. Other bodies, he said, lay in the streets. She heard the roar of American tanks lumbering down the busy, four-lane commercial street near her home. Her sister saw a U.S. helicopter in the distance. On the night of April 8, her entries were short, written in quick succession. Airplanes passed overhead, blasts shook their building, and gunfire could be heard down the street. As midnight drew near, the clouds gathered, and in a trickle, it rained briefly. The water danced across an enervated landscape of browns, tinged in smoke lofted by war and fire.

For a moment, it washed Baghdad.

The next day, a sunny April morning, Amal woke up to news on a neighbor's radio. The entry was shorter than most. It ended with just a handful of words.

"And so," she wrote, "Baghdad has fallen to the Americans."

7

FOR YOU, IRAQ

Before Baghdad fell, the American military tried once more to eliminate the man they had courted through the 1980s, attempted to overthrow by proxy in the 1990s, and now were using 250,000 troops martialed in the region to try to topple.

The strike came at two P.M. on April 7, two days before the capital was conquered. A single B-1 bomber dropped four 2,000-pound bombs on a cluster of homes in the wealthy neighborhood of Mansur, where American intelligence believed Saddam and his two sons, Uday and Qusay, were hiding. The blast that rolled across the city was impossible to miss. U.S. officials were "moderately hopeful" that Saddam had been killed: "It was a leadership target, and it was hit very hard," said Marine captain Stewart Upton, a spokesman for Central Command, which directed the invasion. But again, as it turned out, the Americans had entirely missed their quarry.

The next day there was no official Iraqi presence at the bombing site; Saddam's government had begun its inevitable fall. Kicking up clouds of dust, bulldozers rumbled over the hills of rubble left by the volley of bombs. The machines lurched, careful not to edge over into a crater thirty feet deep and at least as wide. A small crowd hovered on the edge of the destruction, most of them friends or relatives of the thirteen civilians believed to have been buried by the blast, which shook decades-old houses, shattered windows, and hurled debris a half mile away, random as a storm. Some of them sobbed as they watched civil defense workers, still laboring even though their government was not, pull out the dismembered and battered bodies buried underneath the ruins of the three cement and brick homes.

The scene was one of awesome devastation. Near the crater was the Sa'a Restaurant, a venue luxurious by Iraqi standards that was said to have been visited by Saddam on a tour of the neighborhood just days before. It was gutted, its awnings tossed on the sidewalks and its tinted brown windows hurled into the four-lane street. Red-and-black steel support beams had been thrown two hundred yards away, along with doorknobs and furniture. Along the crater, orange trees were uprooted and date palms were split like twigs. Around the corner, along the broad avenue of Fourteenth of Ramadan, not a window was left intact in the grocery stores, boutiques, travel agencies, and electric appliance shops. With a mix of resignation and anxiety, workers piled what was left in waiting trucks: soft-drink bottles, televisions, cartons of eggs, coffee, bags of laundry detergent. Residents said the bombs had sucked air from homes blocks away, as if the neighborhood, in its entirety, gasped for breath. The explosions that followed shook the foundations of buildings, briefly but violently.

"Look at the area," Hassan Amin said, pointing to streets strewn with chunks of rubble, pulverized masonry, palm fronds, clods of dirt, and the detritus of bombing. "Until now, I haven't heard an explosion like that. It was exactly like an earthquake." His eyes squinted in the sun, on a cloudless day, and he looked ahead. "We know how the war began," he told me. "But we don't know how it will end."

A twenty-one-year-old student, Majid Abdullah, stood next to him. He was neither angry nor shaken. He simply turned to me and said matter-of-factly, "Fuck all Americans."

At the crater itself, some neighbors gazed in, their eyes fixed in the absent stare of the weary. A few stood on the periphery, curious. With a sense of duty, others helped the civilian workers trying to recover the bodies. A few of them had toiled, uninterrupted, for twenty-four hours, in a labor that seemed practiced.

At one point, a shout broke the silence that had fallen across the site. "They found something!" a man called out. "They found something!" Neighbors, more in hope than in expectation, ran to help, some of them stumbling over the rubble. The mauled torso of twenty-year-old Lava Jamal was pulled out before they arrived. Moments later, a few feet away, others found what was left of her severed head, her brown hair tangled and matted with dried blood. Her skin had been seared off. The searchers wrapped both head and torso in white blankets trimmed with blue and left her body against a nearby wall, where hordes of flies soon gathered. Under a withering sun, the shrouded corpse soon faded into the sidewalk's tapestry, another scene in a street already deformed by war.

Sitting in a chair down the road, Lava's mother gave up her vigil at the sight of the discovery. She sobbed uncontrollably into her hands, and then, as more flies gathered on her daughter's dismembered body, she vomited.

Less than an hour later, at the crater's edge, another find unfolded. This time, there were no shouts. There were only the cries voiced by custom at funerals: "There is no god but God." Atef Yusuf had found his nephew, six-year-old Raad Hatem, in the debris. He lifted the boy's frail body, coated in a gray dust except for the gaping scarlet wound on the back of his head. For a few minutes, he swayed with the body, rocking back and forth and wailing. Solitary and mysterious, his cry was like a siren interrupting an anxious night. He was alone. He then stumbled to another blanket and wrapped the boy's corpse inside. "Is he a military leader?" he asked me, as I stood a few feet from him, hesitant to come closer. "Are all these people military leaders?" I said nothing.

His eyes red, blood and dirt on his hands, Atef went back to work. Still underneath the rubble were his six other nieces and nephews, waiting to be buried.

THE SITE WHERE ATEF FOUND RAAD WAS FAR LESS GORY THAN THE BOMBING IN the market in Shuala, far less devastating than the attack in Shaab. But it was a terrible reminder of the inevitable disparity between war's grand aims and the reality of their execution. As the invasion progressed, it was more difficult to comprehend the violence that continued to take innocent lives. The early bombing was more strategic and the targets better identified; its precision inspired awe in some of Baghdad's residents. But standards fell; the end was bloodier, and the edges of Baghdad often felt like a free-fire zone as the American forces advanced. The military logic was impeccable and, in its efficiency, the campaign was a remarkable feat to behold. But, just three weeks old, the war felt as though it were dragging on interminably.

Hamza and I were still in Room 622 at the Palestine Hotel. The lack of electricity now added another hassle to the writing and filing of our stories. With remarkable ingenuity, Hamza's driver, Anmar, had figured out a way to string a single bulb from the hotel's generator, producing the equivalent of a night-light. (In a crunch, we could use that electricity to boil water for instant coffee, a requisite given how little sleep we had.) Any other light we needed came from brittle lanterns that gave off a foul black smoke, or small white candles that we stuck next to our notebooks with wax. We charged our computers and satellite phones with car batteries. We still had water for showers, albeit cold ones. More unsettling, the bottle of Glenfiddich was almost empty.

The Iraqi government soon took a turn that competed even with its own record of fantastic delusion. Its public face, Information Minister Mohammed Saeed al-Sahhaf, relished the attention that television coverage brought to his daily briefings and seemed to celebrate the vulgar sense of celebrity the war had brought him. Watching those news conferences, one wondered if he even remotely believed what he was saying. It probably didn't matter. He probably didn't care. At best, he understood the paper-tiger quality of dictatorship: the first sign of weakness, and the charade, in all its brutality and caprice, begins to crumble.

To much of the world, Sahhaf, fielding questions with mendacious bravado, came across as comic. To others, he seemed a sinister thug. (In one briefing during the war, he sucker punched an employee of Iraqi television whose microphone had brushed against the face of Vice President Taha Yassin Ramadan.) His final performances, though, were breathtaking. As heavily armed U.S. troops first pushed into the very center of Baghdad with tanks and armored personnel carriers, Sahhaf flatly denied that any offensive had taken place. Even as he spoke, the journalists asking him questions could see the fighting rage just across the Tigris. "There is not any American presence or troops in the heart of the capital, at all," he told us at a hastily called briefing on the roof of the Palestine Hotel. "The soldiers of Saddam Hussein gave them a great lesson that history will not forget." As he spoke, shelling, tank rounds, and machine-gun fire reverberated relentlessly from the Republican Palace across the river, well within sight of the hotel. Smiling, Sahhaf never flinched. At one point, he even challenged U.S. troops "to double such operations" and promised that Iraqi forces would "slaughter them and bury them in Iraq." He kept taking questions, and he kept answering them, making his cameo in war's theater. "Let me reassure you," he said, nodding, "Baghdad is very secure, safe and in control." His voice then took on a hint of menace. "Don't repeat their lies," he instructed.

Even then Saddam's government retained the power to instill fear. In the war's last week, I found my name on a list of fifty-two journalists to be expelled from Iraq. Nasir had heard rumors from his colleagues that I was suspected of spying. With U.S. forces already on the city's outskirts, the expulsion order was too late, and it was never enforced; only a handwritten posting appeared on an office's glass window off an annex from the Palestine lobby. But the climate was unsettling, and many journalists worried about what would happen in the frenzy of the government's fall.

In the end, the biggest danger to reporters came from the U.S. military, not the Iraqi government. On April 8, on an overcast day, a tank fired a round at the fourteenth and fifteenth floors of the hotel, on the building's northwest side. It killed two cameramen (Taras Protsyuk, a thirty-five-year-old Ukrainian, and thirty-seven-year-old Jose Couso of Spain) and wounded three other journalists. Earlier in the day, a journalist for the pan-Arab network Al-Jazeera—Tareq Ayyoub, a thirty-five-year-old Jordanian—was killed in a U.S. air strike on its bureau in Baghdad, along the Tigris. Al-Jazeera reports suggested that the attack was deliberate. (The year before, the U.S. military had attacked the network's bureau in Kabul, Afghanistan, during the campaign there.) There were three hundred–odd journalists in Baghdad independent of the U.S. military's program of embedding reporters, and these three deaths were the first among them.

In explaining the attack on the Palestine Hotel, the U.S. military said it was responding to sniper fire coming from the roof. Fighting had raged along the river for much of the morning, and many journalists had stood on their balconies to witness the battle. But in the minutes before the round was fired, several reporters said they heard only silence; no one I knew heard shooting at the time. Some saw one of the three M-1 Abrams tanks stationed on the Republican Bridge turn its turret toward the hotel, adjust its position, and fire a round. The aftermath left balconies with shattered glass and chunks of concrete littering the floor. Pools of blood remained on one balcony, and a camera smeared with blood was left sitting in the hotel hallway. In the chaotic aftermath, one of the wounded journalists, Faleh Kheiber, a photographer for Reuters, sat with his colleagues in his hotel room, fielding some informal questions. "This is a black day for journalists," he said.

But these deaths paled before the carnage across the city during the campaign's last days and hours. The hospitals were terribly crowded. Even as authority collapsed, the toll from the war overwhelmed the facilities—hundreds of wounded every day, a hundred every hour in the most pitched fighting.

Each visit to the hospital during the next few days seemed worse than the one before. At Kindi, a grim, dilapidated facility that treated many of Baghdad's wounded civilians, doctors accustomed to pressure worked with increasing speed, shuffling patients onto stretchers smeared with blood. Signs of wear were everywhere: overhead fans worked lazily or not at all; doctors borrowed pens from journalists to fill out patients' reports; patients were brought blankets still soiled with the blood of others. In each ward, a tattered piece of paper taped to the nurses' station listed the names of the wounded. Outside the morgue, on a sidewalk, six bodies in black bags sat in the street. The bags were tied with plastic on each end and at the legs, waist, and chest. Some were nevertheless open to the air, and flies had descended.

Inside the hospital, the wounded kept coming, inexorably. Doctors in blue scrubs worked night and day. One brought in a stretcher bearing Sayyid Hamid, a twenty-four-year-old from the village of Fahana, on Baghdad's outskirts. "There was a missile that landed in front of my house," he told me from his bed. His face was blank, uncomprehending, the shock of his wound still settling in. Just before, doctors had amputated his left foot. Down the hall, a woman in a black *abaya* sobbed. "Oh, Mother! Oh, Mother!" she cried out.

Some patients were left to their own devices. Hussein Obeid carted bags of intravenous fluid for his brother, thirty-four-year-old Saad, who was struck by shrapnel in fighting near his home in Dora, on Baghdad's southern outskirts. Like others, he seemed confused. Articulate and well-informed, he insisted to me that U.S. and British forces had made clear in Arabic-language broadcasts on the BBC that civilians would not be harmed. He didn't understand what was happening. "That was the promise they gave the Iraqis," Hussein said. "They always said we had nothing against the civilians. We didn't do anything to them." His words came out jumbled, emotions bouncing off one another. He was hurt, disoriented, and angry. "I was sure one hundred percent they would not shoot at a civilian," the twenty-two-year-old said. "Now I'm one hundred percent sure they will."

In the emergency room was a toddler, no more than eighteen months old, with a flop of thick black hair and eyes like glimmering black pools. In three places, shrapnel had torn her soft brown skin like paper. She was still alive. But her cries were absolutely piercing. After my return to the hotel, I stood outside for a moment, on our sixth-floor balcony that overlooked the placid waters of the Tigris, to take a break from the reality.

THE NEWSPAPERS ARRIVED THE MORNING OF APRIL 9, AS THEY HAD EVERY DAY since 1979. They were the standards—*Al-Shaab, Al-Qadisiya, Al-Iraq*—with the usual portraits of Saddam, grinning in green khakis and black beret, pontificating in tailored suit and tie, firing a rifle in his best, self-conscious Godfather pose. And there were the headlines written in florid Arabic, speaking to a daily vision of grandeur that never matched the reality of suffering and dictatorship. "The faithful sons of Iraq continue their heroic resistance against invasion," one pronounced.

But dawn brought a day unlike any Baghdad had experienced in a generation, perhaps far longer. As the sun rose over a city scarred by war, traumatized by tyranny, and haunted by Saddam's visage, five million people witnessed the rare, indelible scenes that make history as they happen. Relief at war's end and jubilation at the dictator's fall were accompanied by defiant words never before spoken in a country that had closed one chapter and now braced for another.

It was a day that began with fear.

"Don't cry! Don't cry!" pleaded Ali Mohammed as doctors at Kindi Hospital bandaged a shrapnel wound on the face of his eighteen-month-old son, Ali, who looked at his father, his gaze deadened. Then his brown eyes flooded with tears.

The hospital ward was littered with blood-soaked gauze, the stretchers and blankets themselves bore scabs, and the wounded kept pouring through the doors, just as they had the day before. There were young and old, men and women, and they begged for the war's end. "Can you just ask them to stop bombing?" shouted Ali Mizhar, a thirty-eight-year-old who arrived with five children wounded when a blast rocked their home that morning in the neighborhood of Zayuna. "Why are they still bombing?" he asked. "The resistance is over, it's totally over!"

And it was. Overnight, the city had emptied of the authority that once had instilled fear so deep that parents would lie to their children about their own loathing of the leadership. Gone were the swarms of Baath Party militiamen, in their mismatched uniforms, who had fanned out across the city at the war's beginning, manning every corner and intersection. Uniforms and boots were discarded in the streets, as many of the men hastily donned civilian clothes. Weapons and military trucks were abandoned, some with their ammunition spilling out of trunks. Under a bridge, surface-to-air missiles stood unmanned. Ministries were deserted, blue-uniformed traffic cops disappeared, and the streets crackled with the edgy anticipation of the unknown.

In a few hours, the anarchy that many in Baghdad had long feared arrived. With my driver, Karim, I headed back to the Palestine. Gangs of young men, some slinging Kalashnikovs, ambled down the streets, sometimes letting off a few rounds to make a point. Flying white flags, cars ignored traffic lights and many drove down the wrong side of the road. Nearly all of them barreled through Baghdad with a reckless desperation, fearful of being caught in the crossfire that had killed and wounded so many over the previous week. "Go back! Go back!" one driver shouted at us, going in the opposite direction. He pointed behind him to what he said were American tanks coming down the bridge.

For many, the sign that the government had collapsed came with the looting unleashed by early morning, when overcast skies gave way to a blazing sun. From government offices, state-owned companies, and U.N. buildings came computers, appliances, bookshelves, overhead fans, tables, chairs. From military bases came new Toyota pickups, minus license plates; we saw them careening through Baghdad all day. An elderly woman made her way down Saadoun Street, her back sagging from a mattress she was carrying. Others rode on top of white freezers wheeled down the road on ramshackle carts. Hour after hour, trucks piled high with booty roamed the capital. I thought this anarchy was what the sacking of a medieval city must have felt like.

"People believe these things belong to them," said Faleh Hassan, the fifty-one-year-old owner of the Abu Ahmed restaurant in Karrada. I met Faleh in the afternoon. By then, I had gone back to the hotel, checked in with the overnight editor at the *Post,* and decided to return to the streets. I guess I realized later than most that the war's end had finally arrived. I walked to the nearby neighborhood of Karrada with Larry Kaplow of Cox Newspapers, and we talked with Faleh at his restaurant over lunch—kebab and *kufta* grilled on a charred stove crafted from an air-conditioning duct. We sat on rickety wood benches while he spoke with an ease that seemed to delight him, a tantalizing moment of saying in public what he had believed in private. Our conversation amounted to my first unfettered, sincere interview in Iraq.

"The situation has changed," he told us, "so even our speech is different." A gaunt man with a mustache and graying hair, he looked out at a street crackling with the anticipation of both an end and a beginning. "I can tell you the fear has lifted from people's hearts."

Faleh, like so many in Baghdad, had his grudges. In the war with Iran, he had deserted the army, risking a death sentence if he was captured. His brother, Ahmed, had been killed in 1984 by thugs from Saddam's hometown of Tikrit. He struggled to make ends meet at his restaurant and provide for his sixteen-year-old daughter and two sons, aged seventeen and five. Over tea, he looked back at more than three decades during which, he said, the government had turned one of the world's richest countries into a nation of paupers. "It's a long story, the history of Iraq," he said.

Faleh spoke his mind. He was tired of the fear, tired of the repression, tired of the isolation that had claimed his English. (He had once been fluent, but had been unable to practice.) Since the war with Iran, he said, he had not even left Baghdad. He was thankful for Saddam's end, but in a sentiment I heard often that day, still suspicious of the Americans. "We feel peaceful and we feel relieved, but we are still frightened by tomorrow," Faleh said, dragging on a cigarette, the smell of grilling kebab wafting over our white plastic table. "We will see the American and British intentions over the next few months. People were oppressed for thirty years. They're looking for hope.

They hope there will be a change, because people are fed up with what has happened."

He shook his head. "Every day was worse than the one before."

There was a current of ambivalence racing through Baghdad that day, even amid the scenes of jubilation. Relief was tied up with anxiety, joy with trepidation. What next? many seemed to ask. I had seen this uncertainty and ambivalence time and again since my first visit to Baghdad in 1998. Then it was spoken in the shadow of repression. Now I heard it through the first gusts of liberation. It was the sentiment that defined the war and, as I would see, what followed. Faleh, a little weary, hoped it was better, and he gave voice to the sentiment that seemed to prevail. "I want to feel that I'm a human being, I want to feel that I'm free and that no one can take it away," he said. "I want to work, so that my family has enough to live. I want to live like everyone else in this world who lives in peace."

Across the street, a little while later, a scene erupted in Baghdad that many had not seen in their lifetime. In the streets—their voices raised, their opinions pronounced—people debated.

"Believe me, I have waited for this moment for thirty-five years," said Majid Mohammed, a forty-seven-year-old electrical engineer, whom Larry and I met after leaving the restaurant. We had yet to see U.S. soldiers; nor had we seen any remnant of the government. "You must bring these words to the American people. Thank you, thank you very, very much."

Zuheir Girgis, a thirty-two-year-old who hesitated before giving me his name, said he would wait and see. "Nobody hates freedom, and if they bring freedom, nobody will hate them," he insisted.

Dhikran Albert, a little older than Zuheir, shook his head. "If they've come as invaders," he warned, "nobody will welcome them."

Majid, a burly, cheerful man, delighted in the moment. No one was looking over his shoulder, no one was dreading a question. The Baath Party cadres in the neighborhood were in their homes, dressed in civilian clothes. The soldiers had fled, some leaving weapons behind. "We are now free, so everybody has an opinion," he said, as we chatted in the street.

But even in freedom, as the conversation continued and as more people approached us, the shadow of Saddam could be sensed. One man asked me how he could be certain I was not a spy. Jubilant as they were, others hesitated to answer my questions about politics, about their brushes with iron-handed security forces, about the fate of Saddam himself. "I think he has nine lives," Majid said, his tone now softer. "Maybe he will come back and have his revenge."

In a way, he already had.

"I'm sad," Majid's twelve-year-old daughter, Sara, said as we left the group and walked down the street. "The Americans have stolen freedom."

Her words pained her father. Here was the legacy of Saddam's attempts to mold the people in his image. Liberation or not, his shadow remained. With a grimace, Majid turned to me and lowered his voice, until then exuberant. "Until now, I haven't been able to speak my feelings about him."

IN LATE AFTERNOON, SOMEONE DOWN THE STREET YELLED THAT THE AMERI-cans had arrived. The curious and the jubilant ran down the road, and Larry and I followed. As citizens gathered, a line of tanks and armored vehicles paraded down Saadoun Street, toward a twenty-foot statue of Saddam in Fir-daus Square. As bloody as the days before had been, the American military's final entry into Baghdad was unfettered and uncomplicated, perhaps danger-ously so. There was nothing truly epic about it; the march into the garrison and symbol of Saddam's three-decade rule brought an end to Sahhaf's boasts about the funeral rites Iraq would hold for dead U.S. soldiers. The more accurate appraisal came from the retired Marine general Anthony C. Zinni, the former head of U.S. Central Command, in charge of the Middle East: "Ohio State beat Slippery Rock sixty-two to nothing," Zinni said after the war. "No shit." Past Baath Party slogans on the wall and portraits of Saddam, past shuttered shops, and past the barricades set up for a battle that never hap-pened, the armored column rumbled down a deserted street. From a micro-phone atop one of the vehicles, an Iraqi exile shouted, "We're bringing freedom for everyone, we're making a free Iraq."

The moment had little to do with me, yet I was overwhelmed by it. For a few minutes, I could barely move, stopped by a flood of emotions inspired by my role as a journalist and my identities as an Arab-American and an Ameri-can. I gazed at the tanks, their engines whirring; I glanced around me, at a crowd seized by jubilation, confusion, and unease. I stared at the U.S. flag atop a Bradley Fighting Vehicle, fluttering proudly, and I looked at the myriad emotions on the faces of those around me—Iraqi and American—intersecting in a street of the most fabled Arab capital. It was the convergence of cultures across an immense chasm, brought together in Baghdad, their fates inextricably linked as long as their presence was intertwined.

As a journalist, I understood I would see such a moment only once in my lifetime. Even then, I had a feeling that I would be covering the repercussions of this event for the rest of my career. At that instant, I was overcome by the story, by its magnitude alone. I asked myself how I could ever hope to capture such an event with a few hours of reporting and a few more hours of writing. That fear soon passed—there was too little time to reflect on it—and I then felt an exhilarating sense of relief. I was tired of the war, I was exhausted by the work, I was repulsed by the bloodshed. And, perhaps most powerfully, as I saw the tanks roll down Saadoun Street, I knew that I would survive. For the first time in three weeks, oblivious to the war ahead, I knew for certain that my life was no longer part of the equation. For the first time since the start of war, I felt at ease.

My emotions as an Arab-American were more complicated, but abstract. Here was Baghdad, an ancient city whose name evoked a proud, enduring memory, fallen to a foreign army. I felt neither anger nor joy; in a way, I felt grief. Not at Saddam's demise, but rather at the fate of a city, a destiny that brought about its conquest in the name of its liberation.

"When I saw the Marines coming into Baghdad," Hamza told me long after the war, in a sentiment that still echoes with me, "I did not exactly feel sorry that Saddam was gone. Not at all. But I felt that a very important chapter of modern Arab history was being written, and it wasn't exactly a chapter that makes you optimistic, or look to the future and the days to come with a positive attitude." He turned more reflective. "Baghdad to me is not Doha," he said, "it's not Riyadh, and it's not Dubai. Baghdad is like Cairo and Damascus, a great Arab city with traditions, a thousand years of history, two great rivers, a great people, a country that admittedly went astray and had gone astray for quite a long time. For the U.S. Army to be in the heart of the city, it didn't hurt me, it didn't make me feel like, 'Oh no, we shouldn't let this happen.' But it was shocking, even though we all knew it was going to happen."

I was in awe of the power of my country, America. What other nation, driven by ideology, its existence not threatened, could conquer an entire country in a matter of weeks? As a reporter abroad and as an expatriate, I often felt divorced from U.S. politics, removed from its debates, even stateless in a way. I could no longer enjoy that anonymity. My country had taken over another country, and I was watching it happen. The United States now controlled Iraq's destiny; we would now decide its fate. And we understood remarkably little about it. Deep down, I worried that we would never try to know it, either. At best, we would try to force it into our construct and pre-conception of what a country should be. At worst, we would not care, giving in to overly emotional impressions distorted by differences in language, culture, and traditions, and by conceit. In between, the ambiguity that so defined Iraq for me—the uncertainty, the ambivalence, the legacy of its history—would become too complicated to unravel.

Crowds lined the streets, erupting in cheers at the sight of the armored column, their battle tidily won. Women put their hands to their mouths and ululated, a sign of joy in the Arab world. One man asked me if I could go over to the tank and find a soldier to marry his daughter. Others tossed chocolates and candy, cigarettes, flowers picked from a nearby park at the soldiers—members of the first foreign army to enter Baghdad in triumph in more than fifty years. When the column stopped, many ran to the soldiers to shout hello, to shake their hands, and, for a few, to kiss them on their startled cheeks.

"Did the war end?" asked Kamel Hamid, as he stood on the road. "Is it over?"

"It is a liberation," shouted Abbas Ali, holding his daughter's hand.

Others, more reserved, held back from the curb, gazing at a mysterious horizon. Their questions poured out urgently: Would Iraqi dinars, emblazoned with a portrait of Saddam, still be used? If not, when would they change? Others asked when the United States would restore electricity and phone service.

Some said the Americans wanted Iraq's oil and predicted that the U.S. troops were here to stay. "This is my country and this is an occupation," said Stefan Abu George, a fifty-nine-year-old. "I can't imagine what the result of this is going to be." A friend, Wathiq Abzara, answered him. "Like Palestine," he said.

Down the road, Mazin Hussein, a doctor at Ibn Haitham Hospital, and two colleagues, Saad al-Kaabi and Hussein Hanoosh, gingerly approached a parked U.S. tank. Over the roar of its engine, they asked the soldiers to take down the American flag flying behind it. The soldiers could not hear them and, after a few minutes, they gave up, walking back to the curb.

"This is not the liberation they told us about," Mazin said to me, his voice raised over the din, as we stood on the side of the road. "It's not the right time to raise flags."

Saad interrupted him, his face full of a sentiment that, in the months ahead, I would hear voiced time and again. It was pride. "This is not the right way to change things," he said. "Iraqis should free themselves, not the foreigners."

Hussein shook his head. "We wish we could do it ourselves."

Americans threw packaged meals down to the crowd, the thick plastic pouches sliding across the asphalt. They almost set off a riot. A friend of Mazin's brought him one. "I will not eat from them," he said, with a look of disgust, before turning away.

A few feet down the road stood Nazir Mustafa, forty-six. He gazed at the tanks, his face caught between shock and joy. In a few weeks he had lived a lifetime's experiences, and his emotions were a tableau of contradiction. He worried about what was ahead. "It's up to the Americans what this becomes," he told me. "Every person has an opinion. Maybe it will be colonialism, maybe it will be liberation from the regime." He looked at the carnival in Saadoun Street. "The truth will soon become apparent."

THERE WAS LITTLE REFLECTIVENESS IN FIRDAUS SQUARE; THE SCENE THERE has become the lasting image of the American entry into Baghdad. In a way, it was a parable of the relationship between the Americans and Saddam, whose regime, unpopular as it was, could only come tumbling down through the intervention of the world's greatest military power.

Built in 2001, the park was one of Baghdad's newest; its manicured gardens were reached by a series of short stairs. In its center was a metal statue of Saddam in a suit, his hand outstretched in Stalinist fashion. Like an arena of spectators, columns of descending height encircled him, each bearing the initials "S.H." on their cupolas. By early afternoon, hundreds swarmed around the statue with one task in mind: bring it down.

They threw a heavy rope, tied like a noose, around its neck. Many hurled rocks at it, each volley bringing cheers. Some threw their shoes at it; others whipped it in vain with chains. A few minutes later, someone in the crowd showed up with a sledgehammer, and residents, their faces sweating, some with tears in their eyes, took turns pummeling the purple granite at its base.

"Scum, son of scum," shouted Yusuf Abed Kadhim, as he swung at the pedestal. "I'm forty-nine, but I have never lived a single day. Only now will I start living," he said to me, after taking a break and giving the sledgehammer to a man behind him. "Now, God willing, I can die at peace with Saddam gone."

He watched the men try to bring the statue down. "He destroyed us," Yusuf said bitterly. "Enough. He destroyed us."

As they toiled, groups of religious Shiite Muslims gathered on the side of the square. "There is no god but God; Saddam is the enemy of God," they chanted. Some seized the opportunity to pray in the open, no longer at risk of suspicious stares. Others beat their chests in a ritual of grief known as *lutm*. It was the first time I had seen such a display of religious practice in public in Iraq. "We will not forget Imam Hussein," they cried. Another knot of men, standing near them, shouted another slogan. At the time it meant little to me—a reference to an ayatollah slain by Saddam's men in 1999, whose name I had heard maybe once or twice and whose significance I had not begun to understand. Within weeks, that name would, in many ways, define the war's aftermath. "O Saddam, the blood of Sadr will not go in vain," they shouted.

An hour later, though, the statue of Saddam still wasn't budging. It defied the blows of the sledgehammer, the tug of the rope, the cascade of rocks, and the plentiful invective. It stood there, impervious. Its expression was unchanged. For a moment, it seemed permanent. As the sun began its descent, several more men scurried up the rope to try to push it down from above with more force than before.

They couldn't do it.

Finally, the U.S. soldiers decided to come to their aid. A bulky Marine M-88 tank recovery vehicle plowed through the circle, crushing two flights of the stairs and a flower bed in the middle of the park. Taking the most direct path, the vehicle stopped for no one; given its power, it didn't have to. When it arrived, residents helped set its cable around one of Saddam's legs, then tied both. They worked feverishly, as if dusk's approach had created its own deadline.

A few minutes later, the Marines brought out an American flag. Two of them climbed the statue and draped it over Saddam's visage. A hush rolled through the crowd, and the cheers became subdued. More acclaim came when someone from the crowd, surprisingly, produced an Iraqi flag, a version from before the 1991 Gulf War, and hung that over the statue too. But even so, the statue was still standing. Iraqis finally tied a heavy chain around its neck and tethered it to the Marine vehicle.

"It's a strong statue," said Shidrak George, a thirty-eight-year-old standing nearby. He shook his head in dismay as he watched the attempts at its demolition. "If Saddam was watching this scene, he would be laughing at us," he told me.

For a moment, Shidrak and I stood and observed an instant that we both knew was historic. As countless Iraqis did, in homes across the capital, in Saadoun Street, among the few hundred gathered in the square, he reflected on what the day meant and might come to mean. By that point in the evening, his words had almost become clichéd. In those few hours, I had heard glee at a liberation, anger at an occupation. Far more common was what he suggested: everything remained *ghamidh*; it was all still mysterious and unclear. "We don't know what's next," he said. "They rid us of our repression, there's no question about that. But we want to know how it turns out. Are they here for our sake? They said they came to save us. Now they have to prove it."

Finally, two hours after it all began, as dusk finally arrived, the Marine vehicle brought the statue down halfway. With another pull, it crumbled to the ground. At 6:55 P.M., all that was left was the twisted metal of his feet, two rusted pipes jutting out. The statue itself was hollow. Shouts of joy went up, and the crowd converged on the wreckage. They kicked it, pummeled it with a chain, rocks, and a sledgehammer, and slapped it with shoes—a great insult in the Arab world. Its head was gleefully carted down the street, pulled by ropes. On its body Iraqis jumped up and down. Even if others had brought him to the ground, at that moment, they would all celebrate his fall. At that moment, only his demise mattered, an ephemeral joy shearing it of context.

From the crowd went up a chant familiar in Saddam's Iraq, when his very name was transformed into an object of veneration. But this chant was different, the subject of praise a country, not a man. And for the first time in thirty-five years, people seemed to mean it. "With our spirit, with our blood," they shouted, "we sacrifice for you, Iraq."

PART THREE

AFTERMATH

8

DRY BREAD WITH TEA

The veil had been lifted, but no one was sure what it revealed.

By April 2003, Baghdad, conquered no less than fifteen times in its history, was called free, but the city was a furious storm set down. Emotions—euphoria, vindictiveness, desperation, confusion—surged up from the people after years of silence and restraint. Some observers spoke of anarchy: armed civilians had begun to crack the monopoly on violence held only weeks earlier by Saddam's government, his soldiers, and the American military forces. Baghdad seemed like a dazed inmate stumbling out of his cell and squinting into the harsh sunlight.

The storm started on April 10, the day after the battle ended in Baghdad. Deprived by sanctions, hardened by wars, and brutalized by Saddam, thousands of residents—many, but by no means all, poor and young—hurried to plunder everything from trucks and wood carts to the urinals, copper pipes, and electrical wiring of public buildings. They sought payback and spoils; in a way, they sought relief. Hospitals and embassies fell prey, along with ministries, government offices, Baath Party headquarters, and the stone houses, faced in onyx, of Saddam's henchmen—Tariq Aziz, Taha Yassin Ramadan, Mohammed Saeed al-Sahhaf, and the dictator's sons, Uday and Qusay, all of whom had vanished.

From the General Union of Iraqi Women, in downtown Baghdad, the crowds hauled away chairs, tables, a vase with plastic flowers. From ministries came copiers, lamps, stoves, ceiling fans, and overhead projectors, vintage 1970s. From Yarmuk Hospital, one of the city's largest, came beds, medicines, and CAT, MRI, and ultrasound scanners. Looters emptied a youth center in the neighborhood of Zafraniya of black-and-white soccer balls; some of the thieves were grinning boys on teetering bicycles. From the palaces of Saddam and his men came scuba gear, racing-car tires, shining eight-burner stoves, and hand-crafted tables imported from India. Young men galloped along downtown Karrada Street on sleek, muscled horses that had once grazed in relative luxury at stables in Jadriya.

Cars broke down, burdened with lumber, stoves, sinks, and food warmers on their hoods. Eight people pushed a stalled, loot-laden Volkswagen down one street, past women in black *abayas* with stolen chairs perched on their heads. Ambulances were hijacked, as were the public buses that had plied their routes without fail until the very moment of the government's collapse. Most memorable and devastating to Baghdadis was the ransacking of the National Museum of Antiquities, whose collections of art and artifacts encompassed the region's history from the beginnings of ancient Sumer in 3500 B.C. to the end of the Abbasid caliphate in A.D. 1258. The very record of humankind's awakening was stolen. For Iraqis with memories of past conquests, the waters of the Tigris River were again, more than eight centuries after Hulugu led his Mongol forces in sacking Baghdad, running red and black.

It kept on, into another day and then another, mayhem unparalleled in Baghdad's modern history. Cars barreled the wrong way down streets deserted by the traffic policemen in their familiar blue uniforms and the party militiamen in green who had once scrutinized drivers with steely gazes, like birds hunting their prey.

Most of the lawlessness seemed to target institutions of Saddam's government, in a kind of revenge. After being picked clean, the fortresslike Ministries of Trade, Industry, and Irrigation were set on fire. Black smoke billowed, and flames danced along the windows. Graffiti was painted on walls: "The people are stronger than tyrants," "Death to Saddam," or in a telling variation, "God curse Saddam and the Americans." Portraits of the fallen dictator were defaced, burned, torn, or ripped away.

In an overgrown grove of apple trees and date palms along the Tigris, a group of men worked with beehivelike intensity, ransacking one of the government's palaces. They had arrived in rickety cars, flatbed trucks, and battered taxis—pilgrims of sorts, approaching a promised reward—and fanned out across the compound. On the floor, Saddam's portraits were already scattered, trampled, or discarded. Nearby was a clock portraying him seated at work. One of the looters picked it up. "This is a gift from me to you," he told me, his grin at once elated and vengeful.

For Mohammed Falaeh, a forty-two-year-old carting away a small imported lamp, the looting was vengeance, a final accounting of a miserable past.

"We don't have anything in our houses. No refrigerators, no televisions. Is it thievery when you're hungry?" he asked me. "Look at the riches, and look at how people have lived for thirty-five years." He surveyed the room, in disbelief at what he had been deprived of, what he coveted, and what he would soon claim. "Everything here is for one person. This house, these rooms for one person. Now people will take it to their homes."

But Mohammed and his colleagues were actually a minority in Baghdad. Most in the tattered city were frightened, ashamed, angry, and anxious over the scenes being broadcast to the world. Across town, near the burning Ministry of Higher Education, a man named Abu Omar turned to speak, his face creased with anger and unease. "I want to ask you a question," he said, an edge to his voice. "How long do we have to stay like this? What they are doing now is taking what belongs to all the people of Iraq—not one person—and I don't like this. It's shameful."

Leaning out the window of his blue minibus, he continued to attempt to take passengers and require them to pay their fares, as if the old rules still applied. "If they want to change the regime, they have to put another government in its place," Abu Omar insisted as he stared at the looters in the ministry building. "Liberty like this is not good."

Baghdad after the fall brought to mind a description of Germany in 1918, another nation in defeat. The observer was Walter Rathenau, a German politician and industrialist: "The doors had burst open, the wardens ran away, the captives stood in the courtyard blinded and unable to move. Had it been a real revolution the forces and ideas that had brought it into being would have continued to exert their influence. . . . All the people wanted was peace and quiet."

Yet there was no peace and quiet, and it would soon become clear that there was no vision in the revolution that had overtaken Iraq. Instead, the word uttered by many was *fawdha*—disorder, chaos. In those days and weeks, it was hard not to recall the scene at Abu Ghreib, five months before the war, when an arbitrary decree emptied the prison in hours. Now what had been unleashed was the unchecked madness of a country bound and imprisoned for decades. No one knew how long it would last. No one knew what shape it would take next, or where it would lead. And no one grasped anyone's intentions, least of all the intentions of Baghdad's occupiers, who seemed as much at a loss as anyone, as the toll from the capital's ransacking climbed into the billions of dollars. Defense Secretary Donald Rumsfeld shrugged: "Stuff happens"—words that would be repeated ruefully by Baghdadis in the weeks ahead. "Freedom's untidy. And free people are free to make mistakes and commit crimes and do bad things."

While supremely prepared for war, the American military was singularly unprepared for its frenzied aftermath. There was never really a plan for post-Saddam Iraq. There was never a realistic view of what might ensue after the fall. There was hope that became faith, and delusions that became fatal.

To many in the U.S. government, the dictator's collapse had stood as the aim of Operation Iraqi Freedom. According to the ideology that drove that crusade, everything would fall into place after Saddam's departure. U.S. leaders dangerously misplaced their faith, believing in their own rhetoric of liberation. Exiles like Ahmad Chalabi, whose Iraqi National Congress wielded enormous influence in the U.S. Congress and the Pentagon, told Bush's men what they wanted to hear: sweets and flowers awaited the American troops. With Saddam gone, jubilant Iraqis would embrace those who had freed them. Together with the exiles, the Americans would create an outpost of democracy and prosperity in a region with little of either. This vision colored every decision.

Before the invasion, the army's chief of staff, General Eric Shinseki, had offered an estimate that an occupation might require several hundred thousand U.S. troops. "Way off the mark" was the reply of Deputy Defense Secretary Paul Wolfowitz. ("It's hard to conceive," he testified to a congressional committee, "that it would take more forces to provide stability in post-Saddam Iraq than it would take to conduct the war itself and to secure the surrender of Saddam's security forces and his army. Hard to imagine.")

In fact, within days of Saddam's fall in April, as the city reeled in mayhem, top U.S. commanders were already considering plans to bring the 140,000 troops down to almost one-fifth that number by September. Fearful of military commitments that could drag on for years, Bush's advisers hoped to avoid saddling the armed forces with the task of rebuilding a state. But no one seemed to recognize that the troops already in Baghdad were, even then, looking ill-equipped to deal with the surging tumult. Their armored columns were designed to fight Saddam's mechanized army, not legions of gaunt, exuberant looters coursing through an edgy and unsettled city.

With mouths agape, many in Baghdad waited for the equivalent of the Marshall Plan that had resurrected Europe after World War II. Soon enough, it was obvious that there was none. For a year, sixteen groups of hopeful Iraqi exiles, coordinated by the State Department's Bureau of Near Eastern Affairs, had labored on a sprawling report on potential problems in postwar Iraq. The project's mandate was broad: it looked at questions of justice, amnesty, and war crimes; economic and budget planning; and threats to public health, water, agriculture, and the environment. But the sober report that resulted, thousands of pages long, never became more than a report.

Two months before the invasion, with National Security Presidential Directive No. 24, President Bush had turned over responsibility for postwar Iraq to the Department of Defense. Soon after, Rumsfeld and his men hastily put together a team of soldiers and civilians in the newly designated Office of Reconstruction and Humanitarian Assistance. The man chosen to lead the postwar operation was Jay Garner, a competent, well-intentioned retired lieutenant general who had led the largely successful effort after the 1991 Gulf War to save Kurdish refugees in northern Iraq.

In the few weeks he had to plan for the aftermath, he prepared for a similar humanitarian disaster. He predicted the worst-case scenario: refugees pouring across the border, displaced people washing across Iraq, epidemics, famine, and perhaps the grisly effects of weapons of mass destruction. None of this occurred, though what did happen was probably no less destructive. Unsuspecting and overwhelmed, Garner and his team were almost comically ill-prepared. Garner himself did not actually arrive in Iraq until two weeks after Saddam's fall.

By the time Garner was replaced in May as the civilian administrator of

Iraq by L. Paul Bremer, a hard-nosed, well-connected career diplomat who had served as ambassador-at-large for counterterrorism in the Reagan administration, the looting had proved far more destructive than the war, and Baghdad seemed far easier to dismantle than to reconstruct. It was all a harbinger of everything that was to come. As Bremer arrived from the airport, hospitals were still wrecked and ministries still smoldered. As he remembered it, "Baghdad was on fire, literally." Scared police stayed off the streets. Lawlessness was the status quo—the looting was most dramatic, but along with it came a debilitating wave of street crime, blamed on the tens of thousands of hardened thugs, psychopaths, tribesmen bent on revenge, and petty criminals whom Saddam had released along with political prisoners in October 2002. They were a new professional class in armed robbery, carjacking, kidnapping, rape, and, if the price was right, murder. They could often outgun anyone who tried to stop them.

With the lawlessness came discomfort. The Americans had failed to account for the state of Iraq's infrastructure, aged, decrepit, and worn down as it was by more than a decade of sanctions. For weeks, the capital's two antiquated power plants were barely running, and the long blackouts in searing heat that began toward the war's end remained the norm. Everything followed from electricity, the cornerstone of modern life. With electricity went water, sanitation, air-conditioning, and the security brought by light at night. With electricity went faith in what the Americans, so powerful in war, were prepared to do after.

On the first day of the occupation, Mustafa Kemal, a stocky man with a full head of black hair, stood in his jewelry store in the southern neighborhood of Dora. A man with a wry sense of humor, he wanted to know whether the Americans, having conquered Baghdad, would open the bars and close the mosques. "Saddam Hussein is finished, he's gone," Mustafa said as the first confusing day of freedom played itself out. His gold was in a safe; his glass display cases were bare. "Nobody knows what's ahead," he said portentously. "They just don't know. We're like sheep. The shepherd's gone and everybody goes in their own direction." He thought for a moment, then asked: "When will the Americans put an end to the looting?"

The sense of the unknown and the unimaginable coursed through almost every conversation in Baghdad. Those old enough to recall life before Saddam's rule looked to Iraq's history for precedents, recalling the dates of Iraq's periodic coups d'état, bloody putsches, and mislabeled revolutions—1958, 1963 (twice), 1968, and then 1979, when Saddam, the vice president, had stripped his boss of all his positions, placed him under house arrest, and seized all power for himself. Many now expected some familiar pattern to be followed: first score-settling and executions, then a curfew, and soon a new government, all to happen in weeks, if not days. Power might change hands, but life would not be upended. Never had chaos lasted so long. A ruler had always appeared to settle scores and restore a semblance of normalcy, however iron-fisted.

THE SUN IN IRAQ IS RELENTLESS. IN BAGHDAD, IT BATTERS. IN THE DAYS AFTER the fall of Baghdad, it often seemed to show little mercy, despite the shade offered by the city's abundant palm trees—towering, elegant figures topped by fronds so green and primeval that they evoked ancient Mesopotamia. In the bright sunlight the labyrinthine intricacies of the turquoise tiles adorning the city's minarets, a courtesy of Persia's culture, appeared soaked in dazzling color.

The sculptor Mohammed Ghani stared out his car window at his occupied city. He looked in front, behind, and to the side. "*Allahu akbar*," he muttered, "God is greatest," a phrase that often heralds anger, but from him, suggested resignation. On the other side of his window passed a city's stories. Men sold jerry cans of black-market gasoline along the curb; vendors hawked cheap, Jordanian-made cigarettes; trucks unloaded blocks of ice for about $2 to keep food cold. Chaotic stalls selling bananas, watermelons, and apples spilled into streets, knotting traffic. Trash and soggy leftovers piled on corners ripened in the heat. U.S. soldiers in the street nearby pointed their M-16 assault rifles toward the cars. "Love Machine" read the slogan inscribed on the barrel of a tank.

Religion, long repressed during Saddam's relatively secular reign, had reasserted itself on walls stained by time. "No Shiites, no Sunnis, Islamic unity, Islamic unity," read one slogan. "Yes to Islam," said another. More resonant was a saying popular in the war's aftermath: "The people are stronger than the tyrant." Along the Republican Bridge, the unemployed marched with banners, demanding work or, barring that, compensation. Near the once upscale Palestine Hotel, women demonstrated, calling for rights that seemed more elusive than ever. Traffic, celebrating an anarchic reading of freedom, plowed the wrong way down bustling streets. Horns honked, and cars swerved. Ghani clicked his tongue.

He seemed to reflect. His life had spanned the British occupation, which ran from the end of World War I until 1932; the monarchy the British installed; the coups that followed; and, finally, Saddam Hussein's bloody, methodical ascent to power. Now the artist was acquainting himself again with his city after having spent months abroad. "My son told me that it is better for me not to see Baghdad," Ghani said. "But I insisted." His words were unhurried, their slowness almost narcotic by contrast with the chaos outside.

"I swear to God, Baghdad is a beautiful girl, but her clothes are dirty," Ghani said, tugging on his shirt. "Her hair is tangled"—he pulled at his hair—"but her nature is still beautiful."

Ghani, a sprightly seventy-four-year-old man with bushy black eyebrows, a Semitic nose, and a bald head framed by a mane of gray hair, had spent the weeks before and after the war in the Persian Gulf state of Bahrain. "I never thought the war would come so soon," he explained, too proud to admit that he had been fearful, that he had not wanted to be in his city at the moment the bombs fell. In exile, cut off from the capital and his friends, he had occupied himself in reading the history of his country and, as the invasion progressed, sitting passively before a screen, watching the detached images of bombing, all sound and fury, on Arabic satellite networks—Al-Jazeera, Al-Arabiya, Abu Dhabi, and Al-Mustaqbil.

"Days became very long for me," he recalled wearily. "I could not do anything. It was not easy. It was really not easy. . . . I came back," he told me, as we drove in the car that summer day, "because I'm a Baghdadi."

Ghani was not simply a Baghdadi, a son of the city. As an artist, he had played a small part in defining the modern capital: his monuments, most in bronze and built over thirty-five years, dot the sprawling landscape, drawing on those eleven millennia of history that Iraqis like to boast of, with their spectacular succession of Sumerian, Babylonian, Assyrian, and Islamic civilizations. At a once-luxurious hotel stands a sultry, three-meter-high marble statue of Ishtar, the Sumerian goddess of love, pouring water into a fountain. ("I built this one as a sexy woman!" Ghani exclaimed.) In a roundabout once known as Ali Baba Square stands his bronze statue of Kahramana, the slave girl who outwitted the forty thieves of A Thousand and One Nights. She persuaded them to hide in jars, then killed them by pouring burning oil inside. As we drove by, Kahramana still leaned over, but the fountain no longer worked. She could pour nothing on the thieves. ("It has become a symbol of Baghdad," Ghani insisted.)

Down the road was another of Ghani's works, a flying carpet, stretching upward, its ascent meant to symbolize the flight of the city's residents from war. Behind the sculpture on the day of our drive was an actual American tank, draped clumsily in green camouflage netting. ("Strange," Ghani said; then he shrugged.)

Sometimes elegant, sometimes kitschy, Ghani's works bring a certain nostalgia to a city of five million dominated by shoddily built housing projects, broad avenues where Saddam's now missing military had paraded, Los Angeles–style flyovers, and lingering Stalinist odes to Saddam Hussein. Nearly everything in the modern incarnation of the city is colored brown or the gray shade of concrete. In contrast, Ghani's works represent an idealized Baghdad, imbued with legend and anchored in history.

All of Ghani's statues suggest nostalgia except one: the Monument of Freedom, in Liberation Square, which celebrates the overthrow of the British-installed monarchy. Designed by the revered Jawad Salim, it is one of the city's most recognizable icons. Ghani, then a young sculptor fresh from training in Italy, was chosen to assist Salim during its creation. Set across creamy stone, Salim's fourteen giant bronze reliefs do not fail to inspire with their torches of freedom, helmeted soldiers, workers with sledgehammers, women at harvest, and prison bars bent back. Forty years ago, the work looked ahead to the universal dreams of a buoyant Third World: prosperity, renaissance, and a boundless future. Now its hopefulness taunts.

As we passed portraits of Saddam, doused with white paint or riddled with bullet holes, we spoke freely about the dictator for the first time. As he had before, Ghani cautioned that he himself was not political, only an artist—a distinction often crucial in the Arab world.

"You cannot say you're glad the war happened. But life had to change." The sun beat through the car's windows. "Everyone was waiting for the moment for the party to go, for Saddam to go. In my life, I never saw such bad things in Iraq," he said, his words slowing. "At least you can breathe now, you can breathe freedom. There's no Saddam, there's no fear. People couldn't sleep before because of the fear."

Convoys of Humvees rolled through the streets, past palm and eucalyptus trees. A third of the U.S. troops were in Baghdad, and the heat added to their inevitable edginess.

"It makes me sad," Ghani said, watching a military convoy pass. "You know what occupation is. No one likes occupation. Even when we were under the Ottomans, the people were always revolting. When the English came, they rebelled many times against them. They always make trouble."

Ghani's speech was peppered with Italian phrases, a legacy of his student days. He seemed to be searching for words to express the ambivalent sentiments of his city. He began to speak about a man he knew whose wife had been searched by American soldiers, an act that left the husband crying with shame. "This man could do nothing," Ghani said. "Only cry. They destroyed his honor."

He recalled another who struggled as soldiers tried to force him to the ground on a crowded street. He described an image of a soldier's hand atop an Iraqi's head, the Iraqi resisting, upset, and he grew more emotional as he continued to speak. "They treat us like cowboys," he told me; still his tone was more introspective than conversational. "They use guns. They don't respect us. They don't know anything about the Iraqi character, the culture of Iraq, the history of Iraq. They know nothing. I'm a Baghdadi, I'm an Iraqi, and they've destroyed my country, my city. Saddam destroyed the character of the person, now they've destroyed the country.

"This is a dirty war," he went on with increasing animation. "This is a dirty war, really."

We passed lines of cars snaking half a mile to Jadriya Bridge, waiting to fill up with gas, on our way to Karrada Street, which runs through a spit of land along a bend in the Tigris. Sharp and Panasonic televisions, Samsung air conditioners, and a gaggle of refrigerators, washers, satellite dishes spilled over the sidewalks and into the road.

Ghani admitted that he was too afraid to drive his own 2000 Nissan; that fear was not unwarranted. In some of Baghdad's tougher neighborhoods, a Russian Kalashnikov was running $90, a Czech knockoff $50. Pistols and revolvers were plentiful. At some arms markets, a black ammunition clip, glistening in the sun, cost about $1, and a bullet was going for 50 cents. Nothing seemed secure—not cars, not homes, not daughters, nothing.

"You know, we always have bang, bang, bang," he told me.

In the famous collection called A *Thousand and One Nights*, set in the Baghdad of Harun al-Rashid, the king marries a new young woman each day, takes her virginity during the night, and has her killed in the morning. Then comes beautiful Shehrazad, who tells the king a tale that never ends—not that night, the king's anticipation her reprieve, nor the next, when another story is seamlessly unfurled. Tale after tale, for a thousand and one nights in Baghdad, she captivates him. For the tales' countless tellers, a number one higher than one thousand suggested the endless stretch of infinity. Such infinite nights and infinite tales could unfold only in Baghdad, an eternal city where time, where greatness, would never come to an end.

Ghani's statue of Shehrazad telling her stories to a reclining King Shehrayar kept vigil over once libertine Abu Nawas Street along the Tigris, where we finally arrived. As we sauntered toward it, Ghani looked out at the wasteland, once a stretch of riverside parks, restaurants serving the Iraqi fish specialty called *masgouf*, and bars with ample stocks of *arak*, an anise-flavored spirit that Ghani liked to call lion's milk.

"All of this was gardens," he remembered, but now there was trash, uprooted trees, discarded bricks, a chain-link fence along the river. Up the street were burlap receptacles filled with sand and rolls of wire. Their metal caught the sun's glint; the barbs snared wayward rubbish. The scene was like Baghdad, in flux and out of order. "Look at it," he muttered. "No one takes care, no one comes."

This was the first time since the invasion that Ghani had seen his prized statue—her almond eyes, long flowing hair, and revealing dress—and he breathed a sigh of relief. There was still something left. His Baghdad was a lonely landscape marred by looting, the scars of bombing, and the grinding burdens imposed by blackouts. But not all was lost.

"Look how beautiful she is," Ghani said, again speaking to himself. "No one comes here anymore, but Shehrazad remains."

As he left, he went up to a young boy sitting under a cardboard lean-to, selling soft drinks from a Styrofoam cooler. He pointed to Shehrazad, rubble piled underneath her willowy figure. "Take care of the statue," he told the boy, whose face was already wrinkled by the sun. "If thieves come here, go tell someone. Don't let them take her away."

▪ ▪ ▪

"WE DON'T KNOW WHAT'S GOING TO HAPPEN IN THE COMING DAYS," AMAL wrote in her journal on April 10, the day after Saddam's fall. "Looting, robberies, and thievery continue while the fear over theft continues, too. Oh, God, why does this agony surround us? The Iraqis steal without any remorse or thought."

Then she asked a question that I heard often in Baghdad: "What are the Americans going to do with us?" The entry ended succinctly: "God, have mercy on us."

Amal looked to her mother for guidance, but Karima was too frightened to offer it, and knew too little to make predictions. Amal tried to make sense of events but then realized there was no logic now. Her entry for April 11, 2003, was chaotic and confused: "The hospitals are being looted and no one is protesting! Why does the St. Rafael Hospital have an American tank protecting it? Is it because it is a Christian hospital? What about the Alwiya Maternity Hospital? What about the pregnant women there?" she wrote. "Oh, God, what shall we do? Why all this destruction? Why has it befallen Iraqis? Wasn't it enough to loot government offices? Now the hospitals and even homes?"

The next day, her mother told her that even the schools had been looted. "God, what has happened!" Amal wrote.

There was an attitude in Iraq in those months, shared by fourteen-year-old Amal, that seemed to condemn the occupation from the start. Many in Baghdad had been in awe of American technology during the war. Especially during the conflict's first days, the U.S. assault was as precise as it was devastating. There was an almost divine quality to American power; it was merciless in its practice, flawless in its execution. Saddam had ruled for nearly twenty-five years, behind the scenes for far longer; the Americans had toppled him in less than three weeks, and relatively few of their soldiers had died in the task. How could these same Americans be so feeble in the aftermath?

Like others, Amal confronted a city that was collapsing. Some armed themselves when they went outside; others traveled in groups, hoping for safety in numbers. Few parents let their daughters walk alone in the streets, and Amal's family spent most of their time in the apartment, huddled in the stuffy living room, sweating. Electricity remained intermittent, sorely inadequate as the temperatures climbed. Phones were still not working, their networks shattered by bombing. Money, each denomination still bearing Saddam's portrait, was scarce. Prices soared further, and shortages were everywhere, affecting everything from food to fuel. Overnight, tens of thousands lost their jobs as the bureaucracy disintegrated, some government offices in flames. For many, Amal's family among them, living conditions worsened.

"Where is the help that Bush spoke about?" Amal wrote. "No one knows."

As during the war proper, rumors raced through her family's apartment building, and neighbors traded stories that grew more terrifying with each retelling. Had she heard about the three girls kidnapped as they walked to church? About the two neighbors killed by a cousin who coveted the booty they had stolen from one of the palaces of Uday, Saddam's sadistic oldest son? One of her brothers told her he had watched three men armed with AK-47s seize a car in the street below. When school resumed, only fifteen of the forty girls attended. The rest were kept home by their families, who feared their daughters would fall victim to the rash of kidnappings being carried out by armed, marauding gangs.

"There is fear everywhere," Amal wrote.

"There is no gas, no kerosene, no security. Even if there were buses to transport the girls to school, there is no fuel. We are a country of oil, but people have to stand in line to buy fuel. My God, what is this? There is looting, people steal, and there is gunfire in the streets. What's going to be the future of Iraq? Can it be good? No one knows."

During the war, Amal had already begun asking questions. Now her thoughts were becoming more subtle, more complex. At times, she wrote with grim gallows humor. In one passage, she remarked that Iraqis would sleep through the dawn prayers even on Friday, the Muslim Sabbath, yet they would wake up with enthusiasm if they could steal from others. In another entry, she told a story of a friend of her brother Mohammed, the ne'er-do-well. The anecdote, perhaps an urban legend, was filled with irony that she seemed to appreciate. Irony was appropriate in those days. The friend, she said, had visited their apartment and told them how he had helped loot one of Uday's palaces. With others, he went to the stables and stole one of Uday's horses, named Asad, Arabic for lion.

"It was a very beautiful horse," she recalled him saying.

She then recounted his story: "He gave it bread to eat, but it refused. He gave it milk, but it wouldn't take it. It refused hay, too. So, for two days, the horse didn't eat anything. It stood sleepless. He wanted to feed it, and it refused. Eat, and it wouldn't eat.

"After two days, he brought it bananas and apples, and it devoured them," she wrote. "He became angry and cursed it, saying, 'You son of a bitch. We eat dry bread with tea, living in misery, and you eat apples and bananas! This is unfair, this is *harram*, forbidden.' Then he fired two shots at Uday's horse, killing it instantly."

The Americans had entered a land of dry bread and tea, and Amal sought to see them through the many lenses that Iraqis had inherited from the decades of dictatorship and deprivation. It was easy for Iraqis to recall the descriptions that medieval Arab historians had given of the Crusaders, soldiers of conquest who arrived in 1098, inspiring fear and, for decades, seeming invincible. They were seen as fair-haired giants, sheathed in heavy armor and laden with weapons. The stories made the current intimidation seem familiar.

"Every time American tanks pass, or I see them, I feel scared," Amal wrote.

She stayed far from the gear-laden soldiers in the streets, peering at them from her balcony and even returning waves, but always reluctant to speak. Her vivacious younger twin sisters were more curious. One Saturday in the occupation's first month, a tank was parked on the street, and Duaa and Hibba went to say hello to the soldiers, who gave them chocolates. A few minutes later, there was the crack of gunfire, in staccato bursts.

"Hibba tried to ask the soldier what was happening. He told her, 'Go! Go!' But Hibba didn't understand the American language. Out of fear for Hibba, he carried her to our building. They are nice, but they are misled by Bush, the dangerous one," Amal wrote.

Two days later, the twins saw another group of U.S. soldiers in the streets, their desert camouflage melting into the city's palette of browns. "They wrote their names on the children's palms. Hibba's hand had names of American soldiers on it. Hibba and Duaa were very happy. They said the soldiers were very friendly and they were delighted with them. Is it true they are good?" Amal asked. "Who knows? Only God knows."

▪ ▪ ▪

EVER SO SLIGHTLY, AMAL'S WRITING BEGAN TO CHANGE. DURING THE WAR, infused with the government's propaganda, she had spoken, at least to me, with the force of a loyalist. Precocious, the smartest of Karima's girls, and an enthusiastic inductee in her school's Baath Party group, she had competed with her sisters in pledges of fealty to Saddam, even if her diary was more reflective. In April, a week after his fall, as her fellow Shiites celebrated his demise, Amal still held tenaciously to her old views. Saddam was all she knew. ("Until now," she said, "the collapse of Saddam was not good. Until now, we still say 'his excellency, the president.'")

But privately Amal seemed baffled, and she gave voice to her confusion in the diary. A war she had dreaded was over and a revolution she did not understand was just beginning; she tried to reconcile her experience with reality, as churning, unpredictable, and menacing as it was. Just as she questioned her views of the U.S. soldiers, she began to reconsider her beliefs about Saddam.

"We used to have trust in President Saddam Hussein," she wrote on April 11, two days after his fall, "but now we don't know whom we trust."

Saddam still cast many shadows in Iraq; he would do so for months and years to follow. Almost immediately, the mass graves of those he had persecuted began to be unearthed, sprawling sites that were found to number in the dozens, the victims numbering in the tens of thousands, perhaps hundreds of thousands. Often the corpses were found with their arms lashed, bullets in the back of their heads. With their discovery came an accounting of the dead. Days after Saddam's fall, photocopied pictures of men declared missing or executed and now martyrs began to crowd for space in markets, offices, and mosques bringing memory to nameless, faceless victims put to death under dictatorship. Their dark eyes, lonesome, stared at the streets before them. The people gazed into their eyes.

So began the process of demystifying Saddam, a menacing presence in almost every conversation that occurred in the country for thirty-five years. To many, he was still "the president" or, more often, simply "him." They referred not to the repression of the Baath Party, but "to the story we all know." Saddam's name was still whispered; who knew if danger remained, if somehow he might still be listening, waiting. Was any of this actually real?

The gossip was fevered. Saddam was spotted often—in the neighborhood of Adhamiya in Baghdad, in the Sunni villages, with their idyllic palm groves and orchards along the Tigris, where he used to draw his support. Many insisted that he had dispatched his family west to Damascus in two or three buses two weeks before the war's end. Others speculated that he and others had gone north to Iraq's third-largest city, Mosul, or to the region where he was raised, around Tikrit. Some said he had sought refuge with the Sunni Muslim tribes on which his government had showered patronage—cars, guns, and money—since the end of the 1991 war.

As the days since the ruler's collapse slowly passed, Amal's questions multiplied. She was disoriented by the sudden change in attitudes. "Everybody is talking about Saddam Hussein. They curse him more and more," she wrote. "They don't like Saddam Hussein. Why?"

Secrets soon poured out, and Amal digested the horrors of the government she had once seen as indestructible. Weeks after his fall, she and her family watched some of the fifty-cent videos that had flooded the market. They detailed Saddam's ornate palaces, in their style of kitschy Arabesque—"all with gold and silver," Amal wrote—the gassing of five thousand Kurds in 1988 in the northern Iraqi city of Halabja, and Uday's notorious habit of abducting women he fancied.

"Saddam's elder son, Uday, is the most corrupt person on earth," she wrote after watching the videos over two days, a viewing interrupted by blackouts. "Any girl he liked, he would take. No one could say anything because he is the son of President Saddam Hussein. His other son, Qusay, is also cruel, like his father and brother."

The same, she wrote, went for Saddam's other relatives, men like his cousin and lieutenant Ali Hassan al-Majid, who razed hundreds, maybe thousands of Kurdish villages, served as governor of occupied Kuwait after the invasion in 1990, and crushed the Shiite uprising in southern Iraq that followed the 1991 war. Most notoriously, he was blamed for the massacre at Halabja, an atrocity that earned him the nickname Chemical Ali. At his palace in Baghdad, on the banks of the Tigris, crowds rummaged for days through room after room of the warehouse, which sprawled across an area the size of a football field. There were light fixtures and vases, chessboards and water skis. Medals bearing Saddam's image and a promise of "unity, freedom, and socialism"—the Baath Party slogan—were exchanged as mementos. In boxes were the trivialities of a smaller-than-life man: videotapes of *Les Miserables*, *Lethal Weapon II*, and *Lifestyles of the Rich and Famous* were scattered among portraits of Saddam, scattered, trampled, and discarded.

"No one realizes they are gone, all of them, forever," Amal wrote.

IN MAY, NEARLY A MONTH AFTER THE WAR'S END, AMAL WENT BACK TO SCHOOL. She returned to a building once short on education and long on Saddam's indoctrination. Now, for the teachers as well as the students, what he had left behind was exciting and confusing, intoxicating and menacing. Most telling, it was mysterious.

> I got up at seven this morning, put on my school clothes, hung my bag on my shoulders. So did my sister Zainab. And we both went to school very happily. . . . When we arrived at the schoolyard, I didn't see many of my girlfriends, because only a few came to school. The headmistress met with us and said, "We are no longer worried about the regime, the law, or Saddam Hussein. Any pictures of Saddam should be burned or torn up. Rip them out of your book. And Saddam's instructions, you can cross them out. Don't wear tight pants, or anything tight, because there are some who are abducting girls." Everyone is scared because of such people who don't respect any laws. My girlfriend said some Americans are nice. The teacher said the Americans entered the Sharqiya School for Girls and inspected it. There were pictures of Saddam Hussein, which they burned. They found three rockets inside the Sharqiya School for Boys, and she talked about the looting that took place. We went back home at 12:15. The teacher said school hours would be from 8:30 to 12:00, and every girl should have her mother come to pick her up, to ensure safety for the girl. I came back home and there was nothing, and the day ended without any problems.

AT THE INVASION'S CLIMAX, IRAQ'S ARMED FORCES HAD COLLAPSED FROM within. Soldiers deserted in droves, and commanders of even elite units refused to push their fighters into a battle that would almost certainly prove a slaughter.

Nearing the end, even those ordered to fight fell back from street corners, bridges, and intersections across the capital. They changed into street clothes, left their weapons behind, and went home, past the slogans that still lined the walls: "Iraq, victorious, victorious, victorious, it is victorious with the permission of God."

The dissolution of the Iraqi military was spectacular, though not unexpected. Always suspicious of the regular army, one of the oldest institutions of an independent Iraq, Saddam had devised an array of special forces to circumvent it—the Republican Guard, the Special Republican Guard, the Fedayeen Saddam, and the Quds Army (this last meant, in rhetoric at least, to fight Israel). He bestowed generous gifts and salaries on them, leaving the regular army disenchanted, demoralized, and poorly equipped. They were in no mood to die for Saddam, not after fighting three wars for him, each bringing its own particular brand of disaster. Death in defending Iraq was one thing; suicide in the name of Saddam was another.

In time, even Saddam's specialized units fell apart. The remnants of the vaunted Republican Guard played so small a role that Baghdad, the nexus of Saddam's rule, fell far more easily than the restive cities of the south. By April 9, droves of Fedayeen were hiding in their homes, wary of American retribution more feared than real. More than a few made a strategic decision to abandon the battle, choosing to fight the Americans another day, on their own terms.

Among the soldiers who chose to flee was Amal's oldest brother, Ali, a laconic but pleasant conscript. Two days before the American tanks arrived in Baghdad, he deserted his unit north of Mosul. At 10:30 P.M., like others, he left his weapon, donned civilian clothes, and boarded a bus, ahead of U.S. troops and their Kurdish allies rolling south. Whenever American bombing was at its fiercest, the bus stopped—in all, pulling over more than a dozen times along highways and back roads. Ali arrived in Baquba thirty-six hours later, having traveled two hundred miles. Then he walked southwest to Baghdad, a thirty-five-mile trek through farms irrigated by the Tigris and along roads clogged with refugees hauling a life's belongings in trucks, cars, and carts pulled by donkeys and horses.

"Half of Baghdad was in Baquba," he recalled weeks later.

His trail home was through a junkyard of war, littered with its judgments.

Burned-out tanks, their horrors now cooled, blocked the way. The roads were cratered and corpses lay along his path. The bodies of some of his fellow soldiers were charred, he said, caught in postures of agony; others were ripening in the sun. There was no one to bury them. No one had the job anymore.

"If God writes that you'll live, you'll live," Ali told me as we talked at his mother's apartment, sitting on a wood bench with a sheet thrown over it. The saying was common in Arabic, but he spoke it as if the thought had new meaning to him. "If God writes that you'll die, you'll die."

Cries of joy had met his arrival—dancing and tears, embraces that went on all night, smiles that lasted for days. But, a few weeks after the fall of Saddam, the euphoria over his return had waned. Hopes, dreams, and gratitude were overshadowed by life's hardships. In Karima's building, the water remained off, so the children took turns lugging buckets from a working faucet in the entryway downstairs, near a pool of black, brackish water. For days at a time, the family had no kerosene for cooking. When kerosene was available, it sometimes sold for twenty times its prewar price. The family relied on the occasional goodwill of neighbors, but soon these same people ran short of kerosene themselves. Food prices skyrocketed: Karima groused that a kilogram of cucumbers had tripled in price since the war's end; tomatoes had more than doubled. The family staved off hunger only by way of the monthly food rations that were still distributed to each family after the government's collapse: Karima's family of eight people got about twenty pounds of flour, a little more than six pounds of sugar, the same quantity of rice, more than a pound each of powdered milk and beans, plus tea, cooking oil, salt, detergent, and soap. Almost as if to add insult to injury, the overdue rent still loomed, and the landlord was growing impatient.

Ali, looked to by his mother and sisters as the family breadwinner, had no work. Draped across the bench, with eighteen months in the army and with a war behind him, he was none too eager to find it.

"There won't be a government for one month, for two months. I don't think there will be stability for two or three years," Ali said. He repeated a line I heard often, varied slightly, as he looked ahead. "Nobody knows what's going to happen in the future." This was the feeling that defined Baghdad now; it was a city with no idea about what shape to imagine for the weeks and months ahead. Conventional expectations had been so long decimated and now this. Before the invasion, anticipation of the war seemed to artificially freeze time, creating a pause in people's lives. The uncertainty now did something similar; no one could prepare for a future they knew so little about.

Ali and his sisters talked about the most dangerous parts of the city, the places marked by the worst lawlessness. Their eyes grew wide when they talked about Mareidy, by reputation the toughest neighborhood in Baghdad, part of a slum once known as Saddam City.

"Whatever you want is there," Ali said, shaking his head, as if he were surprised by that himself. "Bombs? You can find a tank there! Whatever you want."

"People don't respect each other," said Fatima, the oldest of the five daughters. "It's like a jungle. Baghdad is a city of five million Ali Babas."

Ali nodded. "Everybody is carrying a pistol or a rifle," he said.

For years, Ali Baba, the woodcutter from *A Thousand and One Nights* who springs open a lair of forty thieves, had come to serve as Baghdad shorthand for a criminal. It didn't matter that, in the story, Ali Baba was not one of the thieves but their nemesis. Now the confusion seemed fitting to the circumstances as the use of the name exploded in the war's aftermath, as crime spiraled out of control, aided and abetted by the tens of thousands of convicts released by Saddam before the war. People would smile as they uttered the name of Ali Baba, even though there was such shame over the thievery, over what had happened to Baghdad.

Karima did not mention Ali Baba. She spoke of *bahdhala*, a word she used to sum up her city's predicament. *Bahdhala* was the mess they were all in, the outrages visited upon them. Along Karrada Street, modern appliances were spilling into the street. The market selling them had appeared courtesy of the unruly overnight end of once burdensome customs, taxes, and bribes, and of the rise in the value of the Iraqi dinar, buoyed by a deluge of U.S. dollars that shifted the exchange rate in its favor. Karima's apartment overlooked the display. She saw it every day. *Bahdhala*. It was all confusion and frightening.

"Ever since the war started, I've earned nothing," she said, her voice flat. "Everything has gone from us. Electricity, we don't have. Water, we don't have. We are anxious, and we are scared." Like others, she said she couldn't understand how a country as powerful as America could not distribute gas or electricity, or provide security or work. Where was the government? Where would she earn money for her children? What would she tell the landlord? Already, she said, she had sold Fatima's gold necklace for about sixty-five dollars, a few dollars of which went to buy three wooden school desks looted by her neighbors. For a time, they used the desks as chairs in the apartment's biggest room. A few more dollars would go to put her daughters through school, paying for clothes, notebooks, and pens. The rest went to getting by. Somehow, Karima always managed to get by.

As she often did, she stopped, turned silent for a moment, and looked to the floor, as if to signify "What more can be said?"

The room, lit by a morning sun and alive with conversation, turned quiet again. In respect, Karima's children deferred to her; they would let her speak for them. She did, uttering a sentiment that I would hear from her time and again. During the occupation, it became her mantra, and she spoke it in moments of unease. She said it in the resigned voice of someone who knows that her wish will never be fulfilled. The words expressed a hope, but sometimes sounded like a curse.

"We want security and we want stability," Karima told me. "Anybody who comes along is fine as long as he brings security and stability."

This was the Iraqi version of the trains running on time. The country, she said, needed a strong hand. Freed from fear, she had little good to say about Saddam, though he still seemed to lurk in the background. "All the people hated him," she insisted. But amid the anarchy, she recalled the order he had brought, in language reminiscent of Amal's diary entries. If you stole a chicken or a car, if you stole one dinar or one million dinars, Karima said, Saddam would throw you into Abu Ghreib. "There must be a leader," Karima nodded, stating a truth. "Only a strong leader can rule Iraq."

Duaa and Hibba played at the side of the room. Zainab busied herself tidying up the apartment, more crowded with Ali's return. Mahmoud, her frail young son, napped next to Karima, cross-legged on a thin mattress on the concrete floor. A sheet colored in greens, blues, and whites had been tossed over her seat. Mohammed, tougher than Ali and at ease in the edgy streets, was gone. Ali, Fatima, and Amal listened to their mother in the hot room. With no electricity, the fan was motionless.

"My son was a soldier," she said. She motioned with her hands, palms upturned, a universal gesture of helplessness. Like her words, the gesture would become familiar. "If there was a government, he'd return to the army. But if there's no army, what is there to return to? Now he sits." The look she cast at Ali was neither sympathetic nor critical. "He looks for work, he finds nothing, and he comes back and sits."

ACROSS TOWN, FUAD MUSA MOHAMMED, THE SHIITE PSYCHIATRIST WHO SUP-ported America's cause, was reveling in what seemed to him a hopeful moment. His wife, Suad, had returned from Beirut, where she had spent the war with relatives. Yasmine, his daughter, was visiting with her three children from their neighborhood of Jadriya. Crime wave or not, the steel gate that led to his driveway was open. Fuad's garden was in full bloom, verdant with citrus trees and rose bushes. Palm trees towered over the chest-high wall. His was a tranquil redoubt in a city with little composure.

This was my first time seeing Fuad since the government's collapse, and he was jubilant. "There's victory! There's victory!" he proclaimed. "All of us are reborn again." With familiar exuberance, his optimism untempered, he threw out his arms and raised them toward the ceiling, provoking the smiles of those around him. In the same breath, he dismissed the naysayers as inveterate pessimists, still stumbling before Saddam's shadow even with the dictator gone.

Lines for gas snaked along streets, even in Fuad's wealthy neighborhood of Mansur, and his home was still cloaked in dark, as it had been during the bombing. But Fuad, far more avuncular than on our previous visit, seemed unscathed. He reclined on his sofa, never losing his smile. He was reassuring; at times, he even seemed giddy.

America? "I call it my government," Fuad boasted.

Bush? "From the bottom of my heart, I really respect, I adore this man, more than you," he declared. "I have a new birth certificate from the tenth of April."

"Don't talk to him," said his wife, Suad, shaking her head. "He's an American."

An effervescent woman with a sharp wit, Suad was as skeptical as Fuad was optimistic: they occupied the positions that shaped the two most familiar ends of the spectrum of opinion toward the aftermath. With familiarity and affection, she bantered with Fuad across that gulf of perception.

Electricity was on her mind. As we sat over a bowl of small candies and tiny cups of Arabic coffee, she insisted that it was all she wanted to talk about. As in most conversations those days, the room was lit by a sun filtered through curtains. The light was soft, but misleading, as the heat stagnated in a room with no circulation. The heat was making Suad uncomfortable, and she directed her irritation at Baghdad's new rulers.

"They brought tanks by an airplane. They can't bring generators, from Kuwait or Turkey? They brought everything. They can't bring generators for the people?"

Fuad smiled again, the same look of reassurance that I remembered from the war. He was always bent on instilling optimism. "It takes small steps," he said.

She looked at him, uncomprehending, and shook her head. It had been weeks, she exclaimed. "It's so hot!" she said. "We can't sleep at night."

She talked about the new quarters for the Americans: the Rashid, once the city's premiere hotel, with its now-dismantled mosaic of George H. W. Bush that guests traipsed over as they entered, and the Republican Palace, whose domed centerpiece encircled with busts of Saddam was left unscathed in the war's bombing. She said she suspected there were indeed generators in those places. She complained that rubble still littered Baghdad, that trash, grown fetid in the heat, clogged its streets.

Fear prevailed at night—Suad's brother-in-law, a neurosurgeon, had been killed by thieves who stole his new Peugeot, and a gang had tried to abduct the daughter of a well-to-do friend who had a factory in Karbala. Already, she suggested, there was a hint of nostalgia for Saddam's iron-handed security. "Everybody is afraid," she said.

"People say Saddam is better, just to make themselves feel better, but I can never say this," Fuad said. He took a psychiatrist's view: Iraqis were traumatized, he said. It would take years, perhaps decades to recover. But with patience, with realism, the country he knew as a child, the capital he remembered from the 1970s, could exist once more. If not in his time, then in his grandchildren's.

"After this generation will come another generation," the doctor said, shaking his head, his eyes almost pleading, "and life will be better."

Suad's concerns were more immediate, and she feared that the future was impossible. She pointed to Order No. 2 issued in May by L. Paul Bremer, less than two weeks after he assumed control as the governor of Iraq. By this decree, Bremer had disbanded the Iraqi army and dissolved the Ministry of Information. The latter decision provoked resentment, as its employees were thereby left without pensions and salaries. The former decision was almost universally regarded as an impetuous, astonishing mistake. The army had, of course, disintegrated and there was not much left of it—about eighteen tanks and a few artillery pieces. Yet it still evoked pride in many Iraqis, and it was less tainted by the Baath Party than other institutions. The net effect of Bremer's decision was to send more than 350,000 officers and conscripts, men with at least some military training, into the streets, instantly creating a reservoir of potential recruits for a guerrilla war. (At their disposal was about a million tons of weapons and munitions of all sorts, freely accessible in more than a hundred largely unguarded depots around the country.) Order No. 2 would come back to haunt the occupation, as a ruthless insurgency unleashed carnage across the country.

In some ways, though, Suad deemed her country already destroyed, even before the May decrees. Leaning forward in her chair, she described her return to Baghdad after the war. She recalled the charred hulks of cars wrecked in the fighting, the scars of bombings, the wounds from looting, and a city left dark at night. Nobody was out after nine P.M. "It was horrible," she remembered. "I cried, I cried."

Fuad listened, then spoke again, seemingly somewhat at random.

"People think the Americans can do everything," he said.

"Not everything! Not everything!" Suad retorted, her frustration growing. "Just the electricity. Sick people, newborn babies. I'm not talking about myself. Telephones. We haven't got telephones. We have to go outside. Bring mobiles. Why can't they bring mobiles?"

"People want everything at once," Fuad answered.

"This is just simple electricity," she said to him sharply. "We can't call our daughters. We have to cross the bridge to Jadriya to talk to them."

Fuad nodded. He would not be persuaded, even if he was still listening.

They talked about their son, Firas, in the United States, who was completing his medical residency in Baltimore at Johns Hopkins University. He was expecting a daughter in September, and they hoped to get a visa to visit.

"They should let us travel to America. We are Americans now!" Suad exclaimed. "I'll tell Bremer that we are Americans."

Everyone in the room laughed, a brief break in an uncompromising conversation.

"I'm proud of it," Fuad said a few moments later, refusing to relent. "As long as America is here, everything will be better, and the future will be brighter."

"Fuad, you say this, but the people don't," his wife said, shaking her head. "The people can't accept it. This is not me. This is the people."

"The people?" he countered. "What do the people want? They want to be happier. They want luxury. For thirty-five years, we didn't get any benefit. What did he do for Baghdad? He did nothing. Thirty-five years." He dragged out the last words, in a voice that suggested a lifetime lost.

Suad paused, looking down. "I don't like Saddam," she said. "But if Saddam were here, he would fix the telephones in two months. I don't say Saddam is good, but . . ." She left the sentence unfinished and shrugged her shoulders.

"They will bring new telephones in one month," Fuad said. "Of course, they will."

As the conversation ended, Suad laughed and looked at her husband, then turned to me. "Take him to America!" she said, flipping her hand dismissively.

MOHAMMED GHANI LIVED IN THE SAME NEIGHBORHOOD AS FUAD. WEEKS AFTER our last visit, I found him there in his sweltering studio, which, like Fuad's house, was cloaked in dark. His Shehrazad was still telling stories to King Shahrayar along Abu Nawas Street, but her likeness in the studio did not manage to survive war and what followed.

"Look, this is Shehrazad," he said grimly, holding up a shattered bust, a spiderweb of plaster holding the pieces together. He surveyed the detritus, then picked up a plaster jaw and nose, the remains of a statue of Kahramana, Ali Baba's slave girl who killed the forty thieves. Ghani held it in one hand, gazing on it with exaggerated appreciation. He turned it, then grimaced. "Look how beautiful this was," he said. "*Tack, tack, tack.*" He motioned as if swinging a hammer. The looters had "hit it again and again."

Next he gestured toward a line of sculpted doors scattered across the concrete floor. They reveled in their arabesque—an array of arch after arch,

designs in geometric splashes, squares, and circles, with graceful Arabic calligraphy dancing across them. But there, too, was the disorder of destruction.
Door after door had been patched with plaster, then stacked against a tarp of
browns and grays.

"Look how they destroyed the doors," Ghani mumbled to himself. He
nodded in disbelief, casting his eyes around his two-story studio.

His studio was only a hundred yards from the Sa'a Restaurant in Mansur,
where the U.S. military had dropped four 2,000-pound bombs in an unsuccessful attempt to kill Saddam. The blast had shattered the windows of his
studio and nearby home, hurled debris into the walls, and blown his wooden
front door off its hinges. In the looting that followed, many of Ghani's works
in the collection of the Saddam Art Center—137 bronze and plaster pieces
in all—were stolen or wrecked. He brought about fifteen pieces to his studio,
where they crowded for space like bloodied patients in triage.

Since then, he had struggled to make sense of them. His hands were white
with powder from plaster he used to mend them. His brown shoes were
unlaced. He wore a gray T-shirt that was either wet with sweat or blotched
with white after it dried. His khaki shorts hung down to his knees. On his
hand was a blue turquoise ring. Mohammed flashed it as he pointed to his
inventory, an exercise that only seemed to punish him more.

He picked up a broken horse head. It was black, wires protruding from it
like the cartilage that dangles after a slaughter. "I found only this. I will show
it this way, only the head." And on he went, bringing forth his own funeral
procession as he showed me piece after piece. There was a lamp of Aladdin,
its green and gold offset by the red of an exposed and rusted iron rod. "Look
what remains," he said.

Next was a bust of Mansur, then another of Harun al-Rashid. Near them
was an array of other shattered pieces in greens, creams, and grays, scattered
on the floor as at a bombing site. Legs, heads, and torsos were splayed about,
wires tangled among them that once gave form to the plaster. He ended by
picking up a statue of the former slave Zaryab, one of his favorites. An artist
and virtuoso, Zaryab had carried the classical music of the oud from Abbasid
Baghdad to Umayyad Córdoba, from where it developed into the lute of
Europe. The instrument's handle, colored in white, was gone, broken, and
like much of Ghani's work, lost.

"Look how they destroyed him," Ghani said. "Look how many times they hit him."

As in Fuad's house, the heat was stultifying, made worse by the blackout. The browns of Baghdad, the color of wet earth, seemed to absorb the sunlight, then grow hotter. There was not a wind, not even a breeze, and I sat soaking. Sweat fell from my forehead and onto the pages of my notebook. Drops splashed on the black ink, turning handwriting into a watercolor. I was miserable. But not Ghani. He saw my misery, and he laughed, the humor of a hard man.

"The heat of Baghdad is better than the humidity of the Gulf," he said proudly. "It's fresh air. You can breathe clearly. This is the nice Baghdad." His words seemed cheerful and lighthearted. Despite the destruction, there were still a few survivors in his studio; some works remained whole. On one wall, there was still a sculpture of Bahraini women, destined for the market. On another, there remained a sculpture of Christ, not yet delivered to a Catholic church. I remembered the miniature of the flying carpet, the inspiration for his work downtown. And then there was a sprawling representation of a family—smooth, still white, still undamaged. "They could not steal it," he said, breaking into a weary smile. "It was too heavy." But these things were exceptions. Ghani's studio was wrecked, as was his Baghdad, now a lonely and unfamiliar landscape.

9

THE BLOOD OF SADR

Ali Shawki, a bearish Shiite Muslim cleric with the kind of swagger that a pistol on each hip brings, strode with an air of mission through the no-man's-land that the capital had become in the occupation's early weeks. In words and action, he left little doubt that there was a new authority in town and it was his. At the Prophet Mohammed Mosque, in the Baghdad slum where he lived, the forty-seven-year-old Shawki led prayers in a room stuffed with booty confiscated from the looters' rampages. He never removed his guns.

Later, accompanied by an armed retinue—one guard carried a machine gun with rounds slung around him, bandolier-style—the cleric pressed the flesh at a health clinic that he had ordered opened after it had been shut down for days. In between the two events, Shawki sketched out his plans for the sprawl of more than two million people on Baghdad's eastern edge, an anxious, unsettled turf once known as Saddam City. They included armed patrols at night, an eight P.M. curfew, and a ban on all gunfire. He would broadcast these injunctions by mosque loudspeaker through the quarter's crowded warrens.

"We order people to obey us. When we say stand up, they stand up. When we say sit down, they sit down," Shawki remarked as he sat at his mosque, his head swathed in a turban and his beard long. "With the collapse of Saddam," he declared, a statement as bold as it was accurate, "the people have turned to the clergy."

With those words, Shawki approached a question whose answer would help determine the political success of the U.S. occupation. The question was that of legitimacy, a quality always easier to deny than to bestow. The Americans never understood the question; Iraqis never agreed on the answer. Who had the right to rule? As important to Iraqis was the question of where that right came from—God, the gun, money, law, tradition? For Shawki, never reticent, the power came from the clergy, specifically the conservative, traditional Shiite religious leadership that had often opposed Saddam and that had emerged in force once he was gone.

"The Americans," he declared, "should not neglect the place of the clergy."

In the weeks after the war, Shawki claimed authority, spiritual and otherwise, over quarter after quarter of the slum. In all, he estimated that sixty thousand people, perhaps twice as many, lived on his turf. His two hundred men—some posted at the mosque's entrance, two on the roof—patrolled the streets.

By the time I met him, the Prophet Mohammed Mosque was overflowing with goods seized by patrols determined to stanch the looting. Stacked haphazardly along one wall were hospital beds, copiers, car batteries, a typewriter, computer monitors, a red fire extinguisher, black office chairs, sirens, running shoes, a motorcycle, rotary-dial telephones, and a kitchen sink. The men gathered around Shawki, without exception, carried AK-47s. They had a stockpile of rocket-propelled grenades, "just for an emergency."

At the dawn of the new Iraq, Shawki was just one of the clerics who stepped into the chaotic breach, under the leadership of a semi-underground grassroots religious movement that, while influential and revered inside Iraq, had gone largely unnoticed abroad during the 1990s. Their morale and unity intact despite years of repression, the clerics set up one hundred roadblocks to deter looters in Saddam City and other poor Shiite neighborhoods in Baghdad, which together made up their stronghold. They put their congregations and the men they could mobilize in charge of protecting hospitals and maintaining security on the streets. In time, they organized popular committees to restore civil services and order. Prayer leaders themselves took to patrolling their neighborhoods, greeting residents, dispensing homilies, and forcing bakeries to provide free bread.

In ways, the writing of the new order brought by Shawki and the others was already on the wall. Hastily painted slogans in black conveyed a less than subtle message: "Stealing is forbidden by God." Across the city, graffiti replaced the twenty-eight-year-old name "Saddam City" with "Sadr City." The new designation honored Grand Ayatollah Mohammed Mohammed Sadiq al-Sadr, the charismatic cleric who had led the religious movement in the 1990s, before Saddam's men assassinated him and two of his sons in 1999. On the day I visited, a young man was painting a greeting in green on the slum's entrance along Habibiya Street. "Sadr City welcomes you," it said.

The neighborhood, at once sprawling and claustrophobic, cast in the dreary browns of poverty, had long been restive under Saddam. Envisioned as a huge housing development, to be laid out in a grid, it was built in the early 1960s by Iraq's military strongman General Abdel-Karim Qassem. Its original name spoke to its ambition: Revolution City. But in the ensuing decades, waves of dispossessed Shiite Muslim immigrants from southern Iraq—natives of poor towns like Nasiriya and Amara—swept across its broad avenues in search of subsidized housing. Crowding into apartment buildings, they transformed the place into a slum that its embittered residents believe was willfully neglected by Saddam, even as they were forced to call it by his name after he took power.

The neighborhood was destitute. In its dwellings, an average of ten people crowded for space in two, maybe three rooms. Herds of goats and sheep picked at scraps of lettuce, orange peels, bread, and tomatoes tossed with trash on the side of the road. Men sold cigarettes, shoes, and hardware on burlap mats spread along the sidewalks. Overhead fluttered green, red, and black flags, the religious banners of Shiite Islam. I first visited in 1998, and on each successive trip, with a rare uptick from time to time, the neighborhood had seemed to grow worse: spare tires and plastic bags awash in shin-high pools of green sewage, now mixed with drinking water and eddying into apartments.

For eleven years, Shawki had served as the imam of one of the slum's eighty mosques. Under Saddam's watchful eye, he was, as he freely admitted, exceedingly careful, to the point of submission. He acknowledged that he used to visit Baath Party officials once a week, but insisted that it was only out of fear, not as a collaborator. He said he was warned by the party's enforcers that they would "rip out my mouth" if he didn't pay homage to Saddam in his weekly sermons at the mosque on Friday. He disavowed politics, politics being, after all, the easiest way to get killed under Saddam.

When I met him, though, that fear had evaporated. Time and again as we talked, one of his hands stroking his bushy, black beard, the other atop his formidable belly, he insisted that his job was no longer solely to supervise daily prayers and ask quotidian questions about proper behavior. His ambitions were far greater.

"The religious man is not confined to the pulpit," Shawki told me. "He can act as a military, political, social, and spiritual leader. I want to stress this point."

He turned and looked at the young men gathered around him.

"True?" he asked them.

"True! True!" they shouted back at him, in unison.

He looked at me again, knowingly, as we sat cross-legged on a Persian carpet. "They respond quickly to the clergy," he said, nodding. "They listen to my words."

There was a thuggish quality about Shawki that I would see often in Iraq, among the men who emerged to fill the vacuum left by Saddam's demise and the Americans' inaction. As he talked, I kept thinking of a line in the Rolling Stones song "Jigsaw Puzzle": "Yes, he really looks quite religious, / He's been an outlaw all his life."

For men of Shawki's generation, background, and affiliation in the slum, weapons often accompanied the clergy's frayed robes and billowing turbans, the Shiite equivalent to a priest's collar. Shawki paid homage to the Quran but, streetwise as he was, proudly pointed to the two 9mm pistols slung loosely in a leather belt around his ample waist. He felt no shame, no need to be meek; he was in charge.

"I pray with my guns," he told me, with barely a smile. He had strapped them on, he said, the day that Saddam fell.

SHAWKI WAS A MANIFESTATION OF ONE OF THE OCCUPATION'S MOST LASTING legacies: a resurgence of Shiite identity, cast in religious terms. Like the occupation itself, the revival produced consequences that no one could predict, much less anticipate.

In truth, the term "revival" was a misnomer, as the word suggests rebirth or a renaissance: Although they are a minority in the Arab world, Shiites have been a majority in Iraq, at least since the country's independence in 1923. Never, however, have the Shiites claimed a share of political power commensurate with their numbers. For centuries, they have lived in the shadow of Sunni Muslim overlords, from the Abbasids in Baghdad and the Ottomans of neighboring Turkey to the elites fostered under the British occupation. During Saddam's narrowly sectarian reign, the community, concentrated in southern Iraq, withered under the worst persecution yet. All in all, the story of Shiites in Iraq is a millennium-old saga of martyrdom.

The schism between Sunnis and Shiites dates back to the seventh century A.D., to the very dawn of Islam, and it begins with a political dispute. To Muslims, Mohammed was the last in a succession of God's prophets that began with Abraham and continued through Moses and Jesus. His revelation, delivered from the inhospitable and rugged climes of western Arabia, is believed by Muslims to be the most perfect and complete message of God's will. His authority, over political and spiritual matters, was unquestioned. Yet when Mohammed died—on Monday, June 8, 632—the nascent community he had founded fell into a divisive dispute over who should succeed him as leader of the *umma*, the community of believers. Discord over Mohammed's intentions followed, with authority eventually passed on to a circle of his closest companions, known traditionally as the rightly guided caliphs. Together, Abu Bakr (632–34), Omar (634–44), Uthman (644–56), and Ali (656–61) transformed a provincial community of the faithful into a world power poised for conquest.

Sunni Muslims venerate and respect all four men—as political, not spiritual, leaders—and look to their reigns as a golden age of Muslim history. Shiites, whose name comes from *shiat Ali*, "partisans of Ali," see their history far differently. They view the first three members of the circle—Abu Bakr, Omar, and Uthman—as usurpers of Ali's divine claim. They believe that Ali was blessed by the Prophet to lead.

Ali was a cousin of the Prophet; at thirteen, though some accounts of his age differ, he became one of the first converts to Islam after hearing Mohammed's early revelations. Today, he is remembered for his piety, nobility, and learning. Stocky and powerfully built, he was a soldier and a thinker who often led the early Islamic army and who gained fame as a generous and magnanimous warrior. His matchless sword, known as *dhu al-fiqar* and shaped like a forked tongue, became iconic. His sayings, sermons, and speeches were compiled more than four centuries later in a book called the *Nahj al-Balaghah* (The Way of Eloquence), which served as a model for Arabic much as the speeches of Cicero once had for Latin.

Even Sunnis acknowledge Mohammed's close relationship with Ali, who married Fatima, the Prophet's daughter. Yet Ali's tenure as caliph was troubled. He faced rebellions and insurrections, and his enemies were many; his attention was consumed by conspiracies. In a theme that would become familiar in Shiite history, Ali's reign ended prematurely in 661 when he was stabbed in Kufa, near the Euphrates River in southern Iraq, by one of the surviving insurgents, Ibn Muljam. The assassin carried out the deed with a poisoned dagger, at the demand of a woman who, it is said, made Ali's death a condition of marriage. Ali died two days later. Today, Najaf, the city where he is buried, is home to a towering gold-domed shrine that serves as his tomb. Built of brown and blue brick, with turquoise-tiled porticoes, it stands astride a white marble complex that is one of Shiite Islam's most venerated sites of pilgrimage.

For Ali's followers, his family's claim to leadership of the Islamic community, or *umma*, did not end with his death. They believe his authority passed to his offspring by his wife Fatima, the Prophet's daughter. Those men are known as imams; most Shiites in Iraq believe there were twelve who followed Mohammed, and that their line ends with the Mahdi, known as the Hidden Imam, who will reveal himself at the end of time, bringing order and justice and taking revenge on God's enemies. In all, six of the imams are buried in Iraq—in radiant tombs in Najaf and Karbala, in Baghdad, and, to the north, in Samarra. To Shiites, the men possess a spiritual and political preeminence; they are endowed with graces, miraculous powers, divine knowledge, and blessings that God has given no one else. They serve as intermediaries between man and the Almighty.

Perhaps none of the imams is as beloved as Hussein, the second son of Ali and Fatima and a grandson of the prophet Mohammed. His life and, more important, his tragic death constitute the central, most powerful drama of Shiite faith. Nineteen years after his father's assassination, Hussein resolved to press his claim for leadership of the *umma*, his right to the caliphate. In 680, he left the Prophet's hometown of Mecca, in present-day Saudi Arabia, with members of his household, closest companions, and other followers, destined for Kufa in neighboring Iraq, where he was assured of support. Reinforcements joined him along the way.

Soon, though, he was vastly outnumbered, surrounded by an army of four thousand on a dusty plain at Karbala. Cut off from water for eight days, the odds impossible, Hussein's party skirmished with the enemy before the Prophet's grandson himself mounted his horse and went into battle with his men. Hussein was decapitated, as were his seventy-two companions, and his head was carted off on a stake to Damascus, from where Yazid, his enemy, ruled. Their headless corpses were left on the blood-drenched battlefield for two days, under a desert sun, until residents of a nearby village buried them after the force departed.

In the centuries that followed, Sunnis saw this episode as deplorable: Hussein was, after all, a beloved figure and a grandson of the Prophet. But his death, to Sunnis, is history. For religious Shiites, Hussein's martyrdom on the plains of Karbala became the motif around which the community's perspective revolves, the heart of ritual and iconography and the defining moment of a narrative that, among the more pious and in Christ-like fashion, remains powerfully resonant. To the devout, Ashura, the anniversary of his death on the tenth of Muharram, is the most tragic and sorrowful day of the year. A time of centuries-old ritual with frenzied mourning, it is most spectacularly marked in Karbala, where Hussein's shrine sits next to that of his half-brother Abbas. The grief not only marks Hussein's death more than thirteen centuries ago; it also commemorates a history, perceived and real, of dispossession and injustice. To this day, the memories intersect.

The sectarian cast of Iraq and the recollection of the history of the imams have shaped politics from the street to halls of courtly deliberation. For centuries, the learned debated and the neighborhood rabble fought, but the question unleashed in the seventh century after Mohammed died remained unanswered: Who has the right to rule?

The authority of Mansur, Baghdad's Sunni Muslim founder, was challenged by Shiites when his city was just twelve years old, but their leader was executed. In the years that followed, Mansur himself interrupted the construction of Baghdad, twice, so that he could put down Shiite revolts led by descendants of Imam Ali. Inside his city, across centuries, clashes punctuated Baghdad's history: for one hundred years, the Shiites of al-Karkh and the Sunnis of the quarter around the Basra Gate kept up their feuds even after the provocations were long forgotten.

The Sunni-Shiite battles were by no means the sole spasm of sectarian violence. Many of medieval Baghdad's street gangs had a doctrinal stamp, and the city's Christians and Jews were known for their own bloodletting in the streets. But it was the Sunni-Shiite battles that were most ferocious. In one of the moments of anarchy that became more common in the tenth century, militant Sunni street gangs loyal to a literalist theologian named Ibn Hanbal staged their own inquisition, impaling and burning alive Shiites they captured. Some Sunnis still suggest that it was betrayal of the caliph by a Shiite minister that brought the Mongols into Baghdad in 1258 and ended five hundred years of occasionally glorious Abbasid rule.

Modern Iraq can be read, albeit superficially, through this sectarian perspective. The region entered the last century as a backwater of the Ottoman Empire, whose Sunni Muslim rulers discriminated against its Shiite inhabitants. The British, arriving in World War I, relied on the same Sunni elite and then imported a Sunni monarchy from distant western Arabia to rule. Republican Iraq saw moments of reconciliation between the sects, but those moments were few, and Saddam was, by far, the worst of the community's oppressors. Under his rule, Shiites suffered the brunt of the Iran-Iraq war's devastation, providing the fodder for its carnage. On the whole, however, they remained loyal, despite the fact that tens of thousands were expelled across the border to Iran, their nationality questioned.

After the Gulf War, they finally rose up. On March 3, 1991, an Iraqi tank commander returning from Kuwait fired a shell through one of Saddam's portraits in the main square of Basra. The act ignited the uprising, which in days consumed much of southern Iraq, all the way to the approaches to Baghdad. The rebels were convinced that President George H. W. Bush's call for the Iraqi army and people to overthrow Saddam meant military support for them, but when they appealed to U.S. troops then deployed in the Euphrates valley, their desperate pleas for help were spurned. Unprepared for the rebellion, fearing that the Shiites were pro-Iranian, and uneasy at the prospect of instability, the United States allowed Iraq to send Republican Guard units into southern cities and to fly helicopter gunships. The rebels were mercilessly crushed. Saddam exacted his revenge, leveling historic swaths of Shiite towns, bombarding sacred shrines in Najaf and Karbala, and executing thousands on the spot. Perhaps as many as 100,000 were massacred in reprisal killings.

Saddam would never forgive the Shiites. In the south, with sanctions worsening their plight, they were shortchanged in the distribution of food and medicine. Clerics, from junior activists to senior ayatollahs, were murdered. In a spectacular environmental crime, Saddam directed the draining of the sprawling southern marshes, displacing hundreds of thousands of Shiite Marsh Arabs and destroying one of the world's oldest, most storied cultures. Throughout his reign, he repressed their rituals, the very acts of worship deemed subversive.

To this day, many Shiites, particularly the devout, recall with anger the American lack of support, a memory of betrayal that colored their view of the U.S. occupation. (The son of a senior ayatollah in Najaf once put it to me bluntly: "If the Americans had finished the task in 1991, the Shiites would have received them with flowers. We have a previous experience with foreigners. Is it possible to trust them?")

To a searing degree, the feelings engendered by distant and more recent pasts live today; history and the present are intertwined. For many Shiites, the suffering and repression of previous times provided a framework for understanding what they suffered under Saddam. Saddam was Yazid, the nemesis of Imam Hussein, and centuries-old tragedies had a contemporary retelling of suffering, with a new generation of martyrs. In April 1980, Mohammed Baqir al-Sadr, an inspired, unorthodox scholar, as remarkable as any in Iraq in a century, was executed with his sister. As the story goes, he was forced to watch as men raped her; his executioners then drove nails into his forehead. At dungeons like Abu Ghreib, the numbingly routine torture of Shiites was commemorated after the fall of Saddam with posters bearing the names of Saddam's victims. When Saddam fell, religious Shiites exploded in the euphoria of salvation. Baghdad had not witnessed such scenes in a generation.

AS IF IN THE SOULFUL DRUMBEAT OF A FUNERAL PROCESSION, HUNDREDS OF men swung their arms to heaven and crashed their fists down on their chests. At once mournful and joyful, the cadence echoed off the white marble floors and ornate turquoise tiles of Kadhimiya, a Shiite shrine I had visited in far more subdued times before the war and returned to on occasion after Saddam's fall. Overhead were the sect's banners — green to denote the noble lineage of the prophet's family, black to symbolize grief over the fate of Ali and his progeny, and red to represent the blood of their slain imam, Hussein. The banners swayed in a breeze that carried the piquant scent of incense wafting over the moments of celebration, jubilation, even ecstasy that were bathed in the glimmer of the sun off the shrine's golden dome. Resuming rituals that Saddam had banned, repressed, or simply discouraged since the 1970s, Shiites chanted the names of their medieval saints in unison, an act of worship that now seemed to recall more modern martyrs. "By God, we will not forget you," they intoned.

In a capital racked by looting and lawlessness and marked by the rise of men like Shawki, infused with dangerous confusion born of mythic times and tragic wrongs — this explosion of ritual was a true sign of actual liberation and uninhibited spiritual rebirth. Here was a remembrance of things past and present, of all the losses across time conjoined into one. In chants and banners, the symbolism was unmistakable. Here, as astonished American soldiers watched, was the reclamation of a 1,300-year-old faith.

"The oppression is gone, however long it took!" the crowd chanted, their voices rising as they surged toward the Kadhimiya shrine, its four minarets newly draped in black banners, its courtyard taking on an air of carnival. "The tyrant is gone!"

Just hours after Saddam fell, Shiites young and old, mostly men but a few women, had begun flooding into the neighborhoods around the shrine, where two of the twelve imams are buried, making it the spiritual heart of Baghdad's Shiites and, for centuries, a destination of pilgrims from Iraq, Iran, and beyond. As the days passed, the crowds continued to build. Some waved swords and carried black flags that read "O Hussein." Some men slapped their foreheads, others beat their chests in the mourning ritual known as *lutm*. A few held aloft the Quran. They marched to the sound of trumpets, cymbals, and wood-and-leather drums. Every so often, they invoked another name of Imam Ali, "Haidar," which means lion in Arabic.

"Haidar!" was the chant, followed by six drumbeats. "Haidar!"

A fire truck seized from the government plied the battered streets — horn honking, lights flashing. "This vehicle belongs to the Kadhimiya shrine," a banner hung on the truck declared. Along the street, soaked in sewage and strewn with trash, the neighborhood's Shiite residents looked on with a mix of mourning and awe, the ancient grief over the ceremony's commemoration of saintly martyrdom mixed with jubilation that the ceremony was happening. Some beat their chests to the instruments' rhythm. Others looked on solemnly, at scenes many probably had never imagined.

"I can't express my feelings. All I feel is joy," Sami Abbas, a forty-six-year-old Shiite reveler, told me as I wandered through the crowds of worshippers gathered under the gold-leafed domes of the shrine. "This is the first time I've seen this for thirty years."

A crowd gathered, and voices tumbled over one another in the anarchy of bliss, in streets surging with faith and fervor. Some apologized for shouting at me. "I can't stop. I'm happy! I'm happy!" said Azz el-Din Hassan, his voice still loud. Others spoke of revenge. The Americans must bring Saddam to Iraq for trial, said Mohammed Abdel-Amin, "so that we can punish him." Yet others displayed artifacts that they had believed would always have to remain hidden. In the crowded, narrow streets of a nearby alley, as I followed the procession, Ali Aidan showed off his ceremonial silver sword with its red-and-gold strap adorned with a red tassel. His uncle Aboud Jawhari had made it and Ali had carried it last in 1975. Since then, it had been tucked in a wood box, gathering dust, in the cellar of his house. "I brought out my sword the first day after Saddam's fall," Ali told me, over the din of the crowd. "That was the first day of our freedom."

On that afternoon in Kadhimiya, there was no talk of "the leader," or even of "Saddam." Here, he was simply "the tyrant." His pictures had come down, replaced by the icons of their faith. Portraits of revered ayatollahs graced the shrine. Black, green, white, and red flags, once signs of subversion, fluttered from the shrine's walls. Nine of the shrine's custodians considered too close to the fallen government had fled, replaced by members of prominent families who had kept their distance from the Baathists. Within days of their departure, the government dictates that had hung at the entrance were removed to make way for the edicts of the clergy, issued from their headquarters in the sacred city of Najaf: there was to be no looting of government property; there would be no stealing; and no women were to enter the shrine unveiled or with makeup.

As the procession marched through Kadhimiya's streets, festivals erupted at each intersection, with roving men spraying rosewater to cool the crowds. Unsolicited, residents offered me cups of sweet, scalding tea. People held aloft stylized portraits of Imam Ali and Imam Hussein, pictured as handsome, bearded men with almond eyes, in leonine poses, their skin a honeyed brown. Some waved replicas of Ali's sword, *dhu al-fiqar.* Young boys sold green flags for a few cents, and vendors offered *dahina*, a pastry of flour and sugar sprinkled with coconut. At other spots, merchants sold prayer stones made from the sacred mud of Karbala, where Hussein was buried, along with cassette tapes of sermons by leading clerics. Many pilgrims made their way to the mosque's grand entrance, kissing the door's brass handles or sliding their hands along its wood, a gesture thought to bring blessings. Inside, families sat contentedly on blankets spread across the floor.

Into the evening, the banners fluttered in the gentle wind. One read "Hussein is thirsty," a reference to the days he and his companions spent cut off from water on the Karbala plain. "We will not forget Hussein, the beloved of God" was written across another. On a banner was scrawled a motto, insurgent in its meaning, familiar from the Iranian revolution: "Every day is Ashura, all the land is Karbala." A green flag, exuberantly flapping overhead, read "The time of Hussein."

This time, I thought, it was their Hussein.

On one banner was a name that kept showing up in those days—in Shawki's renamed neighborhood, on portraits that graced the walls of the Kadhimiya shrine, in my conversations with the devout and my interviews with their leaders. It was a name I had heard, knew little about, and could soon not forget.

"The blood of Sadr will not go in vain," the banner read.

Mohammed Mohammed Sadiq al-Sadr, the beloved ayatollah killed with two of his sons near Najaf, was dead. The career of his youngest son was about to begin, a meteoric ascent that would in time write the epitaph for the American occupation.

BY THE STANDARDS OF IRAQ AND ITS SHIITE MAJORITY, MUQTADA SADR WAS a blueblood. His black turban signified his descent from the prophet

Mohammed, and his lineage traced its way through the especially revered sixth Shiite imam, Jaafar al-Sadiq, who was famous as a scholar, teacher, and fountainhead of hermetic sciences in the eighth century. For decades, Sadr's family, from the shrine neighborhood of Kadhimiya, had given Iraq some of its most revered clergy: these were men, it must be understood, whose word, blessed by God, was unquestioned by their legions of followers.

Like a badge of honor, Sadr bore the deep scars of Saddam's government, which ordered the assassinations in 1999 of his father and two brothers and whose henchmen had driven nails into the forehead of his cousin in 1980. When I met him soon after the war in April 2003, the thirty-year-old Sadr, his hands still soft from a life of religious study, had inherited by birth and by choice his family's respected mantle. His words lacked the usual subtlety of religious discourse and his message was clear: he was both a political and a religious leader, whose banner bore the still-resonant Sadr name. The future of Iraq, he insisted, was in the hands of the majority he claimed to represent.

"I accept the burden and the responsibility," the squat Sadr, his youthful beard not yet bushy, told me at his home in Najaf. "We are with God, and God is with us."

It was one of his first interviews since Saddam's fall—or, for that matter, ever. He spoke words that would define his legacy and go far in shaping the record of the U.S. occupation. He uttered them less than a month after Saddam's fall: "I advise the Americans to ally with the Shiites, not to oppose them." By "Shiites," he meant himself.

Looking to the ground, his body draped in a black cape over a white tunic, he dismissed my question of whether he viewed the Americans as occupiers or liberators. "This is not a question to ask me," he said, his delivery still unsure. "It is a question to ask them. I don't know their intentions. Only God does." He then recalled the Shiites' history, from Imam Hussein to Saddam, and the oppression and suffering in between. Added to that, he said, was the national character of Iraq, where rebellion and dissent date back to Imam Ali. "You can read history," he said. His face was melancholy and humorless. "They will reject any government brought by America, any leader, any state. They have rebellion in their hearts. The people will not be silent."

Sitting atop a cheap mattress with a floral sheet draped over it, he looked back at the floor, as he often did during our two-hour conversation, and nodded. "What is a few months of suffering," he asked, "when we have suffered nearly fourteen hundred years?"

Even by the standards of a country as unpredictable as Iraq, Muqtada Sadr's emergence in the days after Saddam's fall was startling—both to the Americans, who underestimated the sway of the Shiite clergy, and to many Iraqis, who underestimated Sadr. Before the war, his name was little known even among the seminary students in Najaf who were entrenched in the clerical rivalries and arcane scholarly disputes. But in the tumult that followed the American invasion, Sadr emerged by virtue of one lasting, resonant legacy: the life and infamous murder of his father, who became known as the martyred *sayyid*. (A *sayyid* is a descendant of the Prophet.) For Sadr's legions of followers, that legacy translated into a legitimacy whose magnitude the United States never fully appreciated.

An elderly and revered ayatollah, with a snowy, untrimmed white beard and a black turban, Mohammed Mohammed Sadiq al-Sadr had been a new kind of religious leader in Iraq. No one doubted his clerical credentials: he was an acknowledged grand ayatollah, the highest Shiite rank; his family was venerated; martyrs filled his family tree. But through an activist ministry that began after his release from Saddam's jails in 1992, he became as much politician as spiritual guide; in this way he contrasted markedly with his far more reserved colleagues in Najaf. (Abul-Qassim Khoie, a reclusive grand ayatollah in Najaf who died in 1992 at the age of ninety-three, was known for answering guests in either one- or two-word phrases: *"Yajuz"* or *"La yajuz,"* "Possible" or "Not possible.") Like Egypt's Gamal Abdel Nasser, who swelled his populist appeal in the 1950s and 1960s by relying on colloquial Arabic, Sadr was informal and relaxed in his speech. He called people *habibi*, a casual term meaning "dear friend." He was at ease in crowds and, while he fostered a virtuous and righteous image, his reputation suggested a fighting saint. Some of his followers recalled a fierce temper, but that was more than offset by the warm and affable way he had with his admiring students and devotees.

In the disfigured politics of Saddam's Iraq, Sadr's ministry had reshaped Shiite activism through a sprawling, grassroots movement that, over a decade, had redrawn notions of politics and religion and, most important, the clergy's place in both. Owing to Iraq's isolation, few beyond Baghdad and its southern

Shiite cities were aware of the movement, perhaps one of the most decisive in the region in a decade. But through the 1990s, Sadr built up an energetic and devoted mass following through his control of clerical schools, a network of social services, and a fiery message of resistance, usually metaphorical, to Saddam's rule. He catered to, then mobilized, the poor and disenchanted in slums like Saddam City.

Sadr was a maverick, too, within the rigid hierarchy of religious Shiite leadership, bound as it is by centuries of scholarship, tradition, revenue, and the influence of neighboring Iran's power and prestige. That he was a proponent of a homegrown Arab and Iraqi leadership within the clergy put him at odds with his more recognized conservative rivals in Najaf, often men of Iranian descent. The struggle would persist long after his death, and would be reinterpreted and revived when his youngest son led the movement after the war. In 1997, the elder Sadr reinstituted the Friday prayers, long deemed a heresy by traditional Shiite jurisprudence, and led millions in performing them, riding a wave of growing piety in Iraq. (Some accounts say those services could draw as many as 250,000 people on any given day.) His message was not doctrinal; it was populist, driven by the authority and legitimacy of his lineage. Likewise, his focus was not the clergy, but the community. As one scholar put it, the sometimes fiery sermons provided "solace, comfort and motivation" at a time when many in the neglected south were suffering relentless repression by the government as well as deprivation imposed by the international sanctions.

In the early years of his leadership, the elder Sadr had been dogged by charges that Saddam's government had actually encouraged his ascent, being keen to see an Iraqi rather than Iranian leadership emerge in Najaf and take hold among the country's Shiites. To the government, Sadr was an Arab, his rivals were Persians. Yet in the long run he proved hostile, dangerously so, to the regime, reviving links between the isolated clergy in Najaf and neglected peasants and the urban poor in places like Baghdad, Nasiriya, and Basra—a unity that Saddam's government had spent years trying to disrupt. As his influence grew, he became less timid and cautious, going so far as to don a white funeral shroud, a gesture his followers saw as expressing his willingness to die.

By the late 1990s, the government found him an intolerable threat and began to respond to his blossoming ministry as it had to his cousin's in 1980.

It began cracking down on his networks of charitable services. It restricted his movement. And, finally, in February 1999, it acted against the ayatollah himself, whose followers had begun to call him *al-laith al-abyadh*, the White Lion. On a road near Najaf, followers recall, Sadr was riding in a green 1982 Mitsubishi with two of his sons, crossing a sparse, desolate landscape, interrupted by lonely eucalyptus trees and crops irrigated with too little water. Mouamil, the eldest, was driving. His father was in the front; another son, Mustafa, was in back. When the car was sprayed with gunfire, Mustafa sprang toward the front, trying in vain to shield his father's body. Mouamil swerved to avoid the hail of bullets—also in vain.

The bullet-riddled corpses of the three, their clerical robes drenched in blood, were taken to what was then called Saddam General Hospital, in Najaf. (Like many streets, neighborhoods, bridges, hospitals, and schools, it was renamed for Sadr following the war.) Muqtada Sadr, the youngest son, thrust by the assassination into the family's leadership, described that day at our meeting. His recollections were slow, unsure, the memories still visibly painful. For hours, he told me, the city of squat buildings, colored brown like much of Iraq, was awash with rumors—that the three might still be alive, that they had somehow survived the ambush. "The first thing I wanted to know was if it was true or not," he told me.

When the young seminary student headed for the hospital, Baath Party officials refused to let him enter. "They prevented me," he recalled, shaking his head in disgust. Confirmation of the deaths soon followed and, despite government orders for residents to stay indoors, wrenching scenes of grief soon exploded into an uprising in Baghdad. The Republican Guard, said to be under the command of Saddam's son Qusay, crushed the unrest, killing dozens and arresting far more.

Virtually all of Sadr's followers would remember where they were that day. One of the mourned leader's lieutenants, who would later marry Sadr's daughter, raced to the hospital and managed to enter, glimpsing Sadr's body, the back of his head torn off by a bullet. Sheikh Abbas Rubaie, another disciple, was so disturbed that he refused to ever wear a cleric's robes again. He told others that he no longer recognized the seminary without Sadr's presence.

Two days after the 1999 assassinations, the government closed down the elder Sadr's office in Najaf, the nexus of his movement; Muqtada Sadr himself, say some accounts, was placed under house arrest or grudgingly left free but routinely harassed. His father's movement quickly went underground, held together by a dynamic clique of young clerics: Sayyid Riyadh al-Nouri, Sheikh Qais al-Khazali, Sayyid Mohammed Tabatabai, Sayyid Mustafa al-Yaacoubi, and Sheikh Jaber al-Khafaji. With them, Sadr's son bided his time—patiently awaiting the moment that, when I met him, had finally arrived.

In our first meeting after the war, Muqtada Sadr was reserved, even uncommunicative. At first, I ascribed this to clerical modesty, perhaps feigned. But as our conversation went on, it struck me how young and awkward Sadr actually was. He seemed overwhelmed. Even as his father's recognized heir, he spoke without confidence. He was given to slang, a habit unusual among clerics, who pride themselves on the eloquence of their formal, even arcane Arabic, which is considered by Muslims to be the language of God and thus is revered. His black turban rode a little high on his forehead, somewhat uncomfortably. He hunched his shoulders over a frame that was squat and pudgy. He possessed no particular aplomb.

This young, even bashful man had been thrust into the limelight solely on the strength of his father's legacy. Through the memory of the martyred *sayyid*, his son commanded the loyalty of the rebellious, largely young clerics who bridled at the reticence and conservatism of the mainstream clergy and who maintained the cohesion of the elder Sadr's movement after its founder died. Through his father, Muqtada was an acknowledged icon, who was expected to lead a community searching for leadership. But how, I wondered, could the young Sadr ever hope to reach his father's eminence? He was a low-ranking cleric, at best a *hujjat al-islam*, a junior grade well below an ayatollah. Because of his age—some of his detractors insisted he was younger than thirty, perhaps just twenty-two—the more established ayatollahs, for whom maturity is a requisite, would never treat him as an equal. His lack of scholarship forced his movement to defer on religious matters to a more senior cleric in Iran, Kadhim Husseini Haeri, a lieutenant of his father whose relations with Muqtada's movement were always precarious.

The young man's lack of political history had even led some of his father's more senior disciples to break away and form movements of their own.

The more established in cities like Baghdad and Basra quickly dismissed him as an upstart, as did some of the more prestigious Shiite families: the Bahr al-Ulums, Shirazis, Askaris, Jawahiris, and Kishf al-Ghitas. The clerical families in Najaf and Karbala—many of Iranian descent, many affluent by virtue of their ties to the lucrative commerce associated with pilgrimage to the sacred cities—deemed him a rabble-rouser at best, a threat to their order at worst.

Of course, these old, respected families were not Sadr's constituency, a fact that would soon be underscored. Faithful to his father's populist vision, his organization had become a kind of street movement, from the Iraqi equivalent of the barrio, imbued with a profound antagonism to traditional Shiite authority and to the power those families represented. While his father commanded respect by age, learning, and name, his son had only the name, albeit powerful in itself. But Sadr himself shared much with the disenfranchised to whom he catered, the lumpen Shiites. Unlike the returning Iraqi exiles who were suddenly vying for power in Baghdad—men like Ibrahim Jaafari, Ahmad Chalabi, Ayad Allawi, Mohammed Baqir al-Hakim, and al-Hakim's brother Abdel Aziz—Sadr had stayed in Iraq during its worst repression. Like the poor Shiites, Sadr had suffered loss: his father, his brothers, and many of his other relatives were martyrs of the community. He spoke like the dispossessed; he even looked like them.

Throughout his career, Sadr employed the vocabulary of the seminary, known as the *Hawza*, a classical Arabic word that means "centers of religious learning" but that came, in an amorphous, imprecise way, to denote the religious leadership in Najaf. He drew on the symbols of the faith, on the authority of the religious hierarchy. But he spoke the language of the street—his street; the street that his father had mobilized. It was the street that would deliver his family the religious authority he deemed its right.

"One hand with the *Hawza*, and one hand with the people," he told me the first time we met at his house. The room's walls were bare except for a clock and a portrait of his father, eyes pacific, shoulders draped in a funeral shawl that matched the white of his beard. As Muqtada spoke, he seemed to be replaying a conversation he had completed countless times with his father's men. "I found a vacuum, and no one filled that vacuum."

Soon after Saddam's fall, politics began to infuse the sermons of Sadr and his men. From the beginning, they were blunt in their criticism of the United States, blaming the new liberators for failing to support the Shiite uprising in 1991 and for allowing the looting and lawlessness unleashed after their arrival. They erupted in anger when the United States made clear in May, after the war, that it would lead an occupation; the Arabic word, *ihtilal*, is shadowed by humiliation, notions of resistance, and still resonant memories of the occupation by the British eighty-five years before. Soon after, suspicions were voiced that the United States would deprive Sadr and his men of power and handpick a government from the once exiled parties of Allawi (the Iraqi National Accord), Chalabi (the Iraqi National Congress), and Hakim (the Supreme Council for the Islamic Revolution in Iraq) that it had supported, for years, along with the two main Kurdish parties in northern Iraq. Early in the occupation, Sadr's lieutenants railed against the importation into Iraq of a corrupt, materialistic culture exemplified, in their eyes, by the West and in particular the United States.

In quieter tones, in jabs directed at their less militant clerical counterparts in Najaf, Muqtada Sadr's supporters suggested that the traditional Shiite leadership had a hand in the murder of his father, endangering him through their reluctance to stand behind him. In louder voices, they accused the same leadership of being too reticent under Saddam, and now too accommodating to the Americans. With no hesitation, they dismissed the exiled parties, bristling at their condescending and overambitious expectations to take the reins of power in Iraq. "The people who deserve to rule are the ones who stayed here," Sadr told me during that first meeting, offering his reading of legitimacy. He quoted his father, who he said had been urged to go abroad to save his life in 1999: "I should stay here and suffer with the people. If I go abroad, I will pave the way for others to go abroad like me."

Yet Sadr's growing movement never became truly ideological, unless intra-Shiite divisions and implacable hostility to the occupation can be called an ideology. They never outlined a real vision of an Islamic government (except to reject the model offered by Iran's Islamic Republic). Their prescriptions for society rarely amounted to more than a hazy notion of religion's primacy in life (and denunciations of Western consumerism and American-inspired globalization). It was street activism—the grassroots style of the elder Sadr—that defined the movement, not ideology.

When I asked him what he represented, Sadr paused, then ticked off the ways his men had filled the governmental vacuum, citing the kind of work that Shawki and others performed in Sadr City, in Najaf, in southern towns like Nasiriya and Basra, where they exploited the postwar chaos to exert their presence. They endeavored to restore water and electricity, he said, with admittedly only mixed success. With the force of arms and the power of persuasion, they sent guards to protect hospitals and government buildings. They returned stolen cars, set up checkpoints to prevent looting, helped deliver kerosene and flour, and, for a time, he said, paid the salaries of municipal workers. They asked police to return to their stations and begin to restore order to the streets. When the needy asked for money, they provided it, from dozens of mosques.

Surrounded by a coterie of young advisers, Sadr remarked, "What I can do, I do."

AFTER MEETING SADR, I HEADED BACK TO BAGHDAD WITH NASIR, WHO WAS NOW working with me as an employee of the *Post*.

In the war's last few days, Nasir had been trapped with his family at his home, which was caught in some of the fiercest fighting along the city's southern outskirts. Through a cascade of gunfire, tank shells, and rocket-propelled grenades—a deafening assault that lasted hours at a time—they huddled in a bedroom at the back of the house, the two children—Yossi and Ahmed—crying in fear. I was far away in the Palestine Hotel. After the American troops had arrived, our relationship had effectively ended. I no longer had to keep up the pretense of working with a minder. The Information Ministry that Nasir worked for no longer existed, its senior staff having fled with money they bilked from reporters, the ministry building charred by bombing and, more destructively, looting. Nasir had no car, no way to leave. And for a moment, I hesitated about rekindling contact. Only for a moment. Looking back, I suspect I missed his company, even after only a few days. Amid all the turmoil of the war, despite the fear and distrust, grief and anger it bred, we had become friends.

Soon after Saddam fell, I had driven with Karim to Nasir's home to make sure his family was safe. Nasir met me at the door, smiling the same subversive grin that I had seen so often during the invasion and exuding the same bluster that was always a cover for a soul at once gentle and deeply vulnerable. "I thought you might come," he said.

I offered him a job, which he accepted, and we began an enduring collaboration—part friendship, part professional. In time, I would learn about Iraq through his eyes. What I was taught by Nasir was not the stuff of high politics or the arc of the country's history. His lessons were more mundane yet quite helpful in terms of being a journalist there. I learned that throwing water behind departing loved ones wards off evil and hastens their return. I was told to hold the tiny cup of bitter Arabic coffee in my right hand and to shake it, ever so slightly, if I didn't want it refilled from the swanlike spout of the kettle. I understood that the person on the right enters a door first when two or more people approach. I was reminded never to yawn without covering my mouth. I was taught respect. Small gestures, but in work that requires at least some degree of trust, they mattered.

A few days later in Baghdad, we headed to what had become the most dramatic sign of the emergence of Sadr's group as the first popular, mass-based movement in postwar Iraq. This was Friday prayers at the Muhsin Mosque in Sadr City, a mosque that had been closed soon after Sadr's father was assassinated. The convocation would come to represent the group's vision of activism and its success as a street movement. Part street theater, part religious revival, the prayers would draw me time and again.

When we got there, in late morning, tens of thousands of worshippers had already arrived, with towels thrown over their heads to protect them from the sweltering sun. They trudged through dusty streets and filled a four-lane thoroughfare for nearly a mile. Over their shoulders were prayer rugs, from intricate Persian designs to cheap weaves to soiled plastic mats of oranges, reds, and blues. Mosque workers milled through the crowd, spraying mists of water over the men's heads to cool them. A few stopped to share a glass of water from a white ceramic bathtub set up on the sidewalk atop a blue metal frame before settling into rows in front of an open-air pulpit. Other stands, no less decrepit, offered *leben*, a yogurt drink, and prune juice, *khoukh*, for a few cents.

Impromptu markets, the inevitable offspring of any crowd coming together in the Third World, catered to the prayergoers. Vendors hawked plastic-sheathed compact discs of sermons by Sadr's father. A few feet away were stands of perhaps a hundred varieties of perfume, in a kaleidoscope of colors. (The Prophet had enjoined followers to wear fragrance by his example.) Across canvas mats spread religious literature—booklets, paperback books, hardcover tomes—much of which had been illegal just weeks before.

On the sidewalks, in a capital once replete with pictures of Saddam, was the iconography of the movement—posters spread on the soiled mats, weighted with rocks against the wind. They were the Shiite version of pop art, each selling for thirty cents or so. As always, there were traditional, resonant images of Shiite spirituality—portraits of Ali, Hussein, and Hussein's half-brother Abbas, who heroically died with him in Karbala, forging an image of Arab chivalry that persists today, particularly among the tribes of southern Iraq. All of the men wore beards, their eyebrows majestically arched and their turbans colored the green of their lineage. Often, under Ali, was his sword, *dhu al-fiqar*. Hussein was usually pictured in scenes from Karbala, before and after battle, his horse magnificent or bloodied across a landscape colored in scarlet. Another poster portrayed all twelve imams, seated in a garden, halos over their heads. In front sat Ali, again with his sword, at the head of the revered household.

Just as abundant were other, more modern images that suggested a contemporary notion of suffering and struggle, Hussein reinterpreted. In one poster, Sadr's father held his palms upward in prayer. Below him was his cousin Mohammed Baqir al-Sadr, his beard streaked in white. He was portrayed writing in a notebook, a picture that seemed to have been taken shortly before his execution with his sister. Underneath the two men were images of other clerics still living—Grand Ayatollah Ali Sistani, an Iranian-born rival of both Sadr and his son, in Najaf; Mohammed Baqir al-Hakim, another rival and former exile, who would be killed in a horrific car bombing in Najaf in August 2003; then, finally, Muqtada Sadr himself, praying before a crowd that stretched behind him. The poster bore a variation of a saying once rendered as "God preserve Iraq and Saddam." This legend, against the backdrop of a red, white, and black Iraqi flag, read, "God preserve Iraq and its people."

On that day and at Friday prayers in the weeks ahead, some of the most powerful images were those of Sadr and his father. His lieutenants, well aware of the father's legacy, relentlessly and powerfully drew the connection in the posters, sealing the son's legitimacy. The two men were almost always pictured together—the son's glare determined, as if preparing for a fight; his father's eyes wide, as if he awaited his death. In one, Sadr, his face grieving, cradles his dying father, whose wounds are portrayed in wrenching, graphic detail. Against a background painted in the black of mourning and the red of martyrdom, blood flows down the father's white beard from a wound in his forehead. His chest is soaked in red, as are his hands, which grasp a Quran. His eyes remain open, refusing to concede death. In another, Sadr's father is pictured with a dagger in his back, an allusion to the assassination of Imam Ali. Over his head is written, "Peace be upon those who wear the funeral shrouds."

Even in those days the first signs of a personality cult around Muqtada Sadr had begun emerging. Timid at first, it would gain strength as the year progressed, eventually taking on messianic overtones. The posters usually depicted Sadr with others. But occasionally he would be shown alone. In one such poster, Sadr's picture was superimposed on a scene of a sprawling demonstration, awash in the red, green, and black flags of Shiite spirituality. The legend read, "No Shiites, no Sunnis . . . Unity, Islamic unity." Sadr was its proponent, at the head of a national crusade.

Nationalism—or, at least, a notion of a distinctly Iraqi Shiite Islam that would defend the country from its foreign enemies—was important to the movement. Sadr's father had been an advocate of such a force during his seven-year ministry, known for playing down sectarian differences between Iraq's Sunnis and Shiites, as part of a distinctly Iraqi notion of politics. He had self-consciously distinguished himself from other ranking clerics of Iranian descent as a proudly Arab scholar. Muqtada Sadr stayed loyal to that ideal.

Along with the posters of Sadr, the Iraqi flag became another symbol of the nascent movement. Other religious groups had a certain disdain for it, deeming it a symbol of Saddam's rule. Not Sadr's men. The organization always gave prominent display to the flag, emblazoned with the slogan "God is greatest." To them, it was a symbol of a united Iraq. In any portrait of Sadr, the flag was usually represented in some form—by its colors, its slogan, or the flag itself flying over a crowd. His followers flew it at their offices, carried it at their demonstrations, and featured it in their posters.

At the Muhsin Mosque, as the morning drew toward noon, the sun relentless, worshippers held the array of posters over their heads—from Sadr to Imam Ali, the prophet Mohammed's cousin and son-in-law, it was an unbroken chain. Soon, a quiet began to fall, the men's boisterous talk turning to an audience's murmur. As it settled, Sheikh Kadhim al-Abadi, the prayer leader, strode confidently to the pulpit, cloaked in a white funeral shroud. Before him sat a few dozen clerics, all from the Baghdad neighborhood that was firmly in Sadr's grasp and that would emerge as his stronghold. They were draped in the black, white, gray, and brown robes of their profession. Descendants of the Prophet wore black turbans; others wore white. Among them was Ali Shawki, this time without his guns.

"It is time for Islam to emerge and spread its wings!" declared Sheikh Kadhim, a slight man with a wispy brown beard, his tinny voice carried by loudspeakers.

As usual, his words were political, not ideological; the sentiments were everyday, not pedantic. In sermons sometimes arcane, his delivery was clear and simple. His ambition was modest: he sought to be understood.

"They declared that they are occupiers of this country, Iraq, and they are not liberators," he said to the crowd, listening raptly, as a rare breeze blew across. "We will not allow this. We want them to leave soon. This country has many men who can rule and administer it. This country will preserve its faith and traditions." He railed against the threats he believed the Americans posed to those mores and ridiculed "their glittering slogans that are without substance."

"The enemy has tried to introduce corrupt foreign ideas," he said. In quick succession, he listed them: pornography, Western books and films, cosmetics, compact discs, even foreign words. "This is not good," he said, wagging his finger, prompting a murmur to ripple through the crowd. "These are not our customs and traditions."

He called for street-level activism. (With varying degrees of success, Sadr's men would issue similar appeals for mobilization in the months that followed.) He directed followers to form vigilante committees that would enforce morality in streets where the only other authority was an occasional detachment of Humvees on patrol. Liquor stores were warned to stop selling alcohol, even to non-Muslims. "We will not warn them again," he said darkly, a hint of the intimidation and thuggery that would become a hallmark of the movement, as arms poured in and a soon-to-be-announced militia swelled its ranks. Muslim women, the sheikh instructed, should immediately begin wearing the veil.

Most of the crowd were young men, their bodies sweating, their clothes cheap, sometimes tattered. As the sheikh finished, they broke out in chants. "Yes, yes to the *Hawza!*" they shouted. More bluntly, others yelled, "Hear us, Muqtada, and know that we are all swords in your hand." A few simply declared, in a line repeated over and over, "Long live Sadr!"

Ibn al-balad means "son of the country" or, less literally, "salt of the earth." In the chants that rolled over the prayers, in the movement's iconography, in the posters that were copied for cheap and sold for a little more, Muqtada Sadr was an *ibn al-balad.* So were the men he mobilized.

NEITHER MOST IRAQIS NOR THE AMERICANS KNEW WHAT TO MAKE OF SADR'S movement. (Hume Horan, then an official with the U.S. occupation whose flawless Arabic and intuitive knowledge of the region made him one of the leading American diplomats in the Arab world, characterized Sadr to me as "a young upstart and rabble-rouser" and, in a not unfamiliar underestimation that would haunt the U.S. occupation, dismissed him as a fringe player and a "distraction.") At the time, neither Iraqis nor the Americans were even sure what to make of the larger phenomenon, the explosion in Shiite ritual that Saddam's fall had unleashed. The scenes of faith and fervor unsettled some of the more secular in Baghdad, especially Sunnis, who perhaps saw a harbinger of the fall from power that Saddam's demise ensured.

Many Sunnis feared a loss of the prestige they had enjoyed since the Ottoman Empire. Iraq's small Christian minority worried that its relative freedom under the Baath Party would be destroyed in a wave of religious intolerance reminiscent of the Iranian revolution. Kurds, most of them Sunni Muslims, remained focused on their homeland in the north, but cast a wary eye at the south's growing religiosity, which had little interest for them. For their part, Shiite leaders were aware of the anxiety, taking pains to reassure other groups that, even as the majority, they would respect minorities. A mantra was that no real differences divided Muslims, that Sunnis and Shiites were of the same faith, the same country.

Wamidh Nadhme and I had lost touch near the end of the invasion; it was too dangerous to drive across town. But I visited his house soon after the fall of Saddam, and found him angry and hurt, his pride wounded. He spoke with bitterness. Wamidh remained a nationalist—defiant as an Iraqi, proud as an

Arab—and foreign troops were barreling down the streets of his capital in their columns of armor.

"I prefer to be shot rather than cooperate with the invaders," he told me irefully.

He looked out his window as a haze of pollution and shimmering heat settled over the river, then reflected on what had happened. He was carrying a pistol these days. It was not bravado; he felt he had to defend himself.

"The Americans are behaving in a mad way. What sort of people are they? Who can take them seriously? They're just mad," he told me. As always, he served me tea and offered a cigarette. His anger notwithstanding, he would always remain hospitable, and he probably suspected that my Arab heritage helped me, at least to some degree, to understand his sentiments. "They promised they would bring democracy and liberation to Iraq. Where is the democracy and liberation? We have seen looting, we have seen the burning of hospitals, we have seen the robbery of the central bank. The Americans, up until now, have failed to win the support of educated, respected, credible people."

How long did they have? I asked him. Two to three months, he told me. Judging by what I had seen in Baghdad so far, I wondered silently whether they had even that long. I wondered if the window hadn't already closed.

Wamidh's anger was not directed only at the occupation. He was also furious at Saddam—not necessarily for his defeat, but for the shameful way he thought it unfolded. The army—treated poorly by Saddam, filled with conscripts—fought more valiantly than the supposedly crack troops of the Republican Guard. How could the capital fall so quickly, surrendering overnight? How could a government just evaporate? "There is something dubious, something unclear, something unexplainable about what happened that night," he told me, rolling his hands. "I can't understand how the Baathists ran away and fled. This is beyond any standard of manhood."

We spoke about the rumors current in Baghdad. In an atmosphere rife with suspicion, some people suggested that Saddam had been betrayed by his defense minister, Sultan Hashim Ahmed. Wamidh had heard others whisper about a gun battle that supposedly erupted in a meeting of Saddam's lieutenants the night before Baghdad fell. Like Amal Salman, he had heard speculation that Saddam, seeking revenge, might use chemical weapons against his former capital. "He's angry at the Iraqis themselves and he wouldn't mind to hurt the

Americans as well. I don't think this is a reasonable possibility, but this is what people are saying, that he might do something horrible to Baghdad."

What seemed to trouble Wamidh least was the Shiite awakening that had roiled Baghdad. His appraisal: the outpouring was an understandable response to the years of Saddam's rule. "Look," he told me, "these people were deprived from the ceremonies for so many years. This is not a provocation. This is an outburst after years of repression. These people were deprived of their rights. Allow them."

It was this perspective that made me hold Wamidh, a Sunni Muslim, in such high regard. He bristled at the occupation. Given his background and views as an Iraqi and Arab nationalist, why wouldn't he? But when it came to his country, he was, at heart, a patriot, and he sought its unity above all else, even at the sake of tactical compromises. Shiite and Sunni, Arab and Kurd— to Wamidh, they were all Iraqis, and they would have to surrender some principle to collaborate together. It was a tolerance that set him apart from many of his countrymen. "My impression is that with very few exceptions, caused by the pressures of the regime, the Shiites are genuine Iraqis and Arabs," he said. "I believe they are Iraqis above everything else." He went on, "For me, I don't know why Iraq should not be governed by a Shiite. I would vote for a Shiite candidate; I wouldn't have any hesitation."

And Sadr? I asked. Wamidh shook his head. He knew of Sadr's father and respected him. But Wamidh was still trying to make sense of the movement. He was certain of one thing, though—that Shiite activists like Sadr who stayed in Iraq under Saddam believed it was their right—not the right of returning exiles—to govern the country. He did not necessarily share their politics, nor did he subscribe to their vision, but he respected their claim of legitimacy.

IN THE ASHES OF SADDAM'S RULE, SADR'S MOVEMENT PURSUED THAT RIGHT. Like Iraq itself, his organization was defined by God, guns, and money. In time, guns would emerge as the most important of the three. In the early days after the government's fall, God and money gave birth to the movement's street credibility and assured its ascendance as a powerful force in the still amorphous politics of the Shiite revival. His men were from the community, and to the community they returned. Their style was the everyday, almost overlooked work of Ali Shawki, writ large. They spoke the vernacular of the neighborhood; they grasped, almost intuitively, its concerns; and they offered answers to countless questions, in face-to-face conversations in the cramped rooms of street-corner mosques. Through their work, Sadr and his men laid claim—vigorously contested—to leadership of the emerging community.

As a motto and an approach, they quoted a popular Quranic verse, as the clergy are want to do: "Those sitting are not equal to those struggling, even though each has been promised well by God." Their style was activism, hardened by years underground under Saddam. Their headquarters was the Hikma Mosque, a modest place in the heart of Sadr City's sprawl, bordered by a watermelon stand and a shack selling ice on sweltering days.

In those weeks after the fall of Saddam, men and women seeking help lined up every morning outside its walls, plastered with portraits of martyrs and slain ayatollahs. On one side, a graffito read, "We are the supporters of Islam, not America, not Saddam." Inside the mosque, ceiling fans whirring and walls adorned with banners of saints stitched in vibrant reds, purples, and blues, sat Sadr's lieutenants, speaking in hushed tones as if in a monastery. Almost without exception, the men counted themselves as disciples of the elder Sadr. In their twenties and thirties, they were energetic, mid-ranking clerics with several years of study behind them. Almost without exception, their wizened faces and gaunt builds made them look at least a decade older. Torture and jail time, they routinely explained.

Sheikh Abdel-Rahman Shuweili, the head of the group's outreach committee, was one of them. A short, wiry man with a steely gaze, he had been jailed for two months in the wave of persecution that followed the assassination of Sadr's father. He was released, arrested again, then sentenced to fifteen years in jail. He won his freedom three and a half years later, in the amnesty at Abu Ghreib in October 2002. On the morning I visited, his day had begun at eight A.M., when he took his place on a cheap Persian carpet along the mosque's wall, stroking his bird's nest of a beard that was uniformly gray despite his mere thirty-five years. This was the signal that he was ready for business, his enactment of the populist legacy of Sadr's father.

A middle-aged Iraqi man in a black blazer approached. He wanted to know whether he could take part in the new local councils the U.S. administration was setting up across Baghdad. His question amounted to an everyday, almost incidental reflection on living an upright life in an uncertain world. It revealed where real authority lay. "Is this permitted under Islamic law or not?" he asked, holding a piece of paper.

Shuweili studied the document, his furrowed brow knitted even more. It was drawn up by the Coalition Provisional Authority, that is, the U.S. occupation. All employees of the CPA had to sign it, but its contents—in particular, a clause that stated they would obey "all decrees, orders and instructions" of the authority—had angered the more religiously minded. Their protests pointed to that constant question, the one that bedeviled the occupation and eventually undid it.

"If you just obey their orders, then you're doing no more than following their wishes," Shuweili said, sitting barefoot against the mosque's marble walls in his blue robes. "Their orders should take into account Islam. Would you sell liquor in the streets? Every country has its own traditions—Syria, Iran, America, and Africa. They should respect Islam and our traditions."

Shuweili told him to cross out the nettlesome clause. He pointed his finger. "Write, 'I will work with the authority to serve the Iraqi people,'" he instructed.

At that moment, an American jet flew overhead, its engines loud. Shuweili paused and shook his head, and a colleague mentioned that it was the third day in a row one had passed over the neighborhood. "They're trying to provoke us," Shuweili said, his words spoken in the formal Arabic that the clergy often employed.

After each man left, another surged forward, seeking Shuweili's attention. The questions ranged from the mundane to the abstract—requests for equipment at a brick factory, help in tracking down a stolen trailer, assistance to reinstate a dismissed teacher, permission to open a medical clinic, queries about religious taxes. Money flowed freely—from a few hundred dinars to ten thousand, depending on the request. Often Shuweili answered, "*Ala rasi*," "At your service." Other times, he said simply, "God willing." Unlike U.S. administrators, already blamed by many Iraqis for promising too much, Shuweili was careful. He never promised more than he could deliver. Polite, logical, and formal, carrying the authority that his turban and robes brought, he was never ruffled.

The conversations with Shuweili lasted three hours, until noon prayers (the clock was dwarfed in importance by the call to prayer in ordering the day). Through the morning, clerics in pressed tunics, black-and-white turbans, and flowing robes gingerly approached the gaggle crowded on the floor around Shuweili. They murmured into his ear, brought tattered and creased papers for him to sign with his silver ballpoint pen trimmed in gold, and even whispered a joke. Others refereed rambunctious discussions, as many as three of which were happening at any one time, under portraits of Sadr's father and banners bursting with reds, yellows, golds, greens, and blues and inscribed with the names of God, his prophet Mohammed, the Prophet's son-in-law Ali, and the other Shiite imams. Supplicants waited patiently outside, near a blue-tiled fountain used for ritual washing before prayers.

By summer, Sadr's movement would build an office along the main thoroughfare of Sadr City, a boulevard with a stately design whose reality mocked its pretention. Through the summer, though, the tan brick Hikma Mosque served as the nexus of the movement, and it bore the stamp—a rigid hierarchy, a honed organization, enforced discipline—that would mark the movement for the months that followed, in its various incarnations.

The men organized themselves into twelve committees, each with a staff of ten to fifteen, many of whom had been cadres for more than a decade. Shuweili's outreach committee was one of the most active. Others dealt with Friday prayers (like those that spilled out before Muhsin Mosque each week), health services, media, religious edicts, Islamic law courts, and, somewhat ambitiously, electricity and telecommunications. Among the best-known—and most feared—was the vice and virtue committee, charged with encouraging the veil for women (sometimes forcefully), closing liquor stores (many of them owned by Christians), warning the capital's nine theaters not to show risqué movies, and promoting what it saw as Islamic behavior, usually at night after evening prayers and often with the barrel of a gun. As the vice and virtue committee's director, Sheikh Hadi Darraji, who in time would become a prominent leader of Sadr's movement, told me, "In some places, the light of the *Hawza* has not yet reached."

The Hikma Mosque would report to the headquarters in Najaf, where Sadr and the senior religious Shiite leaders had their offices. Often, communication was by satellite phones until suspicions grew that the Americans were monitoring calls. That encouraged Shuweili and others to make the ninety-mile trek to Najaf in person twice every three weeks. Orders came from Sadr's office once or twice a week, a piece of photocopied paper usually taped on Hikma's walls with a floral stamp that read, "In the name of God, the merciful and the compassionate."

The movement's money, ostensibly at least, came from an all-important religious tax known as the *khoms*, which helped to fund the charity that Shuweili doled out to supplicants. (Sadr was long rumored to receive money, as well, from Iran and militant Iraqi Sunnis who shared his anti-Americanism; the scope of his activities, in Sadr City and elsewhere, certainly suggested additional revenue.) Dating to the days of the prophet Mohammed, the *khoms* is a religious tithe that Shiites pay to the ayatollah they choose as their *marja al-taqlid*, or source of emulation, a venerated cleric endowed with the ability to arrive at original and unprecedented decisions on theology and law. Once an ayatollah is chosen as a spiritual guide, his decisions carry the force of law among his most devout followers. For centuries, the tax has represented power in Shiite politics. In essence, whoever has the largest following as *marja al-taqlid* has access to the most cash and to the influence that comes with distributing it.

For years, that leader was Grand Ayatollah Ali Sistani, an Iranian-born rival of the elder Sadr who was recognized by most as the preeminent Shiite religious authority in Iraq and elsewhere. But Muqtada Sadr's office still received its share, a legacy of his father's influence. Sheik Adnan Shahmani, a spokesman in the Najaf office, estimated that the group collected $65,000 a month. Of that, he said $10,000 to $13,000 a month went to the poor and another $13,000 a month to support religious students. The rest went to the office's activities in Najaf, Karbala, Nasiriya, and Baghdad, where Shuweili and the men in the Hikma Mosque worked.

As I watched the activism—the almost mundane gestures of a movement generating support—I realized that I was witnessing a rare phenomenon. In much of the Arab and Muslim world, Islamic movements like Egypt's Muslim Brotherhood, Lebanon's Hezbollah, and Palestine's Hamas had distinguished themselves with their social work, creating a reservoir of goodwill and building the foundation for their success in recruitment, in gaining popular support, and in winning elections. In Turkey, activists went door to door in the shantytowns known as *gecekondu*, providing logistical and financial help for weddings, funerals, and even the Muslim pilgrimage to Mecca. In the refugee camps of Gaza, where the fetid streets are a shoulder-span wide, Hamas ran kindergartens, orphanages, sports clubs, and libraries. The arcs of that activism played out over years and decades. In Iraq, I was watching it evolve over days and weeks.

IN POST-SADDAM IRAQ, THERE WAS ONE MAN WHO STOOD IN THE WAY OF SADR and his movement. He was Grand Ayatollah Ali Sistani, a tall, ascetic cleric who had been in virtual isolation for years and whose emergence in the invasion's aftermath was as much a consequence of time and place as of his own character. Sistani was a study in contrasts to the far younger, coarser, more radical Sadr: they were diametrically opposed personalities a generation apart, with dissonant readings of history, conflicting notions of the clergy and its role in society, and competing conceptions of the *Hawza*, the very institution both, with varying sincerity, claimed to represent.

If Sadr was a son of the street, Sistani was a son of the seminary. After Saddam fell in April 2003, he ranked first among equals of four venerated ayatollahs in Najaf who believed their age, scholarship, following, and standing meant that they—not a young, rebellious junior cleric—should guide Iraq's Shiites. Even Sadr's followers could not contest the respect and authority Sistani enjoyed.

In both his origin and his advancement through the hierarchy, Sistani embodied the traditional clergy that Sadr's father had contested. Born in 1930 in Mashhad, a city in northwest Iran that is home to the country's most sacred Shiite shrine, Sistani came from a prominent clerical family. According to his official biography, he began learning the Quran at age five, then entered studies of Islamic law and philosophy at age ten in Mashhad. At nineteen, he was on his way to Qom, a seat of scholarship in western Iran. Less than three years later, as a twenty-one-year-old, he traveled across the border to Najaf, where he would live—except for one yearlong interruption—for the next five decades.

By all accounts, Sistani proved a brilliant student, methodically advancing through the clerical hierarchy. He studied under the leading ayatollah in Qom, then became a disciple of one of the most powerful ayatollahs of his age,

Abul-Qassim Khoie, in Najaf. Khoie granted Sistani—then just thirty-one years old—the right to judge religious questions; it was one of only two such certificates he awarded. By the 1980s, in subtle but symbolic ways, he had begun grooming Sistani as his successor. In 1992, when Khoie died, Sistani was asked to lead the funeral prayers, a gesture strongly suggestive of Khoie's intentions. Within a year, with the death of two rivals, Sistani had emerged supreme among the traditional clergy in Najaf. Sadr's father, deemed more of a renegade, would oppose his elevation. But Sistani inherited Khoie's endowment and, among the powerful families in Najaf, many of Iranian origin, he was the acknowledged leader, and the best financed. After the government assassinated Sadr in 1999, his position was left largely undisputed.

An austere man with thick black eyebrows and a long gray clerical beard, Sistani spoke in a formal ceremonial Arabic accented by his native Persian. He was known for his reserve, which ensured his survival under Saddam. He did business in an office known as the *barrani*, a well-guarded, unmarked two-story brick building up a winding alley near the Imam Ali shrine, past a gaggle of barbers, bookstores, and small hotels. Overhead stretched a web of tangled wire, and oversized balconies blocked the sun. Inside, the decor was simple. In one room hung a picture of Mashhad; under it stood the furniture: two wooden tables and a few mattresses.

His followers portrayed Sistani as a deeply ascetic man, who wore inexpensive clothes, paid rent, decorated his sitting room with cheap carpets and a lone bookshelf, and had not bought a refrigerator until the mid-1990s. His colleagues said he would cut short guests who engaged in the effusive praise of formal Arabic. Others said he hesitated when followers, adhering to custom, sought to kiss his hand. Yet in private, he was known as a forceful personality, with a sharp intellect molded by the seminary's emphasis on logic. Sistani seldom smiled, they said, nor did he get angry.

In the years under Saddam, his followers say, he endured harassment. With other senior clergy, he was imprisoned in Baghdad for a short time after the 1991 Shiite uprising. His official biography says he was repeatedly threatened with exile. He twice faced assassination attempts—the more serious in 1997, when two men in turbans entered his *barrani* before the evening prayers. Carrying bags said to contain money, they requested a meeting with Sistani. Sistani never showed, and the men eventually pulled out pistols, killing a worker who served tea and wounding another assistant before escaping. But through the 1990s, in a style that became a hallmark of his personality, Sistani remained an inconspicuous, rather private figure in Najaf. The few who recognized him occasionally saw him walk down Prophet's Street on his way to pray at the shrine of Imam Ali. That was exceptional, though. After the attempt on his life in 1997, he rarely if ever left his *barrani,* staying with his family—his wife, who was Iranian, and their two sons, Mohammed Rida, who became his confidant, and Mohammed Jawad, who entered a quiet life of religious study.

In Shiite theology there is a concept called *taqiyya,* dissimulation, the principle of hiding one's beliefs to avoid persecution or harm. Many of Sistani's followers attribute his almost unbroken reticence in the years under Saddam as a version of *taqiyya.* An Iraqi official once recalled to me a visit his sister paid Sistani in 1995. Her son had died, and she had brought several thousand dollars to give the elderly ayatollah for charity as a way to bring blessings. At a time when Saddam was seeking to cut the clergy's finances, Sistani refused to take any of the money, arduously avoiding any provocation of the government. "He was playing it very, very careful," the official told me. "What happened to Mohammed Sadiq al-Sadr didn't happen to him because he was sitting at home. He didn't challenge the regime at all."

Sadr and his lieutenants remembered that. While Sistani remained reclusive in the 1990s, Sadr's father built his movement. As one of Sadr's men, Riyadh al-Nouri, told me, "Mohammed Sadiq al-Sadr gave his blood for his faith. He followed the example of Imam Hussein." That Sistani survived those turbulent years, Sadr's men believed, was a stain on his record. It was the genesis, too, of the struggle between him and Sadr's son, a conflict that would emerge as one of the axes on which Shiite politics revolved.

Sadr and Sistani never disagreed, in a fundamental way, on the kind of religious questions that dominate the life of clerics. They both brought a conservative interpretation to Islam, and Sistani was no less strict: he sanctioned birth control, but forbade the playing of chess and backgammon; he said men and women should not mix socially, rejected music for entertainment, and insisted that women veil their hair.

In rhetoric at least, their politics were similar, as well. Both feared the importation of Western consumerism, which they deemed decadent. (In a

written interview with me, Sistani once described secularism as Iraq's greatest threat. "There is a grave danger in obliterating [Iraq's] cultural identity,
whose most important foundation is the honorable Islamic religion," he said.
This response, like all his communications, was written by hand by his son
Mohammed Rida.) Neither Sadr nor Sistani advocated Islamic rule along the
lines of Iran's Islamic Republic, the archetype for Shiite Islamic activism
since the 1979 revolution, although what they endorsed was, perhaps pur-
posely, left open to vigorous interpretation. And both had a deep suspicion
of the U.S. occupation, a position that, as the months dragged on, became
almost indistinguishable, even as Sistani charted a far more conservative,
even reactive path. In the end, the crucial difference was that to enforce his
views, Sadr would resort to arms in a bloody war that cost thousands of lives.

The greatest distinction between the men lay in their conception of the
clergy itself. At heart, the question was: How assertive a role should clerics
play in society? Sadr and his men were maximalist in their answer. Steeped in
the language of the traditional clergy even as they directed a campaign
against it, they led what they described as the "vocal *Hawza*," a term propagated by Sadr's father. The vocal *Hawza* was interventionist and activist,
catering to the street. Anyone who disagreed with Sadr was on the other
side—in the "traditional *Hawza*" or, more dismissively, "the silent *Hawza*," a
group that came to include men like Sistani who, in the words of one cleric
I met, "will not say anything until asked." I often heard, from the men in the
Hikma Mosque, the remark, "It is not possible for the *Hawza* to be silent
before the people."

"Some people prefer to sleep and some people prefer to be active. We
thank God that there are many active people," Nouri told me. "The dictatorship of Saddam, the oppression of Saddam, and the violence of Saddam were
made more severe because people kept silent."

I met Nouri soon after Saddam's fall. A strapping thirty-three-year-old cleric,
Sadr's relative by marriage, he wore a black turban, like his brother-in-law,
and hints of gray specked his black beard. His life was a counterexample to the
paths of advancement often trekked by the sons of senior ayatollahs, themselves
sons of revered clerics. A handsome, engaging man, Nouri was one of seven
children and grew up in the hardscrabble streets of what was then Saddam
City. His father was a low-ranking policeman, and their house had only two

rooms. In 1995, Nouri left Baghdad for Najaf, beckoned, he said, "by the taste of faith." There, he met Sadr's father and, from that first meeting, fell into his orbit, eventually emerging as a decisive figure in his movement.

We talked for hours, sitting on mats tossed over a concrete floor. His two sons were on either side of him—five-year-old Jaafar to the left, three-year-old Mohammed Ali to the right. Behind Nouri's turbaned head was a portrait of Sadr's father, dressed in a funeral shawl. His loyalty to the elder Sadr was matched only by his resentment of Sistani.

Nouri and Sadr's other lieutenants—only in private, out of avowed respect for his position—ridiculed Sistani's Persian-accented Arabic. They dismissed what they called his traditional, apolitical approach: it was weak, at best; it risked the interests of Iraq's Shiite majority at worst. ("From Saddam until now, he has not intervened in anything," Sadr said of Sistani in our first meeting in Najaf.) They suspected that he favored Iranian students over their Iraqi counterparts and questioned where he spent the vast revenues he received from the *khoms*. "Not even a dinar" goes to the people, Nouri insisted. Most important, they thought the fate of Iraq, an Arab country, should not be in the hands of an Iranian.

Sistani and his allies were no less dismissive of Sadr. Their offices were only a couple of minutes apart, but for a year, Sistani declined to meet him. At times, Sistani's representatives stopped short of even acknowledging Sadr's existence: to do so would undermine a world where only decades of rigorous Aristotelian scholarship brought clout. Recognition of Sadr's movement would, in effect, reformulate the very idea of what constitutes power within religious Shiite politics. Meeting him would signal that Sadr could break the rules and still earn respect.

"Who is he?" Hakim said in an interview when I asked him about Muqtada Sadr. "I don't have any comment on this question." The response of Mohammed Rida, Sistani's son, was similar. "I don't have any comment on that person," he told me.

At times, the rivalry between Sadr and Sistani turned violent, a familiar motif in Iraqi politics. On April 10, a day after Baghdad fell, an angry mob at the shrine of Imam Ali in Najaf attacked Abdel-Majid Khoie, a moderate cleric who was the son of Sistani's mentor. With U.S. funds, Khoie had left exile in London and returned to Najaf on April 3, in hopes of asserting himself within clerical circles.

Given his lineage, Khoie was already influential, and the U.S. government envisioned him as a candidate who might moderate Najaf's turbulent politics. Sadr, no doubt, saw him as a competitor. When Khoie visited the shrine of Ali, accompanied by a cleric who had served as the shrine's caretaker and was deemed a collaborator with Saddam, a mob attacked them. They were beaten, stabbed, and dragged to the mosque's gate. Khoie managed to break away from the group and ran to Sadr's nearby office, banging on the door in hopes of refuge. According to a subsequent U.S. investigation, Sadr refused to open it. Khoie passed out after passersby helped him into a shop across the street from the mosque. The mob then entered, purportedly at Sadr's command, dragged Khoie by his feet down a concrete staircase, and shot him to death with a single AK-47 round to the head. The Americans and allied Iraqi officials would later charge Sadr and his men with the murder. They denied any involvement, but the U.S.-ordered investigation concluded that Sadr had ordered the death.

Sadr's followers were accused, too, of trying to intimidate Sistani into leaving the country in the chaotic first days of the war's aftermath; for a time, a crowd of men said to be Sadr's followers surrounded his *barrani*. Sadr himself again denied any role, but the logic was clear: as long as Sistani remained, Sadr was overshadowed. Whatever his appeal, Sadr could not contest Sistani's clout within the clergy, within the *Hawza*.

Perhaps, though, he wouldn't have to. Perhaps his path to power lay elsewhere.

I saw Sadr again later, at the Kufa Mosque, where his father once preached. Crowds waving paintings of both Sadrs surged along a sun-scorched pavement toward the mosque's mud-brick wall and blue tiles. One poster read: "The blood of the martyrs of Sadr's family." The sidewalks, buckling and dirty, were awash in portraits of Muqtada, selling for fifteen cents. As usual, vendors crowded the parking lot, selling prayer stones, baked mud prayer beads, white funeral shrouds stamped in gold with a Quranic verse, and other tokens of devotion. Within the mosque's wood doors was a vast courtyard of sand and concrete, ringed by tiles of looping flowers colored in blues, greens, purples, and turquoise and arched windows whose edges were inscribed with names of the Shiite imams. A gold-domed clock towered overhead, its hands stuck at three P.M. Murmurs in the crowd gained strength: "Where's the *sayyid*?" "Has he come yet?"

And there he was, walking out under a cavernous wood-roofed portico, flanked by his men, all of whom were young. In the customary funeral shroud, he stood before the pulpit, his tentative gaze cast out at row after row of sun-drenched worshippers, thousands of them, perhaps the largest gathering of people since Saddam's government had fallen. His sermon was awkward, his voice a monotone. Shadowed by his nervous bodyguards, their heads on a swivel, he rarely looked up from his notes and occasionally stumbled over his words. In contrast to some preachers, men like Ayatollah Ruhollah Khomeini who could electrify audiences with their imagery, Sadr appeared a novice. At one point, he lifted his hand to wipe his forehead, and the text of his speech fluttered in the breeze. But as the sermon dragged on for over a half hour, it became clear that the worshippers were more interested in Sadr than in his words. The sermon was an excuse to see him. They referred to him by his first name, a sign of familiarity that suggested a relationship more political than religious, less dependent on the seminary of Sistani's than the street. As Muqtada's followers pointed out, whatever he did, he remained his father's son; whatever he said, he was still one of them.

"We consider him what remains of the *sayyid*," one of them told me.

Another worshipper, twenty-seven-year-old Hassan Faleh, standing in the courtyard, turned to me. He wore a beard, a sign of religious devotion that was becoming more common in Baghdad and other cities.

"Muqtada has the light of God," he said. "Our leader will always be Muqtada."

I asked him why. His answer was simple: "He deserves it."

PART FOUR

THE OCCUPATION

10

A VERY, VERY, VERY, VERY BAD NEIGHBORHOOD

On May 22, 2003, the American occupation of Iraq officially began. Of course, for all intents and purposes, it had begun six weeks earlier. Yet it wasn't until May 22 that a U.N. declaration, passed in a 14–0 vote with only Syria abstaining, granted the United States and its wartime ally, Britain, sweeping formal authority as occupying powers in Iraq. It was a long-expected conclusion to the invasion, ending thirteen years of sanctions and setting the stage for the resumption of Iraqi oil exports to finance the country's hoped-for reconstruction. It cleared the muddy waters of authority—the United States, not a provisional Iraqi government, would be in charge; it would hold a formal writ as an occupying power. "The council has taken decisive action to help the Iraqi people," said John D. Negroponte, the U.S. ambassador to the United Nations, who would serve as the first U.S. ambassador to post-Saddam Iraq the following year.

The resolution—its terminology, its implications, and its very symbolism—was perhaps one of the most decisive gestures of the American experience in Iraq. It almost single-handedly changed the cast of the aftermath, beginning the *ihtilal*, or occupation, a term that leaves no room for negotiation, less for compromise.

The American experience had obviously started poorly in Iraq, chaos and confusion persisting well into the summer. The looting had diminished but it was like a knife dragged across the city, digging wounds that would never heal. While the Americans were not fully responsible, Iraqis perceived them as allowing the plunder and pondered whether the condition of their country was the result of malicious inattention or inattentive malice. Either way, many Baghdadis had soured on their new overlords. The current of skepticism would only deepen, creating a divide that had become impassible, perhaps as early as April.

The May 22 declaration exaggerated the divide. For many Americans, even Europeans, the term "occupation" probably evokes the aftermath of World War II and an American-led vision of cooperation with like-minded peoples forging a common destiny. But for Iraqis, and for most Arabs, the term, seared into the collective memory, brings to mind Israel's record in the Middle East. Some recall Lebanon and the Israeli occupation that endured there, in one fashion or another, from 1978 until May 2000, when the last Israeli soldiers departed through the Fatima Gate on the Israeli-Lebanese border. More spectacularly, the term calls to mind the region's most incendiary issue: Palestine. If the very name "Vietnam" suggests to Americans a decadelong war in Southeast Asia, images of harried U.S. soldiers in rice paddies, fiery napalm swelling across tropical tree lines, the hard angles of American helicopters set against the soft beauty of an Asian landscape, *ihtilal* suggests years of Palestinian resistance to the Israeli occupation in the West Bank and Gaza. The images are persistent: hulking Caterpillar bulldozers demolishing homes of stone and concrete in the squalor of Gaza; American-built Apache helicopters hovering over West Bank villages along rocky, terraced Palestinian hills; imposing Merkava tanks crashing across refugee camps as haunted faces in black-checked kaffiyehs watch them pass. This has become the Arab notion of occupation; those images define *ihtilal*.

When the U.S. government shifted the legal jurisdiction of its presence in Iraq, it inadvertently answered a question that had long dominated Iraqi conversations before and during the war: *Would it be an occupation or a liberation?* Even by American admission, it was now an occupation. And in an *ihtilal*, ambitions of a common destiny, promises of collaboration, pledges of shared aims and goals are rendered impossible. By definition, *ihtilal* denotes inequality, a relationship of two unequal powers, the weaker submitting to the will of the stronger. By imposing an occupation, the Americans declared that the situation was different from what most Iraqis perceived it to be—for, even if Iraq's leader was gone, few Iraqis viewed their nation as fallen.

As the situation began to deteriorate further, the words of one fell on the deaf ears of the other, leaving meanings uncertain, confusing, sometimes imposed. Each side heard what it wanted to hear and acted accordingly.

ABOUT A WEEK AFTER THE U.N. DECLARATION, MY COLLEAGUE THOMAS E. Ricks, one of the *Post*'s best reporters, suggested we follow soldiers from Bravo Company in a battalion of the army's 1st Armored Division through one neighborhood, in one corner of Baghdad, on one day. Over a little more than two hours, Tom would walk with the patrol, while I would trail behind, speaking with residents as they came to grips with the reality of a foreign army patrolling their streets. It was a rare opportunity for us as journalists. Since far more reporters were embedded than not embedded, Iraqis were all too often voiceless. Now we would truly see both sides, in real time.

The day began at ten A.M., with temperatures creeping up through the nineties, as the patrol moved out through the concertina wire that protected the U.S. soldiers' outpost and past two Bradley Fighting Vehicles parked out front.

"Everybody likes us," Specialist Stephen Harris, a twenty-year-old from Lafayette, Louisiana, declared to Tom Ricks. Harris and the others in Bravo Company considered themselves a welcome presence in a friendly land. They were there to help the Iraqis they had liberated, then head home. Tom asked Harris whether the people in Baghdad wanted U.S. troops to stay. "Oh, yeah," he said, taking a slug from his canteen. He then delivered his assessment of the neighborhood they were about to enter: "I'd say ninety-five percent friendly."

I followed fifty meters behind. There were a few waves from the residents. Most just stared. I walked past a stand selling cheap plastic sandals, past a boy selling packets of Kleenex to cars caught in traffic, past a few stands built from cheap wood, with Pepsis and Miranda orange sodas atop. An armored personnel carrier thundered by, setting off a car alarm. Around the corner was a man named Mohammed Ibrahim, standing on the sidewalk as Tom and the ten-man patrol passed his gated house.

"Despicable" was the way he described the U.S. presence. In a white dishdasha, a long Arab robe, the thirty-four-year-old winced as the soldiers moved
along his street, nine carrying automatic weapons slung across their chests,
the tenth a medic. Ibrahim's grimace was personal, the kind of contortion an
insult brings. "We're against the occupation, we refuse the occupation—not
one hundred percent, but one thousand percent," he told me. "They're walking over my heart. I feel like they're crushing my heart."

Ibrahim's sentiments were, obviously, not the only ones I heard that day.
Some residents welcomed the troops, not least in hopes that they would provide a measure of security after the weeks of looting. There was still relief over
Saddam's demise—jubilation that persisted despite the hardships of everyday
life. But a week after the U.N. resolution was passed in New York, with only
token input from Iraqis, many expressed ambivalence or outright anger as the
troops walked by. The hostility ran especially deep among Sunni Muslims,
who made up the neighborhood's majority and who had greeted the invasion
with the greatest skepticism. Along the streets patrolled by the soldiers, they
expressed suspicions over the fate of Iraq's oil and described what they saw as
violations of their privacy.

Iraqis called the area Yarmuk; it was a west Baghdad neighborhood of
middle-class professionals, living in two-story adobe-style houses that would
have fit nicely into a wealthier corner of Albuquerque or Santa Fe. Its sentiments were still colored by its origins in the 1960s as a development to house
military officers—a legacy of a certain era across the Arab world, when whole
neighborhoods were built to house like-minded professionals. To the Americans, the neighborhood was "Sector 37 North," frequently marked as hostile on
U.S. military maps of Baghdad. It was known as a stronghold of Baath Party loyalists, though the more painfully felt undercurrents—the Sunnis' fear of retali-
ation and loss of status—were less well understood by the young Americans.

A week earlier, on the airport highway that marked the southern bound-
ary of the sector, a U.S. soldier had been killed and three others wounded
when their Humvee struck a mine. The attack was an early sign of what
was to gather force over the summer—an insurgency that spiked and ebbed
in intensity, waged by a disparate coalition of forces (loyalists of Saddam,
nationalists, Islamists, and foreigners looking for a fight) united almost solely
by their opposition to the U.S. presence. It would be fought mainly in

Baghdad and the swath of central Iraq dominated by Sunni Muslims that stretches north along the Tigris and west along the Euphrates—in shorthand, the Sunni Triangle. The mine that killed the soldier in Yarmuk would become its weapon of choice. In the beginning, the arsenal would also include hit-and-run raids on military convoys, drive-by shootings of coalition vehicles, and sabotage of power stations, oil pipelines, natural gas plants, and oil installations. In time, though, it would evolve, becoming better coordinated, better planned, and more lethal. Hit-and-run raids turned into elaborate ambushes; makeshift mines became remote-controlled explosives. Helicopters were targeted with rocket-propelled grenades and missiles, whose users benefited by the expertise of officers from the dissolved army, and car bombings were deployed to devastating effect. In cities and towns, militants began to assassinate Iraqi politicians, technocrats, professionals, and members of the nascent security forces—anyone deemed to be cooperating with the occupation. As Tom and I walked through Yarmuk, that insurgency was just beginning. At the time, neither we nor the troops we were with had any idea of its potential.

■ 10:20 **A.M.; 98 DEGREES**

In fatigues colored the brown of the city, the U.S. patrol was configured so that one team of four soldiers was ahead, and another in the back. In the middle, leading the patrol on a slow walk through the broiling streets, was twenty-six-year-old Staff Sergeant Nathaniel Haumschild, of Stillwater, Minnesota, accompanied by the medic. Just to their left was a mosque—like many in Baghdad, now freed from government control, and known for its anti-American sermons. Captain Gerd Schroeder, commander of Bravo Company, said that when he had sent an interpreter to listen to a sermon the Friday before, the theme of the day was "If you're not killing the Americans and the Jew pigs, you're not a true Muslim." The patrol turned right. Specialist Seneca Ratledge, the medic—a talkative soldier from Riceville, Tennessee, who said his Cherokee grandmother had given him his first name—greeted the schoolchildren on the street: "What's up, playas?"

Haumschild turned to Tom and offered an assessment: "Maybe ten percent are hostile. About fifty percent friendly. About forty percent are indifferent."

I asked the same question, as I followed behind. I heard a different answer—at best, fifty-fifty, and at worst, a significant majority hostile. The sentiments often broke down along religious cleavages. Some Shiite residents—among the most euphoric over Saddam's fall—hailed the Americans for ending the Baath Party's rule. With justification, they suspected the party lingered, ready to reemerge—as it, in fact, did over the summer.

"An American dog is better than Saddam and his gangs," said Alaa Rudeini, as he chatted with a friend, Abdel-Razaq Abbas, along the sidewalk. Neither paused in his conversation as the Americans passed and perhaps that was a sign of ease. Farther down the street, Awatif Faraj Salih, a stout matron whose eight-year-old daughter, Rasul, was among the children at the nearby Nablus Elementary School, said she feared what would happen if the U.S. troops departed. "If the Americans left," she said, "massacres would happen in Iraq—between the tribes, between the parties and between the Sunnis and Shiites, of course."

She paused, watching the company. Her next words seemed to contradict her first, but then again, much seemed to conflict these days: "No one who loves their country accepts an occupation. Everybody wants freedom. They want a ruler who is Arab."

▪ 11:03 **A.M.;** 100 **DEGREES**

Private First Class Kasey Keeling, of Denton, Texas, walked second in the patrol, carrying the big M-249 Squad Automatic Weapon, a machine gun. Behind his sunglasses, he looked back and forth, up and down streets lined by homes walled behind concrete and stone. "I scan the windows, rooftops, heavy brush, looking for anything out of the ordinary," he said. The most alarming indicator of danger? An absence of children. "There are always kids around," he said. "No kids, you start to wonder."

There were no children around on Fourth Street in Yarmuk, where the sentiments had seemed to become distinctly uneasy, as the streets became uniformly Sunni. The ideas and the themes came with a regularity that suggested they were voiced over and over in the quick exchanges over meals, coffee, and cigarettes that litter a day.

"We are a Muslim country," Ahmed Abdullah, a seventy-year-old man in a white kaffiyeh, said to me as I stopped to talk. "We don't want anyone to rule us who's not from our country." Standing with his neighbors, feeble with age, he insisted he would fight the Americans. "They said they came to liberate us. Liberate us from what? They came and said they would free us. Free us from what?" he asked. "We have traditions, morals, and customs. We are Arabs. We're different from the West." He squinted into the sun, so intense it seemed to rain light. "If we're to be freed from the regime, we're the ones responsible for freeing ourselves."

As Abdullah watched Keeling and the others pass, he called Baghdad a fallen city, a hint of humiliation in his words. What had happened was akin, he said, to the invasion in 1258 of Hulugu, the grandson of Genghis Khan. The Americans had let the National Library burn and permitted looters to ransack the National Museum of Antiquities; worse, Abdullah believed, was yet to come. "Baghdad is the mother of Arab culture," he said, "and they want to wipe out our culture, absolutely."

■ 11:30 **A.M.; 103 DEGREES**

The patrol arrived at the Rami Institute for Autistic and Slow Learners, a house on a side street with a big lime tree in its walled front yard. On a green chalkboard, written in blockish English and curving Arabic, was this message: "This building is protected by U.S. soldiers. We will use deadly force to protect this building."

Bravo Company was determined to help the school, in part because they said it had been attacked. People hostile to the school, the neighborhood toughs, Sergeant Michael Callan said, "break in, pop shots, terrorize them to get them to leave." The soldiers left their weapons stacked in the yard, under guard. "It scares the kids," the thirty-year-old Virginia native explained. They also left outside the grim expressions they called their game faces, as they entered with Tom.

In the small school, they knelt and talked gently with the children, encouraging them to respond. Callan put his helmet on one child's head, then stopped briefly in all five classrooms. For more than half an hour, he and his men lingered, enjoying the respite from the anxiety—and boredom—of a foot patrol.

As the squad prepared to leave the school, Private Ian Hanson, who had been standing guard out front, was having a playful debate with a teenager who lived nearby. "I'm not a baby, you're a baby," said the nineteen-year-old from the Fox River town of Little Chute, Wisconsin. "You're two years younger than me. I'm a long way from home. You're living at home." As the soldiers walked out, passing Hanson, each looked pleased with himself. They liked helping the school. They admired its teachers. Their hearts went out to the children.

There was little of that goodwill among the group of young Iraqi men standing outside, their expressionless eyes following the soldiers' movements. As I talked with them, on a sidewalk enlivened by palm trees and red bougainvillea, they wondered about men, foreign men, entering a school where women worked.

"We're not against the presence of the school, we're against the presence of the Americans," said twenty-three-year-old Saif Din. "We don't want them here. This area," he said, rotating his finger around the neighborhood, "they don't like the Americans."

He and his friend, twenty-two-year-old Mohammed Ahmed, said they suspected the soldiers were having sex with the women inside, a statement as ludicrous as it was suggestive. To these men, the American presence was utterly vile and their intentions base; they would compete with each other in devising the darkest scenarios. "Only God knows," Ahmed told me. "I haven't seen it with my own eyes. But I've heard about things."

"We don't like it," said Din, wagging his finger. "We don't like it."

For a moment, they debated the occupation—the project itself, not the term. Electricity supplies, however sporadic, were becoming more reliable (though they would worsen as the weeks wore on) and looting had finally waned. But the phones, knocked out during the war, still did not work, and public transportation was a mess. L. Paul Bremer had dissolved the Iraqi army, depriving hundreds of thousands of a salary and sending them to the streets.

Each volunteered a complaint: that U.S. helicopters were spying on Iraqis sleeping on their roofs during the scorching summer months, that the treads of tanks and Bradley Fighting Vehicles were tearing up the pavement, that soldiers used expletives at checkpoints, that soldiers kept their rifles at the ready as they walked the streets.

And the future? I asked them.

"The future is *ghamidh*," Ahmed said, smiling in a knowing way. "Their goals aren't clear."

Din shook his head. "They're clear. They're creating an occupation."

▪ 12:40 **P.M.**; 106 **DEGREES**

The patrol turned a corner a block from their temporary home. "I love it," Specialist Harris said of army life. "Something different every day."

The men passed the two green Bradleys and stepped through the base's concertina wire. A soldier greeted them with cold cans of strawberry soda and cola. They stripped off their helmets, their flak jackets, and the uniform jackets called blouses and set down their weapons. They were sweaty and tired. Some pulled out cigarettes, sharing a pack of Marlboro Reds, and a few leaned against the wall. Others chatted with Tom and me about Iraq, about what Iraqis along the route had said about them, about the months ahead.

A few minutes later, the lieutenant announced that in two hours, they would go back on patrol. A few groaned at the prospect: the heat had not abated. Some were more gung ho. The effusive medic, Specialist Ratledge, spoke up—addressing Tom, me, and his superior. Anyone, really. "They love us," he volunteered.

THERE WASN'T ALL THAT MUCH LOVE FOR THE AMERICANS IN THOSE DAYS, AS U.S. promises propelled Iraqi expectations. Of course, the weather didn't help. Every day seemed to grow hotter as summer arrived in Baghdad, a desert but for the Tigris. The capital was unprepared. In most neighborhoods, residents were almost frantic in their complaints about basic needs remaining unmet—there was still not enough electricity to keep food from spoiling, not enough water to drink, not enough security on the streets.

U.S. Army Staff Sergeant Charles Pollard was thrown into that cauldron, and he had little of the enthusiasm of Specialist Harris, none of the goodwill of Specialist Ratledge. Sergeant Pollard was basically angry, and his first words to me—spoken on a street as desolate as it was dangerous—were unabashed: "U.S. officials need to get our asses out of here." I scribbled in my notebook, trying to keep up with the pace of his invective. He went on, with little restraint. "I say that seriously. We have no business being here. We will not change the culture they have in Iraq, in Baghdad. Baghdad is so corrupted. All we are here is potential people to be killed and sitting ducks."

I met Pollard, a forty-three-year-old reservist from Pittsburgh, by chance. That summer, Nasir and I were chasing down a story on an attack by still-shadowy insurgents on a U.S. patrol in a street in the working-class suburb of Mashtal, and I stopped in to the police station where Pollard's unit was based to find out whether they knew anything. One soldier had been killed, by either a rocket-propelled grenade or a mortar, Pollard told me. Another had lost his arm, severed around the elbow by the blast, which shook the entire block. The toll had left Pollard angry. By this time, attacks on U.S. troops had begun mounting in Mashtal, which he called a "very, very, very, very bad neighborhood." His unit was vulnerable, he said, and their mission was impossible: offering protection to the unpopular Baath Party–era police force before getting them back on their feet and into the unruly streets.

I liked Pollard, even if I found my time with his 307th Military Police Company delivered one of the bleakest, most disturbing judgments about the occupation while I was in Iraq. The soldiers whom Tom Ricks and I followed with Bravo Company were, perhaps, a little naive—across the chasm of occupier and occupied, they simply didn't hear anything the Iraqis were saying. But Pollard was anything but unsuspecting. He looked out across the rift and he hated what he saw. Looking back at him, the Iraqis saw every one of their suspicions and resentments about the Americans embodied in one man. In the station, tensions flared along a divide that was as wide as the temperatures were high. If one man's situation could ever represent a clash of cultures, in a land as battered and troubled as Iraq, it was Pollard's; he had arrived in Baghdad after Saddam's fall, on May 24.

I ended up spending a portion of two days with him, shortly before the military imposed restrictions on reporters' conversations with U.S. soldiers. (Eventually, it was declared that a public affairs officer would have to sign off on any interview.) Of medium height and slim build, with a trimmed outline of a mustache, he wore dark sunglasses that gave him a look of street sense. A twenty-two-year veteran, he appeared younger than his age—his hair was receding but still black—and he was intent on doing nothing that would cut his years short.

"I pray every day on the roof. I pray that we make it safe, that we make it safe home," he said as I stood with him inside the Rashad station, whose newly painted walls seemed a feeble gesture at normality. "The president needs to know it's in his hands and we all need to recognize this isn't our home, America is, and we just pray that he does something about it."

Pollard had thought about retiring before his Iraq tour; in hindsight, he felt he should have. When I met him, he said he didn't know when he could return to his job at the maintenance department at a community college in Pittsburgh. That uncertainty nagged at him. Asked when he wanted to leave, he was blunt: "As soon as we can get the hell out of here." I remember smiling. He didn't.

Pollard was the most outspoken of the men and women I met, but no one seemed in particularly high spirits that summer day. Many of the soldiers in his unit were homesick, frustrated, and miserable in heat that was soaring well into the 100s. As I sat with them in a dusty second-floor room with sandbags piled against the six windows, helmets hung on nails over flak jackets, and a sprawling map of Baghdad on the wall, they debated their departure date. They traded gossip behind a door that was closed so that, as they put it, the Iraqi policemen wouldn't stare at them.

"There's a rumor going around that we'll be here for two years," Specialist Ron Beach said, sitting on a cooler under an overhead fan.

The others rolled their eyes and shook their heads. Some ate pistachios, others tried to nap. "You can put me up in a five-star hotel, and I'm not going to be here for two years," said Sergeant Jennifer Appelbaum, a twenty-six-year-old legal secretary from Philadelphia.

They started talking about what they lacked: hot meals, air conditioners, bathrooms a notch above plywood outhouses, something to do on their twelve hours off other than sweat. They had electricity for one hour, did without for five. Staff Sergeant Kenneth Kaczmarek, Pollard's tall, well-built deputy, called his flak jacket an "Iraqi weight loss system" and said he had shed at least fifteen pounds. Pollard said he had lost eighteen.

Pollard's second granddaughter had been born that month, but he had not been able to call home yet to learn her name. Kaczmarek's daughter, Isabella

Jolie, had been born May 28, eight days after he arrived in Iraq as part of an advance team.

"It makes life miserable," Pollard said. "The morale, it's hard to stay high with these problems."

Largely undefended in the weeks after Saddam's fall, the Rashad police station, with twelve tiles missing from the blue sign over its entrance, had already taken on the look of a bunker. Two cream-colored, armored Humvees were parked outside; another Humvee, with a .50-caliber machine gun, was stationed to the side. Pollard said he wanted barbed wire strung atop the cinder-block wall behind, and an engineering team was preparing to heighten the brick-and-cement wall in front. In coming days, he said he would put sand-bag barricades along the street outside the entrance.

Pollard said he suspected everyone: "I don't trust them, none of them." Two Iraqi journalists, one with a camera, had visited two weeks before, and he was convinced the men had been casing the station. He used to sit at a desk outside, then moved indoors. "Let the Iraqis guard the gate," he recalled thinking. As we stood together next to a sandbagged window, he thought for a moment, looking at the ground, then turned to me again, unrestrained: "I don't build bonds. I don't build friendships. I don't have contacts, with none of them. I just come in and do my job."

The way Pollard saw it, the Iraqi police should be taking risks, not his thirteen reservists at the station. "It's not fair to our troops to build a country that's not even ours and our lives are at risk," he said. "They've got to take control. They may have to kill some of their own people to make a statement that 'we're back in control.' No doubt. They say Iraqi people can't shoot. If they're killing, they can shoot." If not the Iraqis, he said, then NATO forces and U.N. peacekeeping forces should help keep order in the neighborhood of fifty thousand people. It wasn't a job for the U.S. military.

For the most part, the police and Pollard's soldiers said little to each other, and that through translators. The Iraqi police officers disliked Pollard, for what they saw as his unreasonable demands and lack of respect, and he had little regard for them. The neighborhood was dangerous, he said, and fighting crime here might require twice the eighty-six officers the station still had. But of the eighty-six, he said at least half should be dismissed for corruption or ineptitude. To make his point, he led me through the police station, a sordid walk that lasted fifteen minutes and felt like a few hours.

"This is a crooked cop sitting here," Pollard said, pointing to a major in a blue shirt who acted as though he didn't speak English.

We walked on, and Pollard turned to me. "I'll point them out to you," he said, his voice a little conspiratorial. "They know I know."

We moved down the hall, and he leaned into a room with two officers busy at a desk, the air inside stagnant. "Here's a room where they're acting like they're doing real important paperwork," he said. He faced one of the officers sitting at a ramshackle desk with a creaking fan: "There's another lazy lieutenant right there who doesn't want to go out and set an example for the others."

We walked outside to a balcony where three officers were sitting on newspapers and a green burlap sack, one with his shoes off. "This is a couple more lazy cops, sitting down when they should be outside," he said. Without exception, they all greeted Pollard with cold stares, forgoing the traditional greetings that are almost obligatory in Arabic.

A few hours later, near an iron gate where residents gathered in hopes of getting an audience to file a complaint, Shoja Shaltak, an Iraqi lieutenant, brought a brown folder with an order from a judge to release three men in Pollard's custody. Pollard suspected a bribe.

"Tell him he can go, go, go," Pollard said, pausing between each of the last words. "I don't jump at their requests."

The police lieutenant protested, insisting that the order came from an Iraqi judge. The interpreter, Ziad Tarek, answered on his own. "The judge has nothing to do with this anymore," Tarek told the lieutenant. He pointed to Pollard. "He's the judge now."

Sergeant Sami Jalil, a fourteen-year veteran of the force, watched with disgust. Seeing the look on his face, I left Pollard and walked over to him. "It's embarrassing. It's embarrassing for us and for the lieutenant," he told me. "We are police and they don't respect us. How is it possible for them to respect the Iraqi people?"

His complaints were shared by virtually all the station's officers: they didn't receive the flak jackets the Americans wear; they had to check out rifles from the soldiers; they had no uniforms; they had no badges—and they didn't like Pollard.

Asked if he was afraid to patrol, the thirty-three-year-old Jalil shot back angrily, "The opposite! They're the ones who are scared," he said, his eyes narrowing. "I'm ready to go out alone, but they should give me the equipment.

We're facing the danger. We're in the front lines. We're taking all the risks, only us." He shook his head, as we sat together on a curb. "They're arrogant. They treat all the people as if they're criminals." True, he said, there were a lot of corrupt officers, "but you can't generalize to all of them."

Jalil said he was so frustrated that he planned to quit in days. He said he couldn't support his parents, wife, and eight-month-old daughter, Rusul, on a salary of sixty dollars a month. He spent half of that on lunch every day and the thirty-cent fare for a shared taxi to and from work.

With water in short supply or of poor quality, he bought a bottle of mineral water every two days for his daughter—a cheap variety, but still another fifty cents. Sewage flooded daily into his home, where four families totaling thirty people shared six rooms. And, with electricity running no more than six hours a day in his neighborhood, he worried that the heat would make Rusul ill.

"The truth has revealed itself," Jalil said. "The Americans painted a picture that they would come, provide good things to the Iraqi people, spread security, but regrettably . . ." His voice trailed off.

About the only thing everyone at the police station seemed to agree on was that Mashtal was a tough neighborhood. Gunfire crackled at night along the trash-strewn street; a chop shop was down the block. Parked outside the station were six stolen cars recovered by the police. Kaczmarek, the tall sergeant, called Mashtal "Chicago in the thirties" and told me he'd seen someone toting a tommy gun the other day. Jalil called "murder the easiest crime to commit in Iraq." A week before, in his neighborhood, an Iraqi man had hit his twenty-eight-year-old ex-wife with a bicycle, then, as she lay on the ground on a hot afternoon, shot her in the face with an AK-47. "People just watched," Jalil said. "If they interfered, they would be killed, too."

As I left that day, I passed Mustafa Majid, who had been waiting for hours outside the police station's gate for help in settling a property dispute. He was hot, he was angry, and he blamed the Americans for everything. His disappointment was insurmountable. Traffic problems? Caused by checkpoints that the Americans set up, and by roadblocks across bridges. Crime? U.S. authorities were willing to let Iraqis fight among themselves. Lack of electricity? Employing the logic of Saddam's years, he deemed blackouts punishment by the Americans for the escalating attacks on their soldiers. "Is it believable that America, the greatest nation on earth, can't bring order to a small spot on the map?" the heavyset twenty-seven-year-old asked, his blue shirt soaked with sweat. "We cannot believe it."

Over the next year in Iraq, I tried to find Pollard again, but never did. A month later, though, I stumbled on Kaczmarek at another police station, near Mashtal, on a street with graffiti in English ("Backstreet Boys") and Arabic ("I beg God's forgiveness"). Along the wall were portraits of Shiite clerics— Grand Ayatollah Ali Sistani, Muqtada Sadr, and Ayatollah Mohammed Baqir al-Hakim. It was August 2003. At first, Kaczmarek was angry at me, almost confrontational, as we stood outside the police station in a courtyard so dusty the ground was powder. "You're the reporter that got Sergeant Pollard in trouble," he said, pointing at me. After my article quoting Pollard appeared in the *Post*, he told me, Pollard had been relieved of his command, and Kaczmarek didn't want to say another word. I kept asking questions, and he gradually began to loosen up. He was actually more bitter at Pollard's superiors than angry at me. A little subversively, he hinted that Pollard had become a folk hero of sorts at the base nicknamed Mule Skinner, where he was then stationed. Fellow soldiers asked him to sign their green Army-issue T-shirts in black marker, and the article itself was, for a time, posted on the base's walls.

Pollard, he said, was unrepentant—the occupation was going badly, he didn't want to be in Iraq, and he felt he had had to say something. So did Kaczmarck, but with a little less ardor. At the same time that Pollard was disciplined, he was relieved of duty for a day over his crack about the Iraqi weight-loss system, and the experience left him resentful: "I didn't know I lost my First Amendment rights when I joined the military."

DURING THE OCCUPATION'S FIRST SPRING AND SUMMER, AS THE CAPITAL KEPT reeling and the insurgency began to materialize, I often wondered whether the divide I saw in Mashtal could have been bridged. Was it inevitable? Another scenario for life after Saddam was perhaps possible: the ruler falls, to the joy of many; a curfew is imposed in the capital, and a provisional government is quickly constituted; basic services—electricity, water, and sewage— are rapidly restored; security, at times draconian, is imposed in the streets;

and aid starts pouring into Baghdad, as foreign and Iraqi companies compete for the bounty of the reconstruction of a country awash in oil. The occupation might have unfolded that way—but it didn't. Only the first item in the hopeful scenario occurred, Saddam's defeat, and the failure of almost everything else left misunderstandings and misperceptions to define occupier and occupied. It left the more powerful forces of history to shape the relationship between Sergeant Pollard and Sergeant Jalil.

Perhaps history condemned the project from the start. A grim warning lay in Iraq's modern record, shaped as it was by deprivation—Saddam's tyranny, his wars, and the expectations of Baghdadis that they deserved better. The Iraqi impression of America was no less a problem. Whatever its intentions, the United States was a non-Muslim invader in a Muslim land. For a generation, its reputation had been molded by its alliance with Israel, its record in the 1991 Gulf War, and its support for the U.N. sanctions. Not insubstantial were decades over which the United States had grown as an antagonist in the eyes of many Arabs. Iraq had long been removed from the Arab world, isolated by dictatorship, war, and the sanctions, but it remained Arab.

Time and again, no one would hear and no one would see in Iraq; the divide more and more seemed predetermined. Even when the U.S. soldiers were more like Bravo Company than like Pollard, the Americans rarely caught a break. That impression first dawned on me in Sadr City, still early in the summer of 2003, when I spent time with a military unit and employees of the U.S. Agency for International Development, who had chosen an Islamic charity to administer a grassroots project in the neighborhood. The project was brief but symbolic: a sixteen-day, $280,000 effort to clean the slum. In addition to salaries for workers cleaning avenues of hundreds of tons of trash, the sponsors provided money for the drivers of 180 garbage trucks and 130 sewer workers and engineers. The neighborhood's eighty mosques—the majority in the hands of men loyal to Muqtada Sadr—would provide 16,000 workers and supervisors. The charity, known as the Wala'a General Humanitarian Organization, formed by former political prisoners just after Saddam's fall, would provide leadership from among its ninety employees.

At first glance, this was a picture-perfect example of the way the occupation was supposed to unfold. Near a portrait of Iran's Ayatollah Ruhollah Khomeini, a smartly dressed U.S. soldier doled out neatly bound bundles of

15,000 Iraqi dinars to workers chosen by the mosques to clean the sewage-drenched, trash-strewn streets. In the hall stood a Special Forces major, who spoke with the impatience of a soldier used to precision and struggling with the imprecision of translated Arabic. He still managed—with a mix of bravado and bluntness—to cut innumerable Gordian knots. At the helm, overseeing it all, was the charity's director, Sheikh Kadhim Fartousi, a piston of a man with a trimmed black beard, dressed in the white turban and pressed robes of a Shiite cleric, who treated the Americans graciously.

"I believe in the philosophy of crawl, walk, run," the Special Forces officer, Major Arthur P. Vidal III, told me. We were sitting in a room with slogans on the wall that read, "God preserve Iraq." The project, he said, represented the first U.S. steps to engage "the locals" and leave the neighborhood better than when the Americans arrived. "We'll foster a relationship with the imam. He'll get what he needs and we'll get what we need," said Vidal, who often answered questions with a clipped "Check." He was determined, he said, "to play the game."

It didn't take long, though, to see who was winning that game. On the morning I visited, supervisors selected by the clergy waited in the lobby to receive money they would then distribute to fifty workers under them. They queued underneath signs that described the project as a collaboration between Wala'a and the "International Aid Agency." The only reference to the United States was in English. On a nearby street, graffiti scrawled in black read, "We are the supporters of Islam, not America, not Saddam."

"I thank the mosque," said Ibrahim Challoub, a forty-year-old supervisor nominated by the neighborhood sheikh, who had formed a committee to provide security for hospitals, direct traffic, and provide food to the poorest. Like others in line, Challoub, a gaunt, balding veteran of the 1980–88 war with Iran, complained that the Americans had done too little to provide electricity, water, and, most important, security. With a nod, he said he remained suspicious. "We still don't know the Americans' intentions. We'll know their intentions in the future," he said. "I don't trust them."

Standing a few feet from the stacks of Iraqi dinars piled a foot high, thirty-four-year-old Ibrahim Darraj interrupted. "I thank the sheikh, not the Americans," he said, wagging his finger. "It's Iraqi money. We have oil and that's where it came from."

At the Mohammed Baqir Mosque, where lists were posted for worshippers to join the project on a first-come, first-served basis, Sheikh Tareq Obeid disavowed any cooperation with U.S. officials and insisted the money came from the *Hawza*. He said he had been ordered to take part by Muqtada Sadr's office and viewed the work as the clergy's mission to provide service to the people. "The people are with the clergy," he said. "Their voice is our voice. It's one voice." He stroked his bushy beard and went on: "We refuse the American presence absolutely. We didn't invite the American forces. They came to overthrow Saddam. Saddam oppressed us, and we're happy he's gone. But we're not happy the Americans stayed."

Sheikh Kadhim, charismatic and quick to smile though he was, seemed an ambiguous character to me, even as he portrayed himself as America's man in the neighborhood. In the streets, some temporarily freed by the U.S.-funded project of sewage that had run shin deep, residents approached him to kiss his cheek, showing their appreciation. "We thank the *Hawza*, and we thank the clergy," said one resident, twenty-five-year-old Uday Hussein. Around the corner, forty-nine-year-old Shaker Abbas complained that the sewage had prevented them from ritual washing before prayers. He still wanted electricity—his eight children were miserable—but was thankful, to the cleric. "I'm at your service," he told Sheikh Kadhim, who grinned as he dragged on one of his locally made Vigor cigarettes. "Whatever you want."

At each stop, Sheikh Kadhim reminded the residents of the help the Americans provided and told them—sometimes being met with protests—that the Americans were liberators, not occupiers. (His relations with Vidal were good: in meetings three times a week, he would casually throw his arms around the major's shoulder, and had once shared with him an hour-long lunch of the fish dish *masgoof* and goat's milk.) But as he returned to the office, along streets he wanted to be an example for Baghdad, he struck me as ambivalent. At times, he would unintentionally mix the Arabic words for "coalition" and "occupation" (*i'tilaf* and *ihtilal*), making himself smile. As we drove together through the neighborhood in his car, he finally confided a small measure of his own skepticism. "When I was in jail, we thought about how Saddam could be overthrown. I told the other prisoners, 'If Bush gets rid of Saddam, I'll paint a picture of him and hang it in my house,'" Sheikh Kadhim said.

Had he? I asked.

"I won't hang it," he said, "until I'm sure they're liberators, not occupiers."

▪ ▪ ▪

IT WAS THE MIDDLE OF THE SUMMER WHEN I SAW WAMIDH AGAIN. HIS ANGER had cooled since our first meeting after the war, but he was no less insistent. He had refused to take part in a U.S.-sponsored political process, deeming it collaboration. So where did that leave him? "The Americans are trying to keep this dichotomy—it's either Saddam or the American occupation," he said. "Even before the war, I rejected this."

But the fury he had articulated, against the occupation, against the government for surrendering the capital without a fight, had faded. Now he seemed voiceless. What had replaced fury was a gloomier sentiment. Baghdad, to him, was entropic, and he was at a loss, filled with regret. His anger had turned to grief, and his grief was reflective.

"How did we allow such a perversion to come?" Wamidh asked, directing his question at no one. "Why couldn't the country reform the regime of Saddam or put an end to it except by the arrival of foreign troops?" We both shook our heads. "It's a very sad situation in Iraq. Really. A lot of people are thinking the country is doomed. That there's no solution." This was the gloom that, in time, would come to dominate conversations in Iraq. "They think what is coming is going to be worse."

Mohammed Hayawi, a bald bear of a man, was one of those pessimists. Unshaven, his face was beefy but friendly. He often smiled, but the heavy bags under his tired eyes would deepen as the day wore on. He looked much older than his thirty-eight years. By chance, I had met him before the war at his shop, the Renaissance Bookstore, along Mutanabi Street, and long remembered our conversation and how he had seized the opportunity to talk. At that time, he had been unable to understand the American obsession with Iraq and Saddam. Why the crisis after crisis? For weapons of mass destruction? *We don't have any.* If we did, he had declared, we would have fired them at Israel. For Saddam? What, he had asked, does he have to do with *us*?

On this summer visit, my first since Saddam's fall, the narrow stretch of bookstores where Hayawi's is located looked a little shabbier than before. Plastic bags, oil tins, and paper were strewn along the street; some of the rubbish was smoldering and hordes of flies hovered over broken eggs. Horns blared in two lanes of traffic, one more than the street had been built for. An unusual summer breeze prompted vendors to sprinkle water over the road to keep dust from blowing into their shops. At every turn were the lingering scars of looting—arches with their windows broken, yellow brick walls scalded black. Before the war, the market had stayed open till ten P.M., sometimes eleven. Now the street shut down by three P.M., often earlier.

Mohammed sat inside his store with relatives and employees, trying to keep himself cool with a fan, as sweat poured down his jowly face and soaked his blue shirt. As usual, he was unshaven. Over a cup of tea—scalding even on this hot day—he smoked Gauloises cigarettes. I reintroduced myself and he almost immediately recognized me. "Abu Laila," he said, grinning, using the Arabic form of nickname built on the name of one's oldest son. (Since my one child was a daughter, I was "Father of Laila.") He then delivered a line he would say to me almost every time we saw each other:

"I challenge anyone, Abu Laila, to say what has happened, what's happening now, and what will happen in the future." And he shook his head.

Never one to mince words, Mohammed was indignantly disappointed. To customers, friends, and all who cared to listen, he expressed his frustration and irritation. The Americans had broken their promises of prosperity, he complained, and there was still chaos in the streets, albeit less than a few weeks earlier. Were things worse or better than before the war, I asked him. "Worse," he insisted, thrusting his hand in the air. "Truly? It's worse." He dragged on his cigarette with the other hand. "The American promises to Iraq are like trying to hold water in your hand. It spills through your fingers."

Mohammed had worked at the bookstore all his life. His father, Abdel-Rahman, had opened it in 1954, and after he died in 1993, his five sons inherited the business, keeping a portrait of the patriarch, in a Russian-style winter hat, hanging on the wood-paneled wall. His family was Sunni Muslim, but Mohammed played down its importance to his identity. As for his politics, he described himself much as Wamidh did and much as he himself had in our conversation before the war: as neither for Saddam, nor happy with the Americans. Like Wamidh, perhaps a little more bitterly, he was still in shock at how little life had improved.

"The most important thing is credibility," he said. "If the Americans want to do well, they have to gain the trust of the people. Until now, there is nothing. We want to see something *malmus*, tangible." Mohammed used the word *rafahiya* often, as did others. It means prosperity, and it is what Mohammed and most Iraqis thought the Americans had promised would ensue after Saddam's fall.

"The mind of the Iraqi is on electricity. He wants to find a generator to get a little electricity in his house so that he can drink cold water." Other men in the shop nodded in agreement. They sat along shelves lined with books that ranged from Arabic-English dictionaries to brightly colored Qurans to cookbooks. On one shelf was a newly published book by Mohammed Salim, called *Witness to the Fall.* "Every day at the Baghdad airport, the airplanes are taking off and landing. Is it possible the Americans cannot bring generators for power to improve the electricity here? Is it possible these are the same Americans who brought three thousand tanks, who brought three thousand artillery pieces in two days?" I wondered where he got these numbers, but I didn't interrupt. "The tanks, the airplanes, and the supplies, and no generators?"

Mohammed recalled the 1991 Gulf War, and the devastation the bombing caused to Baghdad's utilities and basic services. "Saddam returned the infrastructure to the country in eighteen days," he said. "How long have the Americans been here? It is a superpower and nothing. Zero. Plus there's no stability. Is this good, Abu Laila?" he asked me. "Is this good?"

As he often did, Mohammed would pause after an especially vigorous point. He smiled, in a jovial way. I always found him pleasant, despite his anger, and in his unfailing hospitality, he again reminded me of Wamidh. He ran his hand over his fleshy, sweaty cheeks. "Does this look like the face of thirty-nine years?" he joked.

He clapped his hands, turned his palms upward, then turned grimmer. "Iraq has suffered so much. Since 1968. Since 1968 until now."

As we spoke, I realized that what Mohammed was saying went deeper than frustration or irritation. There was, of course, disappointment; there was disillusionment, too. His pride was wounded; there was a sense of humiliation.

"All we heard was that the Americans came to Iraq to assist Iraq. Before the war, they said they wanted to help the Iraqi people. They wanted to rid us of a great dictatorship. They didn't come as an occupier," he said. "We won't accept them as occupiers. As occupiers, no." He stopped for a moment and sipped his tea. "The word 'occupation' is a huge word, Abu Laila. The Americans shouldn't use this word."

He told me a story that he would repeat to me in the months ahead. In his yellow Caprice, he had been driving to Syria on business and was stopped at a U.S. checkpoint, manned by two Humvees, outside the Euphrates River town of Rammadi, in western Iraq. Through a translator, one of the officers, clad in camouflage and dusty from a desert wind, began to ask him routine questions.

"'What are you doing here?' he asked. I said, 'What are *you* doing here? You're *my* guest. What are *you* doing in Iraq? I should ask you, you shouldn't ask me. You're standing on my land, the land of Iraq. I should ask you!'"

The translator told the U.S. officer what Mohammed said.

"He laughed and he patted my shoulder," Mohammed recalled. "This really happened."

The soldier sent a rueful Mohammed on his way.

11

THE MUD GETS WETTER

Along orange groves and orchards of figs, pears, apricots, and plums watered by the timeless churn of the Tigris, Hashim Mohammed Aani often sat before his birdcage. He had built it of scrap wood and the lattice of chicken-coop wire hung together at angles corresponding to a child's notion of perfection. A chubby fifteen-year-old with a mop of curly black hair and a face still rounded by adolescence, he was quiet, painfully shy. "Awkward" might have been a better word, his family said. For hours every day, outside a brick house perched near the river's sloping banks in a prosperous Sunni Muslim village ordered by the sun's passage and the Muslim call to prayer, this youngest of six brothers and sisters watched his four canaries and one nightingale. The birds were his closest companions, their frenetic motions complementing his bashful reserve.

On a Monday morning in June 2003, after a harrowing American raid that deployed helicopter gunships, armored vehicles, and troops edgy with anticipation, his family found Hashim. Two gunshots had ripped through his abdomen. His corpse straddled a muddy canal and lay next to a bale of hay and a rusted can of vegetable oil. With U.S. soldiers occupying a house nearby, the body remained in that spot for hours, slowly swelling under a burning sun. Lieutenant Arthur Jimenez, a plain-spoken lieutenant who commanded a platoon near the house, said he did not know the details of the boy's death, but in words so cold they were oddly sympathetic, he said he feared the fifteen-year-old was simply unlucky. "That person," he said, "was probably in the wrong place at the wrong time."

Hashim was one of three people killed in the raid on Thuluyah, a lush, oasislike town about a ninety-minute drive north from Baghdad. More than four thousand U.S. troops took part in "Operation Peninsula Strike," the biggest military operation since Saddam fell and the first in what was becoming an aggressive campaign in the Sunni Triangle as U.S. troops set out to crush the insurgency that had begun building. U.S. troops, who still numbered about 150,000 in Iraq, moved through the fiercely conservative towns in force, making arrests and seizing arms. They received help from Iraqi informers, and whenever they appraised the campaign they talked about turning the corner on the enemy.

Yet in those months, the Americans rarely distinguished between battle's unwavering logic and occupation's equivocal reality. While the soldiers predicted success, the raids ignited myriad grievances in villages like Thuluyah, molding a tableau of confusion, fear, and vengeance. As the summer wore on, the armed opposition would never lack Iraqi recruits—or perceived wrongs to inspire them.

In places like Thuluyah, as in other parts of Iraq dominated by Sunni Muslims, an outright war was beginning again, a harbinger of what would follow in Baghdad. Aside from a brief respite after Saddam's fall, combat had actually never ended, but now something new was taking hold. The latest battlegrounds were the once relatively prosperous places along well-watered fields and orchards in the valleys of the Tigris and Euphrates, which cut central Iraq into an arc from the Iranian border in the east to Syria in the west. In this region, fear of the future often arrived in the form of nostalgia for the recent past, when local men filled the ranks of the Baathist government, which had lavished patronage on their communities. Here, occupation or not, Saddam was still the president—a symbol of utter authority in a country with little of it. Newly scrawled graffiti celebrated his rule—"Yes, yes to the beloved leader Saddam"—and some portraits of the deposed ruler still stood remarkably intact.

The escalating anger in the Sunni communities seemed to go deeper,

though. That summer, in places like Thuluyah, there was growing apprehension and anxiety over the fate of a minority that, by virtue of its wealth, its
education, and the favoritism of overlords, had ruled Iraq for centuries,
through colonialism and coups, dictatorship and war. Now the Sunnis were
besieged and leaderless—disenfranchised, in a way. To many, the Arab nationalism that had bound the community together for half a century rang hollow.
Religion, an untested movement in a country whose official ideology had
been secular, was commanding more of their attention. The syncretic result
would, in time, shape the region, reinterpreting and re-creating an identity
that was now self-consciously defined by occupation.

Before the war, Iraq was all too often seen through limiting, simplified
notions. The interplay of history with its sometimes mythic recollection was
rarely appreciated. Neither were the subtleties of faith or the shame and
anger of those who feel that control of their lives has slipped away from them.
That changed with the eruption that defined the war's aftermath. The insurgency brought forth the complexities of that reality and the hierarchy of
resentments, inherited from the past, that had lurked beneath the surface
before the war. In the most sweeping terms, I had misjudged the depth of
loathing among religious Shiites for Saddam, the instrument of another
epoch of suffering and martyrdom. Just as glaringly, I had undervalued the
hostility that Sunnis in rural Iraq would feel for the occupation and the American military presence; looking back, I underappreciated the Sunni sense of
abandonment and siege. As a villager in Thuluyah put it, the Sunnis, longtime rulers of Iraq, were now a *shaab biduun*, a people without. No other
group felt the *ihtilal*, the occupation, in a more visceral way; the word *ihana*,
"insult," punctuated innumerable conversations in the irrigated fields and
mud-brick homes.

In time, Thuluyah, seething in the aftermath of Operation Peninsula
Strike, would become a microcosm of the larger Sunni armed opposition that
the Americans dramatically failed to anticipate and that many hopeful Iraqis
had underestimated, even as it emerged as the flip side of the Shiite revival in
molding their country.

"I think the future's going to be very dark," Rahim Hamid Hammoud told
me. He was a soft-spoken fifty-six-year-old judge in a brown shirt with short-
cropped gray hair and a trimmed mustache, and we were talking as he joined

the long line of those paying their respects to the family of fifteen-year-old Hashim. "We're seeing each day become worse than the last."

Operation Peninsula Strike had been an answer to increasingly sophisticated ambushes and hit-and-run raids in a region that the U.S. military, early on, identified as a bastion of support for the fallen government. It began after midnight. Piercing the dark, the echoes of Apache helicopters and F-16, A-10, and AC-130 warplanes had awoken the boy's kin (four related families) and signaled the start of the raid. Within minutes, armored vehicles were thundering down the dirt road past orange groves to the families' compound. Humvees and troop transports followed. From the other direction, soldiers hurried from camouflage boats onto the denuded banks of the Tigris near a reed-shrouded island. Bodies arched like bow strings, running up a hill near a small plot of green beans and thigh-high okra plants, across a patch of the purple flowers known as the Prophet's carpet, and past a lemon tree. "We came here ready to fight," recalled Jimenez, a lieutenant with the 4th Infantry Division.

At the sound of their arrival, Hashim's cousin Asad Abdel-Karim Ibrahim said he went outside the gate with his parents, brother, and two sisters. In Asad's arms was his seven-month-old niece, Amal. They raised a white headscarf to signal surrender but the soldiers apparently did not see it. Asad, fifteen years old, was shot in the upper right arm. He reeled backward. His hands went limp and he dropped the baby, who started screaming helplessly. Days later, he was still wearing the piece of soiled tape placed on his back by U.S. soldiers who had given him first aid: "15-year-old male, GSW [gunshot wound] @ arm." When he spoke with me, his face was still blank, the interim of fear and relief. "The Americans were shouting in English, and we didn't know what they were saying," he told me. "They were yelling and yelling."

Around the corner, past brick and concrete walls toppled by armored vehicles, residents said soldiers searched the house of nineteen-year-old Fadhil Midhas, who was mentally retarded. He started shouting when soldiers put tape over his mouth. He thrashed, his bulky body jerking uncontrollably, and his brown eyes flared wide with the fear that he would suffocate. The women present tried to explain—more with hand gestures than words—and, residents said, soldiers splashed water over Fadhil's face in an attempt to quiet him. Looking drained and feeble, he pulled back his white dishdasha to show a large red bruise on his left shoulder and stomach that neighbors said was caused when the four soldiers beat him with rifle butts as he lost control.

In the commotion, Hashim, the young boy, ran away, headed toward the thick groves behind his house. Whether because they were afraid that the Americans would return, or simply because it was true, his relatives fervently denied he had a gun. "He was trying to hide," said his brother, Riyadh, who was detained for four days. "He didn't know what to do." When they saw Hashim again, he was dead. "We still don't know why they killed him," another relative said.

More than two dozen homes were raided in the sweep through the town, and a curfew was imposed from ten A.M. to six P.M. Some weapons were seized, but not as many as expected. About four hundred residents were arrested, all but fifty of whom were released after a few days at the makeshift detention center at an abandoned air base, Abu Hleij, seven miles north, whose entrance was guarded by two soldiers and where graffiti in English read, "Welcome to Camp Black Knight." The damage was done. Despite the releases, and the apologies issued by the military as they were freed, many residents of Thuluyah were already speaking of collective punishment when I arrived. Conversations often revolved around the *wadha*, the situation, as the operation was being called.

"They carried out the raid here because we're Sunni and because Saddam was Sunni," Ibrahim Ali Hussein, a sixty-year-old farmer in a blue dishdasha with a white scarf tied loosely over his head, told me. "After this operation, we think one hundred Saddams are better than the Americans."

"We're not criminals," added Hussein Hamoud Mohammed, a fifty-four-year-old veterinarian and Baath Party member. "If they don't come in peace, then we'll attack them with our fists and feet. We'll even bite them."

Unlike some people in the Sunni regions that I visited that summer, the residents of Thuluyah made no secret of their ties to both the Baath Party and Saddam's government; many insisted that they were nevertheless not complicit in the sporadic attacks on Americans that had originated from the groves of date palms along the highway that bisected the town. Throughout his rule, Saddam had been known for courting poor Sunni Muslims, like himself, from small towns along the Tigris, like Thuluyah, at the expense of the wealthier and traditionally powerful Sunnis in Baghdad. Thuluyah had prospered; elegant villas bordered by manicured lawns with vineyards were not uncommon. Commerce was lively: trucks plied the nearby highways, loaded with the succulent watermelons for which the region was famous. Some residents estimated that as many as 90 percent of their fellow towns-people were party members; as many as a fourth were employed by the army, government, or intelligence. As they saw it, Saddam guaranteed their interests and provided them patronage. In a region given to chauvinism and prejudices against Shiites, he had ensured that power would remain in Sunni hands.

"I'll tell you the truth, I liked him, even though he made mistakes," Ibrahim the farmer told me, with no hint of irony. Lounging on floor cushions, he said that Saddam had guaranteed stability, and in a sentiment I heard time and again in the Sunni region, he insisted that only a strong leader could hold a fractious country like Iraq together. He quoted a proverb that expressed the essence of authoritarianism: "He who is scared stays peaceful."

The men in the room began to debate Saddam's whereabouts, the talk in so many towns that summer.

"Only God can know his destiny," one man said.

"He's either outside of Iraq or he was killed," Ibrahim said.

One of Ibrahim's relatives interrupted. "Some people have seen him eating hummus. Some have seen him walking in the street. Some have seen him driving a Volkswagen."

At the condolences for Hashim, where a few of the men still had tags attached to their clothing designating them prisoners of war, guests began to argue over the American intentions in the wake of the raid. Some of them said that retired army lieutenant general Jay M. Garner, the first civilian administrator, had promised that only the fifty-five most wanted Baathists would be targeted. Now, they feared, his successor, L. Paul Bremer, had declared war on all Baathists, even the millions who had joined the party more for its patronage than its politics. They felt themselves besieged. As I listened, I was struck again by the divide. Each side, American and Iraqi, saw their actions as responses to the other's threats. Each side felt the other was forcing it to act. Each side thought the other only understood force. "Now all the people are hunted," said Rahim, the soft-spoken judge, whose thirty-year career had ended with the government's fall. "All the people are being chased. The condition to work in the government meant you should be in the Baath Party. The majority of Iraqis are in the Baath Party."

Over glasses of sweet, dark tea, he shook his head. He spoke pedantically, his years on the bench showing. "The rule is that someone is innocent until proven guilty," Rahim insisted. I wondered whether he had applied the rule when serving under Saddam. "They're stomping all over our dignity. The people can't bear the pressure."

The judge looked at the nods of others around him. "The pressure will lead to resistance, very severe resistance," he said. "It will cause an explosion."

As men in kaffiyehs gathered in the room, smoking cigarettes, a helicopter rumbled overhead, with the familiar thud of gasping air.

"It's better now," Rahim said, nodding. "For a few days, I wouldn't have been able to hear you speak."

Others insisted on the truth of accusations that the military denied—that U.S. soldiers stole gold necklaces, rings, and money from the raided houses, even a string of amber prayer beads and a hunting rifle. One English-speaking relative, a little baffled by what it had to do with Iraq, recalled a slogan he saw written on the back of a Humvee during the week that followed the raid: "We remember 9/11."

Hashim's uncle, Hashim Ibrahim Mohammed, had spent four days in custody. When soldiers entered his house after midnight, he said, they put him on the ground, a boot on his back, and bound his hands with plastic cuffs. Tape was placed over his mouth, a cloth blindfold over his eyes. When he could see again, twelve hours later, he was at Abu Hleij, the air base. He counted on his fingers how many of his relatives had been arrested: fifteen in all. Most were freed a few days later, by the week's end. Echoing other released prisoners, he said his interrogators cast a wide net: Where is Saddam Hussein? Are senior party officials here? Who belongs to the Republican Guard, the military, the Fedayeen? Who has a lot of money in town? At each question, he said, he shrugged his shoulders. "If they shoot at the Americans from any place—fifty kilometers away—they'll come here and arrest us," he told me.

Worse than the interrogation was what Hashim's uncle called the humiliation, a word applied by many residents of Thuluyah to this episode. One recalled how eighty-year-old Mohammed Hammoush, married to his forty-year-old bride only an hour before, was hauled away. Another remembered eighty-five-year-old Faris Abdullah urinating twice in his pants, as he waited in custody at the air base.

At meal times, U.S. soldiers tossed military rations and bottles of water to the crowd. "They treated us like monkeys—who's the first one who can jump up and catch the food," said the uncle, who had been taken prisoner during the war with Iran and spent eleven years in captivity.

The fabric of Thuluyah was stitched by tribal lineages, and the patterns of tradition ran deep. The Jabbour were the largest tribe in Thuluyah, but others were represented too: the Khazraji, Ubaidi, Bujweri, and Bufarraj. As in other towns in the Sunni regions, tribal authority had grown in the wake of the government's fall. On one end of the spectrum, it dictated a deep sense of hospitality. (Even as an American, in a town that had been raided by U.S. forces, I was offered a glass of water and lunch—of chicken, rice, salads, and yogurt—in the same breath as the angry denunciations. Men passed around a tray stacked with packs of cigarettes. My glass of tea was filled again and again.) But on the other end of the spectrum, that tribal code stipulated a brutal frontier justice, which had come to fill a lawless void. This code, rigorous and unforgiving, was paramount.

The sense of honor, pride, and dignity was what made the role of the informer in the U.S. raid so much worse. That man's presence—like a dark family secret—lurked behind every conversation that day in Thuluyah. He had betrayed the village, he had transgressed the law of the countryside, the *rif*, and no one was willing to forget.

Dressed in desert camouflage with a burlap bag over his head, the informer had ambled through a crowd of more than a dozen detainees, as they sat under a sweltering sun, their hands bound with plastic. He had pointed out several, identifying them as suspected insurgents to the U.S. troops. Villagers said they soon recognized the informer's yellow sandals and his mutilated right thumb, which had been severed above the joint in an accident. "We started yelling and shouting, 'That's Sabah! That's Sabah!'" said Mohammed Abu Dhua, another villager who was held for seven days at the base and whose brother died of a heart attack during the operation. "We asked his father, 'Why is Sabah doing these things?'"

The tribal traditions were at work as I spoke to the friends, neighbors, and relatives of the late Hashim's family over those two days. Nearly all of the boy's relatives seemed to know Sabah's identity, but they hesitated to say his name to me or even to say it out loud to one another. He had to stay nameless, even if his namelessness was a façade. Identifying him would encourage vendettas and tribal bloodletting, the chaos that would follow as tribes sought their own justice for the deaths of Hashim and the two other men. Calling him by his name would make more personal the betrayal by one of their own for an enemy who had humiliated and disgraced them. To me, they simply called him the "masked man," a nickname the children outside Hashim's house picked up. Dancing along a dirt path, the children chanted, "Masked man, your face is the face of the devil."

At that point, I realized my questions about Sabah had prompted a stony silence. Men, some belonging to different tribes, on opposite sides of the potential vendetta, exchanged nervous glances. As I leaned back on the wood bench and the background conversations resumed, one of the men turned his head toward me and answered the question I had asked about Sabah's fate. He was trying to be polite, and his voice was soft. "Of course, he'll be killed," he whispered, in an attempt to explain, "but not yet." On my other side, another man made his prediction. His voice was low, too: "They'll rip him to pieces."

IN IRAQ, AN ARAB COUNTRY, TOWNS LIKE THULUYAH IN THE SUNNI HEARTLAND are the most Arab of all—and the least influenced by the grievances of life under Saddam. In the first place, Sunnis had faced little of the withering repression that left mass graves filled with Shiite corpses, bullets in the backs of their heads. In Sunni collective memory, there were few names like Halabja, where in 1988 Saddam's forces had indiscriminately fired chemical weapons at an entire Kurdish village. Sunnis were shaped more by the rest of the predominantly Sunni Arab world. They celebrated its bonds of custom and belief, and they shared its history—the ambitions it once had, as it emerged hopeful from Ottoman domination and Western colonialism, and the frustrations left behind when the pan-Arab and vaguely socialist dreams of independence, strength, and prosperity failed to materialize.

In the preamble to the invasion, the United States had touted Iraq as a potential beacon for change in the Arab world. The Arab world, on the other hand, saw Iraq as the latest victim of an American conspiracy and, even before Saddam's fall, began the inevitable and dangerous conflation of the two very different occupations in Palestine and Iraq. A character on a stage not of its own making, Iraq, in those days, was caught between these two paradigms, neither the U.S. nor the Arab narrative articulating its precise distress.

After the invasion, even in the early weeks of the occupation, the latter narrative had started to seem more relevant, as the Sunni regions began to be pulled toward the Arab conception of Iraq's destiny. Rather than Iraq changing the Arab world, the Arab world, with its complement of impressions, prejudices, aspirations, and resentments, began changing Iraq. As time passed, towns in the Sunni regions began to feel more and more recognizable to reporters like me who had spent years in Arab places. I perceived a new surge of anger after each new catalyst: a shooting deemed unprovoked, a search considered unjustified, or a raid viewed as unwarranted. In three towns that summer—Heet, Fallujah, and Khaldiya—I would hear an Iraqi proverb repeated over and over as the occupation lurched on, violence of all kinds escalated, and more Iraqis were killed: "The mud is getting wetter," the people said. Things are getting worse, it meant. Thuluyah had been the signpost, the beginning.

By early summer, the mud was getting wetter in Heet, a conservative, picturesque Sunni town of 25,000 on the Euphrates 110 miles west of Baghdad. Even before Thuluyah and its endless repercussions, Heet was rising up in anger, beginning what was perhaps the first popular revolt against the U.S. occupation. As so often in the Sunni regions, the catalyst had been mundane.

For U.S. soldiers, the trouble had begun when a rocket-propelled grenade was fired at a convoy on the city's outskirts. The soldiers were rattled but unhurt, yet after two weeks of stones thrown at their vehicles they responded forcefully, transforming what had been a fairly relaxed military presence into a full-blown occupation. In armored vehicles and Humvees, with helicopters overhead, they moved aggressively to search homes—by residents' count, they went through more than thirty—in answer to the attack. Iraqis, perhaps more ready for a fight in Heet than in Thuluyah, declared that a line sustained by tradition and honor had been crossed. Hundreds angered by the house-to-house searches poured into the streets and marched to the police station. They were angry; they felt betrayed. Their town's police officers, who had accompanied the U.S. soldiers, were traitors in the people's eyes. In a tumultuous scene that lasted hours, stones and a grenade were thrown at U.S. soldiers who, in response, fired warning shots, bringing a tense if temporary calm to the confrontation.

By afternoon, the American troops had withdrawn, and the crowd had its way. Having swelled to thousands, the townspeople hauled the police station's furniture to a nearby mosque, then set the station on fire, hurling a few more grenades inside for good measure. The two-story station, its windows shattered, was still smoldering when I arrived a day later. An air-conditioning unit and an unhinged metal door were propped up against the entrance, blocking it. On a wall, a slogan in black read, "God make this country safe."

Men still loitering outside the station, their faces sweaty, gathered around me, shouting their demands: the Americans had to withdraw from the tightly knit community, and they could no longer search homes, particularly not with women inside. I scribbled their words in my notebook, which seemed to satisfy them.

"We will defend our houses, our land, our city," Salman Aani, a forty-two-year-old businessman with an ice-making factory, dressed in a white dish-dasha, told me. "We are Muslims, and we will defend Islam. The first thing we will do is defend our houses."

"The searches made the people boil," shouted Khaled Mohieddin, a mechanic.

Even then, I was struck by the mysterious nature of the opposition. (Choosing a correct name for those who opposed U.S. forces would become an exercise in tedium: one man's terrorist was another's resistance fighter. What was an insurgent? "Militant" seemed a bland term.) American soldiers were now dying in the Sunni Triangle—five in the week before I traveled to Heet—and the U.S. military was blaming what it called former regime loyalists. Perhaps they were, but the armed opposition appeared to be much broader and more eclectic. In Heet, along verdant fields and orchards criss-crossed by canals, the trouble seemed to revolve around the day-to-day details of occupation—an invader, however well-intentioned, unfamiliar with local traditions, running up against a fiercely conservative people infused with ideas of pride, dignity, and honor. Their complaint: foreigners, Christians at that, were not respecting their traditions as Arabs and Muslims. "They are provoking us," said Fawzi Saud, a forty-six-year-old teacher.

I sat with him and his relatives and neighbors in their house, well-to-do by the Sunni town's standards. To a man, they were still angry, unsettled. They traded stories that were perhaps rumor, perhaps fact. Soldiers, they said, entered without knocking and without the men of the houses present. They kept their fingers on their triggers all the time. They spoke directly to wives and daughters—in English, not even in Arabic. No rooms were left unsearched, they said, including bedrooms. "This is a violation of our dignity," the teacher said. "They have no right to enter our house and search it. I'm not a soldier, I'm not a policeman, I'm not a party member."

A day earlier, five soldiers had entered his home at 10:30 A.M. He was not there, but his twenty-year-old son, Ahmed, was. When they knocked, Ahmed asked them to wait. They didn't. Three of them entered with two policemen; the other two circled behind the house. "The Americans made the Iraqis lead them around like dogs," said Abdel-Naser Rashid, another neighbor.

The soldiers stayed for ten minutes, checking the six rooms painted in white and blue. To many Iraqis, with memories of the invasion, the well-armed soldiers remained a fearsome sight, and throughout the search, the teacher's eleven-year-old daughter, Taysir, cried. Ahmad said no weapons were found. The family had hidden their AK-47 assault rifle—nearly every family in the town owned such a gun—in a grove of orange trees and date palms near the house. "We can hide artillery," he said, smiling, then insisting that he would die before soldiers entered his house again. "We have traditions and customs in this city. For them it may be natural, but not for us. If an Iraqi had done this, we would have killed him."

Baghdad had long prided itself on its secularism; for a time under Saddam, religion had played remarkably little role there. But the rural regions, places like Heet, had no such recollections of a time when their lives were not ordered by beliefs and customs deemed sanctioned by religion. The 1970s-era, Baath Party–enforced secularism did not extend here. Like Thuluyah, under the sway of Iraq's resurgent tribes, Heet adhered to a centuries-old code of conduct. Foreigners were respected, residents would say, if they respected them. Gestures of hospitality toward guests were genuine. Many in the town boasted they had accepted into their homes thousands of families fleeing the war. But the teacher delivered a warning that was chilling, I thought, in its implications: the Americans were no longer guests. "They're going to stay a long time, if they have it their way," he said. "But the people will refuse. They won't tolerate it."

Another neighbor, Khairi Abdel-Karim, spoke up. "For us, anyone who comes to rule who is an Iraqi is better than a foreigner," he said.

The men in the room nodded, and the teacher spoke again, citing a proverb quoted so often in the Arab world that it had become a cliché. Clichés, though, can be true. "Me and my brother against my cousin," he said, "me and my cousin against the stranger." Everyone in the modest room, with its unadorned cement floor, nodded again.

Before leaving, I stopped at the American base outside of town. As usual, I found the soldiers sincere, though a little baffled by the turn of events. When they had arrived the month before, they told me, people waved and shouted hello. Now, as the weeks dragged on, greetings were fewer and fewer, and kind words had been replaced by rocks on occasion. When we met, a desert wind blowing and the heat rising, the soldiers had yet to return to the town after the riot at the police station. They asked me about the mood of the place and the condition of the station.

They insisted their intent had never been hostile; in fact, they said, they had gone to great efforts to speak only to the men and avoid being too intrusive during the searches that followed the rocket-propelled grenade attack. "The golden rule applies here just like it does anywhere else," said Captain Andrew Watson, a staff officer with the 3rd Squadron of the 3rd Armored Cavalry Regiment. He and a colleague, Captain Paul Kuettner, said they were not kicking in doors or "smashing up people's homes." They took pains not to be, as Watson described it, "the ugly Americans." But their job, like the job of any soldier, was to go home in one piece. "We try to be as culturally sensitive as possible, but we want to make sure everybody goes home alive," said Kuettner, who served as an intelligence officer. "We're not going to risk the lives of one of our soldiers to be culturally sensitive."

ON JULY 24, 2003, COLONEL GUY SHIELDS, A PERSONABLE OFFICER WHO SERVED for a time as the U.S. military spokesman in Iraq, delivered his assessment of the armed opposition that had surfaced in places like Thuluyah and Heet. "What we've seen is the last desperate reaction by a few people who have no future in this country." They were hopeful words, reflecting optimistic notions. A new day had dawned in Iraq, as U.S. officials liked to say, and once security was restored, reconstruction would follow. A free, democratic Iraq was ahead. The dead-enders—Defense Secretary Donald Rumsfeld's term—were being left behind.

Time and again, though, I was struck by the unintended consequences of Saddam's fall and the country's liberation from his rule. There was the Shiite revival, unexpected in its fervor, empowering men like Muqtada Sadr and Ayatollah Sistani, not to mention a long persecuted clergy that was perhaps the sole institution to survive Saddam's repression. Now, in the Sunni hinterland, I was seeing the first signs of a resurgent religion that refused to fall into easy categories, the tentative steps toward a redefinition of the community's identity.

Religion can be a wild card, as unpredictable as it is powerful, with the potential to redraw the parameters of debate and reconstitute the contours of a struggle. In ten years of reporting, I saw Islam, a politicized version of it, almost completely remake the Israeli-Palestinian conflict. By the 1990s, that existential battle was no longer a distinctly national struggle between largely secular Palestinian demands for statehood and the Zionist vision of a Jewish home on historically Arab land. Instead, the emerging conflict pitted Muslims against Jews in a strictly religious battle. It was the latest manifestation of a feud that dated to the time of the prophet Mohammed when he courted, then banished the communities of Jews after they refused his revelation in seventh-century western Arabia. The view had its mirror image in the messianic, all-or-nothing views of the right wing in Israel. Religion leaves little room for compromise and little room to maneuver. Political demands can be negotiated and concessions offered; tenets of faith are, of course, eternal.

In the summer of 2003, there were hints of that religious absolutism in the Sunni regions of Iraq, where a new ideology—or, perhaps more accurately, a new emphasis—had begun to spring up in conversations. It had less historical grounding and articulated fewer grievances than the vision of Muqtada Sadr, but it was in many ways just as resonant. In the muddle of postwar Iraq, Islam offered direction and meaning when they were scarce in places like Heet and Thuluyah. It provided relentless certainty in unsettled times. It filled a void for a *shaab biduun*, a people without, demarcating the borders of a community that notions of being Sunni, Arab, and Iraqi could all fall within.

I felt this most in Fallujah, a fiercely conservative, traditional place that I had never heard of before the war, but visited often after the invasion. A year later, it emerged as the bastion of resistance (terrorism, to the Americans). The words of the people here struck me like the heat that rushes out after you open an oven door. Fallujah is a dusty Euphrates River town of maybe 250,000 people, bisected by a highway that carries traffic (along with smugglers) toward the Jordanian border and nicknamed by its inhabitants "the city of mosques." The men's eyes here had the threat of anger on a precipice, a fury that I would see more and more.

"I'm angry! I'm angry at this filthy life!" shouted Adnan Mohammed, wearing a soiled blue dishdasha, as I stood with him at the Shaker Thahi Mosque.

"We're becoming like the Palestinians," said another worshipper, twenty-seven-year-old Khaled Abdullah, as the men crowded around me.

"The Americans should get out of our city. It's a Muslim city. We're a Muslim country," cried Shihab Mohammedi, as the muezzins' chants began to echo across the market.

In Fallujah, the tripwire for the cascade of resentments had been a killing. Many killings. On April 28, just weeks after Saddam's government fell, while much of Iraq was still overwhelmed by anticipation over the future and relief at the war's end, protests had erupted in Fallujah over the U.S. presence. Soldiers from the 82nd Airborne Division fired on a raucous, angry demonstration in a residential neighborhood in front of the Leader's School, killing fifteen. Americans labeled the action self-defense and said they had taken hostile fire from the crowd.

Two days later—again saying they had come under fire—U.S. troops killed two more people. The New York–based Human Rights Watch organization differed with the military's version. In a report issued in June, it contended that the military had used excessive force in dealing with the protests. No conclusive evidence of bullet damage on the school where the soldiers were based was found. In contrast, seven buildings facing the school had more than one hundred bullet holes—a finding, the organization said, that was inconsistent with U.S. assertions that soldiers had responded with "precision fire." In the end, the truth actually didn't matter. The residents of Fallujah had already decided what to believe.

It was two months later, a little before one P.M., when I gathered with men from the town at the mosque, a rather ordinary building near a prosperous market. In the market's serpentine alleys, there was the sense of dusk; the punctured corrugated-tin roof allowed in only enough light to create the impression of a nighttime sky. The brick-walled mosque, along the market's edge, was roofless, however, and the sun here was brilliant. A woman in a black *abaya* sat expectantly at the mosque's steel gate, seeking alms. From a doleful, scratchy loudspeaker, the first phrase of the call to prayer was uttered: "God is greatest," repeated four times. The crowd of men gathered in the spacious courtyard of colored tiles paused at the call, a gesture of respect. Only for a moment.

"The Americans are planning, organizing, and working, but they don't realize that they're putting a noose around their necks," said Ahmed Mohammed, the owner of the Islamic Bookstore, across the street from the mosque. Thirty-six years old, with a well-trimmed beard, Ahmed was a soft-spoken man whose politeness shrouded his anger at seeing his country turned upside down. His anxiety stemmed from the presence of American troops in his streets and the unavenged deaths in April.

I asked him whether he was especially religious.

"Everybody in Fallujah is religious. The area is Islamic, it's tribal, and it's conservative," he said. "And we have a proverb: a stranger should be well-mannered."

That proverb unleashed the same litany of complaints I had heard in Heet: how people were hassled at checkpoints by soldiers who didn't speak Arabic, how troops urinated in the streets, and on and on. But surprisingly, Mohammed also ridiculed the Baathists. He dismissed the contentions by U.S. officials that remnants of the party were organizing the attacks in the Sunni towns.

"They're sleeping with their heads under the covers," Ahmed said. "They're scared and they're staying inside their homes. The Baathists were just taking their salaries. They did not believe in the party. They weren't believers in God. If they were believers, they wouldn't have given Baghdad to the Americans in one hour."

Outside, men trickled past wooden stands laden with eggplant, watermelons, onion, cucumbers, and tomatoes and through the mosque's dented blue doors. Some relaxed on cement pillars next to faucets, their sleeves rolled up as they performed ritual washing. Their faces were glistening. Others chatted or shuffled along the floor. Together, they soon gathered inside in rows six deep, their shoes left outside, and performed prayers.

As in any congregation in Fallujah then, complaints coursed through the conversations that followed that afternoon; the mosque was a microcosm of a country coming to terms with *ihtilal*. Their words, the stuff of idle talk, expressed the virtual incomprehension between ruler and ruled, staring across a religious divide.

"Everyone refuses the American presence. Why? It is a Muslim city—not just Fallujah, but all of Iraq—and they are *kuffar*, heathens. They are nonbelievers and we are Muslims," said fifty-year-old Shlash Ahmed, a custodian of the mosque for thirty years. "We don't accept humiliation and we don't accept colonialism."

Abdel-Hakim Sabti sat in the background as I chatted with the men. A dimunitive man with a thick black beard, he preached at the Suheib bin Sinan Mosque on the edge of Fallujah. His front teeth were missing, causing him to slightly slur his words. But his message was clear: he wanted the Americans out, even if he might give them six months to leave. He growled a warning. "If the situation stays as it is, we'll declare jihad. This is what God commands of us."

Saad Halbousi, a fifty-one-year-old former teacher who ran a photo shop, interrupted. "Iraqis consider this period only a truce," he said. "They will eventually explode like a volcano. We've exchanged a tyrant for an occupier."

I knew better than to say a word.

SHARAIYYA: LEGITIMACY. IN ARABIC, IT HAS A RELIGIOUS CONNOTATION, AND ITS meaning is as diverse as its interpretations. Muqtada Sadr's legitimacy came from his father's legacy—a narrative of history, devotion, and suffering. For Ayatollah Sistani, legitimacy was derived from the very institution of the *Hawza*, which he represented. In the Sunni regions of Iraq, legitimacy was a much more amorphous notion. There was no religious hierarchy, no rigid ranking of authority among Sunni clerics. In Fallujah, they still looked to religion, but religion shorn of the rites so familiar in Shiite worship and the age-old narrative of repression and martyrdom.

For many Sunnis, Islam in these days often simply provided the blunt vocabulary of protest: the *ihtilal* was wrong, the Americans were *kuffar*, and those who cooperated with the occupiers had sold their souls. Those collaborators had renounced their faith, an act that was tantamount to a capital crime. People in those towns often could tell what they were against, rather than what they were for; there was an almost nihilist quality to the anger.

Caught in that tangled net of bitter emotions and raw sentiments were the Iraqi police. They had ranked low in Saddam's array of security forces, but emerged as the linchpin of the occupation, the Americans' nominal allies. Fearful of unending commitments, the U.S. military had no intention of serving as the constabulary of the new Iraq—a point iterated by senior commanders just days after Saddam fell. But to extricate themselves, they had to leave an alternative, entirely replacing the vast apparatus of fear that had either disintegrated or been disbanded in the early months of the occupation.

In time, the Americans would envision recruiting and training more than 270,000 security personnel as part of that reconstruction: a new army; a national guard known as the Iraqi Civil Defense Corps; a paramilitary that guarded vulnerable installations like oil pipelines and power stations; and, most important, the police. But the effort that began that summer proved to be one of the greatest, most frustrating, most unpredictable challenges to the occupation. Given the demands of time, not all recruits were vetted well; brought into the ranks were criminals and, as time passed, sympathizers with the insurgents fighting U.S. troops. Morale was low: more often than not, the Iraqis were poorly trained and ill-equipped, especially by comparison with U.S. troops. Many didn't like the perception that they were doing the bidding of their American superiors; those they were supposed to protect didn't like it, either.

In fact, in places like Thuluyah, Fallujah, Heet, and Khaldiya, a town farther west along the Euphrates, the police were seen as collaborators, and they stood at the intersection of all the things that went wrong here after the war—the anger at the occupation, the resentment of the U.S. troops, and the riverbed of religion that channeled those currents into armed opposition, which grew in intensity with each passing month.

That summer, Khaldiya, a farming town on a sun-baked plain, was the first locale where true guerrilla war, in the fullest sense of the term, broke out.

Others would follow—Rammadi, Fallujah, and Samarra. But as early as August 2003, one could see in Khaldiya that attacks on U.S. troops came to embody, in popular imagination, a sanctified resistance; the police, perceived as American lackeys, were caught in the middle.

The catalyst this time was a meeting at the mayor's office in August. Residents believed that U.S. troops were huddling with informers behind closed doors, and rumors raced through the town. (In fact, the gathering in question was a weekly meeting with the mayor, police, and other officials on improvements in the town.) Soon after, two American armored vehicles and a Humvee came under attack; two rocket-propelled grenades were fired from sprawling date groves across the street from the mayor's office, although they missed their mark. The U.S. troops responded and called in reinforcements.

In the search for the assailants, soldiers planted explosives under the corrugated iron gates of two shops along a row of blacksmiths and mechanics, where the men were believed to be hiding. The blasts tore off the gates, incensing a crowd of two hundred that had gathered outside the mayor's office. U.S. troops then evacuated the city's mayor and police chief and withdrew east toward their base near Fallujah. In the ensuing chaos—a staccato burst of escalations that spun out of control, fueled by confusion, misperceptions, and anger—residents held aloft Iraqi flags and began chanting "Islam unites us" and "Yes to freedom, yes to democracy, no to despotism and domination."

A throng threw rocks at the police chief's abandoned pickup, then burned it. Others threw grenades into the newly painted and furnished mayor's office before ransacking it. The looting suggested Baghdad after Saddam's fall or, one generation before, the pillaging in the war with Iran. The people tore doors and windows from their frames. Gone was the new office furniture, along with carpets, floor tiles, and molding painted in bright blues, yellows, and pinks along the ceiling. Fluorescent fixtures and lightbulbs were taken, as were a circuit breaker, a banister, and a bathroom sink. Looters made away with four water tanks from atop the building and started ripping away slabs of concrete lining the roof. Amid piles of half-burned documents, still smoldering, the only fixture left was a squat toilet.

"They don't need that," Said Farhan Abed, a forty-one-year-old resident who was college-educated but unemployed, told me as I looked out at the empty hulk, with a cracked safe at the entrance. "We're sad this building was destroyed. This is our property," he said, "but we feel happy we got rid of the Americans." He surveyed the damage with a hint of embarrassment. "They don't really need all these things," he said, "but if they leave the furniture, the Americans will come back."

After that spasm of anger, U.S. forces rarely ventured back into the city, except to travel the road that traversed a turbulent thirty-mile stretch from Fallujah to Rammadi and was pocked with craters carved by exploding mines. Khudheir Mikhlif Ali, who had replaced the former police chief, met his U.S. counterparts at the base outside town. For their three-day training, police went there rather than have American soldiers come to them. When the police returned, the resistance escalating, they were conflicted at best, angry at worst.

"In my heart, deep inside, we are with them against the occupation," Lieutenant Ahmed Khalaf Hamed said to me, as I sat with them in their beleaguered and besieged police station. "This is my country, and I encourage them."

It was hard to hear those words. Hamed, after all, was an officer with a force trained, equipped, and financed entirely by U.S. authorities. They made possible his livelihood. Then again, this was his town. Thus the ambivalence that would strike me time and again in the Sunni regions. Colonel Shields had his take: he believed he was seeing the last gasp of a fallen regime. The men in Fallujah had theirs: they believed that God would smite the occupiers. And then there was Hamed, snared in between, uneasy about his American patrons and demoralized about his work. The community despised him and his colleagues, accusing them of serving as America's lackeys and spies, charges that weeks earlier had been whispered but were now declared loudly.

Did Hamed, a gaunt man with a mustache, his eyes so black they seemed haunted, sincerely endorse the resistance, or did he say so as a means of surviving? I suspect a little of both. When I asked another officer, Thaer Abdullah Saleh, whether the shadowy armed resistance would succeed, he was uncertain. "God willing," the twenty-seven-year-old officer told me. Other officers in the room hesitated, then spoke up. "It's our right," insisted Dhiaa Din Rajoub, a thirty-eight-year-old colleague sitting on a tattered foam mattress. "This is our country; this is an occupation, and we don't accept it."

"Everybody's upset at the Americans here," Captain Khalil Daham said.

Gaunt and weary like Hamed, he was a thirty-one-year-old officer with twelve years on the job. On the day I sat with them, he was jumpy. When a car blew a tire on the street outside, he said, residents thought the police station had come under attack from angry townspeople. Outside his window sat the charred carcass of the police chief's car, propped on its axle on a pile of sand. If he had the money, he declared, he would quit. "We're sitting here," Daham said, pointing to the window behind him, "and I expect someone to shoot us any minute."

"It's chaos," added Rajoub.

There always seemed to be a sense of siege in Iraq. In Baghdad, the Americans were hunkered down in a four-and-a-half-square-mile area filled with concrete bunkers at the Republican Palace, a quarter that became known as the Green Zone (the Red Zone being the rest of Iraq, a place where some officials of the occupation authority literally never ventured, given the real threats they faced). Set along a wide bend in the Tigris, the marble-walled building, with Saddam's complement of chandeliers, kitschy Louis XIV furniture, and murals portraying imagined Arab glory, was ensconced behind towering concrete fortifications, hulking steel-reinforced bags of dirt and rubble, rolls of razor-sharp barbed wire, and roadblock after checkpoint that themselves became targets of bombs carried by cars and people.

Iraqis in the conservative Sunni areas, bound by tribal traditions, felt themselves no less besieged by the Americans. Who asked them to liberate us? How dare they plow through our streets as if they own them? By what right do they dictate our future? The isolation of the police in Khaldiya was no less intense. In fact, they were beset on all sides: by Americans who expected more, and by Iraqis who expected less.

Their complaints were familiar, being those of fledgling police forces elsewhere in Iraq. They now had uniforms, but they still lacked radios and communications. For a force of one hundred, they said, they had three cars and two motorcycles. Their station itself was a shell of the intimidating, even terrifying post it had been in Saddam's day, when no one dared stare too long at them. Looted soon after the fall of his government in April, the office lacked many of its windows and doors and a single lightbulb lit the hallway. Wires ripped from the wall ran like scars next to a sign that read, "Police in the service of the people." A lone telephone sat on a battered iron cot at the entrance. "It doesn't work," said Mahmoud Ismail, a thirty-five-year-old perched on the bed with an AK-47 assault rifle to his side.

In the middle: the police never escaped that tricky position. Outside the station, several residents told me the police should be fighting alongside the guerrillas against the Americans. "If the policemen work with the Americans, we consider them enemies," said Hakim Talib, a twenty-four-year-old barber. On his storefront window was a leaflet bearing the portrait of a bearded Adnan Fahdawi, described as martyred in an attack on the Americans on July 15. Talib's customer interrupted: "We would attack them just as we attack the Americans." A day later, when I was in neighboring Rammadi, Captain Michael Calvert, a military spokesman, contended that the police should in fact arrest fighters or, at the very least, notify U.S. forces about their activities as a first step toward assuming complete control over security functions. "That's the goal," he said.

When I told Rajoub of this, he threw up his hands. "We are scapegoats here," he said. "How do we satisfy the tribes? How do we satisfy the Americans?" Older than the others, with years of girth to show for it, he shook his head, baffled, knowing no one would understand. "We're sitting here between two fires."

"The people tell us we're selling our country for dollars," said Saleh, a young father of five boys and a girl. "Even our families call us collaborators."

As we chatted lazily across a day, in an office furnished with a lone desk and chair and a black metal frame with a threadbare foam mattress over it, officers said that if they tried to arrest someone with weapons, the suspect would contend the arms were for use against U.S. troops. We're mujahideen, they would say, a religiously resonant term for a guerrilla that police could not contest.

"They claim they are fighting the Americans. If I capture him, he says you're a spy, you're working for the Americans," Saleh told me. "The next morning you wouldn't find any of us. We'll all be slaughtered." He dragged slowly on his cigarette, exhaling exaggeratedly. "We're afraid of them. I swear to God, we're afraid of them."

It was the law of the gun. One day that week, after the policemen had seized two Eastern European–made trucks that were unlicensed, about twelve people showed up at the police station in a pickup, a sedan, and an orange-and-white taxi. The arrivals had red-and-white kaffiyehs wrapped around their faces and carried rocket-propelled grenade launchers and heavy machine guns, and they wanted their trucks back. "They told us to leave or we'll shoot you," recalled Ammar Ibrahim Hammadi, a youthful twenty-two-year-old officer who stood with the other police on the roof that night. "We said, 'We're not leaving. Either we'll kill you or you'll kill us.'" They left, returned half an hour later, then left for good, apparently outbluffed, he said. "They probably would have won," Hammadi told me. "They have RPGs, and we have Kalashnikovs, and we don't even know if they'll work." He lifted his rifle, a gesture at once flippant and discouraged. "This is nothing," he said.

Two days after I left, assailants with their faces masked in red-checkered kaffiyehs ambushed the pickup carrying the force's police chief, Khudheir Mikhlif Ali. They fired more than 120 rounds in the brazen daylight attack. Ali was killed almost instantly, by a shot that tore a cavity through his barrel chest. Three months later, on a limpid morning, a car careened off a road plied by military vehicles and farm trucks and barreled into the entrance of the police station as officers were changing shifts. It was packed with explosives. In a single blast, blinding and deafening, it left a twelve-foot crater. Most of the men I met at the Khaldiya station were killed that day.

In Thuluyah, anger had only mounted in the weeks that followed the raid denoted Peninsula Strike. There was resentment at the Americans, of course, but there was also fury at those perceived to be spies. Most visible among those was Sabah, the informer nicknamed "the masked man" whom the village blamed for the deaths of fifteen-year-old Hashim and two adult men, fifty-five-year-old Jassim Rumayadh and fifty-three-year-old Mehdi Jabbouri.

When I returned to Thuluyah, I learned that Sabah's fate was still unresolved. In a house nestled in a lush farm along a dirt road, I sat with a friend of Nasir's, Qahtan Abdoun, who in terms void of emotion suggested what would be Sabah's destiny. It had become a matter of tribal justice, he said: Hashim was a member of the Aani tribe, and Sabah was a Jabbouri. The Jabbouris were the majority in the town, and Sabah had disgraced them. (His standing was already low in the village: under Saddam, Sabah had served a year in prison for impersonating a government official and was believed to have worked as an informer for the Baathist government after his release in October 2002 in the Abu Ghreib amnesty. Whether that was true or not, they insisted that he had provided information to the U.S. troops—inaccurate information, they might have added—for no better reason than money.) In the vacuum of authority that followed the government's collapse, it was up to the newly resurgent tribes to mete out justice, and Qahtan, sitting in his simple home of concrete floors, was anxious for it to be done.

"I swear to God, it's a disgrace for the Jabbouri people," said Qahtan, a well-built man of thirty-six, prematurely bald and gray. "Some Jabbouris will be killed through tribal revenge. All the other tribes will insult the Jabbouris."

His friend, a thirty-nine-year-old police officer named Ziyad Latifa, spoke up, as we sat on a Persian carpet, drinking tea. "We feel shame and disgrace, shame as Jabbouris. He's no longer a Jabbouri. He's an American. We don't recognize him."

"It's up to the family to handle this matter," Qahtan said.

Sabah was missing, however. His family said that after the raid in Thuluyah, U.S. forces had taken him north to Tikrit, where the 4th Infantry Division was based. Three weeks later, he went to stay across the Tigris in the village of Alim, where his mother's brother lived.

As soon as word of Sabah's travels spread, his brother Salah and uncle Suleiman went to Alim to bring him back. They were desperate. Relatives of the two older men who died in the U.S. raid had made clear what choices Sabah's family now had: either they kill Sabah, or villagers would murder the rest of his family. The logic was cold but, in the context of resurgent tribal justice, flawlessly sound. If the family didn't kill Sabah, an outsider would, setting off blood-soaked vendettas that could last years, maybe decades.

"We sent a message to his family." Abdullah Ali was a stocky retired colonel and brother of one of the slain men; we were talking and drinking bitter coffee at his home near a bend in the Tigris, down a tree-shrouded road from the city's main street. "The message was that it's up to you to close all the doors on this matter." He went on, stretching out a leg crippled by shrapnel during the war with Iran. "If they didn't kill him, the price would be high. We told them if they didn't kill Sabah, we would take twice as many as he was responsible for killing."

Sabah's father appealed, Abdullah recalled; at first, he insisted that Sabah was not an informer. ("All of Thuluyah said Sabah was the informer, but no one actually saw him with their own eyes," the father told me.) But in a town seething with anger, Abdullah and his relatives balked at the suggestion. Trying to buy time, Sabah's father told them he needed permission from U.S. forces before he did anything to Sabah. "We told him that's not our problem," Abdullah recounted. "We told him you must kill your son."

Sabah's brother and uncle brought him back to Thuluyah in July. He never left again. On the day after his arrival, two hours before the dawn call to prayer, the village still shrouded in silence, his executioners entered his room. The decision was already made. Sabah's father and brother each carried an AK-47. And with barely a word spoken, they led him behind the house, nestled in orchards of fig and almond trees, vineyards and groves of oranges and tangerines. His hands trembling, the father raised his rifle and aimed it at his oldest son. "Sabah didn't try to escape," Abdullah said. "He knew he was facing his fate."

I learned of Sabah's last moments from his father, his brother, and five other villagers who said they were told of the account by witnesses. One shot tore through Sabah's leg, another his torso. He fell to the ground still breathing, his blood soaking the parched dust near the banks of the Tigris. His father could go no further, and some accounts say he collapsed. "His father was trembling," Abdullah said. The other son then fired three times, the villagers said, at least once at his brother's head. Sabah, a tall, husky twenty-eight-year-old, died.

"It wasn't an easy thing to kill him," his brother, a wiry man with a goatee, told me.

Sabah's body was buried just hours after the shooting, carried to the cemetery in a white 1980 Toyota pickup. His father and his uncle accompanied the corpse. The brother who had fired the fatal shots stayed at home, next to the family's fields of wheat and vegetables and their orchards, some of which were withering with too little water.

In his simple home of cement and cinder blocks, I sat with Sabah's father as he nervously thumbed black prayer beads, his pace quickening as the minutes passed. We sipped tea. Two overhead fans lazily churned the ovenlike air. Each word of the conversation was labored. Silently I replayed the question I had formulated: Had he killed his son? I already knew the answer. But when the opportunity arrived, I couldn't ask. Even as a journalist, in a job that celebrates provocation and whose standards require confirmation, I couldn't muster the courage to broach the question. In a moment so tragic, so wretched, there still had to be decency. I didn't want to hear him say yes. I didn't want to humiliate him any further. In the end, I didn't have to.

The father's words, deepened by age and grief, were soft, almost a whisper. He dragged on a locally made Sumer cigarette, as he sat cross-legged on the floor against walls painted in yellow with green trim. His eyes glimmered with the faint trace of tears, shimmering.

"I have the heart of a father, and he's my son," he told me, his eyes cast to the ground. "Even the prophet Abraham didn't have to kill his son." He stopped, steadying his voice. "There was no other choice."

12

IF YOU WANT A GAZELLE,
TAKE A RABBIT

In the Sunni regions of Iraq, the summer of 2003 was harrowing. Sabah's killing illustrated how disastrous the trajectory of the occupation had become. Things never seemed to get better, and there was an inexorability to the deterioration. Despite the cheerful, somewhat mendacious veneer that American officials and their Iraqi allies tried to apply to the occupation, violence and unrest were spreading rapidly through parts of the country, and with the identity of the most determined insurgents far from clear, a diffuse dread began to descend over Baghdad. The question of just who was behind the violence was made less abstract by the fact that people, often civilians, were quite definitely dying in ever more spectacular attacks.

There was still a brief moment of optimism in Baghdad, though, where I had returned in October 2003 after a few weeks of vacation in the United States. In the capital, the streets, surprisingly, seemed cleaner, and trash was swept into tidy piles at intervals of a few intersections, waiting to be carted to the city's outskirts. The heat, that airless cloak that had lain over Baghdad all summer, had finally broken, and the city felt like the pacific morning after an especially powerful storm. Curbs were newly painted in yellow and white. A coat of yellow had even been thrown on the traffic signals. They looked better, even if they still didn't work. As each month passed, Baghdad had been looking less like its sister cities in the Persian Gulf—Dubai, Abu Dhabi, Kuwait City, and Doha—and more like distant Khartoum, with which it shared a dusty, dreary feel. But during the peaceful week of my return, I found a city with a fleeting, fragile sense of normalcy. I wondered if the inherent contradictions of the occupation might one way or another eventually reconcile themselves.

I had not seen Mohammed Hayawi, the owner of the Renaissance Bookstore on Mutanabi Street, since the summer, when he had been furious at both the occupation and the reconstruction. Now, he was in a far better mood. Security had improved, he said, by perhaps 60 percent. Electricity cuts persisted, but crime was down. He was making six, maybe seven times more than he had two months before, and was selling books from Lebanon and Iran that had long been banned. The Americans deserved some credit, he said, but Iraqis should get far more.

Dragging on a cigarette and grinning, he quoted a popular Iraqi proverb. I suspect I have never heard a better summation of the occupation: "If you want a rabbit, take a rabbit," he said. "If you want a gazelle, go ahead and settle for a rabbit." He meant that the Americans would give what they wanted to give, and Iraqis might as well take what they could get. Six months into the occupation, Mohammed was feeling okay about the rabbit.

The street where he worked was itself undergoing a kind of renaissance; freedom to some uneasy souls still seemed a bit like chaos. Just weeks earlier, the streets had been deluged with religious posters, akin to Iraqi pop art; Shiite iconography was surging. Now the mix of public expression were more eclectic and exuded a tantalizing hint of what might come: sidewalk displays were crowded with new issues of *FHM*, *Maxim*, and *GQ*, their covers adorned with scantily clad women. (A sign read: "Please, do not browse the magazines. Thank you.") These new arrivals vied for space with landmark works of Shiite thinkers such as Mohammed Baqir al-Sadr (*Our Philosophy* and *Our Economy*) that would have once earned vendors prison time or worse. Not all the recent additions were reassuring to Western eyes: on rickety stands for fifty cents were compact discs of Osama bin Laden's messages and sermons from militant Egyptian clerics like Abdel-Hamid Kishk and Mohammed Hassaan. Also represented was a radical Syrian preacher named Mahmoud Quul Aghassi, nicknamed Abu Qaqaa, whom I would soon learn more about. Down the street were pamphlets of the Communist Party and a Hebrew-Arabic dictionary. Apropos of the bewildering mix, one of the book-sellers quoted a line by Mutanabi, the tenth-century sage and namesake of the promenade where we stood. "With so much noise," he said, striking the tone of formal Arabic, "you need ten fingers to plug your ears."

"From here on, it was forbidden," the vendor, Abu Zeid Ta'i, said to me outside Hayawi's bookstore, waving his hand across the titles. He stood proudly over his display of religious books, jostled by another stand offering posters of the prophet Mohammed's genealogy and notebooks with American pop stars on the covers.

The vendor turned to the traffic that snarled the street and shook his head. Horns drowned out his words, and seamlessly, he tempered his appreciation. In the past, he said, the red double-decker buses had been barred from these streets, as had the trucks that seemingly stopped where they pleased. "Look at it," Abu Zeid said. "America is a great power, and these are simple things." After the good news there was usually the obligatory "but" added to summa-tions of the *wadha*, the situation. Iraqis and Americans would never measure progress in the same way. Even on better days, neither had the same definition of improvement. For the Americans, the comparisons began with the day Saddam fell, or maybe the months before the invasion. Iraqi comparisons were rooted in memories from a generation ago, and Iraqis always expected the Americans to restore those golden days of the seventies.

The issue of security provoked the same conflicting assessments. Hayawi said he felt safer and there were more police in the streets now. But, he said, security has an absolute quality—a person either feels safe or does not—and many Baghdadis clearly still felt uneasy.

A sentiment was starting to emerge—voiced, surprisingly, by some Ameri-can supporters of the war—that Iraqis were better equipped to bring order to a country that U.S. authorities would never completely understand. The Americans would always be strangers in another land; they would never see all the layers and shades of meaning. This was a remarkable shift from the aftermath of the war, when the U.S. military was seen as all-powerful, almost godlike in its technology and force. The Americans were more than human now, and while expectations never flagged, Iraqi faith in U.S. ability did, despite the brief respite I was witnessing.

"The people of Mecca know its canyons." It was a proverb I heard quoted several times on Mutanabi Street after my return. Hayawi was one of those who repeated it. He was fond of larger-than-life gestures and had a flair for the dramatic and theatrical. He would wave his hands, then bring them down in an arc so that they were cupped as he drove home a point. He would shake them; he would part the air. While he made an especially provocative point, his hands would remain still, his words reinforced with a stare. "When you come inside this store, do you know what's upstairs?" he asked me. "You can't, and neither can the Americans. The Americans can never know what they'll find upstairs." He gestured, this time with his head, as the tea arrived on a battered steel tray. "The Americans now are lost. They have maps and guides, but they can't provide security in any area other than by provoking the people."

Outside his shop, construction workers hauled gravel, renovating a street whose history stretches back to the Ottoman Empire. Bags of cement were piled under a scaffolding built from warped timbers. Bakers hawked pastries on sidewalks, and donkey carts competed with bumper-to-bumper traffic. Shoppers stopped briefly at a tea stand, a file cabinet converted by means of a butane tank and a charred kettle. Nearby were posters for *Terminator 3* and *Matrix 2*. Down the street was the storied Shahbandar Café, with its antique water pipes, lazy overhead fans, and ancient-looking wooden benches. Its brick and plaster walls, painted once more in white, were cluttered with the memorabilia of another age: scenes of Baghdad in the 1920s, a portrait of the Iraqi wrestling team in 1936, a picture of King Feisal, Iraq's first monarch, black-and-white photos of singers and poets.

Hayawi's desk was cluttered with Iraqi dinars, bundled tightly with rubber bands. "The Iraqi people want the dinar to be three dollars again," he told me, staring at the stacks of money. (The Iraqi dinar had last earned that price before the war with Iran.) His sentiment suggested to me the standard by which Iraqis were measuring progress.

"It has changed, definitely," he said. "It has changed for the better. But we wish that it could be even better." He smiled at the words, realizing how they sounded. "We don't want to hear explosions, we don't want to hear about more attacks, we want to be at peace," he said. He had dark bags under his eyes, whether or not he'd slept. "The Iraqi person wants to put his head on his pillow and feel relaxed. Iraq has suffered so much."

▪ ▪ ▪

NASIR HAD NONE OF MOHAMMED'S OPTIMISM. IN FACT, HE WAS QUITE PES-simistic, and he freely shared his gloom with me as we drove with Karim through Baghdad, the south, and the rougher parts of central and western Iraq. Nasir's anxious despair stemmed, in large part, from the predictions of a man named Hazem, a fortune-teller whose family Nasir had known since childhood. I would not meet Hazem until much later, but I was always struck by his prognostications, which Nasir would relay to me. They were uncanny, oddly insightful, although it also seemed to me that they could be interpreted in any way that might be appropriate to the situation.

The relationship between Nasir and Hazem went back a generation, to when Hazem's mother, a matron from Najaf with her own twelve children, helped raise Nasir's half-sister, Samah. Hazem was her middle son. Trained as an agricultural engineer, he fought in the war with Iran, where he lost his right arm in a battle in 1984. Near death, and depressed by the amputation, he was nursed back to health by his mother, who eased his anxiety by reciting the Quran almost around the clock. His recovery was a road-to-Damascus experience. Not all that fervent in his beliefs before the war, he became exceedingly devout. He began to display some of his mother's talent for telling the future, too, and a decade on, he had gained a substantial reputa-tion as a soothsayer in his neighborhood of Bayaa. He was known as Abu Ali, Father of Ali, Ali being his oldest son.

Among Islamic mystics, there is a tradition of asceticism and poverty. The term "Sufi" itself comes from the word *suf*, wool, a reference to the rough woolen robes once donned by mystics. In medieval times, some wandered the roads, relying on God's grace and the generosity of fellow Sufis. Some were known for their eccentric spiritual ecstasies, exuberances that flouted the conventions of the day. Often they carried no more than a prayer rug, a rosary, and a beggar's bowl. From the pious poverty they practiced, we have the word "fakir," from the Arabic *faqir*, or "poor one."

By choice or not, Hazem practiced a very pious poverty. His blue dish-dasha was riddled with holes, from the cigarettes that he constantly smoked with a cheap, black plastic filter. He had two teeth above, a few more below, all blackened by decay. He would rarely make eye contact. Usually he cast his eyes downward as he mumbled prayers. Deep in thought, he seemed lost. Then, for a fleeting moment, he would look up, smile, and utter a few words, usually maddeningly cryptic ones.

From 1998 on, at the urging of his sister, Nasir saw Hazem every month, sometimes every two weeks, depending on Nasir's mood. They would meet in the street or inside Hazem's two-room house—one room in which he, his wife, and their five children slept, the other where they cooked. Most often, perhaps being a little embarrassed by his circumstances, Hazem met Nasir at the door, where they would chat. Nasir never paid Hazem for his counsel, never even offered money: that would probably have humiliated Hazem. Instead, Nasir brought him rice, sugar, tea—every Iraqi received rations of these under Saddam—and an occasional chicken, a luxury in the especially grim days of U.N. sanctions. These offerings were more like a gift than a payment for services. "He is like a guide," Nasir would tell me. "He is like a preacher to me."

Nasir liked the fact that Hazem didn't moralize. Despite his devotion, Hazem never passed judgment on Nasir's drinking of alcohol, which is prohibited under Islam. Nasir, in turn, could speak freely with Hazem. At a time when Nasir's father was no longer speaking to him and when he was still reeling from the deaths of his mother and two best friends, Hazem provided stability and comfort. His words suggested utter certainty, an assurance that Nasir appreciated. "God will open the road," he would tell Nasir. "You should wait, you should be patient." Then, of course, he would add, "You should pray."

I credited Hazem with helping me keep Nasir as a partner in those days. Since the war, I had grown to rely on Nasir increasingly. He was what is sometimes called a fixer, and he was a natural. In Iraq, I would look to him for his sense of a situation—was it too edgy, were we unwise to stay? With or without Arabic, I was still a foreigner, and it provided a welcome sense of security to work with an Iraqi who knew the country's canyons. Thanks to his work with the Tourism Board, Nasir often had acquaintances in the towns we visited, and his crucial introductions often opened doors to days of reporting. Occasionally, we could work a scene together, compiling notes afterward. More often, he would help line up the hard-to-get interview, drawing on a little of his Baath Party intimidation, an innate swagger, and a tenacity that

left me in awe. Time and again, Nasir provided the break on a story that probably would have been impossible to get otherwise—from the chance to sit
down with Muqtada Sadr after the war, to my conversation with Sabah's
father in the unsettled town of Thuluyah. Nasir could be very persuasive.

Just as important, Nasir was great company. His jokes were accompanied
by his random displays of extreme vulgarity: "The traffic," he complained, as
we sat in a snarled street in Baghdad. "I love it. Fucking shit." Sometimes his
venom was directed at me: "My hair will be gray because of you. By the end
of the year, we'll be old guys." Or, "You deprive me of my girlfriends, you
deprive me of fucking, you deprive me of everything. I am deprived, and you
are responsible for my deprivation."

More often than not, we shared a fatalistic humor. During the invasion,
his favorite lines concerned what he considered his inevitable incarceration.
"I'll be in prison tomorrow," he predicted, glowering, as he helped me flout
the government's rules for the hundredth time. During the aftermath, he
grew grimmer. "I'll be dead tomorrow," he would say, speculating on how we
might meet death—car bomb, rocket-propelled grenade, machine-gun fire.
No, he would insist, these fates were conventional. Daggers—they would be
our end. And then we would laugh, even after having made and heard the
prognostication many times before.

Although we had spent every day together for a year, I still had no real
understanding of Nasir's politics. His world-weariness seemed to transcend
the upheavals in his country. "It's a beautiful mess, this new Iraq," he said,
enigmatically, around the time we saw Mohammed Hayawi, in the fall of
2003. Forced to survive on his own for so many years, having lost so much he
held dear, Nasir found it hard to believe in anything. Belief would only augur
further disappointment in a country where there was already so much. "I
don't care about these parties," he once told me. "I don't care about Sunni or
Shiite. I'm neutral with everyone. I have my own thoughts going through my
head." For a while, the work we did together, the dissemination of what we
saw as truth, was what he could put his trust in. As time went on, he also put
his faith in our friendship, which, surprisingly, Hazem encouraged.

"You should listen to Shadid," Hazem once told Nasir. "You should do
whatever he says." These were probably the luckiest words ever uttered on my
behalf. When Nasir argued with the *Washington Post*'s Baghdad bureau chief,

Rajiv Chandrasekaran, and threatened loudly to quit, Hazem would counsel patience. "Wait for Shadid," he would say. When Nasir and I fought, around the time of Sabah's killing (an argument worsened by the tension inherent in that story), Hazem tried to mediate. "Shadid's a good friend," Hazem told Nasir, "and he will serve you. He will not forget. When those people see that someone trusts them, they trust you." Hazem offered this counsel long before I ever met him.

In the fall, as the insurgency in the Sunni regions escalated, Hazem's words grew less reassuring. This was around the time of our visit to Mohammed Hayawi, a brief moment of optimism. But Nasir and Hazem both predicted worse times ahead. Wear your flak jacket, Hazem told Nasir, and always keep one of the jackets in the car. Next, he warned Nasir that he was being too pushy pursuing our work, too zealous. "You should be careful," he told him. The warning prompted Nasir, a little desperate, to ask whether he was going to be killed somehow. "No," Hazem said, "but the situation will be messy. It will be scary."

Hazem mumbled his prayers again, then looked up and, as usual, smiled at his friend. "You should be very careful," he said as Nasir looked at him quizzically. "You should be very, very careful."

AS THE OCCUPATION WENT ON THROUGH THE FALL AND INTO THE WINTER, A feeling that recurred often while I covered Iraq came back once more. It was the fear that I was misunderstanding everything, seeing nothing. The longer I stayed in the country, the less I felt I understood the events that were over-taking it. Before the war, covering Iraq had been relatively simple: permission from the government to travel had been difficult to obtain, so I rarely left Baghdad.

The voices I heard in the city were now a thunderous, confusing, swirling din that reminded me of the American reaction to the attacks on September 11, 2001. The depth and breadth of people's emotions continually shocked me. The people I met contradicted one another and themselves. All the old truths had disappeared; new ones had yet to be found. Iraq faced a lacuna: there was nothing to be done to restore the certainties, right or wrong, that had been shattered by the war. Everything was shifting. Nothing was definite.

Morning's hopes were shunted aside by evening's unexpected loss and by silent noontimes of despair.

Over the summer and into the fall of 2003, the Sunni resistance commanded the attention of most reporters, U.S. officials, and even Iraqis. U.S. troops were dying, as were Iraqis, and the divide, perhaps inherent in the conditions of occupier and occupied, was growing wider. Raids like the one visited on Thuluyah became more common in Sunni regions, while the guerrillas became more sophisticated, better organized, and more lethal. No less spectacular was the onset of devastating bombings in the capital that emanated from the darkest recesses of terrorism's cold, calculating brilliance. On August 7, a new chapter of violence opened in Baghdad when a murky underground network—thought to comprise loyalists of Saddam's government, or Islamic militants from other Arab countries who had trekked across Iraq's porous borders, or perhaps a combination—deployed a suicide car bomb at the Jordanian Embassy, killing nineteen people. As with almost every attack, there was a message: Jordan had tacitly supported the American invasion. With the bombing, Jordan and other Arab countries were warned against supporting the occupation with troops.

Less than two weeks later, another suicide bombing—over a thousand pounds of Soviet-made explosives piled on a flatbed truck—targeted the lightly guarded U.N. headquarters on Baghdad's outskirts. Twenty-three people were killed, including the United Nations' chief envoy in Iraq, the respected Sergio Vieira de Mello, whose death was deeply mourned inside the country and abroad. A month later, a second bombing would strike the same headquarters, killing two more people. Another message: if the U.N. was forced to withdraw, the occupation would lose a crucial element of legitimacy and the expertise and resources, both financial and diplomatic, that might pull it back from the abyss. (Within three months, the number of foreign U.N. personnel in Iraq would dwindle from 650 people to about 40. None of them were in Baghdad.)

Perhaps the most far-reaching act of bloodshed that month, though, took place not in Baghdad, but in Najaf, home of Imam Ali's grave. First built in A.D. 791, then destroyed and constructed again over the millennium, this is one of the grandest of Shiite shrines, its very presence inspiring the construction of hospices, schools, libraries, and Sufi convents. Millions of scholars and pilgrims visit each year, crossing a marbled floor shadowed by the lustrous dome and minarets in a gold tiara bordered in tiles of turquoise, blue, and yellow. Each day, funeral processions pass through the crowds, bearing caskets draped in ratty blankets and destined for the Wadi al-Salaam, one of the world's largest graveyards, which lies beside the shrine and has given rise to a profitable industry of body washers, agents to sell plots, record keepers, and gravediggers. Some religious Shiites spend a lifetime saving enough money to be buried within the dun-hued, labyrinthine graveyard; the very internment is thought to bring blessings to the deceased. Through its history, Najaf has been as much a city for the dead as for the living.

The city and its shrine, enjoying a revival in the invasion's aftermath, were an unsettled place in August, as the bombings tore through the Jordanian Embassy and U.N. headquarters in Baghdad. Then, toward the end of the month, came an attack on Mohammed Saeed al-Hakim, one of the four grand ayatollahs in the sacred city. A gas cylinder hooked to an explosive detonated after noon prayers and tore a four-foot hole in the brick-and-plaster wall of the grand ayatollah's office; he was only slightly wounded with scratches on his neck from flying glass, but three of his bodyguards were killed.

Their funeral, a day later, was as much an outpouring of anxiety as a ritual. Hundreds of Shiites surged through the city, the stifling air laden with their sweat and anger. When they arrived at the ayatollah's office, on a street of dusty two-story buildings, the crowd waved the green, red, and white flags symbolic of Shiite Muslim fidelity. Some carried pictures of Hakim, a willowy, bearded cleric in his late sixties, along with black-and-white photos of the three dead bodyguards. Others carried the guards' coffins, cloaked in embroidered black velvet. Rumors coursed through the city; no one ever was sure who carried out the attack—loyalists of Saddam, Sunni fanatics, or rivals in Najaf—and the mystery added to the sense that now, in Iraq, almost anything could happen.

Later, I walked through Najaf's market, past the vendors selling tokens of devotion—boys selling green shawls for blessing, prayer beads with green tassels, prayer stones made from the mud of Karbala, and amber rings arrayed on a green mat atop a wooden cart. Toward the end of the street was Nizar Yusuf, wearing the white turban of a Shiite cleric and the youthful beard of a religious student. He was dispirited, he told me, and very afraid. "It's already started," Yusuf said. "We know from reading history that when it becomes bad, it only gets worse." Nearby was Sadiq Kadhim, a shopkeeper watching over his red-and-blue buckets of pungent pickled cauliflower, carrots, and cucumbers. "There will be more attacks," he told me. "There will soon be something else."

A week later, there was—something worse, a savage attack of awesome proportions whose carnage sent shudders through the country. A car packed with explosives was parked about thirty-five yards from the shrine of Imam Ali, a site all Shiites seek to visit at least once in their lives. The blast tore through the crowded street, killing Hakim's influential and powerful uncle Ayatollah Mohammed Baqir al-Hakim and at least eighty-one others. The bomb was detonated soon after the end of the Friday prayers that Hakim led; it was a moment when the narrow streets and ocher markets of the holy city were teeming with pilgrims, worshippers, and shoppers. From this terrifying event flowed a trail of misery and devastation unparalleled since Saddam's fall. The suspects were the same as in the bombings at the Jordanian Embassy and the U.N. headquarters—loyalists of Saddam, or foreigners, or both—but no one really knew. Speculation ran wild.

The scenes in Najaf that day reminded me of Baghdad during the invasion. Brick façades of shops had been sheared away. Burned, mangled, and dismembered bodies littered the streets and were trampled by others running in confusion and panic for safety. Outside the mosque, where hawkers gathered every day with drinks, religious trinkets, and food, the wood stalls lay splintered in blackened pools of grime and blood mixed with charred metal and brick. Along one sidewalk, men sifted with their hands through shards of glass for silver rings blown from their display cases. Cars had been flipped and hurled onto the sidewalk, and pieces of the wreckage were thrown through the windows of the restaurants and shops frequented by Iranian and Indian pilgrims.

By dusk, thousands of residents, tribesmen, and clerics were milling around the shrine, crowded together in an impromptu wake. Some stretched their necks to see the damage, and others clapped their hands in a gesture of resignation. Many of their faces were grim, and their looks of shock and anxiety suggested more trouble ahead. Into the night, lit by a crescent moon—a good omen—desperate residents dug with pickaxes and bare hands into piles of brick and debris. Shouting "God is greatest," they searched for survivors, an effort motivated more by piety than hope.

The body of Hakim was never found, save perhaps for a few shreds of flesh that a cleric brought in a bag to Najaf's hospital. Throughout the city, rumors arose that he had somehow survived, leaving with his driver and two body-guards in his light blue sport utility vehicle after the Friday prayers. Others found such talk distasteful and offered their own proof. A deputy of Hakim's told me that a single stone from the ayatollah's prayer beads had been found at the site. Others said his amber ring, his pen, or his watch had been found in the street and that his papers were strewn in the muck of charred debris and blood that gathered along the shrine's walls of blue and tan brick. At eight o'clock that night, from the loudspeaker at the mosque, bathed in green and white lights, a voice finally spoke: "We are from God and to God we return," the voice said.

At that moment, everyone seemed to know the news that was to come. A hush fell across the crowd as his death was announced. One man started sob-bing uncontrollably. Another laid his head on a Styrofoam cooler. Along the curb, men cried into their soiled dishdashas or sobbed into their hands. "It will only get worse," said one of them, Mohammed Aboud, as he heard the news.

Hakim had been an enigmatic and alluring character in Iraqi politics. Although he had nothing like the standing of Ayatollah Sistani, he was still a ranking cleric, with credentials that far overshadowed Muqtada Sadr's. As important, he was the scion of one of Iraq's most prominent clerical families, and his father, who died in 1970, had been a respected and revered grand aya-tollah. Hakim himself had gone into exile in 1980 in Iran, where he later assumed leadership of the Supreme Council for the Islamic Revolution in Iraq.

The council attempted to lead the exiled Shiite opposition to Saddam's government, but it suffered from its association with Iran, particularly during the 1980–88 war, when it took part in Iranian attacks on Iraqi soil and was given some responsibility over camps where Iraqi prisoners were held. Hakim's reception, upon his return in May 2003, was muted. But he was one of the rare clerics with both political acumen and a religious pedigree and was thus seen as crucial in U.S. attempts to court religious Shiites. Without him, U.S. officials lost perhaps their most important link with the community at a time that they acknowledged as delicate. Sadr was implacably opposed to the occupation, in any incarnation, and Sistani, as he would continue to do, was refusing to meet U.S. officials.

Hakim's funeral took place the next week, a three-day pilgrimage from Baghdad to Najaf. Largely symbolic, the coffin was cloaked in green and black and covered in red and white plastic flowers. By far, the largest crowds gathered at the funeral's start, in the Shiite neighborhood of Kadhimiya, where a sea of humanity swept across the shrine and its courtyard. Mourners could only guess at the numbers—fifty thousand, sixty thousand, seventy thousand, or, in the exaggeration of a grieving guard, two million. Only a portion could enter the shrine.

As men carried the coffin to the waiting truck atop two poles, it tilted toward the ground, and crowds surged forward to steady it. In the march that followed, men, some of them shirtless, chanted so fervently that they collapsed and had to be carried away by ambulances. The ambulance sirens clashed with the cacophony of grief. Shiite chants blaring from scratchy speakers washed over Quranic recitations from mosque loudspeakers. Drummers led the procession, their cadence mirrored by the rhythm of fists beating chests. Women wearing black *abayas* slapped their heads, sprinkled with mud to signify their sorrow. The truck carrying Hakim's coffin crawled along, escorted by seas of mourners that took three hours to pass any point on the route.

Along the streets, men lined up in rows two and three deep to watch the procession. Some sobbed openly, while others were red-eyed. Many stared ahead, with the blank look that grief brings. One of the men was Qahtan Hamid, a fifty-eight-year-old resident of Baghdad who thumbed amber worry beads as men sprayed water overhead to cool the sweltering crowd. His words of mourning were steeped in Shiite memory: "Every time we present more martyrs," he said to me, "we will gain more strength."

The death of Hakim further buttressed Sadr, who was left as one of the few Shiite religious figures organizing at the grass roots. That Hakim's movement was forced to cede that ground to Sadr proved a disaster for the Americans. As usual, Sadr refused to play by the rules, either those haphazardly decreed by the U.S. occupation or the ancient traditions handed down by the *Hawza*, to which he ostensibly pledged loyalty.

By July, the young cleric was already exhorting followers to expel American soldiers from Najaf and demanding the dissolution of Iraq's Governing

Council, an advisory panel of twenty-five that Bremer had appointed earlier that month. (With a Shiite majority and dominated by leaders of the formerly exiled Iraqi opposition, the panel had received Hakim's blessing, but as the occupation unraveled and the council's lack of real power became apparent, it gradually lost in the eyes of most Iraqis, many of whom saw it as a puppet of the U.S. administration.) At the time of its appointment, Sadr stopped short of issuing a call to arms or urging a holy war against U.S. troops, demands that would have almost surely incited more violence. But in a declaration that would prove pivotal the following year, he issued an appeal to form an Islamic militia to resist "submission, humiliation, or occupation"—code for both the U.S. administration and those he saw as its proxies in the Governing Council.

Sadr's militia was called the Mahdi Army, after the messianic Twelfth Imam, who was said to have vanished in the ninth century. Fearing that the Americans would crack down on an armed movement, Sadr and his lieutenants insisted that its cadres would not carry weapons and that the militia itself would devote itself to social work and the poor. When confronted with observations otherwise, they would simply skirt the questions or dismiss them. (As one Sadr lieutenant put it to me that month, sitting in their cramped office in Sadr City, "We are founding the army without weapons. There is no intention to use any force.")

Indeed, at the time, the militia was not very threatening. Widely ridiculed for its ragtag quality, it was composed of young, unemployed toughs, dressed in trademark black and emboldened by guns. It numbered no more than five hundred. They had looted arms from Iraqi military stores, but they did not often carry these on the street. Their training, what they had of it, called for discretion. But the militia's name alone, laden with symbolism, suggested the mystical devotion that some of Sadr's followers would soon display. And as early as July 2003, long before shooting started between Sadr's men and American forces, the intent of the Mahdi Army was becoming clear. "To those who say we can't expel the occupation forces from Najaf, I say we can," Sadr told tens of thousands of followers at the sprawling Kufa Mosque, where his father had preached. "We must end American hegemony over our sacred place." He insisted that the *Hawza*—meaning him and his followers—should run Iraq. "This mass gathering today proves the biggest trend is support for the seminary, not support for the Iraqi Governing Council," said Sadr, in a white funeral shroud. "The Iraqi Governing Council was set up by the Americans and it must be disbanded."

American officials, whose mantra was to try to keep the Shiites on board, viewed Sadr as a potentially dangerous demagogue. Sadr and his followers, in turn, saw provocations time and again on the part of the Americans. There was truth on both sides. Sadr's populism was often nativist and xenophobic (in particular, anti-Iranian) and, in opportunistic fashion, his men seized on the deeply resonant imagery of faith and family to rally support for political ends. Likewise, Sadr's enmity toward the United States was hardened by missteps on each side that, given the gravity of their consequences, almost seemed premeditated. None were, but they created an inexorable momentum toward conflict, motivated in part by self-preservation, in part by a savvy sense of the street. While Sadr and his men, like many Iraqis, bristled at the occupation, I never viewed the movement, early on, as implacably hostile to U.S. forces, nor the confrontation as inevitable, and I actually saw a change in the movement's position as the months passed and as they felt provoked.

In June, with the occupation already a mess, I asked Riyadh al-Nouri, Sadr's brother-in-law and a pivotal figure in the movement, whether he trusted the American administration. His answer was decidedly noncommittal. "I'm not able to say," he told me, as we sat in his home in Najaf, a simple building of concrete floors decorated with a portrait of Sadr's father. "Their actions will prove our trust or not." He spoke slowly, measuring his words. In moments like these, Nouri struck me as a much more intellectually formidable figure than Muqtada Sadr. "If they finish their work in Iraq—reconstruction, agreement on a permanent government—at that time we can say whether they are occupiers or liberators. We cannot accuse them now before we know, before we are certain what they are doing." I was struck what followed: "In the past, I said if the Americans came, it would be better than Saddam."

Of course, neither side was talking to the other—that lack of communication would dog U.S. efforts in almost every aspect of the occupation—and Sadr himself was often contradictory in his public statements. While Nouri may have appeared relatively flexible, other Sadr lieutenants were far more dogmatic, particularly after the appointment of the Governing Council in July. The conflicting pronouncements by those lieutenants prompted an occupation official at the time to complain of "a degree of confusion and obfuscation."

Seeing all this, I sat down to discuss it with Hume Horan, a storied State Department Arabist who had served as an ambassador to five countries and completed tours in Iraq, Jordan, Saudi Arabia, and Sudan. Before his death in July 2004, he served six months in Baghdad, where part of his portfolio— he was responsible for religious affairs—was trying to unsnarl Shiite politics. It was a formidable job and, of the Americans here, probably only Horan could have tackled it.

Athletic and quiet, Horan was the son of Margaret Robinson Hume, a free-spirited woman from a prominent Washington family, and an Iranian man, Abdollah Entezam, who once served as Iran's foreign minister before the 1979 revolution. He was much more the son of his mother than his father. When I first met him, he struck me as a Brahmin from New England; he had the patrician bearing, a reflection perhaps of his years at Harvard. He was cerebral, fascinated by the arcane. On his off-hours in Baghdad, he could be found reading, in Arabic, the medieval poetry of Ali Zayn al-Abidin, the fourth Shiite imam. As a younger man, he had audited classes in Sharia, or Islamic law, at a university in Libya. He knew what he was talking about.

Horan, to his discontent, worked from the Republican Palace, known as the Green Zone or the Emerald City. The Green Zone had, at this time, emerged as a symbol in Baghdad—as many symbols, in fact. To some Iraqis, it embodied their frustration. It was protected by coiled wire, a maze of mammoth blast walls, Abrams tanks, and Apache helicopters, and because it occupied some of Baghdad's central real estate, its fortifications endlessly snarled traffic, disrupting life. Twenty-minute commutes sometimes turned into ordeals of two hours or more. The Green Zone was also a symbol of the muddled vision that the occupation always projected, as its staff had been chosen more for their partisan loyalty than for diplomatic skills suited to the management of an occupation of one of the Middle East's most strategically important countries. Its confident, bright, and self-assured twenty- and thirty-somethings were drawn from the ranks of Washington lobbyists, congressional staffers, policy enthusiasts, and the public-relations specialists less charitably known as flaks. Their political trustworthiness was unquestionable—most were enthusiastic Republicans—but their experience was woefully lacking.

(At a poker game in Baghdad, I once met two men in their early twenties who had come to Baghdad as volunteers. They were helping oversee nongovernmental organizations in Sadr City. Describing their job, one exclaimed: "Iraqis rock!") Most of the staffers so rarely emerged from the zone's palm-shrouded, formerly manicured villas and palaces that they had no notion of what was going on in the country they were supposed to rule. Adding to their incapacity was the fact that they rarely saw eye to eye with the U.S. military. The military wanted Iraq's reconstruction to be a priority; only improvement in people's lives, they said, would siphon away the frustration that fed the insurgency. With a greater presence in the country's outlying areas, the military felt it spoke with authority. The civilians had their answer: they could not do their job unless security was first established in what had become a truly dangerous place—and security was up to the military.

But to Horan, it was the suffocating isolation the palace came to represent that was most frustrating. The Green Zone was truly a world unto itself. Men and women in shorts—garments never seen outside the palace—jogged along streets wide enough for military parades. Afterward, with rugged chic in the desert heat, some would don cargo pants and safari vests. Others adopted Bremer's wardrobe: smart suits with desert combat boots. At the Green Zone Shopping Bazaar, young Iraqi kids hawked pornographic DVDs to soldiers, and merchants with a knack for memorabilia marketed Saddam Hussein trinkets; watches emblazoned with his portrait were a favorite. While the rest of Baghdad flickered, power in American quarters was always on, and the shuttle buses ferrying staffers around the parklike expanse ran on time.

In a city where streets were sometimes deserted after nightfall, rowdy bars inside the compound stayed open late into the night; CIA operatives drank at their own rattan-furnished bar, where beer flowed freely. At the Green Zone Café, contractors, wearing their sidearms, could smoke water pipes while listening to an Iraqi drummer. One saloon was called the Bunker. Karaoke could be crooned and badminton was available, in between the usually misguided mortars or rockets that sometimes fell inside the palace grounds.

Horan often complained about the place's debilitating isolation, probably the single most important factor in the occupation's short-term failure. "The experience is much more abstract than I wish it was," he told me. In an attempt to rectify this, and even though he was nearing seventy, he strove for a time to travel every ten days or so from Baghdad to Najaf, where he met the second tier of the city's religious leadership (the men right below Sistani), talked about the intricacies of scholarship and the path to advancement within the ranks of the Shiite hierarchy, and drank tea in the *barrani*. He found those he met to have a relatively naive view of what he called the "contemporary" world and especially of the United States. "But I've always had the sense those people are bright, they're sophisticated, they have good judgment of people," he said. "They are intact personalities. They may not be contemporary personalities, but they are intact personalities." With refreshing modesty, though, he acknowledged that his power of persuasion was limited. "I can't say we're making great conversions."

None of Horan's meetings were with Sadr, a man he alternately appreciated (in academic fashion) and dismissed. At one point, he called him "big smoke, no fire." At another, he said, "He's a populist, a critic, and a rabble-rouser and he's gotten awful, awful close to the line." As early as the summer, Horan was worried about the implications of Sadr's movement, which had begun to spread its wings after Hakim's assassination. "If Muqtada Sadr manages to divide the Shiite community between an aggrieved, xenophobic, somewhat nationalist camp and the vast majority of somewhat passive followers, that gap is going to be exploited by Baathists, Sunnis, and Wahhabis," he said. (Wahhabis are adherents of a militant Sunni sect that originated in Saudi Arabia.) "We cannot afford the distraction. Time is limited."

Although he perceived the threat, Horan and others had few ideas about how to grapple with Sadr's movement, and deep divisions within the U.S. administration colored their approach toward it. At all times, they hoped the clergy themselves could stanch Sadr's influence: "We're watching him and some of the big *mujtahids* [ayatollahs] are watching us, and we're both hoping the other does something." Horan described the inaction as paralyzing. "I say to them, 'He is one of yours. This is a family problem. This is your family problem and we're looking for you in the first instance to deal with your own Shiite family problem.'" Their response, he said, was to lean back against the wall, grimace, and "ask for novocaine." "You Americans, you take care of him," he quoted them as saying. "They're hoping for a deus ex machina, which is Uncle Sam, and we're looking for signs from them that they're willing to pull rank on this *hujjat al-islam*." His conclusion, he told me, was that there was "no disposition to grapple with this particular problem." He was frustrated, but part of him understood. "When we reproach them for their passivity," Hume said, "we don't have five to ten thousand people at our doorstep."

It was at about that time—in mid-August, as both sides were sizing up and misinterpreting each other—that Sadr City first erupted, bringing far more than a few thousand to the Americans' doorstep. The slum dropped back to a simmer after that, but with a population so sensitive to slights, insults, and indignities, the incident on August 13 had an indelible impact on the relationship between U.S. officials and Sadr's movement. It colored every event that followed.

The explosion occurred about an hour before noon prayers and began with a U.S. military helicopter hovering over the slum, near a red-and-white six-story transmission tower. A religious cleric I spoke to insisted that a U.S. soldier inside the helicopter had tried to kick the black flag fluttering atop the tower, inscribed with a name for the Mahdi. "How can we sleep at night when we see this?" the cleric recalled asking as he watched the incident.

Within hours, an Arabic satellite station, Al-Arabiya, broadcast images around the Arab world of the helicopter hovering near the flag. At first, the U.S. military denied any wrongdoing. ("Totally bogus, totally untrue," said a military spokesman.) But two weeks later, the commander of U.S. forces in Iraq, Lieutenant General Ricardo Sanchez, acknowledged that the helicopter had, in fact, tried to knock down the flag. The soldiers, who had "exercised poor judgment," would be punished, he said, but he did not explain their motivation.

The incident provoked a day of anger and fervor in a Shiite neighborhood already on edge. Some residents insisted that it was an American woman who had tried to knock down the flag. A few had seen her holding a knife. Instant stories of heroism emerged, cultivated within the Shiite narrative of the weak pitted against the strong, defeat already assumed: soldiers were said to have brandished their M-16 assault rifles at a young boy. The boy had climbed the tower and tried to fend off the helicopter, alone, with a simple metal bar.

Whatever the truth, the damage, in a few minutes, had been done. The divide separating occupier and occupied had widened considerably, foreshadowing a much greater provocation the next year. Protesters angry at what they saw as a religious insult poured out of houses and shops. In some of the worst unrest since Baghdad fell, the crowds grew from one hundred to three thousand, and clashes erupted with a passing American patrol. Iraqis admitted that rocks were thrown at the Americans; the Americans said they faced small-arms fire and a rocket-propelled grenade. As the sweltering evening continued, hundreds of demonstrators, rallied by the clergy and waving flags inspired by faith, moved across streets awash in sewage, calling for a day of reckoning with U.S. troops they said were now unwelcome in their neighborhood.

By sunset, in the heart of Sadr City, youths had climbed up the transmission tower, bedecking it in red, green, white, and black flags. On a fire station below, others had scrawled "Down USA" in English, and "Down with America, down with Israel" in Arabic. Some carried Iraqi flags or portraits of Sadr's father. Banners read, "No, no to arrogance, yes, yes to the *Hawza.*" At times, the crowd broke into chants. "Today, today is peaceful, tomorrow, tomorrow is war," one went, as the sun set over the neighborhood. "We are preparing your army, Mahdi," another announced.

Someone fired into the air and the shots echoed across crowded streets; the sound would grow increasingly familiar in the slum's neighborhoods. With night falling, I wandered to the edge of the crowd, where I found thirty-three-year-old Qassem Khusaf, who was watching the protest. "The Americans want to provoke the people. They have a plan," he told me matter-of-factly. Participants had begun to disperse along the broad avenues, down narrow, winding alleys blocked from view. "They are provoking us to see whether we will fight or not."

Iraqis like to boast of their country as a land of prophets. It is the kind of terrain where legends grow. Two days later, the myths were already being made. I went to the Friday prayers at the Muhsin Mosque, which served as an open-air theater for the Sadr movement's street organizing. In the streets, pictures of the helicopter near the transmission tower were selling for about fifty cents. Other vendors hawked newspapers published by Sadr's group, devotional CDs, pictures of Sadr's father, and portraits of the Twelve Imams. A cleric named Hadi Darraji, a former street enforcer ascending the movement's ranks, delivered the sermon. "What happened clearly shows that America and international Zionism have declared war on Islam," Darraji told a crowd of as many as ten thousand from a wood podium with an amateurish painting of Sadr's father perched in front. He warned that Iraqis would "retaliate twice as hard" against anyone who attacked "us or our sacred symbols" and said the helicopter incident showed that "there is no difference between Saddam and America." Afterward, I turned to an eighteen-year-old cobbler, Mustafa Saad, who was listening to the sermon from across the street. He was neither outraged nor subdued. Instead, he spoke with a hint of reflection. As he, a young Shiite, saw it, the story was familiar. "Saddam could not defeat us," he said, "and neither can the Americans."

THE FERMENT WITHIN THE SHIITE COMMUNITY WAS STILL AT THE PERIPHERY OF the world of Mohammed Hayawi, the bookseller. He knew of Sadr; he had heard of Hakim. But for a Sunni Muslim, Najaf was a distant and somewhat alien city, as Persian as it was Arab. Sadr City was seen as far too dangerous for Sunnis to frequent. Like many well-to-do Baghdadis, Mohammed ascribed every problem—from postinvasion looting to fluctuations in the dinar-to-dollar exchange rate—to street toughs from there. In October, he was still in a good mood—good, at least, by Baghdadi standards.

His hopefulness lasted until October 27, the first day of Ramadan, a month when, by tradition, God's graces seem closer. Ramadan is the ninth month of the lunar year, its name taken from the Arabic for "great heat." For Muslims, it signifies a time of sacrifice that leads to renewal and strength; the widely observed dawn-to-dusk fast helps the faithful understand the suffering of the hungry. While solemn, the month is marked by festivities across the Muslim world, not unlike the Christmas season for Christians. In Cairo, it was always my favorite time of the year. I loved the joke about how Egyptians actually put on weight that month, feasting until the early hours before dawn amid music, conversation, and jokes in cafés that never closed.

On the sunny, clear morning with which Ramadan began in Baghdad in 2003, the air imbued with the crispness of a Mediterranean autumn in a month that had once marked a time of truce, the U.S. administration in Iraq lost some of its last claims to credibility; the people of Baghdad, waiting for peace, surrendered almost entirely to their fears.

In coordinated strikes, unleashed in a forty-five-minute cascade that began at 8:30 A.M., suicide attackers set off powerful car bombs outside the local headquarters of the International Committee of the Red Cross and three police stations across Baghdad. At least 35 people were killed, although the toll was probably higher. More than 230 were wounded, some cut by flying glass, others with limbs sheared off. The attacks had been methodically planned: the Red Cross bomb was packed in a vehicle painted like an ambulance; a bomb outside a police station was hidden inside a truck painted like an Iraqi police car. And at each site, the resulting tableau was similar: twisted metal lined the streets, wires dangled from balconies at gutted shops, bloodied victims staggered, and burning cars unleashed plumes of acrid smoke into the porcelain-blue sky.

Nasir, Karim, and I stumbled across town, each reported attack and rumored bombing coming over our walkie-talkie sending us in a different direction. We finally ended up in the working-class neighborhood of Shaab, a place we had last visited during one of the worst bombings of the invasion. Now the tension and horror had returned. In streets filled with the din of destruction, the last of the red lines had been blurred. The assailants were again mysterious, and everyone felt pitted against everyone else. In the chaos that grief, anger, and vengeance breed, nowhere felt safe, and probably nowhere was. Iraq was cursed by how common death was becoming.

As I ran from the car, I heard the sirens of ambulances carrying the dead and wounded. Windows had been shattered as far as a hundred yards from the bomb. Blood smeared the pavement and soaked the littered ground. Glass being shoveled from gutted shops chimed on the sidewalks. Helicopter rotors beat dully against the air. Along the four-lane street, from the concrete façades of buildings crumbled by the blast, store signs hung askew, shards of plaster and concrete dangled from the roofs, and electrical wires were twisted in the geometry of destruction.

Cries of despair erupted from confused crowds. "This is the work of bin Laden!" one man shouted to no one in particular. A teenager, his face sweaty, glared at an American soldier passing him. "Where were you, mister?" he asked in Arabic. The soldier, not understanding, looked straight ahead. His face red and his eyes swollen, another man ran toward the devastated tan brick police station. Packed in a white Land Cruiser, and detonated at 8:55 A.M., the bomb had torn away the side of the station and the façade of a neighboring apartment house and left a crater ten feet deep and ten feet across. "Where's my brother? Where's my brother?" the man screamed, before a crowd pulled him back from nervous-looking U.S. troops.

A loudspeaker atop a U.S. military vehicle began broadcasting a message in Arabic: "Evacuate the area now. Return to your homes. Thank you for your cooperation."

Across the panorama of devastation, emotions surged to the surface, having festered for seven months of invasion, war, and occupation. The refrain was familiar: confusion, anger, and helplessness warred in a city whose destiny was out of its own control.

"God will not accept this," cried Huda Abdel-Jabbar, standing in front of her apartment, looking at the wake of a hurricane's whim. "This is forbidden!"

Crowds of seething young men, held at bay by the soldiers who set up a barbed-wire perimeter around the station, looked for targets against which to vent their fury. A crowd attacked me and Nasir. We ran to the other side of the U.S. perimeter, but not before Nasir was hit in the face by an assailant. With knives and sticks, others caught up in the mob's menace chased arriving journalists down the street.

As we made our way across the capital that day, I saw the same scenes again and again. They were already familiar from the U.S. invasion, and they would be repeated in the months ahead. The random and the arbitrary had returned. Dread was never fleeting. There was only one difference: back then, everyone had known the war would end.

"Look at this, look at what's happening," Jamil Abu Heidar told me, as he pointed to the snarled rail of a fence that guarded the Bayaa station. It had been hurled into the street fifty yards away. "Anybody can bomb these places. They can do anything they want." He looked around and arched his eyebrows. "Why are we standing here now?"

In the upscale neighborhood of Khadhra, Ibrahim Mohammed gathered with fellow store owners down the street from another devastated police station. They sat in plastic chairs with tattered yellow cushions, drinking tea, with nothing else to do. Glass and bits of cement from the blast littered the sidewalk. Mohammed's anger and bewilderment tumbled out: Who were the assailants? Why would they target Iraqis and the police trying to protect them, if they were fighting U.S. forces? And why now? "It's Ramadan!" he blurted. "Why are they doing this? It's forbidden. Ramadan is blessed."

Another store owner, Raymond Touma, shook his head as he nibbled on pumpkin seeds. "*La hawla wa la quwwa*," he said: The people are helpless.

Nabil Fadhil Mohamed, who owned a plumbing store, interrupted, throwing his hands out in despair. "The Americans are more scared than the Iraqis!"

The bombings had tangled traffic along bridges and intersections. At the traffic circle of Ras Hawash Street, Ahmed Ali, a taxi driver, surveyed the scene in disgust. His city was fraying, he said; its people were losing their way. "There was a man bringing discipline and now he's disappeared," he said out his window, as mourners carried past a coffin draped in black. "No one fired even a bullet in Saddam's time." Next to him, in traffic at a standstill, a frustrated bus driver joined in. "The money's not worth it," he shouted. "I'm going home."

Across Baghdad, knots of people argued over who was responsible, the debates a hint of the overwhelming anxiety the bombings had created. The battle lines were shrouded in rumor. Many pointed fingers at Saddam, in alliance, they claimed, with foreign militants. More common were conspiracy theories, bred by powerlessness: the responsibility for the violence lay with the Syrians, the Saudis, the Iranians, Al-Qaeda, the Israelis, and, on occasion, the Americans themselves. Anger was everywhere. Everyone was to blame. Baghdad deserved better.

"Maybe the Kuwaitis," suggested Hashim Samarai, a fifty-six-year-old retiree. We were standing in a grocery store whose wall had been cracked by the blast in Bayaa, the southern suburb where Nasir lived. "Why them? Revenge. They want revenge from us for the invasion."

"I think the biggest possibility is the Americans, maybe with the Israelis," said the store owner Mundhir Ahmed, shaking his head. The blast had knocked everything in his store to the floor, and he had spent much of the afternoon putting his canned meat, tomato paste, ketchup, cigarettes, soft drinks, and olive oil back in order.

Back in Shaab, Rashid Shuweili had another view. He blamed Saddam and foreigners loyal to Osama bin Laden for the blasts. But he insisted that the Americans were responsible too: as long as they were present, those who worked with them would be viewed as collaborators, making them targets for opponents of the occupation. To the bombers, he said, anyone working with an infidel becomes an infidel. "If the Americans leave the streets, there would be no problem here," he said. "They just give the resistance an excuse."

At Noaman Hospital, a place that became familiar to me during the war and where many of the wounded from the bombing in Shaab that day were taken, Thamer Abdullah, a thirty-one-year-old police officer, lay in his bed. His face was bloodied, one eye swollen shut. "God save me!" he screamed. "God save me!"

His mother, Shafa, was angry and suspicious. A day before, U.S. soldiers had opened the road the bomber used when he raced toward the station and barreled over barbed wire. Why? she wondered. Why were no Americans killed in the Shaab bombing?

"Why are the Americans coming here? Why?" she asked. "They should protect us. They can control the situation! They can impose order!"

Shihab Sadeq, a bandage covering ten stitches to the back of his head, jumped up from his bed and approached her where she sat near her son. "I saw an American hurt with my own eyes," he said. "He was bleeding from his mouth."

She shook her head, unconvinced. "Damn the Americans!" she said angrily.

By late afternoon, Baghdad's streets had emptied, as families went home in fear and to prepare for breaking the fast. A strange calm had descended. In the lull, the city again displayed, as it had so many times in the past, the resilience born of hardship. Fruit vendors and nut sellers served their last customers. Young boys pushed wood carts laden with still-warm bread, *samoun*. On one downtown street, butchers displayed their wares of sheep heads. Next to them were kiosks stacked with Jordanian-made cigarettes. A teenager furiously pedaled his bicycle, lugging a block of ice impossibly propped in back.

At about five P.M., Nasir, Karim, and I sat down with men at the Moawad Restaurant, waiting for the symbolic firing of the cannon that would mark the end of the fast's first day and the call to prayer that follows. Before us were the plates that awaited: dates, pickles, and *zlabiya*, a honeyed pastry. Across the aisle was Ahmed Jaber, a sixty-eight-year-old, playing with his yellow worry beads and biding his time. He yawned exaggeratedly, a gesture that suggested a lack of worry. Even after a day like this, he was reluctant to despair. What good would it do?

"Today there were explosions," he told me. "God willing, there won't be tomorrow."

His was a rare voice. In the days that followed, Baghdad reflected, grimly. I sensed that emotions were running very deep, in dangerous directions. There was a new hopelessness, tinged with nihilism.

The next day, Baghdad went through the motions of doing what it did after every disaster. It began to rebuild. Along a sidewalk where flies gathered on a pool of dried blood, residents restrung electricity wires; helicopters passed overhead. Others shoveled bricks, concrete, and other debris onto the median that bisected the four-lane avenue. Children played along the edge of the crater, which was filling with groundwater. Alleys that ran along the main street had been blocked with stones, tires, and palm-tree trunks, a feeble attempt to foil the attacks that everyone thought would continue.

But conversations would never be the same again, and the perception of the American military in Iraq was taking yet another turn; the all-powerful army imbued with technological prowess had become, first, a callous overseer in a looted capital, then an insensitive occupier in a Muslim land, and now, in the wake of the Ramadan bombings, it was a provocative presence whose visibility only deepened the strife.

At the Kindi Hospital, where many of the wounded from the Shaab bombing had been taken, Mohammed Arsan Zubeidi sat in his bed, his head propped on a pink pillow, a bandage concealing his severed right ear. A recent graduate of the police academy, he vowed not to return to the force. "When I'm on duty, when the Americans are with me, I feel in danger," he said. He ticked off the series of warnings that had preceded the bombing, threats that reminded me of Khaldiya. A week earlier, a leaflet made the rounds of the neighborhood, signed by a group that identified itself as mujahideen, Islamic fighters. The typewritten letter, heavy on religious rhetoric, vowed to kill any officer who worked with U.S. forces. But Zubeidi also held responsible the Americans whom the police were supposed to work with. He thought the U.S. presence was inciting the attacks. "When I joined the police, I thought the Americans should stay to provide us security," he said, grimacing. "Now they're just creating risks for us."

As long as the Americans stayed, he said, the police would never be able to win the respect of the neighborhood. Even now, when he tried to arrest someone, they asked why an American soldier had not accompanied him. "They're scared of the Americans, they're no longer scared of us," he told me. "We can handle the situation. We should not have to depend on the Americans."

The perception of the American military and the submission to fear that ensued after the bombings fed off each other. Four days later, Baghdad was rife with warnings that a "day of resistance" was planned. Few claimed to have seen the plan or know with certainty who had made it. But in a city deeply unsettled by the Ramadan bombings, rumors were enough to reorder residents' daily routine. Schools across the capital reported only a handful of students showing up, and many had canceled classes. Traffic on the day, a gray Saturday morning, the traditional start of the week, was remarkably light, but snarled by newly added checkpoints. Stores opened their doors, but many customers stayed away.

The U.S. administration, usually remarkably slow in gauging popular sentiment, acknowledged the shift in mood. L. Paul Bremer called the events "a tough week here in Iraq." (Two months earlier, after the bombing of the U.N. headquarters in Baghdad, Bremer had admitted the situation was "grim" but declared that "beneath the surf was a swelling tide of good news.") At a news conference, Bremer declared that security remained the occupation's first priority and announced steps that U.S. officials would take to accelerate the transfer of responsibility and authority to newly trained Iraqi forces. It was a theme U.S. officials would return to often, with limited success.

The declarations did little to calm Baghdad. On that Saturday, Nasir, Karim, and I visited the Ibtikar School, on well-known Palestine Street. On any normal day, 1,410 students entered its doors at eight A.M. When we got there, ten students had arrived; the rest had been kept home by parents chilled by rumors that more attacks were planned. Two hours later, even the ten left—heading out the door, down a deserted street, and past a wall bearing this graffito: "By God, this is a warning we will cut off any hand waving to the American soldiers."

The weather had begun to turn brisk. The school was newly painted white, its stucco walls accenting the blue doors at the entrance. It was cloaked in silence—no chattering students, no shuffling along tile floors, no desks banging into walls. This was one of the grimmest moments of my time in Baghdad, suffused equally with fear and melancholy.

"In our mind, there's only death," said Rasmiya Hassan, the short, stout sixty-three-year-old headmistress. Her voice was flat. "We'll die here, we'll die there. That's all we think about—death," she added. "We know they'll do it. They do what they threaten. Maybe they won't do it today, maybe tomorrow. Everything is possible."

At that moment, an irony struck me. Few Iraqis believed the Americans pledges, Bremer's vow to reinforce security. On the contrary, they would point to promises they believed had been broken time and again since the occupation started—hospitals with too few supplies, roads still broken, persistent (though diminished) crime. But they believed the armed opposition, and they listened. They had faith that it would carry out what it threatened. The opposition, not the Americans, was shaping the new Iraq.

"We believe what we see," said Hamid Abed Mohsin, a visiting fifty-five-year-old inspector for the Education Ministry. He offered a proverb tailored to the city around him. "The Americans came to put mascara on our eyes and instead blinded us."

Rasmiya smiled and offered her own line. "The mud is getting wetter," she said.

OVER THE SUMMER, WAMIDH HAD MADE A PREDICTION THAT, AS I HAD COME TO expect of his forecasts, proved uncannily accurate. Many people thought the country is doomed, he had said. "They think what is coming is going to be worse."

"The Americans have opened a Pandora's box," he said, when I saw him again that fall.

Wamidh's gloom had deepened and, his mind always at work, he was trying to bring a critical perspective to what was going on around him. Hopelessness, directed at both Americans and Iraqis, now imbued his perspective.

"What are the Americans all about?" he asked, a little desperate. "What do they want?" He listed what he perceived as the sins of the U.S. government. It had supported international sanctions, which wrecked the country. Despite its insistent prewar claims, no weapons of mass destruction had been found in Iraq, nor had ties been confirmed between Saddam and Osama bin Laden's network. There were more terrorists in Iraq now than before the invasion.

And, as an Arab nationalist, he was disgusted by the lack of even-handedness in American dealings with Palestine and Israel. "How could I have trust in such an administration?" he asked me.

But he was almost as upset at his fellow Iraqis. This was a sentiment I heard more and more often. Saddam had destroyed the body politic, and in the wreckage, Wamidh feared, no one was speaking in the interests of the country. Compromise was a foreign word, the culture too brutalized to embrace it; everything was a zero-sum game. When someone criticizes Saddam, he said, they are accused of being an apologist for the United States. When someone criticizes the American occupation, they are called a puppet of Saddam. "Both arguments are wrong," Wamidh told me. "It is true some people came on top of American tanks. It is true that some people benefited from Saddam. But there are a lot of people who fit in neither category." But in resisting easy categorization, Wamidh was a distinct minority.

"I have stopped believing that Iraqis are capable of sorting out these problems. Fanatics are growing on every side—Shiites, Sunnis, and Kurds. Most of the problems are solvable. But we need political leaders of charisma, wise judgment, foresight, and tolerance. Unfortunately, we don't have such leaders." He dragged on his cigarette, the long ash hanging precariously over his lap. The groups that had opposed Saddam from abroad, the returning exiles, were tainted by their association with the U.S. government, he said, and thus "had no legitimacy or credibility." Those who stayed in Iraq had been jailed, tortured, often executed. "The country is suffering from a serious lack of statesmen," he said. "This is what frightens me. I can't say there is even an embryonic unity in the country."

He stopped again. I wanted to ask another question, but I hesitated to interrupt.

"Who is going to be the catalyst for this unity?" Wamidh asked. "I'm not saying that human nature in Iraq is completely, radically different from what's happening in Western countries. But the amount of spiritual corruption in this country, the amount of looking out for one's interests rather than ideas, is so deeply rooted in this society. I wonder if we can cure this society during my lifetime."

Wamidh was in a particularly grim mood that day because a friend of his, Abdel-Latif Mayah, a professor at Mustansariyah University in Baghdad, had been assassinated a short time before. The murder was well planned. Eight people, their faces covered, stopped his car. They ordered Mayah into the street, then pumped thirty-five bullets into his body. No one knew why; no one knew who was responsible. That was Baghdad now.

We talked about the assassination and the wave of killings that shadowed Baghdad. Many though they were, few were dramatic enough to warrant writing about them for the *Post*. They chilled Wamidh, though, more and more instances of violence in "the continuous, vicious circle of bloodshed in this country."

He mentioned his daughter Qudus, born in 1979, the second of his four children. "She opened her eyes to the Iran-Iraq war," he lamented, his voice reflective. "And until now she hasn't seen one moment of happiness or security."

DREAD WAS EVERYWHERE. AS BAGHDAD BEGAN ITS DESCENT INTO HORROR, I heard more and more decry the city's fate. It was often the grief of parents who knew that their children deserved better.

"I don't know when in history a country has been in war almost continuously for over twenty years. I know there is supposed to be something called the Hundred Years' War in Europe, but twenty years is a long time. My youngest son—one time we were calculating. I think he lived only two years of his life in peace. From 1991 until now, it was not peace. So then, what was it? War, the threat of war. He's only known two years of peace and that was 1988 to 1990. Really, in his life. It's changed the people in the city. Before the wars, people were nicer. Just nicer. People were much more friendly, much more." Gayle Vrozina stopped, leaning back in the couch. "They were nice to each other, there was less greed." She paused. "It's been going downhill since then."

Gayle was the American wife of Adel Ghaffour, a gentle doctor I had met before the war in his clinic on Saadoun Street. Adel had spent ten years in the United States, and was still fond of the country. Born in Cleveland, Gayle had spent more than thirty years in Iraq, where she raised three children and learned the Arabic dialect of Baghdad. (Her first words were "apple" and "orange," taken from an Arabic teaching book she bought at the airport in Miami after she and Adel were married in 1966.)

This was the first time I had met Gayle and the first time I had seen Adel since the war. During our last visit, in his clinic in 2002, he had been anxious about the coming U.S. invasion. President Bush "can invade Iraq, he can topple the government. After that what is he going to do?" Adel asked me then.

Now he almost immediately recalled the conversation: "Do you remember what I told you? I told you, 'God, I hope it will not start.' Honestly, I was sensing what it was going to be after the war. Now our era can be described in one word, chaos. Our country is in chaos. They left the country in chaos, complete chaos, in every aspect of life. We are seeing things I never saw before."

In their simply decorated house, a red Persian carpet lay atop the living room's tile floors and an overhead fan churned air already cool. The walls were white. There was little inside that spoke of Iraq, save a white plate with a Quranic inscription in black atop the buffet. Adel, who was sixty-eight, wore a black knit shirt, buttoned to the top, and gray pants. As we talked, he thumbed worry beads "so that I don't smoke."

Gayle, ten years his junior, wore dark glasses, a light blue blouse, and blue pants. He was still spry, with a quick mind and eyes that danced around the room; she was more deliberate but inquisitive. After thirty-seven years of marriage, the Iraqi husband and his American wife still treated each other with affection, dignity, and respect.

Over her decades in the capital, Gayle had had to continually adapt, groping her way in a mercurial city. "I stayed in the house a lot, and during the regime, I didn't talk politics," she told me. Whenever someone asked her in those days what she thought of the Iran-Iraq war, she remembered smiling and pleading ignorance. "I would say, 'My Arabic is not good enough for politics.' That's how I managed to stay here for so long and to stay alive. I never talked politics."

Now, her country of birth was occupying her country of choice, and her vision was bifocal, sometimes frustratingly so. I asked her if she felt like an immigrant. "I still feel like I have two homes. I've integrated into Iraq but I don't feel a hundred percent Iraqi," she said. "I have learned to understand all the tensions, maybe because I can stand back and watch the nuances of things going on."

She grasped America's power and Iraq's pride. She shared the frustrations of a reeling Baghdad. And she knew the people she had grown up with in

Cleveland had no notion, absolutely no idea of what they had on their hands in Iraq.

Her sense? I asked.

"The war has restarted," she said.

"Stay in," Adel added. "The streets are in the hands of the criminals now. The streets are in their hands, and you are under their mercy."

Their house was quiet, but the day's noise filtered in from outside. Chickens crowed next door, refusing to stop for the call to prayer. A U.S. military helicopter passed overhead.

"My personality is like this," Adel said, setting his worry beads aside as he nibbled at his cake. "If you put me in hell, I'll tell you it might turn into paradise one day. That's why you see me staying in Iraq. But it's very dangerous to live here now. This is the only time I felt in my life that it is unlivable. The first time. War with Iran, no. The embargo, no. We had coups. No, this is completely different. We passed through all these bumps, but something like this? We've never seen it. It is ugly."

PART FIVE

THE INSURGENCY

13

A BAD MUSLIM

The Americans in Baghdad framed the tumult in Iraq from the perspective of their own heritage and expressed them in the familiar vocabulary of democratic ideals. They had come as liberators. "Day by day, conditions in Iraq continue to improve, freedom becomes more and more entrenched," L. Paul Bremer declared early on, with a confidence that was occasionally surreal and that seemed directed to encourage not Iraqis, but an audience back in the United States. The Iraqis, in a country where grievances tend to accumulate but rarely fade, confronted a situation miles removed from Bremer's vision. Molded by their own identities and history, their vocabulary was shaped less by a reflexive celebration of democracy and freedom and more by their own religion, nationalism, and material circumstance, qualities that come into sharper focus when people feel besieged.

Many of the men who, during the early fall and winter, began pouring into the ranks of the armed opposition along the arc of Sunni land in central Iraq asked their own questions from the lexicon with which they were raised: How could they end an occupation they perceived as illegitimate? How could they defend their culture, which, they feared, the occupiers hoped to transform to suit their own purposes? How could they maintain their identity—as Iraqis, as Arabs, and, most important, as Muslims? Other questions were asked, with no less emotion, by the very people the Americans had enlisted in the project to defeat their growing insurgency—the policemen and militiamen who were the foot soldiers in the American reconstruction of Iraq's security forces. It was hard to tell whether they were fighting for the Americans or for the Iraqis. Were they traitors or patriots? How far, and for how long, could they compromise principles of faith, nationalism, and tradition that constituted the very essence of their identity?

As the insurgency gathered force in the Sunni Triangle through summer and fall of 2003, these questions were aggravated. Religion, culture, and centuries of history and oral traditions fed the armed opposition. In the mostly arid expanse of western Iraq, intersected by the valleys of the Tigris and Euphrates and the wadis of the Syrian Desert, the insurgency joined disparate but inclusive ideologies, some devastatingly severe, under the banner of resistance. This union of ideological forces—sometimes nationalist, sometimes Islamist, always anti-American—was yet another unintended consequence of the invasion and occupation. This new insurgent unity now threatened the success of the ambivalent rank-and-file whom the Americans were enlisting to take over the security of Iraq and battle their countrymen for an uncertain future. Among that rank-and-file was the 3rd Patrol of the Iraqi Civil Defense Corps in the northern Sunni town of Baiji.

The faces of these men, torn by nagging loyalties and obdurate realities, were somber. We were sitting outside Baiji's sprawling train station, which had been looted of everything but railcars. No, more than somber: their visages were funereal.

"I swear to God, we'll be killed," said Hamid Yusuf, holding a secondhand Kalashnikov rifle. The varnish of its wooden butt had worn away.

"We all have the same opinion," insisted one of his commanders, Qassim Khalaf, thumbing yellow worry beads in his rough hand.

"One hundred percent," answered Jamal Awad.

"My family's already made a reservation on a plot of land to bury me," insisted the twenty-nine-year-old Yusuf, breaking into a wry grin. "As soon as they leave, I'm taking off my hat," Yusuf said, tipping his red baseball cap emblazoned with the corps emblem, "and putting on a *yashmagh*," the checkered head scarf sometimes worn by resistance fighters in the Sunni Triangle.

He volunteered a proverb that made the others laugh: "Escape is two-thirds of manliness."

The eight men of the 3rd Patrol had been trained and equipped by Lieutenant Colonel Larry "Pepper" Jackson, the engaging and committed American commander in Baiji. When I met him in the fall, he had already outfitted more than 450 Iraqi police, along with 198 members of the Iraqi Civil Defense Corps, including Yusuf and his colleagues. All around the country, inductions had picked up markedly in the previous weeks, spurred by the marketable American concept of "Iraqization," one aspect of the U.S. military's effort to shift responsibility for security from their overstretched troops to homegrown forces under American direction.

Jackson had put the men of the 3rd Patrol through three weeks of training—drilling, marksmanship, first aid, and basic combat skills. "And I'm talking *basic* combat skills," he told me. He dealt, as well as he could, with the language barrier and even established camaraderie with the recruits; some called him Captain or General, whichever sounded more senior. He gave a few of them nicknames, including Baby and Smokey. His superiors had assigned no specific targets for enlistment, but given the mounting urgency of the situation, Jackson was told to "work as fast as you can and recruit as many people as you can." He said he felt the induction was proceeding at "the right pace," but that in the end assessing the pace wasn't up to him. "What's to say what's too fast? I don't know," Jackson said. "That's the thousand-dollar question. What's too fast?"

A reflective man, Jackson understood that the odds were against him in training men like those of the 3rd Patrol. He admitted freely that, as a Westerner, he was in a never-ending struggle to bridge the immense gap between cultures if he was to succeed. He wasn't accustomed to the traditional authority of tribes, which had filled the vacuum left by Saddam's fall, or to the tribal law that still held sway in the countryside. Nor was he used to vendettas that spanned decades over "someone who killed my goat one hundred years ago." Still, he tried to rely on the conservative, traditional values underpinning life in rural places like Baiji to inculcate loyalty among his recruits, who were more often than not motivated simply by the salaries the Americans offered. His idea was to appeal to the men's sense of family. Joining the force, Jackson tried to emphasize, "is a way of taking care of your family and it is a way of having a job and everybody needs a job to take care of their family."

"I try to tell them it's not loyalty to me, it's loyalty to your community," he said. "I tell them, 'What are you going to do when it's just you downtown?

That's what you need to be trained and prepared for, because eventually that's going to come.'"

Jackson tried to imagine how an Iraqi might think, or better yet, how he himself might think as an Iraqi. "At some point, you would prefer to make your own decision and to choose your own destiny," he said. "If you don't allow them to do that, you may get the perception that you are—what's the word?—I guess an occupier, I don't know."

By the fall, when I visited Jackson and the 3rd Patrol, the insurgency had picked up pace. The spasms of anger that had erupted in locales like Thuluyah and Heet over the summer had grown into a simmering guerrilla war as the year went on. The less savvy insurgents, sometimes peasants with little or no training, had been killed; those who survived were, month after month, honing their tactics and techniques, bolstered by former military officers left unemployed by Bremer's decision to disband the Iraqi army in the spring. Hit-and-run raids on military convoys had turned into much higher-profile attacks on electric power stations, oil installations, and liquid-natural-gas plants, a campaign of sabotage that again and again set back reconstruction. Senior Iraqi officials working with the United States were targeted, as were scores of cadres in Iraqi security forces and even Iraqi technocrats, professionals, and translators deemed to be collaborating with the occupation. Early on, U.S. soldiers had ridiculed the attackers' "pray and spray" technique, but by fall they were seeing guerrillas conducting coordinated small-unit ambushes and well-planned attacks on supply convoys. (At one point in the winter, insurgents fired at least a dozen rockets from donkey carts at the Oil Ministry and two well-fortified hotels in Baghdad.) U.S. losses mounted, and for a time, so did the insurgents' confidence.

Lieutenant Colonel Jackson, based in the conservative flatlands along the Tigris, estimated in the fall that attacks had increased by a factor of three or four since the summer. But the resistance still remained a mystery to him. Were the attackers remnants of Saddam's government? Radicals fired by religion? Foreigners pouring over Iraq's loosely guarded frontiers with Syria, Jordan, Saudi Arabia, Iran, and Turkey? Jackson, who was at times remarkably candid, could only shake his head and shrug. "Can I tell you who's behind it, who's leading it, who's funding it?" he asked. "I don't know."

The Iraqi men of the 3rd Patrol, envisioned as part of the security force that would one day inherit the fight for a future Iraq, were afraid, perhaps because they had a better sense of who was out there and what motivated them. A scared, disheartened, and confused lot, they told me story after story. The most recent: some of the men in the patrol were stopped in the market by four men in checkered head scarves riding in a car packed with mortars, rifles, and machine guns in back. The guerrillas delivered a warning: they planned to assassinate the patrol's commander, unless he resigned, and the men in the patrol would be next. Like the men in Khaldiya, the men in the 3rd Patrol threw up their hands, exasperated.

"We have children, we have families, and we need to live," said Yusuf, sitting with the others on a stack of railroad ties, as a brisk wind blew over them. From a family of ten, Yusuf had two daughters, aged three and four, and two sons, aged two and five.

"We don't love the Americans, but we need the money," he said. "It's very difficult, but there's no alternative."

Awad nodded his head in agreement. "There's no work. Otherwise we have to steal. You have to become an Ali Baba."

Baiji sits at the apex of the Sunni Muslim arc in Iraq, about 120 miles northwest of Baghdad, usually a three-hour drive. The Sunni regions delivered Saddam most of his support, and the United States and its Iraqi allies often portrayed their inhabitants as no more than Baathist diehards. Yet its historical links with the former government constituted only part of the story. It was also a region shaped by rural traditions and reflexive nationalism, stitched together by a fierce interpretation of Islam and the certainty it brought. This fundamental identity and its attendant values became even more important as the community sank deeper into the sense of disenfranchisement voiced so often in this swath of Sunni land.

The men in the 3rd Patrol were members of this traditional community, but that was no protection. The clergy in their town had praised those fighting U.S. soldiers as sacred warriors. One cleric, the men told me, had insisted that men like those in the 3rd Patrol could no longer fast during Ramadan. As collaborators with the infidels, the cleric reasoned, they were infidels as well. Raised to accept the clergy's opinions, many of the men said they did not disagree with the logic. Indeed, they concurred with it: they were bad Muslims.

"Under Islam, you should not shake hands with Americans, you should not eat with Americans, you should not help the Americans," said Shakir Mohammed, a twenty-three-year-old and deputy commander of his patrol, who before the invasion had worked as a carpenter.

"Islam doesn't accept it," added Yusuf. A thirteen-year veteran of the Iraqi army, he had deserted his post in Baghdad two days before the fall of Saddam's government.

"But what can we do?" Mohammed asked. "You have to work. It's my job."

The twenty-five-year-old Awad, gaunt like the others, shook his head. It was a gesture at once confused and despairing. "We can quit working with the Americans. Fine." He had two young boys, one just seven months old, at home. "But will the clergy give us salaries?"

Mohammed grinned at the idea.

"They pay us," he said, "and we'll stop working with the Americans."

"Money is good," the witty Yusuf said, kissing his hand with flair. "Clothes and food for my children. This is the good thing. Should I sleep without dinner and not work with the Americans? No. I should work with the Americans and have dinner."

Yusuf and most of his colleagues made $130 a month, a respectable salary in a city where U.S.-provided jobs in security were the few available. The more senior officers in the corps made $140 or $175. All of them came from large families—the smallest with six people, the largest with fourteen. Like Yusuf, nearly all had belonged to the disbanded Iraqi army.

During twenty-four-hour shifts twice a week, stretches of monotony punctuated by minutes of duty, they slept on a cold tile floor in a room with no windows, bringing their soiled and tattered blankets from home. They brewed tea in a charred black kettle and shared a cup fashioned with a pocket knife from the bottom of a plastic water bottle. Each day of Ramadan, adhering to the sunrise-to-sunset fast despite the cleric's judgment, they dispatched one colleague to bring food from the market for the evening meal—tomatoes and potatoes, bread and tea—which they shared next to a gray railroad car.

Like soldiers anywhere, they traded stories about close calls, most hauntingly when, in a case of mistaken identity, they had come under fire from Special Forces troops a month earlier. At least three of them had been wounded. Trails of their blood, blackened by time, were still smeared across the train platform. "Have you ever seen a horror movie?" asked Awad, another army veteran, who had been sentenced to a year in jail under Saddam for desertion. "It was worse than that. Only Rambo could have handled the situation."

Considering how uneasy a place Baiji was these days, some men in the town expressed amazement that the 3rd Patrol was still working. Latif Sayyib, who lived a few blocks away, was one of them. He made two dollars a day as a carpenter, when he could find work. His brother, Wathban, worked in the utility, making sixty dollars a month. No amount of money, they said, could have persuaded them to face the risks in joining security forces that, they contended, were indelibly tainted by the occupation. "If we work with them, under tribal law, they would consider us traitors," Latif said. Wathban agreed. "You can see that anybody working with the Americans can be killed—the governor, the police chief, anybody. This is a warning," he said, "for us."

The men were acquaintances of Nasir's, and I had met them at their house before I visited the 3rd Patrol. The town was small; everyone knew everyone else. They had grown up with Yusuf and some of the others, attending school together or playing soccer in the city's dusty streets. Whether the patrol members were traitors or not, suspicion was so intense in the city that they did their best to avoid contact. Even Nasir, an outsider from Baghdad, could feel the unease.

"I don't want to see them," Latif told me and Nasir, as we sat on cushions against the wall. "I'll see them in their house, but if I see them in the street or the market, I'll only stay a minute or two because I fear I'll become a target." His brother nodded. "Behind their back, people talk," Wathban said. "They say he's just a collaborator, he doesn't know when the time will come that he'll be killed."

"Their destiny will be the same as it was in Vietnam," he added. "The Americans left their allies there and they were killed. I think the same will happen here."

In the streets of Baiji, graffiti cluttered the walls, tinted black by fires at the city's oil refinery. "Anyone dealing with the Americans will be killed," one scrawl warned. "Saddam will be back, you traitors," announced another. Down a ways were other warnings: "No to spies, no to oppressors." And then "Resist the occupation."

"The people here don't forget our faces," said Mohammed, the former carpenter.

When the men in the 3rd Patrol were in training, they said, children threw rocks at them. Awad told me he was hit in the back, hard enough to keep him in bed for three days. Several times, they were pelted with tomatoes as they drove through the vegetable market. They tried to bring civilian clothes with them and change into their uniforms on the job. If they did so, their commander threatened, he would dock five dollars from their pay. Fear had prompted three of the men to leave in the past month, and nearly everyone said he had thought about it.

"Sometimes when I'm in a taxi, I hear the insults," Mohammed said, smoking a cigarette from a pack they all shared. "I hear them say, 'These people working with the civil defense are traitors, they're agents. Their future will be grim.'"

"It stays in our heart," Awad admitted.

"We're scared, I swear to God," Yusuf said. "We don't know at what moment we'll be killed. We don't know what will happen tomorrow."

"Tomorrow?" Mohammed interjected. "In fifteen minutes, we don't know what will happen."

Dusk arrived by late afternoon, as it does during winter in Iraq, and night soon followed. From the grounds that sprawled beyond their station, the men gathered wood for their fire. Dinner arrived—tomatoes, cucumbers, and parsley in a black plastic bag. In a looted warehouse, littered with charred wood and shattered glass and concrete, they gathered around—"like brothers," Mohammed said, in a town remarkably unfraternal. As we smoked cigarettes, I asked them what they hoped for from life.

"I want my children to live in safety," the thirty-three-year-old Khalaf said.

"We want to be like Kuwait. We want to live in luxury." That was Yusuf, again smiling. "We want fancy cars, not the worn-out cars we have."

"Health," Awad volunteered.

Mohammed nodded his head, then added another dream: "We don't want to always be scared."

WHO WERE THE MEN BEHIND THE INSURGENCY, THE MEN CREATING THE FEAR? This remained one of the great unanswered questions of the American occupation. There was no one group. There was, instead, a disparate coalition that included all the groups Lieutenant Colonel Jackson had mentioned: leftovers from Saddam's government; disgruntled Iraqis; militants like Abu Musab al-Zarqawi and hundreds of other foreigners with an extreme interpretation of Islam who had slipped across Iraq's borders; like-minded Muslims from inside Iraq; members of organized crime who abetted the delivery of money, weapons, and, eventually, hostages. There was never a dearth of recruits, from city or countryside, and U.S. military officials, time and again in those months, seemed to underestimate their numbers and, just as important, the extent of their network of sympathizers. It was as if acknowledging the enemy's significance called into question the Americans' role as a liberator.

Most of the insurgents shared a religious ideology that, in message and appeal, was a direct consequence of an occupation that was envisioned as the means of bringing democracy to Iraq. The doctrine that many of the militants had begun to share was at once alien and familiar to me. It was alien in the way it shaped the insurgency in Iraq; it was familiar in its message, one I had heard many times in the Middle East.

In country after country in the region, over the past generation or so, Islam has proven remarkably adept as a political program (or, more precisely, as many political programs) bringing together opposing demands and unifying distinct grievances. Most often, the movements that espouse it understand its pliancy: they begin with a universalist message of faith—a seventh-century revelation remarkable for its simplicity and clarity—and tailor it to specific communities, from the poor in Palestine's refugee camps, to the neglected Shiites in Beirut and southern Lebanon, to those newly arrived from the countryside in the slums of Istanbul and other Turkish cities. For the Muslim Brotherhood in Egypt, Islam is a critique of Western decadence and corruption, a message of social reform that harks back to the Prophet's early ministry in Mecca; in Turkey, pulled by East and West, it serves as an umbrella for Kurds and Turks, creating an identity based on faith rather than on ethnicity; in Palestine, it is a vehicle for resistance to Israel, providing a vocabulary that celebrates martyrdom and exalts violence.

In the Sunni arc of Iraq, in the vacuum left by Saddam's fall, Islam served to unify and motivate a disparate array of factions and currents. The result was a hybrid of religion and nationalism. We were witnessing a fusion of two distinct but mutually reinforcing ideologies, sometimes as critical of Saddam as they were of the Americans. The consequence was a jihad: a prolonged war against the Americans that bled their forces and diminished U.S. standing in Iraq and, no less significantly, in the broader Middle East. For a time, the ideological war served as a rallying cry for the most disenchanted and disillusioned Sunnis in Iraq, drawn to the simplicity of a struggle against the infidels, the veneration of death in sacred battle, and the empowerment that violence sometimes provides.

This new strain of Iraqi Islam—a synthesis of religion and politics—was the ideology of five men I came to know, though I never actually met them, in the western town of Khaldiya, the same place where I had spent a day at the police station later destroyed by a car bomb. The five were unofficially led by one man, Adnan Kamil Mahan Fahdawi, whose family—housed in an austere room of concrete floors, its walls adorned with two renderings of Islam's holiest shrine in Mecca—served as a window on their lives and, especially, their deaths. It was a glimpse into martyrdom and the onset of a home-grown movement that was actually new, despite its familiar militant reading of Islam. His family showed me another unintended outcome of the American occupation.

As the sun beat on Fahdawi's modest home, the streets empty in the silent afternoon, Nasir and I sat inside with his brothers. With care, they pulled out a creased and torn green folder. It was a death certificate of sorts taken from the black body bag in which thirty-one-year-old Adnan Fahdawi's body had been delivered to the local police station. "Multiple GSW," read the blood-stained tag—gunshot wounds. Cause of death: "extrusion of brain matter." Next they showed me a memorial poster, prepared after Fahdawi's mission, that captured the dead man's hard, bearded face. Smoldering eyes, tinted by determination, stared out over a caption that declared him a martyred hero. Next came a letter he and the others had written before they attacked a U.S. convoy under a full moon near the Euphrates town, a mission that, for all intents and purposes, was the pursuit of death.

The paper was embossed with traditional religious invocations in floral Arabic script. "As we write this testament, our hearts ache over the fate of the Iraqi people," began the typed statement. "To all our brothers, friends, and beloved ones: Today, we call on you to join the jihad, to move, not to stay still in silence in the face of this oppression and anarchy. Today, we have sacrificed ourselves to defend our honor and pride. How is it then possible for us to see decadent pigs desecrate our land and honor today. We have sacrificed our souls for the sake of Islam, sacrificed ourselves to get rid of the monkeys, pigs, Jews, and Christians. To all our brothers and sisters, we urge you to be joyful with us, we the ones who sacrificed ourselves for the sake of righteousness and Islam. We want you not to mourn us, but to remember us at all times."

In the streets of hard-packed dirt in Khaldiya, Fahdawi and the other authors of this letter were not all that unusual. From different families and tribes, they were drawn together by a childhood playing soccer, but were most deeply united by the piety that grew after Saddam's fall and that began to blossom in the fields, alleys, and mosques lacing together the landscape of western Iraq. Like others in their town, they became devotees of a militant Syrian preacher who interspersed calls for jihad with images of the September 11 attacks and whose once-banned bootleg tapes and videos I had seen selling for less than one dollar near Mohammed Hayawi's bookstore on Mutanabi Street. Together, they congregated in a small but popular mosque. They went into the attack, their relatives told me, with the belief that their deaths would serve as examples.

"When the neighbors arrived, they said, 'We didn't come to give condolences, we came to give congratulations.' He was a hero," Adnan Fahdawi's brother Salah told me.

Salah, a thirty-three-year-old who looked far older, was sober and earnest. In a family of fourteen, Adnan was the second brother he had lost; another, Khaled, had died in the war with Iran. His father, a taxi driver, had developed diabetes after the U.S. invasion; his feet had already been amputated. Salah looked at me with eyes that appealed for understanding, even if he didn't expect it. "It's difficult to lose a brother," he said. "But now I know Adnan is happy, and I'm happy for him. We wish God would plant the faith in our hearts that he put in Adnan's."

Their town was colored in shades of brown; sewage canals ran by houses of cement and cinder block, the relentlessly utilitarian architecture of poverty. Carrying viscous gray waste, the canals ran like tributaries into bigger, more fetid canals. Outside was what remained of Adnan Fahdawi's construction business: two cement mixers, a red tractor, a wheelbarrow, and a few pieces of lumber. U.S. helicopters whirred overhead as we spoke, a familiar sound in a town where guerrillas had repeatedly attacked American forces and the police chief, considered by many a collaborator, had been slain.

Salah, instinct with a soft-spoken pride, ignored them. "When the Americans came here, Adnan was upset. His wish was jihad. He wanted to fight as a mujahid in the path of God." At thirty-one, middle-aged by Iraqi standards, Fahdawi had yet to have a family—by design, his brother insisted. "He preferred to be a martyr than to marry," Salah said, sitting on a simple couch in a room whose tile floors were covered by cheap Persian carpets. "Adnan truly believed in God," he told me.

For weeks, Fahdawi's poster had hung at the Mashaheer Barbershop, on Khaldiya's main drag, where I first saw it. His picture, bordered by two roses, portrayed a man whose face was stern, framed by a white turban. His eyes were narrowed and, even in the black-and-white picture, tinted a steely gray. His beard suggested youth (it was wispy) and devotion (it was untrimmed, in the style of the most austere of believers). Proper in a conservative way, his dishdasha was buttoned tightly around his throat. Written above the picture was the familiar Quranic saying: "Do not consider those killed for the sake of God dead. Rather they are living with God." He was declared a hero, a religious scholar, and a mujahid, a sacred fighter. Below the photo was the date of his death. He was martyred, the caption said, for voicing the words "There is no god but God."

The men at the barbershop called Fahdawi a formidable, even intimidating presence in town. After his discharge from the military, he formed a fifteen-man construction crew, and he was a familiar sight in the serpentine alleys of Khaldiya on his battered twenty-year-old red motorcycle. In his spare time, he studied Islam with the town's elder cleric, sixty-five-year-old Sheikh Abed Saleh, in the tan brick Bashir Mohammed Mosque, and he brought religious fervor, they said, to almost every element of his short life.

He never missed the obligatory five daily prayers, often performing them at the Nur Mosque. Hotheaded and intolerant, he fired his employees for not doing the same. He refused to eat with residents he suspected of looting in the war's aftermath, and in the month of Ramadan, he would refuse to speak with those he suspected of not fasting.

For him, faith always intersected with politics: he was angered by the U.S. attack in 2001 on Afghanistan, a Muslim country, and no less angry at images of Israeli soldiers dragging Palestinian women, an image that he associated with any occupation.

Fahdawi was the axis around which the others who helped pen the letter revolved. The cell came together for the attack on the convoy. Both working in construction, Adnan met Khalil Huzeimawi, a stocky thirty-two-year-old father of five who had moved from neighboring Fallujah a year earlier. Huzeimawi also worked in construction. With Omar Shaabani, a quiet, twenty-four-year-old father of three, Fahdawi shared a passion for sports. He was a childhood friend of Hamid and Ra'id Kirtani, two orphaned cousins in their twenties who worked together selling poultry from a shack built of chicken wire and dried reeds, with a battered green scale propped on a wooden table.

Although they shared a perspective on the world, each had his own kind of life. Fahdawi was nicknamed the Sheikh, a reflection of his religious study and public demeanor. Shaabani and Huzeimawi were more mature, with families to raise. Hamid, the only one who had not served in the military, was working on a business degree in Baghdad, commuting fifty miles from Khalidya most days. Ra'id, who had been intended to marry a month earlier, was obsessed with soccer, hanging pictures of Argentina's Javier Saviola, Gabriel Batistuta, and his favorite, Diego Maradona, on his wall. But each family spoke of the men's deepening devotion after the war, and of new influences made available by Saddam's fall. As in places like Palestine, Egypt, and Lebanon, the language of Islam—elastic but eternal—began to provide the framework through which they saw their country, reeling as it was from war, occupation, and, in the eyes of many, chaos. In a confusing aftermath, nothing was confusing to the five men: they now lived in a subjugated land, and their faith called them to fight in a sacred battle pitting Muslims against infidels.

Relatives said the men enjoyed listening to Quranic recitation and, during the occupation, began attending the Friday prayers at Khaldiya's Grand Mosque with devotion. At least three of them began to follow the sermons of Mahmoud Quul Aghassi, the militant Syrian preacher. Relatives said two of them, upset and angry, went to the funeral in Fallujah for a man named Laith Khalil, a fiery prayer leader who had been killed weeks before with six religious students in what U.S. officials said appeared to be a mistake during a "bomb manufacturing class" in his mosque. While their neighbors complained of rising prices—cooking gas that had gone from sixteen cents to two dollars, cement that had gone from twenty dollars a ton to ninety dollars—Adnan and his friends railed against the American occupation, which they viewed through the prism of religion, not politics.

This was a message, relatives said, repeated often at the Nur Mosque, its small worship hall perched behind a tidy garden of purple periwinkles and white and yellow jasmine, bordered by a sidewalk leading to the entrance. The walkway passes a chalkboard that reads, "You, the ones who believe, do not take the Jews and Christians as patrons." Inside, along freshly painted walls, is a picture of Jerusalem's Aqsa Mosque, one of Islam's holiest sites. Across the top appear these words: "Jerusalem we are coming." The message inside, delivered to them and later to me, was stern.

Sheikh Aalam Sabar was a thirty-three-year-old cleric with a flowing black beard and a white turban draped loosely over his head in the style of the most austere Muslims. "The Americans are infidels," he declared as we sat on his mosque's spotless gray carpets under overhead fans. "It is legitimate," he said, his voice level, "to fight the Americans."

THERE WAS LITTLE TALK OF LIBERATION AND DEMOCRACY IN THE SUNNI regions of Iraq; instead, the language was that of religion: infidels and Muslims, East and West, Islam and its enemies. The occupation, nationalism, the American presence—all these were viewed through the prism of religion, and, most important, the *perception*, by others, of those who died. The Muslim world had opened yet another front in the ever-widening conflict between East and West. In the pantheon of hallowed struggles, Iraq had now joined Palestine and Afghanistan, Chechnya and Bosnia, all countries where a besieged Muslim population was pitted against a more powerful foe. To many, those who fell in its battles were remembered better by their deaths than by their lives. They were *shuhada*, martyrs.

Around the time that Fahdawi and his men were undergoing an awakening, Omar Ibrahim Khalaf, who lived in a village down the road from Fahdawi's town, was plotting his own act of resistance. His story was, in a way, more complicated than Fahdawi's, his motivations less clear. Beyond Khalaf's home of Albu Alwan, his death was little more than a footnote in a simmering guerrilla war. But like the lives of Fahdawi and his comrades, Khalaf's was a unique part of the tapestry of post-Saddam Iraq, life defined by occupation and resistance. He was recognized by his community—his family, his village, and his local preacher—the way that Fahdawi and his colleagues were. He was seen as a devout Muslim, his death as sacred. His fight was viewed through the lens of faith, the construct through which the aftermath of Saddam's fall made sense.

Thirty-two years old, Khalaf was the second youngest in a family of six brothers and six sisters who belonged to the Albu Alwan, a Sunni tribe that gave its name to the village. He was known for his hot temper, but also for his sense of humor. He had curly black hair and a patchy beard more the product of oversight than grooming. As a twelve-year-old, he lost one front tooth and chipped the other while roughhousing outside.

Albu Alwan was a hardscrabble village of a few thousand, its dirt roads bordered by olive trees, date palms, and muddy canals. Khalaf's education, like that of many boys in the village, ended with elementary school, and he soon began farming hay, barley, wheat, and sunflowers on an eight-acre plot he inherited from his father. He was drafted during the war with Iran, but deserted his post after serving six months in Heet. He married young and struggled to make money.

A few years before Saddam's fall, he landed a $600 contract hauling construction material to the resort of Sadamiya on Tharthar Lake, friends said. But he spent most of his life eking out a living, driving a truck back and forth to Jordan and herding his fifteen sheep and one cow. His brother Abdel-Latif said that before the war he managed to make about $90 a month, enough to get by. During the chaotic aftermath, as burdens mounted after the government's fall, he was making no more than $6 a month. His house, started four years before, remained an empty shell of concrete floors and unfinished tan brick walls. A month earlier, his wife had given birth to their sixth child, a boy named Radwan. "He had no money," said Khaled Mawash, a neighbor who knew the family.

Everybody knew everybody else's business; neighbors said Khalaf was devastated when Baghdad fell in just hours. One shopkeeper said Khalaf told him that he had wept at home all day. Others recalled the anger that he loudly voiced as U.S. patrols barreled down the highway that ran next to his house and fields. The sight, they said, was so repugnant that he quit playing soccer in a dusty field adjacent to the bridge that the convoys transited. A childhood friend, Mawlud Khaled, recalled that as the vehicles passed Khalaf said, "If I had a grenade, I would kill myself and take them with me."

Neighbors said his behavior grew increasingly erratic as the weeks progressed. In vain, he once fired a Kalashnikov at a U.S. helicopter flying overhead in the month after Saddam's fall. One morning a week before his death, heat already hanging like a haze over the village, he ran at a passing convoy dressed only in shorts, neighbors recalled. His family had to restrain him. "He hated the Americans," his friend said. "He didn't care whether he died or not."

In late July, neighbors said, Khalaf wrote the names of three people on a piece of paper. He owed each one money—between ten and thirty dollars. A few days later, on August 1, he woke up early and dressed in gray pants and a plaid shirt. A little before seven A.M., as was his custom, he was seen taking his sheep to graze in a nearby pasture. He left without saying a word to his wife, his family, or anyone else in the village. Not a word. "Nobody knew where he went," his cousin Nawar Bidawi told me.

A nine-vehicle convoy of the 43rd Combat Engineering Company was passing just a few miles outside of Fallujah when the attack began. It was 7:15 A.M. The assailants were hidden about fifty yards from the well-traveled road.

It had already been a chaotic day for the soldiers of the 3rd Armored Cavalry Regiment, which was patrolling most of western Iraq at the time. Three attacks had been reported overnight. Four more would follow. For a region that had previously witnessed just three or four attacks a week, the ambushes and raids marked one of the most violent twenty-four-hour periods in weeks.

Khalaf and at least ten others seem to have chosen their spot for the sake of the canals, which provided cover. They lay waiting in one, and another snaked behind it. Both were filled with stagnant water and overgrown with reeds as much as ten feet tall. The village of Falahat was less than a mile away, but the area of the ambush had only fields of clover and orchards of apricot trees and palms laden with ripening dates.

With a loud hiss, the attackers' first volley sent three rocket-propelled grenades at the convoy. Two missed their mark; a third hit the road underneath a Humvee, damaging the oil pan and transmission and disabling the vehicle. By the book, the soldiers returned fire with .50-caliber machine guns, along with lighter weapons and grenade launchers. The volume of the return fire was so intense that even villagers in Falahat said they sought cover. The U.S. troops quickly called in reinforcements, and Lieutenant Noah Hanners, the platoon leader of Heavy Company, arrived within ten minutes in a tank from a base about six miles away.

The assailants in the canal fired their Kalashnikovs wildly and lobbed badly aimed grenades every couple of minutes. But they were outgunned and out-trained, and the U.S. soldiers were on higher ground. Khalaf and the others, all in civilian clothes, were concealed by the canal vegetation but had no avenue of escape, no way to get away. "You could see the cattails move as they tried to run, so we just put a large volume of fire down on the canals," Hanners said.

The lieutenant said he believed that Khalaf was one of the first to die. When he raised his head above the canal's reeds, he was struck by a .50-caliber round. "His head was pretty much missing," the lieutenant said. Machine-gun fire almost detached his left arm and ankle; his torso was riddled with bullets and smeared with blood and the powdery dirt of the Euphrates valley. One or two more of the men were killed at about the same time. As the assailants tried to escape through the canals, wearing plastic sandals, another two or three were killed. In the lopsided fight, so intense villagers would later call it a glimpse of hell, no U.S. soldiers were hurt.

By the time a second tank arrived at about 7:30 A.M., the fight was over, and the soldiers took the body of Khalaf and two others to the U.S. base near a town called Habbaniya. At least one other corpse, too badly mangled to move, was left behind. The air stagnant, the heat tactile, Khalaf's body and the other two that had been recovered were stored in black body bags in a small cement room for three days. The stench was so overpowering that soldiers at the front gate, about a hundred yards away, burned paper to fend off the smell.

Khalaf's oldest brother, Abdel-Latif, and his brother-in-law were escorted by Iraqi police to the base. Soldiers gave them blue surgical masks, but a stench they compared with that of dead livestock on their farms threw them back out the door. "It was an ugly smell. It was unbearable," Abdel-Latif recalled as we sat in his house in Albu Alwan. He smoked cheap cigarettes and thumbed a string of amber worry beads. "When you faced it, you wanted to vomit."

Soldiers suggested they take all three bodies, but Abdel-Latif said he claimed only his brother, whom he identified by his bloodied clothes and his chipped front tooth. The rest of his face, he said, was unrecognizable.

Once again, the gulf between occupier and occupied, the almost certainly unintended and perhaps unavoidable slights: Khalaf's family was outraged by the fact that his body had been left lying on its stomach, rather than its back: his head had faced the ground, rather than the holy city of Mecca. The body had been left in a hot, windowless room, rather than refrigerated. And it was riddled with maggots. Mohammed Ajami, Khalaf's brother-in-law, said, "The treatment was inhuman," perhaps forgetting that it was his brother, after all, who had instigated the attack.

Khalaf's kinsmen returned in a blue Volvo at 3:30 P.M. and, before dusk, buried Khalaf in a wood coffin at the Kiffa cemetery. Because he was a martyr, he was interred as he had died, in his clothes and unwashed. The wounds, according to tradition, bore witness to his martyrdom.

His family said a convoy of a hundred cars carrying 250 people accompanied Khalaf's body. And in the mourning that ensued, Khalaf went from angry spectacle to hero. The sheikh at the village mosque, Omar Aani, told me that the three men to whom Khalaf owed money forgave their loans. Neighbors collected money for his children, now considered orphans. A family that had battled with Khalaf for a year over the rights to water from an irrigation canal apologized to his family and expressed shame at their enmity. "They recognized that he was a true hero," said Khaled, the childhood friend. "They regretted not talking to him."

On a sun-drenched plain along a bluff of barren cliffs, a cheap headstone made of cement marked Khalaf's grave. His name had been hastily scrawled on it in white chalk; below was the invocation "In the name of God, the most merciful and compassionate." This was followed simply by the date of his death: Friday, August 1, 2003. One word on the marker distinguished his resting place from the scores of others that dug into the rocky soil. Khalaf's epitaph declared him a *shahid*, a martyr.

■ ■ ■

Why did he choose to die?

Hanners, the American lieutenant, speculated that Khalaf was at the end of a chain that began with a paymaster—in the lieutenant's words, "someone we've pissed off lately who has money." The paymaster, in turn, would have been linked to someone else who could find weapons and plan the ambush, usually a military officer from Iraq's disbanded army. Hanners was confident that Khalaf had been paid. But as for motives other than money, Hanners told me, one could only guess: "Pretty much anything you can come up with, any motive you can come up with, is a possibility."

In private, a few residents of Albu Alwan passed on rumors that Khalaf might have been motivated in part by money, desperate as he was for a way to mitigate his grinding poverty. Others vigorously, sometimes angrily shook their heads at this suggestion—a denial based, perhaps, more on respect than reality. "The most important thing is that he was so upset by them. Money wasn't important, because he knew he would be killed," said his neighbor Muwaffaq Khaled. "If I'm Muslim and I respect God, I can't die for money. It's *harram*, forbidden."

"I know him well," his brother Mawlud insisted. "It wasn't a matter of money."

In the villages like Albu Alwan, bound by tradition and populated by Sunnis who bristled most at the day-to-day humiliations (perceived and real) of occupation, many insisted in those days that they were actually perplexed by the question of who was behind the attacks on U.S. troops. Were the insurgents driven by Islam, or by loyalty to Saddam? At one house, a neighbor of Khalaf remarked on fresh graffiti in nearby Fallujah, calling Saddam "the hero of heroes." Other graffiti read, "God bless the holy fighters of the city of mosques," "Fallujah will remain a symbol of jihad and resistance," and more bluntly, "We have the right to kill the foreign American occupiers."

"People are confused. Is it for Saddam or is it for Islam?" asked twenty-two-year-old Saad Kamil. "I tell you I don't know."

For many of the people I interviewed in Albu Alwan that week, Khalaf's death seemed to bring clarity to that question. They knew him, they said, and they knew why he would die. A week after his death, it seemed that Khalaf had been transformed into a symbol of his friends' and neighbors' dismay over the occupation. In words as heated as the village's scorched streets, some of the most outspoken townspeople insisted that he had acted out their own grievances. Through him, they found a certain element of catharsis. A shopkeeper along the village's main road called Khalaf a hero motivated by hatred of the occupation, which all of them felt was an awful humiliation. The speaker was Muslim; the Americans were infidels. There was not the slightest shading of hesitation to diminish the absoluteness of the division. What would follow, the speaker said, was clear. "Revenge is part of our tradition," he said; maybe it was with these words that I knew for certain that whatever the American intentions, that gulf was unbridgeable.

Khalaf's brother enumerated the promises that he believed had been broken by the Americans—a share of Iraq's oil he and others had supposedly been assured of receiving, one-hundred-dollar payments that would accompany better rations each month, jobs and prosperity that were supposed to follow the nearly thirteen years of sanctions. His brother-in-law complained of the daily degradations. U.S. soldiers had often made men bow their heads to the ground, for example, an act that he emphasized should only be performed before God. He recalled American soldiers pointing guns at Iraqi men in front of their terrified children and wives. Khalaf, they insisted, had stood up for his countrymen against these degradations.

As we chatted at the house of Aani, the village sheikh, which adjoined the mosque where he led prayers, he acknowledged that, after Khalaf died, he had had to ask friends just who the man was. "I was asking about what he looked like," he said. But what he found out about Khalaf's life paled before what he came to understand about his death. "Omar sacrificed his soul for the sake of his faith, for the sake of his country, for the sake of oppressed people, not for the sake of the previous regime or for the Baath Party. He has become a model for everyone to follow," he said. "The person who resists this situation becomes an example."

He looked at me for a few moments. He seemed to be trying to read my face, trying to read whether I was more Arab or Western. "He's equal to half the Americans in Iraq," he said, his own face expressionless. I didn't know whether I was being insulted or not.

▪ ▪ ▪

A MODEL AND AN EXAMPLE: THAT WAS WHAT FAHDAWI AND HIS BAND, RADICAL-
ized by the occupation, intended to become as they prepared their deaths at
night in Khaldiya.

Fahdawi's brothers said he told his mother to put henna on the palms of
her hands, a sign of joy and celebration often reserved for a wedding night.
He told his family he wanted no grieving if he was killed—no tents set up for
mourners, none of the wild fusillades in the air from AK-47s that traditionally
mark funerals in Iraq. As a martyr, they recalled him insisting, he would be
alive in heaven.

Fahdawi sat down to a dinner of rice, tomatoes, and eggplant. When the
last call to prayer pierced that sweltering summer night, he got up from the
table, said an abrupt good-bye, and left through a yard of lotus trees. "He
didn't return," said Salah, his brother.

The muezzin's sonorous call, at 9:30 P.M., was the signal for the others,
too. Ra'id Kirtani had taken a bath and put on cologne, then laughed with his
mother before leaving. Shaabani, the father of three, simply bade his family
farewell. Some donned their dark track suits and tennis shoes before they left.
Others wore their camouflage under their dishdashas. Fahdawi had put his
clothes in a bag and taken them to the mosque a day earlier.

They staged their attack near an ammunition depot where U.S. forces
were stationed, between Habbaniya Lake and a canal that snakes along
brown, rocky bluffs interspersed with straggling eucalyptus trees and electric
pylons.

At about 1:30 A.M., Fahdawi and the others lay in ambush as troops left the
depot. U.S. officials at the time said the attackers may have been expecting
Humvees; instead, they confronted a patrol of twelve-foot-tall, 67,000-pound
Bradley Fighting Vehicles. Armed with rocket-propelled grenades, AK-47s, and
knives, they were no less outgunned than Khalaf and his men. Fahdawi and
four colleagues were killed. A sixth fighter was captured. There were no U.S.
casualties.

In the town a mile or so away, residents woke up and clambered onto their
roofs to watch a furious storm of sound and light that some said lasted ninety
minutes, others three hours. But even before the fighting ended—its outcome

was really never in doubt—relatives and friends said they suspected the truth. The men had chosen to die.

"I had a feeling," said Khaled Kirtani, Ra'id's brother.

Fahdawi's brother did, too; his emotion could best be described as resignation. "I thought to myself, 'If he hadn't died today, he would die another day,'" he said.

As the sun rose, relatives went to the moonscape that was the battlefield. The bodies were gone, departed on a journey first to the hospital, then to a nearby base, and finally to Khaldiya. Left behind were hundred-yard trails of blood where the bodies had soaked the dust as they were dragged away. Alongside the trails were spent rounds, soiled shoes, and shreds of crimsoned clothing. Muthanna, Shaabani's nineteen-year-old brother, found the bloodied, bullet-holed head scarves of Shaabani, Fahdawi, and Huzeimawi, one checkered red, the other two black. Nearby were the baseball hats, one emblazoned with the Nike logo, that were worn by the Kirtani cousins. "We took them and delivered each one to their families," Muthanna said proudly.

Within hours, the relatives recalled, the men had crossed the threshold from mundane death to celebrated martyrdom.

Sheathed in body bags and carried for hours in Humvees under a scorching sun, the corpses were delivered to the police station that afternoon. Khaled Kirtani said his brother's face was so mangled, he could recognize him only by his hair. His cousin's belly was ripped open and his right arm had been shredded. Khaled thought Shaabani's body had been run over by a tank. Fahdawi's relatives said that half of Fahdawi's face had been blown away.

But, as is said of martyrs across the Muslim world, the body of Khaled's brother had no odor that could be discerned. "There was no smell," Khaled said, surprised still. "They had gone to meet God." Fahdawi's twenty-five-year-old brother Adel said Fahdawi's blood was still glistening hours after the attack. "A dead person's blood will clot," he insisted. "The martyr's blood stays fresh."

At the funerals, held the same day as the deaths, hundreds of relatives and neighbors paid their respects to the five men. Shaabani's father, forty-five-year-old Ahmed, displayed a yellow-and-black notebook with the names of 40 relatives and 318 friends. Carefully recorded by hand were their names and the sums they had given—from one to fourteen dollars—to mark his son's death. "He has many friends," the father told me.

As we sat together, he thumbed through the pages in silence, an enlarged portrait of Shaabani near him, a piece of black tape placed over the corner of the photograph in a mark of mourning. After a few moments, I asked how he felt about what had happened. "I'm sad, but at the same time, I'm very proud of my son," the older man said as he sat cross-legged on the floor on a gray-and-black carpet. The walls had been newly painted in white. "He was not stealing or looting. He was killed for defending his principles and defending his religion. Only the bravest and the most heroic will expose their chest to the Americans' gunfire." He nodded. "Those are the heroes."

In Fahdawi's house, the family heeded the departed's wishes and refused to cry as they received mourners who numbered—in Salah's words—"two hundred, three hundred, perhaps one thousand." Sitting in stony silence, Fahdawi's mother did not shed a tear. Sheikh Abed, his former teacher at the mosque, told the family not to wash the body, but, as is customary in war, to bury it as it was. He bestowed on Fahdawi, who had never married, an honorific reserved for fathers, a symbol of the wedding that awaited him in heaven.

As the family wrapped Fahdawi's body in a white shroud and then set it in a wood coffin, the sheikh, a reserved man with a gray-and-black beard, declined to deliver the traditional funeral prayers. "A martyr doesn't need the prayers," Salah recalled the sheikh saying. "He's guaranteed to be in heaven. He's already there."

The radicalization of young men like Fahdawi was fed by the changing notion of authority made possible when nearly every institution that had ruled the country for a generation was overthrown, crumbled, or was relentlessly questioned. A vacuum resulted, and in Sunni towns like Khaldiya, religious influences that had been sweeping the Arab world for decades but had lain underground in Iraq emerged into the open and began to fill the void. Those currents were strains of political Islam, sometimes its most extremist and revolutionary strains. In the rest of the Arab world, they had already transformed the essence of religious leadership. Now they were molding Iraq.

In Shiite Islam, religious authority is remarkably well delineated. At the pinnacle of a rigid hierarchy in Iraq are ayatollahs vested with authority in the shrine cities of Najaf and Karbala; to observant Shiites, their pronouncements carry the force of law. For centuries, their Sunni counterparts in places like Khaldiya sometimes enjoyed respect, occasionally even reverence, but they had nowhere near the sway of the Shiite ayatollahs.

The clout they did enjoy rested in their power to interpret the Quran. Steeped in Islamic tradition and the teachings of medieval philosophical masters, they were charged with preserving and disseminating the faith to the faithful. Many of those men are venerated to this day, and some, like Ibn Taimiya, a scholar at the turn of the fourteenth century, have been reinvented as revolutionaries seven hundred years later.

But more often than not, the Sunni clergy, or ulema, have served as an instrument of government power, legitimizing the status quo even in times of despotism, and currying favor with rulers for financial gain or otherwise. Their subservience has diminished their credibility. In contemporary Egypt, from Gamal Abdel Nasser to the present, the Sunni ulema are notorious for their creative ability to bestow blessings on policies dear to the government: peace with Israel, for instance, or the paying of interest on loans, which was thought expressly forbidden by Islam. They did the same in Iraq under Saddam, lionizing a man who never treated religion as more than a vehicle for his own self-enshrinement or as a path to secure elusive legitimacy. That relationship hurt the reputation of the Sunni clerics: at worst, they were regarded by their people as lackeys; at best, they were seen as impotent functionaries in times too dire for weakness.

Among the most reverent in much of the modern Arab world, this invited a backlash against the Sunni clergy. In response, in recent decades, new generations of devout Sunni Muslims had risen to interpret the Quran for themselves. Although the older clergy was still respected by some, a younger, far more militant, activist contingent was gaining force, with its own reading of religion. And whereas Shiite Islam had a rigid hierarchy and preordained protocol for advancement, Sunni Islam did not; so the new contingent could emerge more assertively and did so brazenly in the 1960s and 1970s. Joining these new militants were laymen—youths who resembled Fahdawi and his colleagues in their ardor—who had taken it upon themselves to define Islam, its message, and its meaning within their own context. They had already made their mark in places like Egypt, where in 1981 Mohammed Abdel-Salam al-Farag, an Egyptian electrician of humble origins, wrote a pamphlet that laid the philosophical justification for the assassination of Anwar Sadat.

His argument: Islam, as a religion of revolution, impels its followers to sedition against illegitimate and unfaithful rulers. (Farag was executed for his role in the assassination.) Now Fahdawi and his men, inspired by the American occupation, were also linking their struggle with the militant aspirations of the larger Arab world.

Like many religious movements in Muslim countries, political Islam was elastic in Iraq, in Khaldiya, and in the homes of Fahdawi and his men. They adapted it to local circumstances, molded it to their own context, but drew from it the symbolism and meaning they desired. For Fahdawi and his colleagues, faith was tailored for resistance against foreign occupation and, through religion, they justified their deaths.

To help chart his path, Fahdawi looked to one of the younger, more militant preachers, a man considered neither corrupted by the old ways nor co-opted by the old government. This was Aghassi, the Syrian preacher also known as Abu Qaqaa. I had seen his cassettes and video CDs in religious bookstores in neighboring Jordan before I traveled to Baghdad in 2003, although they circulated only from hand to hand in Iraq before the occupation. By that autumn, they were being freely sold in Fallujah for less than one dollar, vying for space on shelves cluttered with cheaply copied tape-recorded sermons. Relatives said the young men of Fahdawi's circle had rented them for twenty-five cents, sometimes watching them together and trading them among themselves. "If they had spare time, they would watch them," said Abdullah Kirtani, Hamid's brother.

The tall, lanky Aghassi was a stentorian speaker, with a modern style and forceful approach that was familiar to me from other Arab countries. He carefully refrained from criticizing his own government—he lived under Syria's version of the Baath Party—but delivered a message of jihad that characterized the United States and Israel as inseparable allies in a campaign against the Muslim world. As with other Islamic preachers, the Palestinian cause sat at the heart of his rhetoric, and he framed it as a struggle between religions. He gestured with extreme animation, his finger pointing into the air and shaking, his arm crashing down like an executioner's sword. A gifted orator with a booming voice, he punctuated his speeches with talk of traitors and mercenaries. He built to fiery climaxes, then softened to a tone of reason, only to build again to fury.

Many days later, as I tried to decipher Fahdawi's martyrdom, I watched the same CDs that the men had viewed before they died, all of which I had picked up for a few dollars at a small storefront in Fallujah where they were selling briskly along with recorded messages from Osama bin Laden and Abdel-Hamid Kishk, a radical Egyptian preacher who came of age under Sadat.

"We want manhood and heroism," Aghassi declared in one taped sermon, delivered to a crowd that broke into tears. "We want people to love death and yearn for heaven. We want the words 'No god but God' to shake the world." Muslims, he said, should look to martyrdom "as a thirsty man looks to water."

The montage behind the speaker was telling: images of Iraq and Palestine were relentlessly interwoven. Pictures of Palestinian casualties, often graphic, were followed by footage of women and children crying, blood in the streets, stone-throwing youths, Palestinian funeral marches, and Israeli soldiers chasing protesters against the backdrop of Islam's holiest sites in Jerusalem. Images from Iraq followed seamlessly, cataloging the destruction caused by the U.S. invasion, the toppling of Saddam's statue, bloodied casualties in hospitals, looters dancing in the streets with furniture stacked on donkey carts, and American armored vehicles, flying the U.S. flag, crashing through Baghdad.

In a tape made after Baghdad's fall, Aghassi railed against Arab leaders allied with the United States, men "who know nothing but palaces." He drew on Islamic history to recommend tactical retreat and sited the conflict to follow in a clearly religious context—of infidels against believers, of Muslims against others.

"I wept," he said, "for a whole hour as I looked on the American tanks as they were entering the capital of Harun al-Rashid, as if those tanks were rolling over my heart, stepping on our tongues, before the eyes and the ears of the Arab world.

"Show these mercenaries a black day," he went on, his voice dropping low. "Like a dark night, drown them in the Euphrates and the Tigris."

In another CD, its quality poor but serviceable, Aghassi's sermon was juxtaposed with images of planes flying into the World Trade Center and pictures of the White House, Capitol Building, and Kremlin followed by deafening explosions and fireballs. In the background, over chants of "O God!," Aghassi stood with an M-16 rifle in his left hand and a pistol in the other, an almost cartoonish image of an empowered cleric. The sermon, recorded on May 17, 2002, was titled "The Cadence of Justice in the Time of Defeat":

"Tell them that they shall be attacked in their own cities and homes. They will be destroyed. A pledge to you, my Lord, that the believers' hearts will be at peace only after we have seen destruction all over America. A pledge to you, God, to raise your banner, that our blood shall not be shed except at the tree of faith. A pledge to you that we will be your best worshippers, who will not hesitate to advance on death, unblocked by barriers. No trench will stop us. . . . America has tyrannized the Muslim nation. Pour on it your anger and change its strength to weakness, its wealth to poverty, its unity into disunity."

There was no doubt in Aghassi's words, no hesitation. They punctuated the air with confidence, couched in a single reading of destiny. They were new to Iraq, which for so long had been ambivalent, a place of complexity, muffled opinions, and what was *ghamidh.* But there were no layers or ambiguities or conflicts in the sermons of Aghassi, only utter certainty about the cause and what was necessary in its pursuit. There was an utter faith about death, with no fear or reluctance. There was utter conviction in the martyrs' righteousness. What was suicide to Westerners was an act of devotion to them.

That winter, a soldier I met in the Sunni town of Samarra, Sergeant First Class Robert Hollis, would put into words the change I sensed. He had fought an engagement with Iraqi guerrillas in checkered headscarves and dark shirts and pants. In a battle that ebbed and flowed over a day, the guerrillas, shuttling from back alley to side road in orange-and-white taxis, BMWs, and white Toyota pickups, had dared to mass in numbers against the overwhelming power of U.S. forces. The toll was, as usual, asymmetrical: scores of guerrillas killed; no U.S. fatalities. When we spoke, though, it wasn't the victory of his colleagues that he remembered. It was the way his enemies died. It was their absolute conviction.

Through his scope, Hollis said he saw a man lift a rocket-propelled grenade launcher to his shoulder, taking aim. "I'm telling you, these guys taking some of the shots knew they were going to die," said Hollis, a seventeen-year veteran from Pensacola. "But they still under that fire squeezed the trigger even though they knew that was the last thing they were going to do. They were standing the ground and fighting, and our guys were standing the ground and fighting. Both sides were sending a message. We sent a message to them and they sent a message to us, that they're willing to die fighting us."

Hollis was standing on a dirt berm at his base outside the town as we talked. We stepped away from his commanders, and he seemed to speak more candidly. His words were clipped, soldierly, but there was an undercurrent of surprise.

"They're going to hit you and before you hit them, they're going to disappear. That's their M.O.," said Hollis, whose tank barrel was emblazoned with the word "Comanche." "In this case, they hit us and instead of disappearing, they stayed. Did you see those tanks? Do you know the amount of firepower on those tanks? The amount of firepower we had, why would you even think of attacking something like that?"

My last conversation in the two days I spent in Khaldiya was with Khaled Kirtani, the brother of Fahdawi's colleague Ra'id Kirtani. Ra'id was buried with his cousin in a cemetery overlooking a dense grove of palm trees and the green-domed Sheikh Masoud shrine, a local place of pilgrimage. The men's marble tombstones called them "martyred heroes." Ribbons colored the green of Islam were tied at the base.

Khaled was eager to speak. He had a message, I thought, and he wanted an audience. Beginning with confidence, he stated the goals of the Americans: to protect Israel, control Iraq's oil, and, most important, destroy Islam. "We realize the Americans want to do the same to us that was done to the Palestinians. But this is Iraq, and they cannot do it."

This was almost a cliché. But then he turned to the subject of Saddam to deliver a different message, pronounced with no less bitterness or anger. "Saddam Hussein put a tent over the Iraqi people," said the twenty-seven-year-old Khaled. "He cheated the Iraqi people." Slender and stern like his brother, Khaled listed the former Iraqi leader's sins, as if reciting from a textbook. The fallen dictator had started the senseless war with Iran, during which Muslim killed Muslim. He had invaded Kuwait. He had given the Americans a pretext to occupy Iraq. And his army, Khaled said, had "dissolved in minutes."

"Saddam Hussein is behind all our problems," he told me. He was wearing brown sandals, blue track pants, and a black shirt that he said he had inherited from his slain brother. "My expectation is that Saddam Hussein is in the United States on an island. They'll build a monument for him because he made their mission easy."

At the time, one current of opinion in the Sunni town still looked to Saddam with nostalgia for the days when their region was favored at the expense of the Kurdish north and the Shiite south. To some of them, he stood as the embodiment of a recognized past as opposed to an uncertain future. Angrily, Khaled dismissed those sentiments, voiced most often by his parents' generation. Like his young relatives, their conversations peppered with the language of Aghassi, he said they died for God, not Saddam.

"The young people are waking up. I saw it with my brother and cousin," he said, running his hand through his trimmed beard. "They're not Baathists, they're not party members. They did it for God. When they saw the Americans come, raid the houses, steal from the people, they didn't accept it."

At times, Khaled grew agitated and boastful. "There will come a day when the Muslims are victorious," he declared. Then he would relax, lean back in his chair as I sat next to him, and look to his side, away from me. He would invoke the Quran, in quiet tones. He would quote the prophet Mohammed's sayings, recited from memory. And, with utter conviction, he would talk with the fervor of the converted.

"The American people should realize they're going to start receiving coffins," Khaled said, his words sounding like advice. "We're not their slaves." He stopped to catch his breath, shaking his head as if uttering a self-evident truth. "We accept death as easily as we drink water."

ON DECEMBER 14, 2003, L. PAUL BREMER STOOD BEFORE A TIGHTLY GUARDED news conference within the fallen government's vast constellation of domed palaces and marble offices. "Ladies and gentlemen, we got him," Bremer declared. These were words that many Iraqis had waited a lifetime to hear. "The tyrant is a prisoner."

Saddam, after nearly nine months on the run, had been captured.

The end was ignominious, especially for a man who had ruled the destiny of millions, who had sent countless to die in battles with no meaning and in dungeons with no mercy. On a tip from a relative of Saddam's, in a region where clan and family reign supreme, soldiers with the 4th Infantry Division, based in Tikrit near his hometown, found the fallen dictator crouching in a hole eight feet long and less than three feet high. Near a palm grove, the site was a garbage-strewn plot, not too far from the Tigris River and not too distant from Saddam's humble birthplace, where he was raised by his widowed mother and uncle in unforgiving poverty. Five feet underground, the hole, with dirt floors and concrete walls, was barely big enough for his bulky six-foot frame to fit. On one side were a pipe for ventilation and a tiny plastic fan. On the other was a fluorescent bulb that didn't work. The ground over the hideaway was covered with a Styrofoam block, a rubber mat, and flower pots, an attempt to mask the disturbed earth. Nearby were two AK-47 rifles and a green metal trunk filled with $750,000 in $100 bills.

Saddam, the indomitable legend of Baath Party myth, had a loaded pistol but, his vanity gone, his delusions of grandeur fallen away, he offered no resistance. None at all. Once found, he thrust his hands toward the sky and emerged quickly, looking haggard, with a straggling, unkempt beard. The soldiers present reported that their prisoner was nervous, dirty, and disoriented. He called out in halting English to his captors: "I am Saddam Hussein, president of Iraq, and I am willing to negotiate." It was 8:26 P.M. on a Saturday.

One of the soldiers replied, "President Bush sends his regards."

In a moment of such drama, so much was mundane. In the hut in al-Dwar where he spent his last hours of freedom before going to ground, a dozen books were piled near Saddam's bed. There was classical Arabic poetry and Fyodor Dostoyevsky's *Crime and Punishment*. Coarse blankets sat atop rusty beds. On a refrigerator was a cake of Palmolive Naturals soap, a bottle of Dove shampoo, a pot of moisturizing cream, and a stick of Lacoste deodorant "pour homme." To the side were two cans of Raid and a flyswatter. Opened bags of walnuts and pistachios sat on a bookshelf. On the floor was a Styrofoam container with three pairs of white boxer shorts and two white sleeveless undershirts (XL and XXL) still in plastic wrapping. There was a hint of luxury—a gilded face mirror—but only a hint. Rising from the most humble of origins, Saddam ended in circumstances no less mean.

President Bush took the opportunity to declare the end to "a dark and painful era" for Iraq. "A hopeful day has arrived," he said in an address from Washington. "All Iraqis can now come together and reject violence and build a new Iraq."

That was the sentiment voiced by American officials in Baghdad, jubilant at a rare, tangible demonstration of liberation. Perhaps their enthusiasm was more hope. With Saddam gone, why should Iraqis keep fighting? With Saddam's capture as an answer, perhaps occupier and occupied might finally ask the same questions, despite divergent vocabularies defined by their own heritages and ambitions. "The capture of Saddam Hussein is a defining moment in the new Iraq," said Lieutenant General Ricardo Sanchez, the U.S. commander in Iraq. "I expect that the detention of Saddam Hussein will be regarded as the beginning of reconciliation for the people of Iraq and as a sign of Iraq's rebirth."

Saddam or not, though, the two sides' questions still remained different.

The Sunni regions of Iraq can be visualized, more or less accurately, as an expanse that begins in Baghdad, then stretches in an arc north, fanning out east and west to the borders of Iran and Syria. In the days after Saddam's capture, it was an even more unsettled place.

Nasir, Karim, and I set off from a place in Baghdad called the Imams Bridges that arches over the Tigris River and begins in Adhamiya, a Sunni Muslim neighborhood whose venerated Abu Hanifa Mosque marks the burial place of one of Islam's greatest scholars, an eighth-century jurist who founded the most popular present-day school of Islamic law. As if to exemplify the unease, it was shielded behind eight steel barricades. Its twin minarets, clock tower, and tan brick walls interspersed with turquoise still bore the scars of war. The slogans painted along its subdued streets invoked nostalgia and anger. "Long live Saddam," read one, scrawled in black. "Jihad is our way," said another. A dozen or so men carrying AK-47 rifles sat atop the mosque's roof and patrolled the street below, casting a wary glance toward the bridge. "The future? What's the future?" one of them, Ammar Abu Nour Quds, asked me when I stopped to chat. He was just twenty-seven, but his hair was almost completely gray. "We don't have any future."

In its stirring drama, Saddam's capture unleashed a paroxysm of emotion in the arc of Sunni land. The sentiments were grim. Saddam's arrest was the latest benchmark for a community that was besieged, leaderless, and adamant in its refusal to accept the occupation. No longer kingmakers, the community's leaders vowed that they still held the key to stability. But casting a shadow over my conversations those days with men like Quds was a sense of dispossession, of a minority searching for a voice in the contest to create a new state. It was a sense of waiting. In a photo shop near the Abu Hanifa Mosque, Khaled Ahmed put it to me bluntly: "The people are waiting for something, to hear something, to see something." He listened for a moment to the sermon, being broadcast from loudspeakers; it urged restraint and unity. On his wall were pictures of U.S. tanks and Humvees driving by the mosque. "They're waiting for some kind of hope," he told me.

For some, that hope still resided with Saddam, and theirs was the kind of feeling that comes with the death of a relative: refusal to accept the finality of the event. As we wandered up the Tigris, we heard that longing in the talk of the towns, villages, and farms. Some claimed that Saddam somehow had not really been captured. In Tikrit, near his ancestral hometown, young men insisted that the former Iraqi president had visited just a few days earlier and doled out "ten papers"—Iraqi slang for one thousand dollars—to the sheikh of the Bayt Habous Mosque, telling him to distribute it to the poor. They recounted another story, spread at a wedding that week, by which Saddam was sighted in the streets of Tikrit on the day of his capture, wearing a checkered kaffiyeh and greeting the people. In Thuluyah, villagers traded stories of his appearance in Fallujah, Rammadi, Baaquba. Others pointed to the photos taken after his capture—already indelible images in Iraq. Saddam had a scar on his right hand, some insisted, but no one saw it in the pictures.

During this same trip, I returned to Thuluyah, the town where a father had been forced to kill his informer son. In a riverside home, I sat again with the men who had demanded the killing. Former army officers who had risen to positions of influence and prestige under the Baath Party's rule, they were the constituency, in the poor rural areas of the Sunni region, that owed Saddam its loyalty.

"I have some suspicions," Abdullah Ali told me. We were sitting near a window that overlooked the meandering Tigris, sharing a lunch of chicken, rice, salad, stuffed grape leaves, and chicken soup. Abdullah and his brother were puzzled. They had understood Saddam: he was a peasant, imbued with the traditions of tribe, conservative in a clannish way, given to revenge. He was like them. And until his capture a week earlier, they had believed they shared with him ideas of dignity, pride, and honor. How could he not fight back? Perhaps it wasn't him, they suggested. Perhaps he had been drugged.

"If he didn't resist, he would be a coward," Abdullah told me.

"He's supposed to fight with honor, he's supposed to defend his honor," added his brother, Abed.

Abdullah shook his head, a gesture of dismay. "We believed in him, that he would always resist," he said. "We can't believe that he would be reduced to this level, as a coward."

Ihana, an insult. This word punctuated their conversations around a butane heater, where a silver coffee pitcher was kept warm on top. The brothers recalled Baghdad and how it fell with barely a fight. They railed against U.S. soldiers who freely entered their towns in tanks and armored vehicles, barging into homes with women present and forcing men to kneel. And a week earlier, they had seen the images on Arab satellite television of Saddam with his unruly beard. Not just the images but the probing of his mouth, the inspection of his scalp, at the hands of a U.S. soldier. The footage was repeated over and over, like a recurring nightmare, and they themselves were humiliated by it. In a way, they shared his sense of shame.

"No president can accept to be insulted like that," Abed said. "He was a president." His eyes narrowed. They hadn't treated Emperor Hirohito that way after World War II.

"Believe me, the day of his capture was the same as the collapse of Baghdad, maybe worse," Abdullah added.

In their humiliation, the men spoke to the greater forces at work in Iraq those days, the currents embodied in younger, more militant Iraqis like Fahdawi and his men. There was a vacuum of leadership, and there was a crisis of identity for a people disenfranchised. For some, Saddam had filled the role of leader, but his time had passed. The question they now asked was: Who will represent us? It was a question that transcended Saddam's capture; in fact, that it was being asked showed how far beyond the fallen dictator Iraq had already traveled, in just nine months of occupation. Whereas in the United States, the struggle was still often seen as America versus Saddam, Saddam soon became a sideshow in Iraq. The stakes were higher: Who has the right to rule, and from where does that right arise?

For generations, sect and ethnicity had cast a long shadow over Iraq; under Saddam's clan-based regime, Shiite Arabs and Kurds were the most frequent victims of repression. But only in the freewheeling postwar arena had sect and ethnicity come to almost exclusively define politics, with explicit quotas determining the allotment of power and patronage under the U.S. administration. In that contest, the Kurds were represented by the community's two traditional parties, based in the north. The Shiites, in the majority, found a voice through formerly exiled groups or men like Muqtada Sadr and Ayatollah Sistani, who emerged forcefully in the wake of Saddam's fall.

The Sunni Arabs had no charismatic politicians, no lay leadership. The Baath Party, its leadership traditionally dominated by Sunnis, had been outlawed in May 2003 in a decree by Bremer. The Iraqi Islamic Party, whose leader served in the U.S.-appointed Governing Council, struggled to acquire support from a constituency that overwhelmingly rejected the present state of affairs. In the words of one leading Sunni cleric, Abdel-Salaam Kubeisi, the party did little more than "market the occupation." The leaders of Sunni Arab tribes, aggressively courted by the U.S. administration, were seen by many as compromised. "In the past they took money from Saddam," one man in Thuluyah told me. "Now they're taking money from the Americans."

Stepping into the breach were the same forces I saw in Khaldiya, appealing to an Islam grounded in nationalism. The act of Fahdawi and his men was not an isolated incident. As the occupation continued, as the armed opposition mounted, many of the people I met in Sunni regions began to speak more and more to what I was encountering around me, a landscape growing more radical.

Soon after Saddam's capture, I was handed a leaflet after the Friday prayers at a Sunni mosque. The young men distributing the flyers handed out a few others to men around me, then, in moments, faded into the departing crowd. The flyer's title amounted to clarity amid the confusion, direction amid the chaos: "The Disaster of the Occupation and the Duties of the Islamic Nation."

"The goal of the infidels, after stealing our wealth, is to remove us from our religion by force and all other means, so that we become a lost nation without principle, making it easier for the Jews and Christians to humiliate us," it read.

The unsigned flyer—printed on both sides—threatened those cooperating with the occupation, urged support for the resistance, and warned against informing to U.S. forces. Fighting the occupiers, it said, was a religious principle, an individual duty incumbent on every Muslim. Everyone reading the leaflet was urged to make ten copies and distribute them to others. "When God sees us in this condition, he will rescue us from the infidel and enemy," it declared.

As the men left the mosque, many folded the leaflet and placed it in their pockets.

AFTER THE TRIP THROUGH THE SUNNI TRIANGLE, I RETURNED TO BAGHDAD, where I visited Dr. Shahla Kadhim Atraqji, the beautiful thirty-eight-year-old Shiite doctor whose lonely voice had always reminded me of the capital's fortunes. We met, again at the Hunting Club, after Saddam's capture and, for a moment when his arrest came up in the conversation, she was excited, even jubilant. Coming from her, such sentiments were rare.

"We were ready to shake hands with the devil to get rid of Saddam," she told me. We were sitting at the same white plastic table in the expansive courtyard, sipping an orange drink called Rani that was imported from Saudi Arabia, under the shade of towering palm trees. "It was the happiest day of my life. I was alone, and I shouted." Older men passed us with their gym bags and headed for the swimming pool, suggesting a routine of life that Baghdad in these days rarely permitted, with its persistent blackouts, surging crime, and insurgent attacks, along with the specter of more. "He ruined us," she went on. "He destroyed our life completely. I wish I could stand in front of him in court. They have to give us the right. They have to." His palaces—she shook her head—he had built them while he paid Iraqi government employees two dollars a month. "He was a criminal."

To Americans, Saddam's capture was the finale to a conflict that had lasted more than a decade, beginning with Iraq's invasion of Kuwait in 1990. Through those years, Saddam was an almost cartoonish nemesis, in a conflict that was always gratuitously personalized. Saddam was now in custody; President Bush kept the fallen dictator's pistol mounted in a study next to the Oval Office, a trophy of war. Of course, most Iraqis never saw the conflict that way, never as Saddam against America; in fact, many would argue that both Saddam and America victimized them. Likewise, Saddam's arrest resonated differently. For Shahla, it was a time to pause and reflect on what he signified, then turn to what she still faced, a country transformed by eight months of occupation, ideology, and hardship. In a life of war—the memory still burned; of Iranian soldiers being paraded through Baghdad's street when she was a schoolgirl—she saw more strife ahead. Baghdad was always at war, whether Saddam was prowling the palm groves of the Tigris or biding his time in U.S. custody. The drama was not in Bremer's announcement, but in life unfolding around her.

As we sat at the club, alone except for flocks of pigeons and sparrows in the courtyard, I asked whether she was hopeful about her city, about Baghdad. She answered immediately: "No, never. It's finished. It's lost, really." She caught herself and, a moment later, offered another answer, more ambivalent. "It is still there, but it's hidden."

Nearby, workmen swung sledgehammers down on the tiles of a dilapidated patio slated for renovation. Flower beds, with little grace, encircled palm trees, and the white stone borders—crooked, askew, or crumbling—showed signs of neglect. Nearby was a sign that read "Iraqi Hunting Club," written in English in red, in Arabic in blue. The second "n" was missing. In time, as we talked, an explosion was heard in the distance, unusual only in how ordinary it was becoming. "Music, music," Shahla said, laughing. "Every morning I wake up to the explosions. I say, 'Oh,' and then I go back to sleep."

The warbling of birds glided over the strains of Nancy Ajram, the same Lebanese singer who'd been playing the last time we were at the club. Her honeyed voice was everywhere these days. "It is worse now, worse than any of the wars, worse than ever, ever," Shahla told me. "We are not safe. When somebody leaves their home, they don't know if they come back. Nobody knows. Whenever you walk, there might be a bomb. You don't know."

I asked her what Baghdad might be like in five years. She laughed. "We can't predict tomorrow! We don't know what will happen tomorrow!"

Her smile faded. "I hope we live the next five years," she said. "Maybe one year, maybe tomorrow. Maybe there will be a bomb and we will be killed. Nobody knows."

Shahla didn't sound desperate; she seemed anything but frantic. She was, rather, mournful. As a doctor, Shahla was independent, exuding a feminine strength that more conservative, religious forces were trying to extinguish in

Iraq. Insistently unmarried, she said she was lonely, too, although never lonely enough to embrace the future. Like her city, she turned inward, drawing on her own strength as her world crumbled around her.

"The best thing is that I have no children," she told me, her eyes cast down. "I have no family. I couldn't bring children into this. I always told my mother, 'Why did you bring us into this? You're a criminal!'" She laughed at the word, then turned serious again. "If I can't offer my children a good life, I would never bring them into this world."

14

BAGHDAD IS YOUR CITY

The modern thoroughfare to the neighborhood of Mansur was clogged with sentiments that spoke to the past and future, to aspirations and disappointments. "The mass graves are the living proof that Saddam and his collaborators are debauched infidels," one line of graffiti read. Another insisted, "No Sunni, no Shiite. All of us are under the banner: There is no god but God and Mohammed is his messenger." Across Fourteenth of Ramadan Avenue, on a tan brick wall, posters put up by allies of the occupation, then ripped down by those opposed to it, gave a version of the future. Against a backdrop of a blue sky, sketches of birds' wings fluttered across one sheet. "Together under the wing of peace," read the caption. Further down the street, political demands of the religious Shiites lined the walls: "Islam is the basis of the constitution."

It was late afternoon in a lingering autumn, and the congestion of Baghdad's streets had eased. Nasir and I were going to visit Fuad, the Shiite doctor who had been filled with such optimism after Saddam's fall. At Ahmed Hassan al-Bakr Square, two rusted metal poles, one pointing to one o'clock, the other to three o'clock, were left where the statue of Saddam's predecessor once stood. Behind them was a new billboard, installed by the U.S. administration. "Baghdad is your city," it read in bold type. Below the caption was an image becoming more familiar in Baghdad: in the crosshairs of the U.S. military was a man in black mask carrying a rocket-propelled grenade launcher, with black smoke and an explosion's fireball billowing behind him. On the other side was a scene of Iraqis constructing a cinder-block building. Another billboard portrayed a classroom with a teacher and student at the chalkboard. A green map of the country was superimposed over everything, and it was divided into three colored bands. In white, "Progress." In red, "Iraq." In white again, "Prosperity." And then this slogan: "The progress will continue despite these attacks, which are trying to make the future of Iraqis oppressive."

"They don't know anything about Iraq," said Fuad, who six months earlier had considered himself all but an American citizen. We had just been seated. He was glum and, at moments, agitated. His exuberance after Saddam's fall—his predictions of a better future, his adoration of President Bush, his appeals for Iraqi patience—had become trepidation, a nagging sense of doubt, when something as ordinary as electricity could not yet be relied on and the specter of something dreadful—kidnapping, robbery, murder, the carnage inflicted by increasingly effective insurgents—loomed. "I feel sorry for them," he said of the U.S. administration, a hint of both plea and reprimand in his voice. "They don't understand the Iraqi mentality. They stick with the American way of thinking."

"They don't know what they're doing," his wife, Suad, said.

The couple had just returned to Baghdad after spending time in Amman and in London, where their youngest daughter, Balsam, lived. In Los Angeles, the wife of their son, Firas, had given birth to a girl just a month earlier. With a visa they had just received, they hoped to see her for the first time.

On this day, the still-intermittent electricity in their home was working. We sipped cups of Arabic coffee, the sludgy black grounds gathering at the bottom, and water, which had been chilled in the working refrigerator. A gray sky—Baghdad is sometimes overcast in fall and winter—colored the windows, and the mood was subdued. With the couple was their forty-three-year-old daughter, Lubna, who lived across town in Jadriya, and her children. Like her sister Yasmine, who was living in Jordan, Lubna was petite and beautiful. Dark eyes accented her black hair. Clearly, she shared the family intelligence.

Always friendly, always hospitable, these people made me feel at home.

Almost immediately, though, I sensed the transformation in mood since the last time we met; the Mohammeds were far less festive, their optimism forgotten. They were not angry, and there was none of the terror I saw elsewhere in Baghdad. But, like the city, the family was grim, worried about their capital, which was in the hands of rulers whose wisdom, capability, and integrity they questioned.

"From childhood, you hear from your father, your grandfather, your relative, 'America is against us, America is with Israel.' From childhood. This is from *childhood*," the doctor explained. Everyone was happy to see Saddam go, he continued, but the Americans had little goodwill to draw on and could ill afford mistakes.

"They're so . . ." Lubna paused, grasping for the right idea and the appropriate word. "I can't say 'arrogant,' but they're so sure about themselves."

"This is how a stranger behaves," the doctor said.

"Saddam was the worst on earth, but he was an Iraqi," Lubna emphasized. The attitude she refused to call arrogance, Americans telling Iraqis what to do—it hurt. "I don't hate the Americans, I don't hate them," she said. "But I have to admit we're not a free country."

Lubna, three years younger than Yasmine, was an architect by training. Baghdad's plight made her think of its past—the old Baghdad, the city of treasured photos in textbooks, much of it too old to remember. Along the old buildings was the *shanashil*, known as *mashrabiya* in much of the Arab world: patterned latticeworks of carved wood that served as windows for balconies that stretched creakingly over the narrow, crooked streets. In more distant times, the *shanashil* allowed women to stay secluded while viewing the street. They could see out, while no stranger could peer within. The *shanashil* was a metaphor for Baghdad, old and new.

The past Baghdad I remembered was Saddam's capital, a testament to his megalomania, a strange, extended sprawl with an eternal memory and a disfigured sense of grandeur. Saddam's Stalinesque statues towered over the squares. His portraits—in black beret, in jacket and tie, in Arab headdress, sitting with children in a surreal Norman Rockwell reality—hung everywhere in ministries, offices, and galleries. After Saddam's fall, these statues were, of course, removed (rusted poles like those in Ahmad Hassan al-Bakr Square were left). The palaces had been looted and the city was stripped bare to reveal itself as a modern creation of brick and mud, a utilitarian place that barely suggested a capital and said nothing of the past.

Now Baghdad was full of the architecture of occupation, which had fallen like a curtain over the city during the past year. There were barricades in all shapes—some reaching to the waists of passersby, others five, ten, or even twenty feet tall. Some of the fortifications sloped gradually and squatted on the ground; others rose formidably, like a palace wall. But all were a somber gray, like the overcast sky, and all were made of a dull unadorned concrete. They competed for space with brown burlap receptacles filled with sand and rolls of wire, their metal catching the sun's glint, their barbs snaring wayward trash in a panoply of colors. The reason for some barriers was obvious, as with those around the sprawling U.S. headquarters in the former Republican Palace. Others were more mysteriously placed and the choice of location itself attracted notice.

Lubna thought about the city and its present.

"We've learned how to walk in the dark," she said.

Was she being literal? I wasn't sure. I didn't know whether she was thinking of the way Iraqis survived under Saddam's slaughter, or how they endured the Americans' more practical failures from electricity to security.

"We have to be patient," Lubna said, "and Iraqis are not patient."

Her father had always been optimistic and exuberant, never less than certain that the future for his grandchildren would be better. Was he still hopeful?

"Of course I am," he declared. "From the start, I thought if they got rid of Saddam, everything would be all right. Nobody did what Saddam had done. The mass graves, kicking out three hundred thousand people because he accused them of being Iranian, a policeman comes to my house—two or three of them—and takes me away. Certainly it will get better, there's no doubt," he said. "It will take time."

As I left his house that day, through his tidy garden, which he had flooded in order to keep it moist, he followed me to his metal gate, glaring in the sun. As was his habit, he wanted to make sure that my mood was high. Even in grim times, he wanted to shore up my spirits. "Don't worry," he shouted, as I got into the car with Karim. "The future will be brighter. It will be okay."

▪ ▪ ▪

THE DOCTOR'S OLDEST DAUGHTER, YASMINE, HAD LITTLE OF HER FATHER'S
faith. She and her family had weathered the invasion, but not what followed.
During the summer, as the insurgency escalated in the Sunni regions and
violence burgeoned in Baghdad, she, her daughter, Hala, and her youngest
son, Amin, had left the city in a well-packed Chevy Suburban for the relative
safety of Amman. A few weeks later, her husband and her oldest son, Hussein,
joined them after the latter finished his finals at the university. Travelers
feared the bandits who held sway on parts of the highway—the region was
like an Eastern version of *Mad Max*—but everyone arrived in Jordan safely.

"We ran for the lives of our children, then our own, simply to save our
skins," Yasmine wrote me in an e-mail. "Whom do I blame?" she asked. "Of
course I blame Saddam because he is behind all of this, but the Americans
are to blame, too."

During the war, Yasmine had never shared her father's optimism. She
loathed Saddam, but was mistrustful of the United States. Saddam was the
Americans' man, she used to say. After the invasion, her skepticism turned to
a sense of betrayal and her remarks were bathed in anger. "Imagine," she
wrote me. "We were willing to risk the war and all its atrocious destruction if
it would bring back the good old days." (She meant the 1970s, the lost prosperity.) "How naive! And how stupid we were!"

Exile could mean many things in Baghdad in those days. Those who
stayed in the capital during the occupation retreated more and more into
their homes as time went on, buffeted as they were by the carjackings, armed
robberies, assaults, and more and more frequent kidnappings that targeted
people with money—merchants, traders, factory owners, jewelers, and, in
particular, doctors, whose ransoms sometimes stretched into the hundreds of
thousands of dollars. In response, Iraqis created an exile of sorts behind brick
walls, iron gates, and barricaded doors. As society atomized, its fabric tearing,
many fair-minded, conscientious people simply withdrew. Others fled, literally, barely locking their doors behind them. Yasmine's family had left everything inside their house in Jadriya. Their car was still parked behind a steel
fence shaded by a garden's trees.

Yasmine's feeling of loss, the sad sense of the end of home, had grown as the chaos of the summer melted into the fear that had been building since the Ramadan bombings. She told me that many of her more hopeful friends thought they were crazy to leave. "Are you out of your minds leaving your home, your possessions?" they wrote her. "You will see how our beloved Baghdad will turn into a safe haven. You will see how Baghdad will recover from its long illness and retrieve its health." These people believed that change would come because the Americans intended it. "My only wish at the time was to prove them right," Yasmine wrote me. "Now those very people and ten times their number have left Baghdad after us."

Like many Iraqis in exile, she thought about what made Baghdad beautiful. To her sister, it was the *shanashil*. For Yasmine, it was the groves of palm trees that graced the Tigris, their fecund greens interrupting the sun's intensity. "I feel sorry for it. I feel sorry for the people. It's breaking my heart. It's really breaking my heart," she wrote. "I love everything about it. I love the trees, I love the water. I love everything about it. But I love my children more. Now my daughter, when she gets up in the morning, says, 'It's so nice to wake up when there is electricity and hot water!'"

Whom to blame for the failures? The question was asked more and more through the occupation, as Iraqis debated about who should be accountable. For many, blame lay with the Americans themselves, and Iraqis' disappointment and disillusionment ran so deep that many suspected conspiracies were being hatched. No country with America's power could fail so miserably unless it meant to. To an outsider, it may sound like nonsense, another one of those conspiracy theories with which the Arab world is famously obsessed. But even those of us who were visiting from the United States shook our heads when, month after month, electricity—the very basis of modern life—still flickered in and, more often, out. Other Iraqis looked to their own countrymen. Iraq was ungovernable, some said. The least charitable insisted that only someone like Saddam could impose the iron fist that Iraq—unruly, prone to violence, and predisposed to discord—has needed through its history.

Drawing their share of blame, too, were the exiles who had fled under Saddam's rule and returned to Iraq in the months after his fall. To many Iraqis, their presence in the country was embodied in the twenty-five-member Governing Council, an advisory group appointed by Bremer and subordinate to him. It was composed of American allies and political neophytes, the majority of them newly returned to the country. Throughout the occupation, the Americans turned to the council for help in navigating the transition toward an elected government, and it often served as the U.S. administration's eyes and ears. But it usually saw and heard what was most opportune to its own political fortunes, and it tailored to those fortunes the message that it delivered to Bremer and his lieutenants. As the occupation's failures accumulated, the Governing Council and the exiles served as another lightning rod for anger, and their political prospects withered. Many Iraqis loathed them for escaping Saddam's repression abroad, then expecting to seize the reins of government on their return.

"They all talk about Iraq," Yasmine wrote of the exiles, "but it's not the Iraq I spent three decades in. They have no idea what the Iraqis living in Iraq for the past twenty-five years have been through or turned into.

"Like many Iraqis, I attribute some of the misbehaviors, mistakes, and wrongdoings that the Americans committed to the fact that they have been misinformed by Iraqis who had left the country decades ago," she wrote. From informing the Bush administration that Iraqis would welcome U.S. troops with flowers to urging a methodical and comprehensive de-Baathification program under which tens of thousands of people lost their jobs through guilt by association, she said, the errors in the exiles' counsel only mounted and multiplied.

Even from afar, Yasmine could feel every bombing and every killing. I suspected that she felt great guilt, since her fellow Iraqis had to endure fear and carnage that she had avoided thanks to her family's wealth and circumstances. She cited her children again and again to explain her departure. But there was always that hint of shame. She was one of the exiles now.

"If I was still living in Baghdad," Yasmine wrote in one letter, "I would be spending most of my time going to funerals and paying condolences.

"Do you remember when I told you that what Saddam turned us into is only a normal consequence of years of the abnormal circumstances he put us through?" she asked. "My worry is that the scars of the past year will be deeper and will take longer to heal. Can a year change people so much?" She left the question unanswered.

For weeks that fall, I had been trying to find Omar, the thirty-two-year-old son of Faruq Ahmed Saadeddin, whose family I had spent a day with during the bombings. Faruq, a Sunni diplomat, and his brash son had sat stoically in their two-story house during the invasion, their anger at Saddam surpassed only by their resentment of the United States. They had reveled in Iraq's tradition of toughness. Faruq would remind me of his nation's record of survival over eleven thousand years; but neither he nor his son had predicted what would follow. Ultimately, Omar and his wife, Nadeen, had left the country.

Omar propped his beige 1990 BMW on blocks under a green tarp at his father's house. They left their furniture "as it was." He and Nadeen packed two suitcases and headed for Mosul in September. Two weeks later, they drove one and a half hours to the Syrian city of Qamishli, caught a plane to Damascus, then drove two hours to Beirut, all on the same day. In November, they arrived in London, where Nadeen's brother Ihab lived.

"You're starting from scratch," he told me by telephone after I tracked him down through his parents. "It feels weird. It's something you're forced to do because of the situation. I love the country. I love Baghdad. I love working there. I don't like London at all. I don't feel myself here at all. There's just no other choice."

I recalled a moment at lunch during the invasion, when Omar had become upset. Interspersed with the cacophony of war were the sounds of ordinary life, and they seemed to move him to an emotion he could not entirely articulate. A cart passed the house, its horn blowing. The driver had come to empty the trash and refill the kerosene tanks. "I should be able to live like other people are living," Omar said glumly, as the cart passed. "I shouldn't fear bombs falling on my head, I shouldn't be hearing sirens. Why should I have to live like this? Why should this be normal?"

"It's going from bad to worse," he said when we spoke by telephone. "There's no rebuilding, there's nothing with infrastructure, there's no water, electricity. Look at the situation now. It's worse than before. It's a lot worse, a lot worse. The Americans aren't doing anything about it," he said, "and they don't care."

He relayed a wisecrack he had heard from friends in Baghdad: "Neither Sadr nor Sistani, we want our old fucker back." It was a rare lighthearted moment in our grim conversation.

Before the war and even later, Omar was often angry but defiant, like countless young men I had met in Arab countries—nationalists, proud as Muslims, and imbued with a gut-wrenching sense that they're on the receiving end of justice. Now he was angry and helpless, negotiating the loss of his family, his old life, and his country. He was on the other side of the *shanashil*, on the outside looking in. In a way, he had become a stranger.

Nothing would get better in Iraq for the next five years, he predicted, his voice changing. "I can't believe what's happening. It's ridiculous. The thing that really pisses me off—we've been under sanctions for thirteen years, every-thing we underwent for thirteen years, everybody had to sell everything." There was silence on the line. "For nothing," he said finally. "For nothing. It was all a big joke. I have no hope anymore."

Yasmine could visit Baghdad from Amman; it was a twelve-hour drive, arduous but possible. Not Omar. In London, he looked for work and he searched for news about Iraq, but there was too little coverage in the British media. So he checked the Web site of the Arab network Al-Jazeera daily. He tried to talk to his parents once or twice a week. "Otherwise, I'm just cut off," he said. "You listen to the news and you're helpless. You can't do anything about it. And that's what's frustrating."

More frustrating was the longing for what was taken for granted. For Yasmine, it was the Tigris and its graceful palms. For Omar, it was a life that he perhaps never appreciated until it was gone—the hamburger from a favorite locale in Jadriya, or being able to fill his gas tank for a dollar. He missed the Baghdadi tempo of life, that almost unnoticed rhythm by which people live, in war or peace. At a temporary job in London, he told me, no one said hello in the morning. In a grocery store he visited every few days, he had yet to learn the cashier's name or exchange even a few idle lines of con-versation. "These are the things I miss," Omar told me. "You don't find it here.

"I look at Nadeen every day and I say, 'We used to do this, we used to do that,'" he continued. "'We used to be doing this right now, we used to be doing that right now.' That's what I miss. I don't want to do it here. I want to do it with my family, I want to do it with my friends. I want to be there. I want to be with them."

For weeks, Omar had tried to persuade his sister to leave Iraq. His mother and father would come next, he hoped. "I'd rather be with my parents. I left them there," he said, then paused. "I know my father loves the country. But the situation is horrible. I'll try to get him out, even if I have to come down and get him. I'll bring him out."

"I WISH WE COULD LEAVE THE COUNTRY," OMAR'S MOTHER, MONA, SAID TO ME. "I want to go out. I don't want to stay in the country."

"I will not," Faruq said.

"But Faruq will not," she repeated.

"How long we live is set by God, so it doesn't make much difference," Faruq said. "We'll die here or we'll die there, but it's not up to us." Seamlessly, taking the long view of fate, he turned to the future. "If I leave and someone else leaves, who's going to help the country?"

"It's not death," Mona said, shaking her head, speaking almost under her breath. "It's not death that frightens me. If someone bombs the house, what do we do? The kidnapping. What's going to happen?"

"You can't just cut out and run away," Faruq interrupted. "This is our country, and sooner or later our children will come back. The resilience of the people, that's what eleven thousand years means," he said. "Someone who has eleven thousand years, one hundred years to lose here or there is not that much."

Silence followed and I asked them whether they were glad Omar had left for Britain.

"I'm very happy," Mona said.

"I'm not," Faruq answered.

"I always said, 'Omar, try to leave,'" Mona said. "'I don't want you to stay here. It's not safe anymore.' Omar, he's my only son. I don't want him to be kidnapped by criminals or something happen to him. I would die," Mona said. "Now I'm scared about my daughter."

"We again have different points of view," Faruq said, smiling.

It was a blustery winter day and I was visiting Faruq and Mona in their neighborhood of Jihad. They sat in their dark house, reluctant to turn on a generator and endure the racket it threw up. I sat alone on the couch, with Faruq in a chair to the left. Mona served us a warm soft drink, then sat to my right. Almost predictably, the conversation began again with the weather. A little wistful, they mentioned that it had snowed for the first time in a hundred years in Mosul, Faruq's hometown, and that the winds had brought another year of unusual storms.

"*Everything* has changed," Faruq said.

Faruq, the Sunni diplomat, and Fuad, the Shiite doctor, had never met, either during the war, when I met them, or in its aftermath. They had no reason to. But in my conversations with them over the year, I was struck by how their opinions were beginning to coincide. Baghdad, their city, served as a crossroads between promises of a country remade and the reality of a country too broken.

At the war's end, the doctor had proclaimed victory. "All of us are reborn again," I remembered him saying in the spring. But Faruq had seen humiliation and defeat, tempered perhaps by a moment of hope. A passing moment. Now, in the winter, he recalled watching Saddam's statue fall in Firdaus Square: "I felt as if a heavy burden was lifted off my back when I saw the toppling of the statue. But the minute somebody went up with the American flag, the whole thing changed. I started saying, 'No, no, no, shoot the bastard!'"

Just sixty-six but feeling his years, diabetes taking its toll, Faruq leaned back in his chair. "Why wasn't a curfew imposed," he asked, "as it was done in every change of government, at least five of them over the last fifty years?" What if a new government had been decreed in two or three days, he hypothesized, with the top echelon of the former leadership dismissed, imprisoned, or executed?

"If it had gone smoothly from the first day, honestly, I believe this a hundred percent: ninety-five percent of the Baathists, the registered Baathists, would have cheered, hailed America." He then shook his head. "But when we saw the burning and looting, that was like raping the city, that was like raping my country. I cried when I heard the news on the radio. I was so pissed off. And I cried. I honestly cried. That was the golden opportunity to win the people and they messed it up."

During the war, Mona, an elegant, soft-spoken woman, had worried most about bombing that seemed to move ever closer to her house; as Faruq talked politics that day, she had stayed silent. On this day, she quietly revealed to me her true feelings about Saddam: she had secretly loathed him. Perhaps, she thought, he was even an American agent.

"I was one of the people excited about change," she told me. "I used to hate Saddam. I used to hate him personally. I never liked him, for many, many years."

"We are more nationalist than her," Faruq said, again smiling. "We didn't like Saddam, but we didn't want an occupation."

"But now I say no, he was much, much better," Mona went on. "Especially when they destroyed all the ministries. That hurt me so much." After the war, Omar had driven her around the capital, where the looting and fires had produced a climate of ruin. "I cried so much in the car," Mona said. "I couldn't bear it. Why did they destroy all the ministries and let the thieves go in? They kept Saddam's palace so they could live in it. Then they let them destroy all the ministries. They let the thieves in. Let them go in. Go in, Ali Baba. Go in and destroy. They never stopped them. They burned everything. All the documents." She looked down, remembering. "It was terrible."

"People forget the bad things of before very quickly," Faruq said, nodding in resignation. "And that's the sad thing."

Faruq, like many Iraqis, spoke of being caught between forces shaping his city. A neighbor's house had been searched by U.S. troops. They broke down the door, she said, and shattered vases. Afterward they apologized, Mona said, and gave the family one hundred dollars. "Isn't this ridiculous?" Mona asked. Down the street, the son of another neighbor was kidnapped by men posing as Iraqi police, who demanded a $400,000 ransom. Luckily, the kidnappers accepted $100,000. Another kidnapping, this one of a relative's nephew: during Ramadan, nine men with guns stopped his car, beat the driver, and took the nephew captive, holding him for more than two weeks. He was ransomed and released, and within hours, the extended family had fled overland to Jordan.

"You hear this all over town," Mona said.

The hours passed as we talked, and it was finally lunchtime. Faruq and Mona invited me to the dining room. During the invasion, it had served as the bedroom for Omar and Nadeen, being judged safer than the upstairs bedroom since it was on the ground floor. The flour, rice, beans, and powdered milk the family had stockpiled then were gone. Back on the walls were sketches and a painting from Faruq's time as a diplomat in East Asia. Yet the room itself felt somber and mournful, empty, now that the couple lived alone. The windows were still X'd with tape, and at least four others were cracked from bombings during the invasion. Mona asked if I would like them to turn on the generator, so that the room would be lit while we ate. I told her it didn't matter. Like Baghdadis, I was getting used to the dark.

"I just hate the sound of the generator," she said. "Drrrrrrrrr."

The lunch was as magnificent as the meal we had shared during the war, in circumstances less harried. There were traditional meat dishes: *kebab malaki, kibbe,* and chicken with peanuts. Plate after plate was stacked with *dolma, tabouleh,* and a bean dish, *fasuliya bi zeit.* Dessert was in the waiting: oranges and bananas, along with *maamoul* and baklava from the famed bakery of Abu Afif in the central neighborhood of Karrada. Soon after we started eating, as if on cue, the city's electricity resumed.

"Oh, now we have light," Faruq said.

"I just felt the heater," Mona added. This was followed by a thud in the distance, probably a roadside bomb targeting U.S. troops. It echoed off the house and shook the rickety metal gate outside. Unlike the war, when blasts would roll over the horizon like thunder, explosions those days were more indeterminate, the danger a little ambiguous. A pause would usually ensue. Had that been a bomb, or a door slamming shut?

"That was a bomb," Mona said conclusively.

"That's our Geiger counter," Faruq said of the gate. "That's how we know."

As we ate, Faruq recalled conversations with a close-knit group of four friends, all doctors, before the war. One had predicted that after Saddam's fall, Iraq would be as like Abu Dhabi. "'Perfect,'" Faruq said, quoting his friend's description.

"Now I joke with him. 'Look Abu Ahmed, where are your American friends? What happened?' He said, 'Well, they turned to be different than we thought. We made a mistake.'"

"We thought Iraq would be like heaven," Mona said.

"And we don't see the light at the end of the tunnel," Faruq added.

BY FEBRUARY 2004, ACROSS TOWN, THE GOOD-NATURED FUAD, ALWAYS QUICK TO laugh, was in despair. "We were expecting so much from America, and we haven't got anything," he told me. "Only fear." He threw up his hands, slowly. "They need someone like Saddam," he said, only half-joking.

"No, Dad, that's not fair!" interrupted Yasmine, who had come with her children from Amman for a ten-day visit over the holiday of Eid al-Adha.

Fuad looked out the window on a city that still bore the scars of the postwar looting. Bombings had picked up pace since Ramadan. Unemployment had surged, thanks in part to Bremer's decision to dissolve the Iraqi military and the government's intelligence services. A year after the United States had started rebuilding Iraq's police, crime still shadowed the streets and entered almost every conversation. "It has been a disaster," he said ruefully, to no one in particular. "Whether it was deliberate or not, we don't know."

Yasmine shook her head, then quoted an Arabic proverb: "The servant went, and now comes his master." She smiled. "Saddam went, and the Americans came. What difference does it make?"

It was another gray day. Fuad and Suad had just returned from a trip to Los Angeles, where they saw their new granddaughter. One day a blackout struck the city, shutting off electricity for five hours. Sharp-witted and friendly Suad, telling the story, laughed at the thought. "Oh, we're back in Baghdad, I said. All dark. Half of Los Angeles."

All these months later, electricity was still the one thing Suad wanted to talk about. It was her barometer for the occupation's success and failure, her measure of the Americans' goodwill, and it had gotten little better while they were gone. "It's still bad," she said, exasperated. "We came back, we went, we came back, and it's still bad.

"We thought it was getting better," she exclaimed. "It's getting worse!" She looked at me, in disbelief. "What are they waiting for?"

On that day, as on most days, talk of civil war lurked in Baghdad, just as it did in the Sunni Muslim countryside, in places like Thuluyah. Few people were actually predicting civil war, but it seemed the natural result of the mounting chaos that so many felt in their lives. Both Faruq and Fuad, patriots and stubborn optimists, discounted the prospect. The doctor was fond of pointing out that his three Shiite daughters were married to Sunnis, as was his son, Firas. They were all Iraqis, he insisted, and Iraqis wanted to live in peace.

"Religion is a matter of every person for himself. It has nothing to do with politics. You are Christian? It's okay. It is between you and God," he said, in the voice of a therapist. "Everybody has his own way to stand before God."

Fuad was flexible, tolerant, and reflective, not the qualities I associated with Baghdad just then. He refused to surrender to the prevalent pessimism. Never, he would say. Even now, as gloom settled over Baghdad like a coarse woolen blanket, he tried to remain hopeful. The salaries of doctors and teachers had increased, he pointed out. A medical resident used to get 5,000 Iraqi dinars a month, "with all the weight on his shoulder." Now residents were paid 300,000. "That's a big difference," he noted.

In the old days, Fuad had been ashamed as an Iraqi when he went abroad; he felt humiliated by Saddam, embarrassed by his country's image. Now he felt prouder as he went through the routine that makes anyone from the Third World nervous: approaching immigration control in the First World with passport in hand. One always met skepticism and suspicion. Saddam's fall in itself, he believed, improved his countrymen's image. And as bad as Baghdad was becoming, Fuad would never forgive Saddam for the crimes he had committed.

"We had enough from Saddam," he said. "We had enough. Whatever we saw, we just blamed Saddam. We had no faith in him. Thirty-five years and he governed Iraq and look what happened to the country. Really, I hated Saddam."

Yasmine nodded in agreement. "He didn't fire one single bullet," she said of his final confrontation with the United States. "He didn't have the decency to fire one single bullet in the air. He would have been killed. Give us one good reason that he should stay alive."

But the drama of Baghdad had spilled off the stage on which the Americans and Saddam acted it out before a passive Iraqi audience. To Fuad, the stakes were now higher, the dangers greater. Saddam had become a sideshow, the invasion a fading memory. Where was his city headed? Fuad asked. What was the fate of his country? They had arrived at a turning point, but no one knew the axis.

"Everybody thinks America can do everything. Not only in Iraq, but all over the world. America has the power to do everything in the world. We were expecting that. This is America." He shook his head. "Don't tell me this is Russia, Germany, or England. This is America, this is the United States. It's been nearly a year, we're waiting nearly a year," he said, his voice rising. "We thought America was different."

He complained of corruption in the ministries and among the twenty-five members of the Governing Council. We used to have one Saddam, Suad joked, now we have twenty-five. They complained of the barricades and barriers that littered their once manicured neighborhood of Mansur. Suad spoke of the shoddy service on newly arrived mobile phones. With bitterness, Fuad lamented the lack of draconian justice and a strong hand required to administer it.

"In Iraq, if you know this person is a killer, you must give justice at once," he said. "You must make the others afraid. You must create fear in others so that they don't do it. This is the way Saddam did it. No one's afraid of anything. If you don't see what happened to that man who committed a crime, you're not afraid."

Did the Americans not understand this? he asked. "Why do they permit these things? Deliberately? Do they know what they're doing? Do they want people to kill each other? I don't know."

Suad served cups of Arabic coffee, glasses of water, and small chocolates in a glass bowl. Two space heaters glowed red in the living room, giving off a dry heat that offset, somewhat, the biting, rainy cold outside.

"I felt hopeful; so did you," Fuad said to me. "Do you remember? I was cheerful, relaxed, optimistic. I said 'our President Bush.' I used to tell you that.

"Why was I so happy? I felt empowered. America got rid of Saddam. We thought America could do anything. Now we've waited all this time and nothing happened. Why? You begin to wonder if America had fingers in this problem. Do they do it deliberately? Was it planned? Do they want all this to happen? Why are they standing and watching? Don't tell me America doesn't know. They can, they can do everything.

"I don't want to be gloomy," he said, clicking his tongue. "I don't want to be pessimistic, but things that are happening now make you feel that way.

"America wanted it this way—that's one explanation. In the beginning, I wouldn't have said it. Now when I see how they govern people, the policy, I say why not. Maybe it's true. One year. Next month will be one year since they took power. What happened in one year?" He stopped, staring at the coffee, a whiff of steam still coming off it. "Really, it's amazing. Electricity. Is it that difficult for them? Is it that difficult? These things make you wonder. Are they genuine? Are they truthful?"

Conspiracy theorizing this might be, but Fuad was right in saying, "Everybody's started to think this way."

The room fell silent. He spoke again. His face seemed taut, his eyes harder. And almost as if angry at himself for what he said, he echoed the thoughts of Faruq, almost to the word.

"It's the nature of human beings to forget. It's their nature," Fuad said to me sadly, his voice dropping lower. "It's easy to forget what happened in the past."

15

OIL AND PUNKS

Like the 1980–88 war with Iran, the U.S. invasion that toppled Saddam and brought the occupation never had a real name. The Bush administration called it Operation Iraqi Freedom, a label that became the butt of jokes in Iraq even as combat raged. Predictably, Saddam's own name for the invasion, Ma'rakat al-Hawasim, "Defining Battle," was similarly grandiose, a product of his delusional reading of his place in history. This was, after all, the man who christened the 1991 Gulf War the Mother of All Battles.

Like many in Iraq, Karima and her family simply called the war the *suqut*—"the collapse," or "the fall," a name that probably made more sense than any other. It designated the end of thirty-five years of pitiless Baath Party rule. In a way, it suggested, too, that another beginning had yet to be inaugurated. Ma'rakat al-Hawasim lingered in the wreckage of the government's fall. The war remained open-ended, its muddled aftermath as inconclusive as the toppling of Saddam's statue seemed climactic. For Iraqis, *suqut* meant an end without renewal, a seemingly endless interim.

Each time I visited Karima and her family, I was newly moved by the way religion continued to sustain their lives. The blue porcelain plate that read simply "God" still hung on the grimy wall of the Salmans' home. A poster of Imam Hussein still stared down, joined, at times, by portraits of his father,

Imam Ali, or his half-brother, Abbas, the slain warrior of Hussein's family. Always, the Almighty was the meter of Karima's family's language. He filled pauses and hesitations, served as an answer to questions, and provided the period at the end of sentences. "Only God will solve our problems," Karima would say, looking to her ceiling, her hands turned upward. "Only God."

She would often pause, then again say, "God."

Like others, Karima and her family struggled to understand the *suqut*. For a year, they had been powerless and frustrated as its ramifications reshaped their lives, sometimes in the quietest of ways. Now they gave witness to a life imposed, not chosen.

"I am scared of the future," Amal Salman wrote in her diary in the summer of 2003. She was still fourteen, although she seemed much older than when the war began. "Everybody is asking about the future, the future of Iraq," she wrote. "Some are asking where is the future. Others say Iraq has no future anymore. These are all opinions, but no one knows what the truth is."

Amal's diary was becoming more and more tattered, as she filled each page with the record of her search to make sense of the world around her. To bind the worn book together, she wrapped it in a newspaper in which editorials cried out against the occupation. "U.S. soldier loots citizens," one headline read. "The U.N. criticizes the occupation," said another. Some of the pages were creased, a few corners torn. The writing itself was filled with highs, the glimmers of hope that had passed, and the more enduring lows that always seemed to return.

"God is greatest! Praise to God!" Amal wrote one day when electricity returned to their apartment. "There was rejoicing in the whole building, people saying to each other, 'Electricity is back, thanks be to God.' We slept, feeling happy because of the electricity."

And then, a few pages later: "We are now sitting, waiting for electricity to come back. What happened to the promises?"

In almost every entry, the weather made its mark and often served as a measure of the family's misery. During electricity cuts, water would go as well. To take a bath, Amal had to carry bucket after bucket upstairs from a tap near the sidewalk, filling the tub. She would soak her feet, swollen from the climb up and down three flights of stairs. "Today is very, very hot, and there is no electricity," she wrote in a typical passage. "Sweat is dripping down because of the extreme heat. The air is very hot and unbearable. There is no water in the roof tank, and we have to fill it with water from the faucet outside."

As oppressive as the lack of power was the crime that seemed to have taken over Baghdad and the fear that it had aroused everywhere—carjackings and, more commonly, kidnappings whose ransoms would fetch tens of thousands of dollars. A poll around this time by an Iraqi foundation found that three out of five people felt unsafe; about the same number had little or no confidence that U.S. forces were making conditions safer. The fear was as diffuse as the sun, which beat down day after day with no hint of dissipating.

"No one can walk down the street at 9:30 P.M.," wrote Amal. "No one can do that at this hour, and the streets are empty except for cats, and even cats are scared after 10 P.M. You can see neither cats, nor humans nor dogs, not even cars passing by. Only the sidewalk."

In the worst days of the invasion, Karima once said something I never forgot. "It's like we're part of a play on a stage." Her tone was reflective. "Life's not good, it's not bad. It's just a play." As the occupation unfolded, those words, acknowledging her powerlessness, seemed to take on new meaning. The script had already been written. People like Karima sat as spectators, watching the performance. In part, this feeling of powerlessness had been fostered during the reign of Saddam, when endless litanies of "God, country, and leader" were transformed by his lieutenants into a kind of omnipresent fear as pervasive as his image, which adorned every street and government building. Saddam, of course, came to be the all-powerful personification of all three. But the feelings of futility and helplessness among Iraq's citizens were deepened by the occupation, when contact between ruler and ruled sometimes amounted to a sighting of a white sport-utility vehicle leaving the Green Zone. Mediating the reactions of occupier and occupied were rumors, which created their own dynamic, their own cycle of hope and disappointment.

"I heard that this summer, hospitals will be free, and also medicine," Amal wrote. "But it turned out everything is a lie. Nothing more, nothing less. Many diseases are appearing now in Iraq because of garbage accumulating in the street. The Baghdad municipality is refusing to collect unless the workers are paid money—not a little money, but a lot of it. What are we to do? Die from hunger or from disease?" In another entry, she wondered about relief.

"Every day, they say that humanitarian aid has arrived, canned food and all the other needs of the Iraqi people. But where is this aid?"

The past months had been trying, bringing one disappointment after another for Amal and her family. Neither Karima nor Ali, the oldest son, could find work. Fatima, the oldest daughter, had to stay home to help take care of her sisters, and the rest of the children were in school, which had finally resumed. Prices for even basic items kept spiraling upward; a canister of kerosene for cooking, which would last up to ten days, now cost thirteen dollars. At times, with no electricity or water, the family brewed tea in the home of their neighbor Um Haider. Rent was always two months or more late, and the landlord stopped by the apartment every few days, angrily demanding money. Without gas, Karima could no longer bake bread for neighbors and thus could not earn the few dollars that would halt his visits for a time.

The pressure was taking its toll on Karima, who often burst into tears in front of her daughters. Just thirty-six years old, she was developing cataracts and staying in bed, exhausted or ill. She looked for work at the city's main hotels—the Meridien and the Sheraton—but could not make her way through security. She spoke no English; often the U.S. soldiers manning the entrance spoke no Arabic. Their translators dismissed her as more riffraff from the street.

"My God, what can we do? Everything is difficult. What can we do?" Amal asked in another entry. "Where can we get the money? Oh, God, help us out of this problem, let everything be like before. Praise be to God for everything."

At the time, Mohammed, Karima's second-oldest son, was up to no good. Imprisoned under Saddam for wrecking a car while drinking, he had more recently been arrested by U.S. soldiers for firing a gun in the street. Karima paid visits to friends, relatives, even the American base near their neighborhood in a vain appeal for help. Amal prayed, and relatives stayed overnight to provide support. Then, days later, when Mohammed was released, his erstwhile friends threatened to attack his house unless his family paid the equivalent of four hundred dollars for the gun, which the U.S. troops had confiscated.

"My brother was very scared, and fear is filling our hearts," Amal wrote. "What can we do? We have no one but God. God is greatest! God is greatest!"

During the war, the neighbors in Karima's building had set aside the old, trivial disputes that arose in their cramped quarters. They shared what they had, food and tea, and, in moments of the most ferocious bombing, they huddled together in a hallway darkened by the blackout. In the streets outside, taxis would sometimes forgo fares as a gesture of solidarity.

All vestiges of this mutuality had by now disappeared; the crisis had gone on so long. The civility and solidarity that Karima and her family recalled from the invasion were nowhere to be found among their fellow Baghdadis. Now reigned confusion, chaos, and, most often, pettiness. The same families who had prayed with them in war, creating bonds that had not before existed, refused to help Karima and her family hijack electricity from other buildings. At times, Karima's was the only apartment in the building that couldn't secure an electrical connection. The family had to sit in the dimly lit hallway if they wanted light.

Amal directed her anger at one neighbor in particular, Abu Seif, who lived down the hall. He rebuffed each of their pleas for help—he had too little wire, too few tools, or not enough time, he would say. There was always some excuse. Once he refused to help because he was installing a satellite dish for his own apartment. To Amal, such men were manifestations of a society that seemed to be fraying, crumbling, where a quarter of people survived only on monthly rations, usually with too little money for food or rent. Even under Saddam's terrifying grasp, the city had never felt so dangerous or out of control.

"He is very rude," she wrote of Abu Seif. "If we had electricity, and he didn't, we would give it to him. . . . Why does he do that? Aren't we all neighbors and everyone cooperating for the welfare of all? Why does Abu Seif discriminate against us? We are in the midst of darkness and I am writing by the light of a candle, and the smoke has blinded my eyes. I never knew that Abu Seif was so mean, rude, and lacking in any love for others. He only cares for his own interests. When his wife used to go visit her family and he was alone, we used to prepare lunch and dinner for him, just like one of the family. But now? He won't give us electricity. My God, why is this so?"

As their circumstances spiraled downward, Karima, in desperation, went to the family of her late husband's sister along Abu Nawas Street. Karima needed help—money for rent and food. After fighting and humiliating her, the relatives tried to get U.S. soldiers stationed down the street to arrest her, but the translator with the troops was a neighbor of Karima's and sided with her. Karima returned home.

"Why would my aunt do that?" Amal asked. "She is our aunt and we are like her own children. But the times have changed. Life has no mercy on anyone in this world. Even the same family won't have mercy on each other. Why? Why? I think of this every day. My name is Amal Hussein Alwan Ameer al-Shameri, and my aunt is named Amal Alwan Ameer al-Shameri. Look at the names, her name and my name. She is the sister of my father. Why did she do all that? Because of money? She is a teacher and she is in no need, but we are. If my aunt has no compassion for us, who will? We can only depend on God. God have mercy on us."

To Amal, this episode became symbolic of her family's plight: they were alone. "No one stands by our side," she wrote. "Even my father's brothers and sisters hate us, don't help us, and are always saying bad things to my mother. But she is the best mother I have seen in my life. She made great efforts to raise us. I don't know why they hate us. . . . They don't care whether we are hungry or thirsty."

The moment of her aunt's rejection seemed to mark a turning point for Amal. Applying her experience to her perception of the lives all around her, she became determined to understand the broader world, as frustrating as it proved. She was no longer writing for herself; her voice, which had been singular, became plural. Her perspective broadened, and she gave voice to her awakening.

"I cry for the children, who are living in the street without hope, without relatives or family that can protect them from this dark period of hunger and deprivation," she wrote that summer, her sentences urgent. "The tears of those children cover the streets of Baghdad. Where are the humanitarian organizations, where is the aid? Why don't they help Iraqi children? Why don't they hear the cries of children? Why? Why? They are crying and shouting. Why don't you hear their calls? They are calling on you—we, the children of Iraq, are calling. Do you hear us? Where are you? I am crying now, and shouting, but no one is listening. I am writing my diaries to reveal the truth about an Iraqi family suffering from poverty and deprivation. Not only my family, but many, many others, suffering from the same thing. Please listen to my appeal. I am writing this with a pen, but others are writing with their blood, which is bleeding from their wounded hearts, many wounds that we cannot treat. Why do the people of Iraq have to suffer so much?"

In a diary usually somber, sometimes exasperated, and occasionally angry, there was a moment that was especially hopeful. In the summer of 2003, Amal, her sisters, and her youngest brother, Mahmoud, went to receive the grades from their final exams. Mahmoud had passed. So had Zainab and the twins, Duaa and Hibba. So had Amal.

"I am very happy I passed," she wrote on that day in July. "I want to finish my schooling because it is the only weapon that I will have to defend my family and the only way that I can provide for my mother to compensate her for what she did for us."

IN AMAL'S WRITINGS, THE MEANING OF LIBERATION WAS PERSONAL; PERHAPS she was unaware of it herself. But her mind was flowering, her raw intelligence exercised by her consideration of her country's experience. Amal's hard-won wisdom seemed the quietest of triumphs in the days after Saddam's fall.

In a society that equated wisdom with age, the once impressionable girl had begun thinking critically about, first, Saddam, and then the invasion, the occupation, and the ambitions that drove the Americans forward. There was an irony in her awakening: she was free to speak, but it was her liberators whom she criticized with her new candor.

"People are exhausted and conditions are harsh. We are now living on false dreams and in a failed democracy," she wrote. "Satellites were banned in the past, and they are now permitted, but who can buy a satellite? Those who have money can buy, but those who don't can't buy anything. This is democracy. I used to think that democracy was something that benefited the people, but what has democracy done? Where is democracy? It is a question that should be asked of everyone."

Well-intentioned U.S. officials would often remark that they had come to forge the conditions in which prosperity and progress could flower. They were there to throw open the gate to a democratic, pluralistic future, but the Iraqis themselves would have to walk through it, on their own. Time and again, the Americans were frustrated when Iraqis didn't start to walk through the gates. Some of the less charitable grew angry at people they characterized as unprepared to help themselves.

There was, of course, an element of truth in this. Iraqi society was battered and beaten down by wars and dictatorship. Sometimes it seemed that the initiative of Iraqis had been entirely vitiated by Saddam's government, which didn't sanction resourcefulness or originality and which fostered a depen-

dency that many in Iraq were willing to embrace. As in other oil countries—
the welfare states of the neighboring Persian Gulf: Kuwait, Qatar, Saudi
Arabia—people had grown accustomed to turning to the government for
life's essentials—infrastructure, education, housing, even income. This tendency sometimes seemed particularly pronounced in Iraq. By eviscerating
the economy, international sanctions had tied an already dependent population ever more closely to the government, which ministered to its most basic
needs by providing monthly rations. When the Americans arrived, motivation appeared to be in short supply, and in many quarters it actually was:
people were desperate for relief.

The U.S. administration may have complained that Iraqis expected too
much too soon, given the state of the country, the resources at hand, and the
challenges inherent in a postwar environment. But the Americans had to
take, or at least share, responsibility for raising the people's expectations in
the first place: Iraqis might forget the date, perhaps even the person who
spoke the words, but they remembered the pledge uttered on March 10,
2003, by President Bush. When he promised that "the life of the Iraqi citizen
is going to dramatically improve," his words were not forgotten. One of those
who remembered was young Amal:

"Please, tell us, when are we going to live a life of security and stability?
Listen to us, hear us, you people out there, we have cried and shouted. What
else can we do?"

Although her entries became less frequent over the summer, Amal's writing became clearer, her sentences longer and more complex, her vocabulary
more sophisticated. She gained confidence in her ideas, as she observed life
around her. "They talk about democracy. Where is democracy? Is it that
people die of hunger and deprivation and fear? Is that democracy?"

I VISITED AMAL'S FAMILY WEEKS AFTER U.S. TROOPS IN MOSUL HAD KILLED
Saddam Hussein's sons, Uday and Qusay, in July. The brothers had holed
up in a building and for hours held off an assault by two hundred American
soldiers supported by attack helicopters. Finally they succumbed to a barrage
of antitank missiles. There was little question of their deaths, and the U.S.
military took a step it acknowledged was unusual and released grisly photos of

the bloodied and battered corpses. Nevertheless, Baghdad was alive with rumors that the men had somehow survived and escaped.

Fatima suggested it, then shook her head skeptically. "But they were brave," she insisted. "They fought the Americans for hours, and they died as martyrs. The Americans couldn't even kill them with planes and missiles."

Amal, who usually deferred to her older sibling, had heard enough. "They weren't martyrs," she said quietly, looking to the ground. "They were just defending themselves."

It was early morning when I arrived. The sky was still gray, in the interregnum between dawn and day. The stairwell to Karima's apartment was cloaked in black from another electricity cut, although I could make out places where cracks and fissures had been patched with sloppy cement. Less formidable ruin was swabbed with paint. Another day had begun, as the children scurried around the apartment.

"Bring the bread," Karima called out to Hibba, one of the twins.

Fatima finished talking with me, then filled plastic bottles from a faucet downstairs, the water tanks on the roof having run out. In one of the bedrooms, Zainab gathered blankets from the floor. Amal brought in tea and a single fried egg. They shared this and some *samoun*, sitting on a cheap Persian carpet near the space heater propped next to the television. Karima threw yesterday's trash out the kitchen window to the street, where someone had scrawled in red on the wall, "God's curse on anyone who throws trash here." Next to it was a fiercer statement: "The son of a dog who throws trash."

As they ate, the twins opened their school bags and practiced English lessons from a textbook whose pictures of Saddam had been ripped out months ago. Amal and Hibba liked history class best. Duaa's favorite was English.

"This is a glass. This is water," Duaa read from a passage she had already memorized. "These are glasses. This is water."

Hibba pulled out a note that a twenty-nine-year-old U.S. soldier had given them during the summer. The note was always tucked inside her canvas bag, a gift from the U.S. Agency for International Development, whose symbol of two hands clasped was emblazoned on the front. Inside was a calculator, its buttons colored pink, purple, yellow, and white. Other pockets were filled with pens and pencils. The note she grasped had been folded and unfolded a dozen times.

"To: Duaa and Hibba," it read on the outside.

Written inside in English was "To Duaa and Hibba, I'm going to miss the both of you twins, xoxoxo Diaz." Along with it was a copy of his driver's license, giving his full name and address. They asked me to translate this.

"He was nice and beloved," Hibba said.

Duaa chimed in. "He was smart, too."

He gave them sweets. They smiled at him. Neither spoke the other's language.

"But he understood us," Duaa said.

Karima smiled, a wan expression that was proud but weary.

"When all my children are around me, when they're all together in the house," she said, in her usual black veil and black dress, "that's the best moment in my life."

I had known Karima less than a year, but in that time, her face had grown more lined; her eyes were heavier, and her shoulders had lost their wide arch. She rarely smiled; I don't think I ever saw her laugh. Her faith in her daughters was unstinting, but her appraisal of life was that existence was merely a contest for survival. After the children went out to school, she circulated through the city looking for work, usually from ten A.M. to noon.

"I look and I look and I don't find anything," she told me.

Outside, past the graffiti denouncing those who littered, markets were bursting with everything from glistening eggplants to Korean-made suitcases and kitchen utensils imported from Syria, and the streets were vibrant with an infusion of money: under the American administration, the salaries of the most senior bureaucrats had gone from $10 to more than $330.

Along the brick sidewalks were shirts, some still wrapped in the plastic from their manufacturers in China. Styrofoam coolers were brimming with soft drinks. Nearby were canned goods stacked in pyramids—mushrooms, olives, sardines, sausage, and hummus. On a rotating wheel hung brown and black leather belts for sale. On tarps laid down along the street were leather shoes, sunglasses, lingerie, socks, and briefs. Down the street were children's toys: plastic machine guns and camouflage tanks, binoculars and fake cell phones colored green, red, and blue. There was a "Super Mega Heavy Metal Fighter," and a doll that, when squeezed, played "It's a Small World." On another stand, a sheet of wood propped up on bricks, were posters of Shakira,

Britney Spears, and Eminem, Ehab Towfiq, Nancy Ajram, and Asala. In a row below were portraits of Shiite icons—Imam Hussein, his half-brother Abbas, and their father, Imam Ali.

"There's work for government employees, but for people in my circumstances, the simple people, we just stay as we are," Karima said.

"Those people are making one million," Duaa interjected.

"All of them are carrying mobiles and driving cars," Ali said.

Ali had just awoken and his eyes were sleepy. He and Karima were as dejected as the twins were exuberant. Since the war, he, too, had been out of work. As a former soldier, he was entitled to some income—forty dollars every three months—but he had resolved never to collect it again: in October, he and his mother had been caught in a melee between frustrated ex-soldiers waiting in line and U.S. troops and Iraqi police. The clash lasted hours, closing the streets. Ali said he saw people die in front of him, among them one of his friends.

Karima shook her head. "No one's scared of anybody. There is no security. There is no stability and there's no government to bring order to things. Before, one person ruled, one president ruled all of us. Now there's one thousand."

Ali shared Karima's sorrow, but was even more cynical. He was upset by everything around him. As attacks mounted in both the Sunni regions and in Baghdad, he felt angry at his fellow Iraqis. He recalled seeing an American tank on whose barrel he insisted was written, "We are building, you destroy." "This is true!" Ali declared. "This is true!

"I'll tell you the answer. A foreign ruler would be better than an Iraqi," he added. "Even a Jewish ruler would be better than an Iraqi."

His sisters smiled, enjoying his iconoclasm. "I say the Americans are better than the Iraqis," he said, shaking his head, his expression wavering between a grin and anger. "We live in a country that is impossible. The Iraqis prefer *fawdha*," anarchy and chaos. "They won't let themselves be helped."

WHEN THE DAMP, SOMETIMES GUSTY COLD OF WINTER ARRIVED, KARIMA'S family sat on mattresses and shabby brown blankets. Pictures of Arabic pop stars lined the walls, along with the usual religious portraits and invocations. As the family often did, they talked about the lawlessness in their neighborhood. Baghdad remained locked, physically and emotionally, in the fear and unease the Ramadan bombings had so dramatically ushered in. During those days, Nasir and I would repeat to each other a proverb I had once read in a book on Iran: "Since we're already in hell, why not go one step further." Sometimes we smiled at this. There was little humor outside, though. In one poll, more than half of Baghdadis would say there were too few police to protect their streets. In another, across the board, people reported more shortages in electricity, gasoline, drinking water, medicine, and food than they had endured before the American invasion. Nearly a year on, almost two-thirds said the U.S. administration had turned out worse than they had expected.

The months between my visits to Karima's family were an unsettling mix of high politics above and grim deterioration below. In November 2003, Bremer had declared the Americans' intention: the occupation—at least, the formal occupation—would end in summer 2004. The U.S. administration hoped to manage the political transition by choosing a provisional government through caucuses in each of Iraq's eighteen provinces. At every turn, it struggled with the opinion of Ayatollah Sistani, who was suspicious of U.S. aims and determined to see the Shiite majority inherit political authority for the first time in Iraq's modern history. He insisted on immediate, direct elections and, to back his demands, he deployed the power of the Shiite clergy, which had emerged from the vacuum left by Saddam's destruction of civil society as the most influential and popular institution. In the end, neither side won. A caretaker government was chosen, in a process nominally led by the United Nations, and a nationwide ballot was delayed until 2005. But the debate itself was a telling sign of how political power was shifting.

Debates such as those rarely filtered into Karima's apartment in those days. Even the big moments, such as the visit by President Bush on Thanksgiving Day, 2003, or the capture of Saddam in December, were a sideshow. Daily life was its own drama, high politics a luxury, somewhat frivolous. When politics was mentioned, it was as little more than a means to express their growing disillusionment, their disdain.

"What are we going to do with democracy when we don't have anything?" Karima asked, echoing a passage in her daughter's diary. "They haven't done anything in a year. What do we do with freedom? The words are empty. The Americans don't understand anything, they don't understand at all."

She went on: What did elections matter when thugs had tried to abduct Amal and Fatima in the street the other day? (They ran, and their assailants luckily decided not to give chase, allowing them to escape.) Then there was the daylight robbery that she and Ali saw in Shurja market, where a bandit pulled a man from his car and shot him for his satellite telephone. "Not one person said anything," Karima noted. "No one spoke, no one interfered," Ali said.

While traveling around Baghdad, I often saw an advertisement for the U.S.-funded Iraqi television network, Al-Iraqiya, not too far from Karima's apartment. The ad was posted on a building with several gaping craters in its façade—five below the sign angling left; three others to its side. Against a blue-and-green background, the advertisement featured a large eye. Its caption read, in Arabic, "Prepare your eyes for more." That was exactly Karima's fear.

"The joy is gone," she told me then. "People have lost joy. It was stolen from us." The situation was *muzri*, she said, miserable. "If we were a poor country, no one would come here, no one would covet what we have," she said. Her youngest son, Mahmoud, weak and often sick, clung to her back, his head resting on her hunched shoulder. "But we're a rich country, and this is our fate."

Her best day? I asked.

"When nothing happens."

In February, Karima had finally found work as a maid at the Palm Hotel, cleaning fifteen rooms from nine A.M. to two P.M. The local employment agency was a racket and it took a third of her wages. That left her with about thirty-three dollars a month.

"Since I was young until I got old, I worked. I baked bread here, I washed clothes in the house. Now I'm working in a hotel," she said. "I just want to provide a future for my daughters. I'll be weary when I die."

Karima often would speak to me that way. She wasn't addressing me, really. Rather, she was reflecting on her fate, and one word kept recurring: *taaban*. It means "tired"—better yet, "weary"—and Karima said it often. The context was often prices, the subject of almost every conversation we had.

"This costs a thousand dinars," she said, shaking dirty ice that she had poured into a blue thermos. Potatoes, she pointed out, were more than twice as much. Tomatoes, more than four times their price before the war. Onions had doubled. "We don't buy meat," she said. She was silent for a moment, then added, "One day we have, one day we don't."

Her rent was hiked from $33 to $40. She threatened to leave, but learned that a smaller apartment nearby would cost four times as much. In February, her freezer broke. She estimated the repairs would cost no less than $50.

In February, Ali, too, had found a job, serving tea in a real estate office from nine A.M. to six P.M. He made about a dollar a day, "depending on the baksheesh." As in the autumn, he remained angry at his fellow citizens. But with bombings claiming more Iraqi victims, the conspiracy theories that threaded through Baghdad infused his conversation. One of Karima's mantras was "Security and stability." When Ali said it, I thought it meant organized fear—the identifiable, demarcated lines of government repression. Now he and his family faced dangers that were far less predictable.

We sat over a small kettle of tea, brewed by Fatima, and a plate of a kind of cheese called Abu Thufira, served on a dented metal tray. The carpets were out, spread over tile floors that chilled during winter. Blankets were tossed over thin mattresses against the wall. The bathroom sink was leaking and water trickled from underneath the flimsy door and into the living room.

The twins attached stickers of soccer players to their school notebooks, while Zainab studied in another room. The other children traded copies of the leaflets that were circulating in the streets at the time. "An American soldier cries in Baghdad," one of them declared over a picture of an American fighter with his hand held to his eyes. The leaflet was from one of the numerous insurgent groups, and it cataloged the opposition's latest, if fictional triumphs: three planes and fourteen U.S. tanks destroyed on a single day. "The mujahideen," it read, "will continue fighting until the American forces and their allies are chased away." Another, handed out by the U.S. military, featured a picture of a fighter clad in black, wearing a black ski mask and carrying a rocket-propelled grenade launcher, against a red background. It implored Iraqis "not to permit terrorists or loyalists of the previous regime to take away your new freedom. Notify Iraqi police or coalition forces about any terrorist activity," it urged.

Karima's family believed one, not the other. They talked about the fear they had seen in the eyes of U.S. soldiers near their home. They exchanged rumors of desertions from the U.S. military, troops fleeing on the road to Syria or Turkey. "All the explosions are their fault," Karima said of the U.S. officials ensconced in the Green Zone. "They are the reasons for the bombing."

"It's apparent," Ali said, as an Egyptian serial, *Alexandria*, played loudly on the television. "Only Iraqis die in the explosions. No Americans ever die."

As we talked on that cold afternoon, I thought back to my conversations with Faruq and Fuad. They had converged on an idea that both uttered in almost the same words: it is the nature of human beings to forget. Karima and her children had not forgotten; in those grim days, they began to remember what they wanted, what they had been told was coming. And, as each day passed, they resented, more and more angrily, what they instead had.

Ali mentioned the U.S.-appointed Governing Council, conspicuous in the white sport-utility vehicles that had become Baghdad's symbols of status and objects of resentment. "Look at them," he said, flicking his wrist. "They have sixteen cars and one hundred bodyguards. What's the difference from Saddam? I swear, Saddam is better than them. He was Iraqi, it was our country, and he is better than those guys."

Ali's answer was to emigrate. "If I had fifty papers or sixty papers"—Iraqi slang for hundred-dollars bills—"I'd go to America or Australia and work there." Baghdad, he said, was *mahjura*—forsaken or abandoned.

He uttered a line so dismissive it was an indictment. "We've gone from a *balad nafti* to a *balad ufti*," he said: from a country of oil to a country of punks.

Karima shook her head. "Saddam did not do good things," she said. "He made the people suffer. But there was fear. And with fear, there was security. He was strong."

"Now only the Americans know what will happen," Ali said

He called civil war a prospect. "It's possible," he said. "It might happen."

"It might be a gang war in the streets," Karima suggested.

Amal interrupted, raising her voice for the first time that day. "I don't think it will happen," she countered.

Growing ever more confident, Amal volunteered her own view of the country's confusion. "If I say the Americans are better, someone asks, What have the Americans done? What have they done for us? All the Americans have done is bring the tanks," she said. "If I said the time of Saddam was better, they say, What? If he didn't like you, he would cut off your head. He was a tyrant."

"I don't know what to say," she admitted.

I returned to see them a few days later. As we sat next to the space heater casting a yellow glow over the room, Amal had thought about the previous conversation. "In any country, there's good and bad. There's no government—foreign or Arab—that's just. In any ruler, there's something good and something bad."

"People must be optimistic," Amal went on. Sometimes her dark brown eyes were cast to the floor. At moments, though, she looked up, her voice clearer, her ideas more insistent. "There must be hope. Even the Quran says we should be optimistic. If you hope, you can get an answer. If you study more, you will find more success. If you have more hope, you can be assured of more and more progress."

She looked down to the ground again. There was a suggestion of defiance in her words. "If not for my generation," she said, "then the generation that's coming."

Karima sat next to her and looked at me. She spoke softly, though Amal seemed to hear her. "They're still young," she said, shaking her head. "They don't know what's ahead."

OVER THE YEAR, ICONOGRAPHY HAD PROLIFERATED IN KARIMA'S APARTMENT. More posters went up of Shiite saints, consoling portraits. On religious holidays, beckoned by tradition, Karima traveled to Karbala, a sacred city. Even the troublesome Mohammed, whose devotion was suspect, set off with his friends on foot on his own pilgrimage, a trip banned when Saddam still ruled. In Karima's apartment, her twin daughters learned chants over the holidays from fifty-cent CDs by Bassam Karbalai, a famed reciter whose work had once been clandestine. Always festive, eagerly grinning as the words tumbled out, they raced each other in completing a one-minute rendition.

"They said for thirty-five years you couldn't say that," Hibba said afterward, her eyes growing wide. "They said Saddam would slaughter you. They said he would pour boiling oil on your head."

It was the time of Ashura, the most hallowed day in the Shiite calendar. The culmination of ten days of mourning, it marks the medieval slaughter of Imam Hussein and his followers at the hands of the iniquitous Yazid in A.D. 680 on the site of present-day Karbala. The commemoration evokes grim memories, but the rituals this year were festive. The celebrations had been discouraged under Saddam, Yazid's modern incarnation. Religious Shiites were now free; their ceremonies were unencumbered, and holidays such as these were a respite in difficult times.

"We were feeling down because of the conditions, but the holiday swept away from my heart all the notions of sadness," Amal wrote in her diary on one such day. "My heart became full of assurance, and peace, and I am no longer worried."

The air was crisp on this night, and the streets were alive with colored lights strung along buckling sidewalks. Quranic chants and Shiite laments from scratchy cassettes bounced off stores doing brisk business in Karrada. Shops were draped with black banners marking the day. With her daughters, Karima headed to the Abdul-Rasul Ali Mosque, where dozens engaged in ritual mourning. They held hands, their walk brisk and jaunty. It was the Shiite equivalent of Christmas season.

Together they wandered into the mosque, through a blue, floral-tiled portico and past wood doors. They entered a moment of community, a constant in changing times.

"Your heart opens up," Karima whispered to me as we arrived.

The sheik, Sadiq Zayir, beckoned other arriving worshippers inside. His voice was jubilant. "God's blessings on you," he shouted. "Enter! Enter!" Every so often, the crowd would reply, "God's prayers on Mohammed and the family of Mohammed." Orange drinks were passed around, as were apples and sandwiches of kebab, as men sat beneath calligraphy invoking God, Mohammed, and Imam Ali and banners depicting the martyrdom that Ali's descendants endured. Chandeliers lit the room, and lazy fans circulated the sweaty air, stuffy with so many people in the room.

In time, men began *lutm*, the ritual beating of their chests. Mournful chants retelling the story of Imam Hussein's martyrdom reverberated over speakers, the cadence interspersed with sobs. Younger men, many of them unshaven and burly, lightly dropped chains on their back, a symbolic gesture of solidarity with Hussein.

"My imam, O Hussein, all eyes are crying for you," they repeated. The words built to a climax. "Hussein!" one group shouted. "Hussein!" another answered.

In the upstairs room, where the women gathered behind windows, Karima looked at ease. Like the posters in her apartment, her face was pacific. There was succor.

"These days are beautiful," she said to me, as we left the ceremony, her shoulders straight. "It's the first year it wasn't forbidden. It used to all be forbidden. Did you see the people?" she asked, a rare hint of excitement in her voice. Her children skipped alongside her. "They had joy. All of them had joy."

The ceremony occurred two days before a string of suicide bombs and explosives in the sacred city of Karbala killed scores of Shiites and wounded far more in the bloodiest day in Iraq since Saddam's fall.

16

MYTHS OF RESISTANCE

Before the March 2, 2004, bombings, Karbala and Najaf, the twin capitals of Shiite sanctity, seemed the most vital examples of uninhibited liberation rising from the occupation. While Baghdad mourned its losses, the cities boomed as they had not in generations. This was a breathtaking revival of fortune for places ground down by Saddam's oppression. After his fall, it seemed as if a carnival was under way in these old cities. Freedom brought celebrations and a newfound confidence that was palpable in the streets.

Millions of tourists—most of them from overwhelmingly Shiite Iran, but also others from smaller Shiite communities in India, Afghanistan, and Pakistan—poured in. Intersections were snarled with vans and buses bringing the faithful, who had for so long been deprived of the opportunity to practice their rites in great numbers in these holy cities. In the squares, rickety stands offered the beads and prayer stones of rituals long discouraged. Streets overflowed with money changers, jewelers displayed the carnelian rings thought to bring blessings, kiosks brimmed with hummus, cardamom, and olives, and pastry shops offered delectable sweets. (These included flat cookies called *sahoun*, a pistachioed treat known as *mastaki*, Turkish delight, and a baklava-like pastry called *burma*.) Along the walls of the two cities, posters offered courses for those who desired to memorize the Quran; the best students would win a trip to Mashhad, a Shiite shrine city in Iran. Advertisements announced religious lessons taught by Iraq's leading ayatollahs. Wares of bookstores spilled onto sidewalks, offering landmark titles by Ayatalloh Mohammed Baqir al-Sadr (the young Sadr's cousin, who was executed with his sister in 1980), along with tracts by Ali Khamenei, the spiritual leader of Iran; more books by his predecessor, Ayatollah Khomeini; pamphlets of the Dawa Party (so reviled by Saddam that he decreed the death penalty for membership even before the party was actually banned); and the literature of Muqtada Sadr's movement.

There was a celebratory cacophony, as the calls to prayer clashed with the sounds of the cities. In Najaf's covered market—bombed, then looted by the Iraqi army after the 1991 Shiite uprising—Iranian pilgrims haggled with vendors, nearly all of whom spoke some Farsi. "Visit me! Visit me!" a merchant shouted to other visitors in English. Along the sidewalks, televisions blared footage of passion plays from Iran and the training of Shiite militias. Vendors hawked cassettes of ritual chants of grief, plying their wares. With drums and banners, the faithful converged in often spontaneous parades toward the shrines—for Imam Hussein and his half brother in Karbala, for their father, Imam Ali, in Najaf—past slogans declaring Saddam an infidel and banners proclaiming the primacy of faith. "Heidar!" phalanxes of men shouted fervently, invoking a popular name for Ali. "Heidar!"

At times, though, the chants and slogans were more political. A popular poster pictured Khomeini, his fist raised. "Absolutely no to Israel, absolutely no to America," the caption said. In another, Mohammed Baqir al-Hakim, the long-exiled ayatollah killed along with dozens of others in a car bombing in August in Najaf, looked out with a halo around his head: "Our submission is out of the question."

The revival, in a span of only months, was reweaving the cities' fabrics, dramatizing the promise of Saddam's fall and making the shrines, as one shopkeeper put it, "roses between the thorns." Long dormant Shiite seminaries reopened, and new religious colleges and centers proliferated and were given names steeped in religious imagery—Imam Mahdi, Imam Ali, Imam Sadiq. ("Space is very limited," one announcement said.) Hotels were being built to cope with the thousands of pilgrims who arrived every day, uneasy over the carnage of Hakim's assassination in August but hopeful that the orgy of bloodshed would stand as the exception. So said the merchants, keen to keep up the flow of income that had doubled, even tripled in the bazaars.

Sitting in a lobby smoking a water pipe, with the grin that comes with dazzling profits, Farhan Thijil was one of these merchants. For two months, busloads of Iranian pilgrims, seizing upon the opportunity of an open border, had kept his forty-five-room hotel in Najaf booked solid. (He would usually, after going to much trouble that was made very visible, find a room for Nasir, Karim, and me.) He had more than tripled his rates, from $8 to $25. His revenue had jumped five times, he estimated, and he no longer paid taxes. Land itself had skyrocketed. Next to Thijil's hotel, a 7,250-square-foot parcel of property had gone from an estimated worth of $25,000 in 1999 to a current valuation of $1.4 million. His only inconvenience: angry pilgrims who, he said, felt they were being cheated. (They often were, but not by him, he insisted.)

Whom did he credit? I asked him.

"It's money from God," said the ebullient Thijil, a stocky man with a quick smile and eyes that danced. "And the thanks after that go to the shrine of Imam Ali. If it wasn't for the shrine," he added, blowing as he flicked his wrist, "nothing." Thijil smiled again. "You should open a hotel," he suggested. "That's my advice. Only God knows how much we're going to earn."

On March 2, the day of Ashura, Karbala was as festive and celebratory as its sister city of Najaf. All roads seemed to lead to the city; in small towns in southern Iraq, along the Euphrates, signs pointed the way toward Karbala and its shrines of Hussein and Abbas, which were draped in black for the occasion. Religious flags of green, red, and black fluttered from houses all along the routes approaching the holy city, and chants of mourning from scratchy cassettes and dilapidated speakers filled the streets. (At times, the batteries would run low, making the chants even more mournful.) The neighborhoods surrounding the shrines were teeming with pilgrims, many sleepless, having taken part in festivities that had lasted through the night. Tea and water were served for free, and along the road, bottomless steel vats of *harisa*, a stew served on religious holidays, were cooked over wood fires and blow torches. Iraqi police and U.S. troops hovered in the background, as volunteers and members of militias of religious Shiite parties enforced security inside the city and on its outskirts. "The police work for money," one of the guards, twenty-six-year-old Bassem Aswad, told me. "We work for faith."

Across the street was Ali Odeh, who had arrived with eight friends from the southern city of Basra the night before. "We didn't sleep, we didn't sleep at all," he said excitedly, as he watched the processions surge, meander, and spill toward the shrines. "This is the first year we've tasted peace. It's like we were released from prison."

For many, these early hours were a celebratory moment of reflection on both the old and the new: each ritual commemorating Hussein's seventh-century death was in itself a testament to the contemporary liberation brought by Saddam's fall. As usual, the community's narrative moved seamlessly across the centuries. Some sat in silence before the shrines, reading prayers. Others, particularly the young, were more public in their mourning, and the streets reverberated with their impassioned celebrations. Many did *lutm*, beating their chests to a cadence set by cymbals, and others flailed their backs with chains, their bodies like the taut skins of drums. Through the morning, especially exuberant groups of young men, draped in funeral tunics, slapped their foreheads with swords, spilling blood from small cuts over their faces and white-clad chests.

A fountain outside the Abbas shrine flowed red, a symbol of Hussein's blood. A banner along the shrine read, "Karbala is a symbol of heroism and sacrifice."

Then at ten A.M., under an especially vivid, sunny sky, the festivities came to a shattering end, and with it ended the exuberance over what had happened after Saddam. The blasts ripped through the celebrations in a series spaced about a minute apart. Another string of explosions, almost simultaneous, tore through the Kadhimiya neighborhood in Baghdad, about fifty miles away. On this Ashura, the most hallowed day in the Shiite Muslim calendar, the places of pilgrimage and prayer were infused with scenes of the consecrated and pro-fane. Festival turned to carnage and ritual mourning to wrenching grief. The pattern familiar elsewhere in Iraq was now making its mark in the country's few oases of prosperity and hope. Shockingly efficient, the bombings devastated some of the most crowded spots in Karbala—the road behind the Abbas shrine, packed, at the time, with pilgrims; streets in front of hotels; a bridge spanning a canal where pilgrims swam in the muddy waters; and the entrance to the city, from where pilgrims walked the last mile toward the shrines.

The blood of suicide bombers and their victims splashed the brick walls of nearby buildings. Blood soaked ground that was considered sacred, and the wooden carts used to ferry elderly pilgrims were now stacked with bloodied victims. In a hasty gesture of respect, cardboard and palm fronds were tossed on body parts strewn across the street. Piles of sandals were swept to curbs, where pools of water turned red. At the Hibut Allah Hotel, a wheelchair was tossed on the sidewalk, splashed with blood that drew swarms of flies.

The blood and pieces of flesh had yet to take on the smell of decay. The scent was more metallic, permeated by the powerful odors of the explosives. It was as if a burst of fire had seared street after street, leaving behind burns in red and black.

"It's forbidden!" shouted Hassan Hadi, a twenty-two-year-old guard. He was trying to stop fleeing pilgrims from walking over pools of blood and scraps of seared flesh. "Don't step on the blood. It's forbidden! This is the blood of Shiites."

Down the street, Ahmed Naama, a fifty-five-year-old shopkeeper in a black dishdasha with a green scarf around his waist, was sweeping the sidewalk across from the Shurufi Hotel. His glazed eyes were printed with terror. "I saw the flames racing toward me," he said. "It was like somebody throwing water at me." He patted his ears. More than an hour later, he said he could still not hear.

In the hours before the bombs struck, Arabic had mixed with Farsi in the streets. The crowds had chanted. Quranic recitation cascaded from loud-speakers, intersecting with the clash of instruments and the sirens of ambulances bearing away those exhausted from the rituals. In a moment, all this ritual disorder erupted into panic. Iranian pilgrims flocked to hotels, looking for phones to call home. Few understood the shouts of the Iraqi guards trying to control frightened crowds. "Brothers! God's mercy on your parents! Back up!" the guards cried in vain. Finally, the pulsating city fell into the numb quiet of grief and shock, broken only by the ringing of shattered glass and by appeals over mosque loudspeakers for pilgrims to donate blood to the wounded. As the bodies, most nameless, passed, invocations were pronounced. "God is greatest," a few shouted. Others cried, "O, Hussein," whose martyrdom they had come to commemorate on this day. "There is no god but God," some murmured, the traditional utterance on the death of a Muslim.

As I sat outside the turquoise-tiled portico of the Imam Abbas shrine, I was approached by Saad Hashem Saidi, a thirty-five-year-old pilgrim from

Baghdad. He had seen my notebook and wanted an answer. "Why won't they leave us in peace?" he asked.

Who *they* were was a difficult question. No one asserted responsibility for the attacks, believed to be suicide bombings. Some perceived a disturbing realization of ideas from a letter reputedly written by Abu Musab Zarqawi that came to light in February 2003. A Jordanian militant with professed loyalty to Osama bin Laden, Zarqawi had outlined plans to fuel sectarian strife by striking Shiite targets.

The blame that day was immediate. Anger clouded reason. There was fury over the persistence of violence, over the perceived U.S. inability to bring order, over still mysterious enemies. "You're the reason for the explosions! You're the reason!" one guard shouted at me and a colleague, near the Abbas shrine. "God's curses on you!"

Down the street, men gathered, speculating on who was to blame.

"We say America is responsible," said thirty-five-year-old Abu Ahmed Husseini.

Some suspected bin Laden's followers or Wahhabis, others vestiges of the Baath Party.

"Wahhabis and Baathists," insisted thirty-two-year-old Mahdi Salman.

"America is trying to create a conflict between Sunnis and Shiites," countered thirty-five-year-old Ahmed Hassan. "This is the fundamental goal of America. America wants anarchy, America wants chaos."

I wandered down the street and found Heidar Mahdi sitting alone, smoking a cigarette a few feet from one of the blasts. A twenty-five-year-old baker from Baghdad, he had arrived an hour after the attacks, determined to complete his pilgrimage. He said he was weary from worry. On his mind was not newfound freedom or the celebration of ritual, but rather growing fear, that sense that every moment foreshadowed more death and suffering, more corpses that would join the scores killed in Kadhimiya and Karbala.

"The future is not clear," he said; tomorrow was, as I heard once again, *ghamidh*. "These events, we see them as a warning. They're a warning about the future."

NIGHT ALWAYS SEEMED TO BE DRAWING NEAR IN IRAQ, AND NOW THE CHAOS AND the sense of the unknown seemed to generate their own momentum. A mournful dread followed the Ramadan bombings in Baghdad, just as it now seemed to permeate everything after the attacks at Kadhimiya and Karbala. Each new spectacle seemed to set a standard for the bloodiest, most destructive, and most lethal outrage in memory. This was unlike anything anyone had predicted. Loss was everywhere.

Moving through the blood-soaked city, I tried to do my job, but at every turn, I was repulsed, overwhelmed with a desire to leave this place and, for that matter, the country itself. I walked past a finger and a piece of scalp with knotted, matted hair; a chunk of brain had been tossed into a pot of still steaming rice. (The kettle was considered cleaner than the ground.) With their own twisted logic, the other attacks over the past year had made sense. The U.N. bombing in August 2003 discouraged the world body from playing too active a role in the U.S.-led occupation. The bombing of the Jordanian Embassy that same month sent a message to other Arab states not to embrace the government the Americans had set up. The assassination of Hakim in Najaf deprived the United States of a crucial mediator between religious Shiites and the American administration. But Karbala and Kadhimiya? There was no discernible target, no strategic aim other than to inflict the greatest number of casualties among civilians who were utterly defenseless, celebrating their own liberation.

But, this being a war unlike any other, victory was defined differently. The logic of violence never envisioned a triumph or an ending. There would be no winner, no agreement, no real truce. No one, not even the most ardent opponents of the occupation, thought the Americans could be defeated in military terms, and of course, that was never the goal. Bloodshed in itself was the ambition; it was a brutal, chilling, but calculated way to produce the perception of American failure. This war, from every perspective, was defined almost solely by its terrible, unforgettable images, searing images: bodies strewn in the streets in Karbala, the charred carcasses left by car bombs that began to be deployed casually, the craters blown wide and the façades of buildings in Baghdad ripped off by blasts becoming so frequent in early 2004 that they would quickly become mundane.

In a tactical sense, the attacks in Karbala and Kadhimiya—like those that preceded and followed them—had no real impact on the American presence in the country. Yet they succeeded, with cold brilliance, in magnifying the sense of U.S. failure in the eyes of most Iraqis and, for that matter, in the eyes of much of the world. It was theater, and people kept dying to create those indelible scenes, a portrait of a debacle designed for world consumption. The carnage itself sent the message of approaching anarchy, of the nearing of an abyss, as if it was understood that Americans could say nothing to mitigate the most recent tragedies or promise anything that would end the violence. The country was neither liberated, as Americans would have it, nor occupied, as the rest of the Arab world saw it. Iraq was subsumed in the logic of violence, ruled by men with guns. Those men, playing by no rules, would soon inherit Iraq.

Around that time, Nasir had come to the *Post*'s bureau in Baghdad, where my colleagues and I lived. It was early, 7:20 A.M., and I was still asleep in my second-floor bedroom. Nasir's face was expressionless but for his eyes, and I knew something was wrong. "I was bombed," he told me.

His voice was unusually calm, even though a trace of fear clipped his words. On that morning, someone had attached an explosive with magnets to the black iron gate outside his home in the Bayaa neighborhood, in southern Baghdad. Soon after dawn, it detonated, the echo rolling down his crowded street where legions of children played. It peeled the gate back like a can and shattered the windows of his two living rooms, the kitchen, and an upstairs room. Like smeared blood, the blast left its dark shadows on the newly swabbed white stucco outside his house and tore through a heavy wooden door at the entrance, tossing it gracelessly inside like a playing card. Nasir and his family had escaped safely, but we knew they were in danger.

For months, insurgents had been attacking anyone believed to be working with the American occupation; dozens, perhaps hundreds, had been killed. There were bombings and executions, sometimes preceded by warnings, sometimes not. Nasir, the staff, and I sat downstairs, speculating: *Was it mistaken identity? Was it a vendetta?* We thought about the people we had met and whether any of them might have had a grievance against us. I wondered whether we had gotten too close to the families of Adnan Fahdawi and his men in Khaldiya, killed in the attack on the Americans.

Nasir homed in on another suspect, an intensely devout twenty-seven-year-old student who lived in his neighborhood. We had visited the student often, seeking help to put us in contact with the families of men who had died in attacks on U.S. forces in Baghdad. With a pleasant face and a well-trimmed beard, he was rigorously hospitable, offering us Turkish coffee and sweets on each visit, but he remained insistently suspicious of our intentions. In the end, he refused to help. "No one knows the truth," he told us, "except the person who died." A week after that conversation, his father, a senior Baath Party member, was arrested by the Americans. Did the son think us responsible, and was this his vengeance? Once again, we had no answers. In retrospect, we still don't.

On that morning of his arrival at our hotel, we returned to Nasir's house. Just weeks earlier, he had spent hundreds of dollars renovating it for his wife, their two children, and his sister, who lived with them. It looked like the scene of any of the numerous attacks we had covered together: shattered glass was strewn across the cement floor; the drapes were torn and tangled; the furniture was tossed as if a storm had swept through the place. The faces of Nasir's family were expressionless as they tried to cope with tragedy.

For a while, we worked to clean up the place, hoping to make the destruction less conspicuous in a neighborhood whose graffiti was growing ferocious. "We will cut off the heads of the Americans," one slogan on a nearby building read. Handwritten in black, it seemed to shout its promise. "Death to spies and traitors!" cried another scrawl. Hurriedly, after we had done what we could with the house, Nasir and his family packed their clothes and a few belongings, and we took his family to the residence of another staff member, Abu Seif, who had invited them to stay with him. Nasir then insisted, somewhat desperately, that he and I pay a visit to Hazem, the fortune-teller.

On a subdued street lined with squat concrete houses, as all of us kept an eye on the traffic, Hazem scolded Nasir for ignoring his warnings. He mumbled, his eyes cast downward, then looked up. "I told you not to remodel your house," he told Nasir. He repeated his words with little emotion, and Nasir shook his head, a gesture of regret at ignoring advice he knew had been wise. Hazem, seeming satisfied that his words had been heeded, then spoke again.

"You must stay away," he told Nasir.

Nasir's questions tumbled out, and Hazem stuck with his answer.

"You must leave," he repeated.

Days later, Nasir and his family packed for the last time. They would leave for Amman. No one disagreed with the decision. In the words of one of our friends, quoting an Iraqi proverb, "Everything short of death is acceptable." But this was exile, and it had been forced on them.

The occupation, though not the American presence, formally ended on June 28, 2004, when L. Paul Bremer caught a flight out of Baghdad, two days ahead of his scheduled departure. But symbolically at least, it seemed to have come to its conclusion long before that, as residents struggled with even the most basic of services, and as violence—both political and criminal—surged. In my view, the American experience—and the hope and promise it perhaps, at one time, embodied—collapsed in twin uprisings that came a month after the bombings in the Shiite shrines and Wasir's departure. Those uprisings— in the Sunni city of Fallujah and parts of the Shiite heartland in Kufa, Nasiriya, Najaf, and the slums of Sadr City—wrote the occupation's epitaph before it actually ended. Helping hold the pen were the young, sometimes brave, usually reckless followers of the Shiite cleric whom I had met in the turbulent first weeks after Saddam's fall: Muqtada Sadr.

In the months before and after the bombings in Karbala and Kadhimiya, Sadr, as was his wont, was organizing his street-level constituency. With an increasing emphasis on the efficacy of the gun, and the seeming conviction that political power grew out of its barrel, Sadr and his followers had continued to develop his movement at the crossroads of his father's populist legacy and an Iraqi nationalism that chafed at occupation. The movement had two aspects, which would ultimately intersect in the uprisings that ensued. There was the grassroots organizing, of which Friday prayers in Baghdad and Kufa stood at the center. No less important was the more thuggish and increasingly dominant power of the Mahdi Army, with its motley collection of militiamen. Each had its own ritual.

The grassroots organizing was on display every Friday on the road to Kufa, a ribbon of black asphalt that snaked from Sadr City to the town where Muqtada's assassinated father had first incubated his following. Every week, hundreds and sometimes thousands of Sadr's followers—mostly men but occasionally women—would gather in the quiet Sabbath streets and head for the assemblage of minivans bound for the prayers and parked near a rusted iron stand selling cigarettes and a rickety white shack that sold blocks of ice during the summer. The men would pack their tattered prayer rugs and money for the seventy-five-cent fare. Still sleepy, they would grab their seats for the two-and-a-half-hour trip south, along roads lined with palm trees and police checkpoints. The police were wary of those they deemed rabble.

"God willing, I'm going to the prayers," Abdel-Rahman Tuama told me one morning as he boarded a minivan. Women in black *abayas* with children in brightly colored dresses wove through the traffic. Drivers shouted their destinations in staccato bursts. "Karbala! Karbala! Karbala!" one yelled, laying on the last word like a carhorn. Another: "Najaf! Najaf! I'm going to Najaf." And finally: "Kufa!"

A few minutes after Tuama settled into a torn leather seat, the van lurched forward and set off the wrong way down a two-lane street. The drivers were notorious for their indifference to traffic regulations. "God's prayers on Mohammed and the family of Mohammed," he said, fulfilling a custom. Tuama and the twelve other passengers dutifully repeated the blessing.

In the front seat, the driver and a passenger fumbled through cassettes cluttered on the dashboard, finally settling on a tape of devotional chants to Imam Hussein. Black prayer beads swayed from the rearview mirror. On the right-hand corner of the cracked windshield was a stylized portrait of Imam Ali with Hussein and Abbas—a talisman of sorts. Through open windows, a cool breeze blew over Tuama. The passengers lazily ashed their cigarettes on the van's carpeted floor.

Sadr's followers were often young and unemployed and usually uneducated. Tuama, a heavyset thirty-three-year-old with a trimmed black beard, was neither. He made a respectable $120 a month welding air conditioner ducts. His family lived in a house with five bedrooms, shared by eight people. Formidably devout, he said he had witnessed both good and bad in the U.S. presence. But occupation was an "ugly word."

Sitting in the front seat, Mohammed Abed overheard this and he cocked his head. "We don't want to feel like the Iraqi people need something from the Americans. Why can't we depend on ourselves to provide security and stability?" he asked. Abed, a bald, bearded forty-two-year-old electrician, stopped for a moment. The minivan hurtled past cans of black-market gasoline stacked in pyramids. Then he voiced a suspicion common to Sadr's followers. "I don't think the Americans are going to leave, ever," he said.

"Only God knows," Tuama insisted.

That morning, I was continually reminded of the power of the legacy of

Sadr's father. The Americans, their Iraqi allies, and the more traditional, conservative clerical leadership in Najaf often tried to dismiss Muqtada Sadr as a too-young upstart, lacking in the scholarship so important to seminaries in the Shiite holy cities. Those criticisms meant little to those who, like Abed and Tuama, were loyal to him as they had been loyal to his father. Each gesture Sadr made in defiance of the occupation and in defense of his father's legacy only buoyed his support. Far better than the Americans, far better than their allies in Baghdad, Sadr knew the Iraqi personality, and he knew what bravery and courage—real or not—meant to his constituency.

"We don't care about his age. It's not a matter of age. Age is not a condition," Tuama told me. "Sayyid Muqtada is completing his father's divine march." He looked out the window as we passed a billboard bearing portraits of Sadr's father and his relative Ayatollah Mohammed Baqir al-Sadr. "When people find someone who is brave," he said, "they are drawn to him."

The gray minivan passed the last checkpoint into Kufa, and the passengers got out. Some jumped to the street; others, a bit older, stepped out gingerly. Each went his own way. Tuama joined friends and they headed toward the sprawling brick mosque where Sadr would deliver the sermon. Abed hurried over to the turbulent displays of religious literature; posters of Sadr and his father; and newspapers, sold for a little more than ten cents on soiled canvas mats weighed down by rocks on this breezy day. One of the newspapers read, "Yes to the army of Imam Mahdi." The smell of grilling kebab and boiling garbanzo beans wafted in the air, past stands selling bananas, apples, and children's toys.

Abed picked up the latest copy of Sadr's newspaper, *The Seminary*, with its lead editorial urging unity among Shiite leaders "before the great flood comes and before the army of Satan readies itself to eliminate you one after another." Then, with hundreds of others, he shuffled into the Kufa Mosque, summoned by the call to prayer. Over the floor of dirt and stone, he laid out his red-and-gold rug, body to body with others in the intimate community of the Friday prayers. As Sadr went to the podium, chants rang out from supporters, some wearing the movement's trademark funeral shrouds: "Long live Sadr! Faith will be victorious."

Sadr's once hesitant voice had matured; it sounded deeper, more forceful. Infusing his speech with calls "to defend the oppressed and the weak and to help the poor," he repeated his insistence on peaceful protest but denounced U.S. troops. "They have shown their wicked intentions against Muslims. Their hearts are full of hatred," he declared.

When followers started chanting their support, he playfully scolded them. "Enough, enough," he said jokingly, employing Iraqi slang that few clerics would use in a public address. "You'll get us into trouble." He (and his lieutenants) bestowed nicknames on the Americans, their allies, and his foes, often as a way to ridicule them. Today Saddam was *Haddam*, destructive.

When the prayers ended, dozens gathered near the mosque's door to wait for Sadr's departure. One man asked excitedly, "Has he come yet? Has he come yet?" Others chanted their fealty, thrusting kaffiyehs, towels, and posters in the air: "We sacrifice our souls for Sadr and his son Muqtada." They broke into another: "We are the army of Mahdi and the followers of Sadr and whoever touches you, Muqtada, we'll cut him to pieces."

Abed stood at the edge of the energized crowd, remaining silent. The Sadr newspaper was under his arm. In one hand, his prayer rug was bundled in a yellow plastic sack, ready for the trip home to Baghdad. He grasped a prayer stone in the other. "I don't have to say it openly," he told me, his voice soft. "It's inside, in my heart."

Hume Horan once said something to me that proved uncannily apt: "When the pot starts to boil over, it boils over very fast." The grass roots of Sadr's movement and its militia arm, the Mahdi Army, began to merge in the wake of the bombings in Karbala and Kadhimiya.

In the first six months after Saddam's fall, neither the Americans nor Sadr's movement really seemed to understand each other. But the eruption after a U.S. helicopter knocked over a religious banner in Sadr City in August 2003 had seemed to unleash further momentum, pushing both sides inexorably toward confrontation. From then on, the conflict never subsided; it only intensified, gathering force from the anxiety and apprehension created by the bombings in Karbala and Kadhimiya. Sadr's lieutenants—men like Mustafa al-Yaacoubi, Riyadh al-Nouri, and Abbas Rubai—no longer responded thoughtfully to questions. They insisted, always without hesitation, that the Americans were on the verge of arresting Sadr, and they were increasingly blunt in their warnings at the Friday prayers in Kufa.

Their fears were not unfounded. Months earlier, U.S. officials had asked an Iraqi judge to investigate Sadr's role in the killing of Abdel-Majid Khoie, the son of Ayatollah Sistani's mentor who was knifed to death in Najaf on April 10, 2003, shortly after returning from exile. After a discreet inquiry, the judge issued warrants in August for Sadr, his top deputy, and eleven other people. But at the time, a decision was made by the CPA not to execute the warrants and risk a confrontation. "I don't see much taste for running out and arresting Muqtada at the Friday prayers," Hume Horan told me then. He and some other officials believed they might be able simply to ignore him and his movement. As Horan put it to me, the strategy was "Let him burn himself out. That's a nice out. You don't have to do anything." Some within the Green Zone and in the U.S. administration's satellite offices in southern Iraq disagreed, and as the months progressed and Sadr's rhetoric grew more hostile, their opinions began to prevail. Sadr's officials feared the worst.

"They're trying in many different ways to provoke us," Mustafa al-Yaacoubi, wearing the black turban of the prophet Mohammed's descendants, told me as we sat in Sadr's two-story office in Najaf. "But if they commit more provocations, people may act spontaneously. They may act on their own, in ways that are not organized. No one can control people's passions, their reactions, and their behavior. What they would do is unpredictable."

Abbas Rubai, stern and direct, spoke similarly in his Baghdad office with its banner reading "With Sadr, we are liberated." Warning that any move against Sadr would unleash "a popular uprising," he ticked off the southern and central Iraqi cities where he expected such a reaction would erupt: Baghdad, Basra, Nasiriya, Kufa, Kut, and Diwaniya. The Americans, he insisted, were deceived by reports telling them that nothing would happen if they acted against Sadr or the movement.

His statements were inspired, in part, by his knowledge of the popular revulsion that follows the arrest of clergy, an attitude that the U.S. military and its civilian associates were hopeless to overcome. Particularly for religious Shiites, such arrests smacked of Saddam's withering repression against clerics. They were men of religion, after all, and they were respected for the suffering they had endured over three decades of Baathist rule. Even critics of Sadr warned against detaining *muammimeen*, the turbaned ones. "The arrest of scholars is a grave mistake," said Abdel-Aziz al-Hakim, the head of the Supreme Council for the Islamic Revolution in Iraq and one of Sadr's main rivals.

Sadr's first line of defense was the Mahdi Army, which by late 2003 and early 2004 had begun to shed its makeshift quality and take on the air of a fighting force with an elaborate hierarchy and formidable organization. Estimates of its strength ran anywhere from three thousand to ten thousand. In public, its black-clad members were often seen handling security at religious festivals and Shiite sites in Najaf, Karbala, and Baghdad. Its iconography, already imbued with the traditional Shiite notions of suffering and martyrdom, was growing more and more militant as contemporary currents began filtering into Baghdad and the south. (The dynamic was not unlike that visible in western Iraq, where Fahdawi and other rural men provided an audience for the imported messages of militant Sunni clerics that had become available after Saddam's fall.) For Sadr and his men, those new influences revolved around the Lebanese Shiite movement known as Hezbollah, whose mantle the Mahdi Army tried to wear inside Iraq.

To the West, Hezbollah remained a shadowy band of militants suspected in the kidnapping of more than fifty foreigners amid the anarchy that defined Lebanon in its 1975–90 civil war. More dramatically, Hezbollah was blamed for two attacks on the American Embassy in Beirut and for the 1983 bombing of a U.S. Marine barracks, which killed 240 soldiers. In the Arab world, not surprisingly, the group's image was far different: the organization had won heroic status for its success in forcing Israel to withdraw from southern Lebanon in May 2000 after a long guerrilla battle across war-scarred wadis. Hezbollah celebrated the victory of *al-Muqawama al-Islamiya*, the Islamic resistance, and the imagery of that struggle—Kalashnikovs and Qurans, bathed in the glow of Hussein's martyrdom—had arrived at the offices of Sadr's movement by early 2004. It was an early, troubling sign of a new direction that movement had chosen. It was also another irony of Iraq: the country's liberation from Saddam's rule had again opened it to influences that were then tailored to fighting the American-led occupation.

At Friday prayers and outside the Sadr movement's headquarters, pictures drawing on Hezbollah's iconography were scattered across the pavement. Some were simple, for example, a portrait of Hassan Nasrallah, Hezbollah's secretary-general, who had been chosen to lead the movement at the age of thirty-two. Others were overtly militant; in one, Sadr's father was portrayed against a red background, with Sadr and Nasrallah beneath him. Sadr pointed with two fingers; Nasrallah lifted a Kalashnikov over his head. In white, the poster read, "Our submission is out of the question." In posters selling for fifteen cents, Nasrallah and Sadr were pictured against a green background, before crowds of worshippers at Friday prayers in front of the Dome of the Rock in Jerusalem. A slogan often used by Hezbollah—"Crush them under your feet"—began to show up on Sadr's own posters. The message was clear: more than a parochial clique, Sadr's men were part of a movement that, while distinctly Shiite, was steeped in Iraq's history and the struggles of the broader Arab world, sharing its enemies. Those enemies were America and Israel.

As the confrontation with the Americans deepened, the celebration of this new militancy and heroic martyrdom began to become more and more visible. At Sadr's office in the southern city of Nasiriya, I witnessed some indelible scenes around the time of the bombings in Karbala and Kadhimiya. Dozens of men clad in black and belonging to the group's militia were crowded inside the place, some of them wearing World War I–style green ammunition belts. Sitting lazily against the wall or crouched in the middle of the room, they clutched among them four rocket-propelled grenade launchers, more than a dozen Kalashnikovs, and an assortment of pistols, rifles, hand grenades, and ammunition clips. (All of these, of course, were banned by the occupation.) One of the fighters was Abbas Abdullah, a smiling, cheerful thirteen-year-old, wearing a black headband inscribed with the militia's name in Arabic, Jaish al-Mahdi. He was not much taller than his rifle.

As I met with Sadr's lieutenant, more militiamen, all similarly clad, gathered in the muddy courtyard outside, their chants audible from inside the office. "Long live Sadr!" some shouted. More troubling was the chant of another group: "We're impatient!" they yelled, drilling in a circle with their rifles. "We want death tonight!"

The words seemed a harbinger; although no one really anticipated just how the increasing militancy of Sadr's men would express itself, there were clues. As the months passed, complaints about the Mahdi Army's more nefarious activities increased. Armed with rocket-propelled grenade launchers, mortars, and the ubiquitous AK-47s, the militia began to act as the long, dreaded arm of the movement, sending out death threats, intimidating people not adhering to its version of proper Islamic dress, setting up its own courts, and, at times, seizing public buildings and beating up disobedient policemen. Its record had instilled fear in some places in Baghdad and the southern Shiite cities—not the diffuse terror that Saddam's government intentionally bred but rather a sense that some things are better not spoken about: Why risk angering someone when you don't have to?

The potential for cruel violence became clear in March 2004, when the Mahdi Army destroyed Qawliya, a Gypsy village in southern Iraq that long had been known as the country's equivalent of a red-light district, a redoubt of gunrunners, and a haven from the law. More than a thousand residents were driven out, and the village, an isolated warren of perhaps 150 concrete and brick homes, was razed. (The Mahdi Army had help from looters.) When I arrived with Karim a few days later, the few sounds of life were made by mangy, barking dogs and by scavengers, who arrived in tractors and trucks to search for bricks in the rubble. Usable bricks could go for between three and seven cents each. The walls of nearly every house were at least partially torn down; the roofs were gone. The doors and the window frames had been removed. Overturned desks, their writing surfaces missing, were tossed around inside a school. Wreckage was strewn through the half-dozen streets, shaded by a few haggard eucalyptus trees. Remnants of daily life littered the wreckage—brightly colored fabric caked with dust; sandals; tins of cooking oil.

The story I heard was that Sadr's militiamen had gone to retrieve a girl from nearby Diwaniya who was either abducted and taken to Qawliya or had sought refuge there. When residents refused to give her up and fired on the militiamen, a devastatingly lopsided fight was ignited. This was the explanation given by Hussein Tawil, a spokesman for the Sadr office in Diwaniya, who wore a pistol slung around his chest when I met him. Two AK-47s sat in the corner of his cramped office; four plastic chairs and a wooden stool lined the walls.

"They provided a fertile land for sinning," said Tawil, a burly man who smoked menthol cigarettes. "There were so many crimes in that village." For months, Tawil emphasized, the office had tried to reform the village. His office had offered to send a preacher to serve there, to provide religious CDs and videos, to hold Friday prayers inside the town, and to send five of its residents to the seminary in Najaf. "Since the fall of the regime, we tried to call on these people to improve," he said. "I wanted to give them an opportunity for a decent life."

He looked out the window that overlooked the street.

"They refused," he said.

THE INSURGENCY AGAINST THE AMERICANS PERSISTED WITH GROWING STRENGTH in the Sunni regions, surging alongside the militarization of the Mahdi Army in Sadr City, Kut, Nasiriya, and Basra. Over the last weeks of March and into April 2004, those forces and other currents converged. It was a time when the U.S. administration could little afford further tremors: the Coalition Provisional Authority was just three months away from formally turning over power to an interim Iraqi government and in the midst of a huge troop rotation, with many new and relatively inexperienced soldiers coming to Iraq. The result would be a climactic storm, devastating and awesome, which was about to rewrite the draft of history that the Americans and the most optimistic Iraqis were composing. My colleagues and I heard the warning signals, as did others. "I have sort of a bad feeling that things are not where they should be," an Italian official with the U.S.-led occupation in Nasiriya told me around that time. "I can tell you what will happen next week, not after that."

The omens began to be fulfilled, it seemed, on March 28, at about 9:30 A.M., in a downtown Baghdad square tied up with its usual traffic on the pleasant spring day. In thirty vehicles or so, U.S. soldiers arrived at the office of Sadr's newspaper, *The Seminary*, which regularly distributed ten thousand copies outside mosques during Friday prayers. ("Bremer follows in the footsteps of Saddam," had read the headline of a recent issue.) Polite to the point of being apologetic, the soldiers ushered the newspaper's staff into the street. Then, moving quickly and efficiently, they fastened a brand-new steel padlock on a chain bound to the newspaper office's flimsy front gate. "American Lock," read the padlock's tooled lettering. One of the officers presented a letter from L. Paul Bremer, written in a sparse, understated Arabic that suggested a literal translation from English, bearing the seal of his administration and ordering the paper to cease publication for sixty days.

"I'm sorry," the officer said. "I'm going to have to close your building."

The closure was more than a simple crackdown on a paper that, for months, had irritated the American administration; U.S. officials saw shutting the newspaper as a way to exert pressure on Sadr to disband the Mahdi Army and lower its profile. With the approaching dissolution of Bremer's administration, his officials were worried that militias—Sadr's and others—would make a free and fair election difficult, contribute to more strife and instability, and bring closer the prospect of civil war. If they could not force the Mahdi Army to disarm, the thinking went, there would be no way to get other militias to do the same. The hesitation that Hume Horan had once voiced about Sadr's movement was giving way to the desire, on the part of Bremer and others, to be more forceful in trying to dramatically steer the occupation in its last months.

In the end, Bremer and his deputies saw the newspaper's closure as a tactical maneuver, the movement of a piece across the chessboard, with the anticipation of unlocking a further series of moves that would turn the game to their advantage. There were few American troops in Sadr's strongholds and no military plans to respond to a backlash; no one envisioned that the closure would create an unmanageable crisis. But Sadr and his men, whose suspicions had been building over months, saw this gesture as the final provocation. As they appraised the situation, it was now a life-and-death struggle, and they were ready, even eager, to simply throw all the pieces off the chessboard. When Bremer moved against the newspaper, the clerics around Sadr acted on the calculus of a showdown. Unless there was a retaliatory show of force, they feared that the U.S. administration would only be encouraged to take further steps. "They wanted to hide the Shiite voice by closing the newspaper," said Fuad Tarfi, a spokesman for Sadr in Najaf. Within hours of the closing, Sadr's office ordered a mobilization of the Mahdi Army in Baghdad and cities south.

Protesters flooded the traffic circle in front of the newspaper's offices, holding a noisy rally that would be convened again over the next two days. On March 31, 2004, three days after the newspaper was closed, the demonstrations escalated. Instead of loitering in front of the newspaper's offices, hundreds of supporters marched in tight military formation to the fortified entrances of the Green Zone. "We are followers of Sadr!" they shouted. "All the people know us! Why is America against us?" Many of the men wore only black, save for their headbands of religiously resonant green. Marshals rushed between the units, warning them to keep their ranks sharp in martial fashion. Clerics in turbans swept down the fringes with a proprietary air. "Today is peaceful!" the men yelled. "Tomorrow will be military!"

In the days that followed, most of the communication between Sadr's staff and the occupation authority occurred only through public statements. The U.S. administration had few if any intermediaries to call upon and showed little willingness to negotiate anyway. Actually, they took the opposite tack. Despite the mobilization of Sadr's followers, the Americans kept up the pressure on the movement.

On Saturday, April 3, under cover of darkness, U.S. Special Forces detained Mustafa al-Yaacoubi, the quiet, lisping cleric who had long been the most accessible of Sadr's lieutenants. With twelve others, he was arrested on the nearly eight-month-old charges stemming from Khoie's death. The repercussions were vast and almost immediate. Escalations—some unintentional, some otherwise—that had played out over months now played out over hours. As positions hardened, both sides prepared for a showdown; from then on, each side would hear the other's contentions and simply shake its head in disbelief. "We didn't choose the time for the uprising," said Tarfi, the Sadr spokesman. "The occupation forces did. It's clear that by arresting Sheikh Yaacoubi and closing the *Seminary* newspaper, they wanted to provoke the Shiites. We didn't want to choose this time for the uprising."

After Yaacoubi's arrest, Sadr's followers began boarding buses and trucks for Kufa, along the same road I had traveled with Tuama and Abed. A protest was scheduled for Sunday, and at three o'clock that morning, buses were still crossing the bridges over the lush green banks of a canal along the Euphrates and depositing young men in the crowded square in front of Sadr's headquarters. More kept coming.

After daybreak, they moved, becoming a mob with a direction and purpose. Hundreds of Sadr's men took over the headquarters of the city's traffic police station and a second government building, both of which were surrendered by local police and officials without a fight. The next target was the headquarters of the U.S.-led administration, which was protected by private guards and Salvadoran troops allied with the United States. Neither side, of course, knew the other's intentions. The guards and troops took up firing positions on the roof next door. Alarmed to see the throng still moving toward them, they fired percussive rounds designed to break up the crowd, which instead enraged it. They may then have switched to live fire. Armed men in the crowd returned fire with small arms, rocket-propelled grenades, and mortars. Accounts of the confrontation differed, as was to be expected, but at one point, witnesses saw a vehicle carrying four Salvadoran soldiers caught outside the gate. Demonstrators overwhelmed the terrified occupants, seizing and executing one prisoner on the spot by putting a grenade in his mouth and pulling the pin. Two of the other soldiers, their faces bloodied from beatings, were seen being led by armed men into the mosque. The firefight lasted for hours, eventually drawing in U.S. warplanes and Apache helicopters. When it ended, one U.S. soldier and one Salvadoran were dead, and twelve others had been wounded. Twenty, perhaps thirty Iraqis had been killed.

The revolt spread. By 1:30 P.M., the loudspeakers of the Kufa Mosque announced that the Mahdi Army held Kufa, Najaf, Nasiriya, and Sadr City. The checkpoint controlling access to the bridge into Kufa and Najaf was staffed by young militiamen, wearing bandoliers and brandishing their rifles. Many Iraqi police, trained and paid by the American-led occupation, had joined the assault on their own building. U.S. officials, informed by Iraqi intermediaries that Sadr's influence was overstated, were stunned. "The response we got from capturing Yaacoubi was unexpected," a senior U.S. Army officer said. "We did not expect it to be as broad-based as it was."

At 4:30 P.M., Sadr issued a typewritten statement calling on his followers to stop the protests, which he described as peaceful. They were futile, he insisted. But he gave a new order, whose phrasing would change the occupation permanently: "Terrorize your enemy," he declared. "God will reward you well for what pleases him. It is not possible to remain silent in front of their violations." Clashes in Amara and Nasiriya, trouble in Basra, protests in Baghdad. Then came a fight with American troops who had dared enter Sadr's stronghold in Baghdad after the declaration.

None of the soldiers in the platoon, from Comanche Company in Sadr City, saw the rocket-propelled grenades fired from an alley into their Humvees. But four of them died there. The survivors radioed for reinforcements. The unit racing from the base camp into the slum was met by a hail of fire from rooftops, alleys, and upstairs windows—in the words of one senior army officer, "a mob with a lot of weapons." Ninety minutes later, a third convoy—this one a tank column—was fired on. Every road was blocked with concrete, debris, and trash. When the gunfire subsided a few hours later, four more soldiers had died and forty were wounded. (Major General Martin Dempsey, the commander of the 1st Armored Division, later called the clash "the biggest gunfight since the fall of Baghdad a year ago.")

By nightfall on that Sunday, both sides had reached a point that neither had anticipated and whose conclusion neither could foresee. In Baghdad, Hazem Aaraji, a Sadr lieutenant, declared outside the headquarters of the U.S. administration, "The people are prepared for martyrdom." The language from inside the compound was no less uncompromising. "This morning, a group of people in Najaf have crossed the line, and they have moved to violence," read Bremer's statement. "This will not be tolerated."

The next day, Bremer called Sadr an outlaw. But there was bigger news—a second front was opening, in territory that had seethed from the first weeks of the occupation.

Before members of the 1st Marine Expeditionary Force arrived in Fallujah in March to replace units of the army's 82nd Airborne Division, they were encouraged to grow mustaches as a gesture of goodwill. (In Iraq, few men are clean-shaven.) In the soldiers' hands was a $540 million rebuilding effort, and there was reason to be hopeful: the Marines prided themselves on educated attitudes and cultural sensitivities far beyond those displayed by their army predecessors. They had received handbooks warning them about taboos against showing the soles of their feet or eating with their left hands. About three dozen men from one unit had taken a three-week intensive course in Arabic. But that benevolence didn't last long in Fallujah, which, like Khaldiya, was entrenched in the religious and nationalist sentiments that had proved such a powerful draw for men like Fahdawi. Quickly, goodwill gave way to God's will, and there was little room for compromise, even with the best of intentions.

On March 26, two days before the closure of Sadr's newspaper, the Marines had entered Fallujah to conduct a rather ordinary raid on suspected insurgents. But what began as an early-morning search operation spiraled into a daylong firefight with residents and guerrillas. When it was over, fifteen Iraqis and one Marine were dead.

It was a chilling precursor to an unforgettable instance of the war's brutality.

That same week, on the city's main road, insurgents ambushed and killed four Americans who worked for the security company that provided Bremer's personal detail. In horrifying scenes that demonstrated the depth of anti-American rage in the city, an angry mob then set on the bodies and mutilated them. One was dismembered and a severed right leg was attached to a brick with string and thrown over a power line that stretched across the street. Two of the other corpses were hung from one of the city's bridges over the Euphrates. Crowds danced and cheered, some throwing rocks at the bodies. Hours later, the dead were cut down, tossed onto a pile of tires, and set afire. The blackened remains were then dragged behind a cart pulled by a gray donkey to Fallujah's main municipal building and dumped there, only to be tied to the bumper of a car and dragged away again.

On the day Bremer called Sadr an outlaw, more than a thousand U.S. Marines sealed off Fallujah and began an operation aimed at tracking down the people who killed the four American contractors. Brigadier General Mark Kimmitt, the milkitary spokesman in Baghdad, promised that the campaign "is going to be deliberate, it will be precise, and it will be overwhelming." As for those who mutilated the bodies, "we will kill them or we will capture them and we will pacify Fallujah."

The operation, at first, unfolded by the book: in the city, the U.S. military distributed leaflets warning people to stay home and declared that a curfew would be in force from seven P.M. to six A.M. With the tough talk of Marines, using bravado as a tactic, they taunted their enemies: "Some have chosen to fight," one statement said. "Having elected their fate, they are being engaged and destroyed."

But an operation conceived as a focused raid turned into a battle for the city and, together with the fighting against Sadr, a second front in the revolt against the occupation. Hundreds of insurgents congregated in Fallujah, a town of 200,000. Concentrated in the Jolan neighborhood, they were heavily armed and strongly motivated; many were well trained, organized by officers hardened in the war with Iran. More important, they were prepared to fight to the death. As the days ground on, the Marines, increasingly frustrated, took blocks or buildings only to have the elusive insurgents take them back. In scenes reminiscent of the initial U.S. invasion, thousands fled the city; traffic snaked more than a mile, waiting to pass through a barbed-wire roadblock. Those who stayed were caught in pitched battles that played out on television sets nightly; the incendiary images were carried by Arab networks like Al-Jazeera and Al-Arabiya. Within a week, hospitals were reporting hundreds of Iraqis dead; the carnage had a profound impact on sentiments in Iraq and beyond.

If the Ramadan bombings marked the utter loss of faith in the American project, April was its practical conclusion, and its epitaph was written in those weeks. The occupation, of course, went on for a few more months. But neither the American effort nor Iraq was ever the same: the reverberations of the fighting in Fallujah and the battles with Sadr rumbled across an already roiling country like staccato bursts of failure.

A battalion of the Iraqi army refused to go to Fallujah to fight with the Marines. The U.S. general in charge of overseeing the development of the forces quoted the men as saying, "We did not sign up to fight Iraqis." In all, as many as one in four of the new Iraqi army, civil defense, police, and other security forces quit in those days, changed sides, or stopped working. The U.S.-financed reconstruction effort ground to an irreversible halt as contractors hunkered down against violence that flared like sparks from the fighting. The Governing Council, already marginalized and ineffective, became more reviled. Those with political savvy knew which side to choose: a senior Sunni politician and American ally, the octogenarian Adnan Pachachi, called the Marines' attack on Fallujah "unacceptable and illegal." "It was not right," he complained, "to punish all the people of Fallujah."

On March 21, 1968, a battle was fought between the Israeli military and Palestinian guerrillas, who were only then emerging on the world scene. It began when an Israeli armored force of fifteen thousand men struck the Jordanian village of Karameh, just across the Jordan River from the Israeli-occupied West Bank. Until then, guerrillas had staged ambushes, mined roads with improvised explosives, thrown an occasional grenade, and lobbed mortar shells. This battle was waged differently: for the first time, the Palestinians stood and fought the Israel Defense Forces. When it ended, the guerrillas, with the help of Jordanian artillery and armor, forced an embarrassing Israeli withdrawal.

In military terms, Israel won the battle, losing at least twenty-eight men but inflicting perhaps ten times as many casualties on the Arab side. Victory, though, is often more a matter of perception than reality, and, for the first time, the Palestinians had repelled the Israeli army. For an Arab world accustomed to humiliating defeats, a draw can assume mythic proportions; despite the vast losses suffered by Arabs in both struggles, the 1973 Arab-Israeli war and the Israeli withdrawal from Lebanon in 2000 are celebrated as victories. So, for a generation, Karameh created the myths that propelled a movement, sending a surge of optimism through refugee camps throughout the Arab world. Thousands flocked to the guerrillas' ranks. Karameh became one of those events whose names alone, devoid of context, denote legends.

The outcome of the battles in Fallujah and in Sadr's strongholds was never in doubt. After all, the U.S. military is perhaps the most powerful in world history. But a far more intricate struggle was playing out in Baghdad, and the players—Sadr, the men in Fallujah, and the audience they courted—spoke the same language, a distinctly Iraqi vernacular. It shared nothing with the stilted cadences of the translated statements from Bremer and his administrators, ensconced behind their armed sentries, concrete barriers, and rolls of barbed wire in the Green Zone.

"I'm accused by one of the leaders of evil, Bremer, of being an outlaw. If that means breaking the law of the American tyranny and its filthy constitution, I'm proud of that and that is why I'm in revolt." So began a statement Sadr made after the twin revolts erupted. It was read out from the mosque in Kufa, the same sprawling building, its history sacred, where his father had ministered to millions in the 1990s, dressed in a funeral shawl. Fusing nationalism, historical allusions, and Islamic motifs with economic grievances, he called for sectarian unity between Sunnis and Shiites and, aware of the deep-seated popular suspicion of American motives, accused the United States of trying to eradicate Islam. His goal, he declared in statements that were issued daily for a time during the fighting, was the ouster of foreign forces and the emergence of an independent and free Iraq.

Those statements were both a rallying cry and a plea. "Let the occupiers know, indeed the whole world, that if America wants freedom and democracy, then it must grant the people of Iraq their freedom," he declared in a statement that bore the official stamp of his movement. "America has unsheathed its fangs and its despicable intentions and the conscientious Iraqi people cannot remain silent at all. They must defend their rights in the ways they see fit. . . . If this disobedience means anything, it is that the Iraqi people are not satisfied with the occupation and do not accept subjugation and submission."

As always, the Americans used one vocabulary and the Iraqis another. Bremer spoke of the law, while Sadr spoke of martyrdom: "I am ready to sacrifice myself and I call on the people not to allow my death to cause the collapse of the fight for freedom and an end to the occupation." President Bush described the fighting as pitting those who loved freedom against those who hated it, while Sadr inverted the relationship and claimed the fight itself was blessed: "They possess money, weapons, equipment and numbers, but this will not weaken our resolve, because God is with us." The Americans talked about independence but were perceived as occupiers; Sadr, like his father, talked about closing ranks in a national crusade that joined the uprisings in Shiite towns with the defense of Fallujah: "You are witnessing the union of Sunnis and Shiites toward an independent Iraq, free of terror and occupation. This is a lofty goal. . . . Our sentiments are the same, our goal is one and our enemy is one. We say yes, yes, to unity, yes to the closing of ranks, combating terror, and ousting the infidel West from our sacred lands."

Sincere or not, the language was more nationalist than religious, always Iraqi:

> One of the leaders of evil has tried to throw the ball in my court—as they say in their lowly language. . . . He said that cooling things down was up to me, as if I were the occupier, the one against whom the people rose; as if the people rejected me, not him, the occupier; as if I were the one who struck at the demonstrators, detained people, cheated the people with promises of freedom and democracy; as if I started the clashes and possess the deadly, destructive arms; as if I am a stranger in the homeland.

In the war of words, the Americans never really had a chance. They prosecuted their campaign; the toll of casualties surged, by hospitals' accounts, into the hundreds in Fallujah. They tried to reclaim territory from the Mahdi Army, which occupied bridges, police stations, municipal halls, and goverment buildings in cities across the south. Scores were killed in Sadr City, as brave but ill-trained insurgent militiamen were far outgunned. They denigrated Sadr; Bremer's spokesman, Dan Senor, called him "a two-bit thug."

But the myths of resistance were already being created, although the battle's inevitable conclusion had yet to arrive. The occupation's epitaph was being scrawled in writing that went from right to left, the slope of the Arabic alphabet so distinct from the sharp angles of English script. Baghdad was at war, as it had not been before.

In Sadr City, his most populous stronghold, Sadr's militiamen set up blockades of concrete slabs, steel beams, rusted car parts, discarded gas tanks, and scrap metal. Smoke from burning tires wafted overhead and shops stayed shuttered throughout the day, some putting steel grates across the entrances. Apache helicopters—which most Arabs associate with the Israeli army in the Palestinian territories—circled overhead. Down the block, no more than a few hundred yards away, two U.S. tanks were parked opposite the Muhsin Mosque, which the Sadr office uses for Friday prayers. On one barrel was written "Anger Mgt." Another read, "Analyze This."

A short distance beyond, a black banner inscribed with white hung over the entrance of the militia-controlled Shahid Sadr General Hospital. "Death in glory is better than life in humiliation," it read. Outside Sadr's headquarters—destroyed by U.S. forces, rebuilt, and destroyed again—were copies of a newspaper that named the revolt "the first Muqtada Sadr uprising." In red type, a banner headline declared, "Bremer opened the doors of hell." Militiamen and Sadr's supporters gathered in front, some of them holding rifles, pistols, or grenades aloft. Others broke into impromptu chants. As always: "Long live Sadr!" was one.

On another street, the charred hulks of two cars had been left near curbs. Through the day, crowds gathered around them, gawking and growing angry. On one car was a small piece of paper, with the names of three victims written in pencil. The mood was combative; questions tumbled out.

"They weren't armed, they were civilians," said Hassan Abdel-Wahid, a twenty-seven-year-old resident, who insisted the car was targeted from behind. "Why did they kill them?"

As the crowds grew, few blamed the Mahdi Army for the violence or accepted the U.S. contention that it would destroy the militia. To many, the American response was an assault on Shiite religious leaders, on a movement that sprung from the neighborhood, on Islam itself.

"They say the Madhi Army is fighting them. They're fighting the Mahdi

Army. The protests were peaceful and they fired on them," said twenty-nine-year-old Hussein Hamdan. "It's worse than Palestine, and the resistance against them will be worse."

He looked at others around him. "Is this our country or is this not our country?"

The crowd joined in, competing to outdo one another in zeal. On the street, black banners in memory of the dead were already multiplying. "Bush talks about freedom and democracy? This is freedom and democracy!" said twenty-eight-year-old Ahmed Jabbar. He pointed to the charred car. "This is the democracy that Bush promises!"

Abdel-Wahid, the most energetic, interrupted. "We'll launch a second Vietnam against the Americans, a thousand times worse," he said.

Down a street in Sadr City that day, near pools of sewage and wet trash, children showered rocks on an M1-A1 Abrams tank. Its force too great for the task at hand, its armaments singularly unsuited to the enemy before it, the tank's turret swiveled back and forth through smoke and dust blown up by a brisk breeze. It swung helplessly, and the children threw rocks defiantly, and this went on and on. In the end, it was a draw.

In Sadr City, I began to hear a sentiment rather different from what I had encountered before. Men stood around me, angry, vengeful, and shouting, desperate that I somehow understand what they had to say. The fight in Fallujah, a Sunni town, was the same as the clashes with Shiites in Sadr City. "They're no different," twenty-year-old Alaa Sarraji said to me. "We're one Iraq."

The mounting death tolls as the fighting dragged on during much of April created a powerful effect in Baghdad. The fighting in Fallujah was more focused than the running battles dispersed across southern Iraq and seemed to strike a deeper chord. New graffiti appeared on the walls, and stories of what had transpired were traded in the street. The clashes redefined, for many, the nature of the armed campaign against U.S. troops. The intense, sympathetic, and often startlingly graphic coverage on Arab channels deepened a vein of nationalism and provoked outrage over the casualties. (Even the wife of Karim, my Shiite driver, just as secular and apolitical as he was, began weeping as she watched footage from Fallujah of bloodied women and children and rows of freshly dug graves on the Arab networks. Still sobbing, she finally leaned forward and kissed the television screen.) The popular response—of Shiite and Sunni coming together to give aid, shelter refugees, and even volunteer for the fight—pushed, however briefly, prevalent fears of civil war to the background. In the months ahead, the bloodshed would grow precipitously, taking on a nihilist quality in a drumbeat of beheadings, suicide bombings, and executions and deepening the country's sectarian and ethnic fault lines. But in those weeks, in the Arab parts of Iraq, there was a moment of common cause, ephemeral perhaps, that they shared the same foe.

As early as April 6, two days after Sadr launched his revolt, residents of the traditionally Sunni neighborhood of Adhamiya, considered by many the birthplace of Iraq's Baath Party, marched with Sadr's followers. Throughout Sadr's revolt, Sunni groups, long angry at Shiites for tolerating the occupation, hailed him as a hero, their proclamation read over a loudspeaker in Sadr City to the cheers of hundreds of militiamen waving pistols and swords. A leaflet made the rounds: "God is greatest," it proclaimed. "Long live the resistance in Fallujah, long live the resistance in Sadr City. No Sunnis and no Shiites, only Islamic unity."

Traffic went both ways. As refugees arrived during a brief truce in Fallujah, both Sunni and Shiite families in Baghdad gave them shelter. Convoys headed to the besieged city carried heavy bags of rice, tea, and flour. (A friend of mine told me that he answered one of the scores of calls from mosques to provide aid to Fallujah's residents. He donated 100,000 Iraqi dinars, then returned with beans, lentils, and sugar. At night, he came a third time with medicine emptied from his cabinet. The next day, at the request of his daughter, he gave one hundred dollars more.)

As some of the convoys were dispatched, men waved posters of Muqtada Sadr and Sheikh Ahmed Yassin, the founder of the Palestinian militant group Hamas, who was assassinated by Israel in March 2003. In Shiite Kadhimiya, a handout was passed around at a tent for donating blood to the wounded. It invoked the martyred Imam Hussein and the battle in Sunni Fallujah. "Prevent killing the innocents in Fallujah by all means available or your turn will come," it read. "Where are the lovers of Hussein and where are the heroes? Go there. Go to Fallujah, carrying food and medicine."

"Saddam is gone," explained Adnan Safi, a spokesman for the Sadr office in Kadhimiya. "Nobody is demonstrating for Saddam. If they do, they are masking what they really want to say. They are demonstrating for Iraq."

These same sentiments were expressed by the graffiti across the city. For months after the U.S. invasion, the slogans largely supported Saddam in Sunni enclaves, or denounced him in Shiite neighborhoods. As the fighting surged, the messages in several neighborhoods took on a new inflection. On a wall in Jihad, the southern Baghdad neighborhood where Faruq lived, four exhortations were spaced about ten yards apart: "Long live Fallujah's heroes," "Down with America and long live the Mahdi Army," "Long live the resistance in Fallujah," and, finally, "Long live the resistance."

Another slogan was perhaps more telling. Many Shiites will recall a phrase they saw written on an Iraqi tank barrel when Saddam moved to crush the 1991 Shiite uprising. "No more Shiites after today," it read. In the tumultuous aftermath of Saddam's fall, graffiti across cities in Shiite-dominated southern Iraq declared bluntly, "No Baathists after today." In April, in Adhamiya, there was this: "No occupation after today."

And the myths, those sustaining tales, began to take shape.

At a Sunni mosque in Baghdad, built by Saddam to commemorate the 1991 Gulf War, posters at the gate read, "Long live steadfast Fallujah." Next to it a white leaflet pleaded with the Almighty: "God protect Fallujah and all the cities of Iraq. God give victory to Fallujah and all the cities of Iraq. God accept the martyrs of Fallujah with the Muslim martyrs of all cities." In the parking lot, shadowed by six minarets in an Oz-like compound of gold paint, white stone, and blue tile, built over a reflecting pool, men held a spirited discussion about the need to take the fight to the enemy, as they prepared a convoy bound for the besieged city with more than a ton of donated foodstuffs packed in a long yellow semitrailer. The men were drawn from all classes: a dentist, a prayer leader, a law student, a lieutenant colonel in the Iraqi police, and a man who until ten days earlier had traveled with U.S. troops as a member of the Iraqi Civil Defense Corps. In the words of one of them: "Our brothers who went to Fallujah and came back say, 'Oh, God, it is heaven. Anyone who wants paradise should go to Fallujah.'"

Across town, at the Friday prayers in Sadr City, on a street littered with newspapers, rags, tires, broken eggshells, orange peels, onion and garlic stalks, soda cans, a pair of pants, an occasional sandal, and piles of rice submerged in flies, thousands gathered in the biggest turnout since the war, drafting their own myths. They ignored the fires burning the trash that wasn't soggy. They trudged past the horses, sheep, and donkeys feasting on the food scraps. Sadr City looked worse than I had ever seen it, but its condition seemed not to register on anyone's face. The sullen stares were reserved for four Humvees that passed.

"No life without Sadr!" men chanted as they lined up in row after row, black-and-green banners flying overhead, their fists in the air. "No country without Muqtada." The crowd was raucous, celebrating the uprising. "No to America! No to occupation! No to colonialism! No to Israel!" As the prayers began, with almost absurd timing the clouds broke and a light drizzle stopped. A few minutes later, the prayer leader, Sheikh Nasser al-Saadi, stepped to the podium, draped in an Iraqi flag and pictures of Sadr and his father. Before him were the clergy. Gaunt and dark, with scruffy beards, bad teeth, and callused feet, they were distinguished from the prayergoers only by their worn clerical robes.

The barrel-chested, gray-haired sheikh, more brawler than pastor, began with a plea in simple, direct Arabic. His style was born of the street, not the seminary. "I can't hear you!" he shouted. "Why?" The chants grew louder and more sustained, with men jabbing their fists in the air. "God's blessings on you," Saadi answered approvingly. Even in the days of strife, the Sadr men would play to their audience. He nicknamed members of the Governing Council: Ayad Allawi looked like Chemical Ali, Saddam's reviled cousin, and Muwafaq Rubaie was the minister of sewers. And he spoke with bravado: "This is a warning: do not mess with us because you haven't seen anything yet."

"Welcome the brave men and damn the silent people," the sheikh declared, over scratchy speakers that carried the booming sermon to the side alleys and back roads engorged with worshippers. "Damn those who sold their country and those who accepted the crumbs from Bremer. Damn you all to hell. We are in heaven."

The sermon wrapped up in an hour. More prayers followed. Then the convocation ended. Within moments, the crowd was gone. The show of strength vanished; the worshippers melted back into the streets from which they came. Life, that mundane project of survival, returned. The walls along the road were exposed again, revealing a faded slogan that had gone up the day after Saddam fell. "Sadr City," it read.

His city.

▪ ▪ ▪

At the end of April, after on-again, off-again mediation, a truce was reached in Fallujah between the guerrillas and the American military. The Marines withdrew from their buildings and bulldozed their earthworks, turning over the fight to a force of Iraqis led by officers once loyal to Saddam's government. The Americans had found a face-saving way out of what was becoming a public relations disaster. A draw to the Americans, though, was a victory to those in Fallujah, who could claim to have fought the U.S. troops to a standstill. Their success became clearer in the months that followed as the city was ceded almost entirely to militants and became, for a time, a launching pad for attacks, many of them horrific, blood-soaked instances of terrorism, and a site of executions, often by beheading. The haven ended in November 2004, when the U.S. military again attacked Fallujah, this time with a far larger force and a far greater willingness to overwhelm its enemy. In some of the most intense urban fighting for the United States since Vietnam, it took the town, destroying vast swaths of its concrete and cinder-block landscape in pursuit of victory.

The revolt by Sadr wore on longer, ebbing and flowing into May with a climactic battle in Karbala, still scarred by the bombings in March. In time, though, the Mahdi Army withdrew from the police stations, government buildings, and streets they controlled, having suffered hundreds of casualties in overwhelmingly lopsided battles with American forces. The men melted back into their communities, biding their time to fight the Americans another day.

During the fighting, President Bush had declared, "Our coalition's quick reaction forces are finding and engaging the enemy. Our decisive actions will continue until these enemies of democracy are dealt with." A more sober assessment came from Wamidh, whom I saw again that month at his riverside home in Adhamiya. As was his wont, he evoked history; his doctoral thesis was about the 1920 revolt against the British in Iraq. His mood had altered: no longer the grim, somber man I had seen just weeks earlier, he was hopeful, even emboldened.

"What is striking is how much has changed," he told me, in a way that suggested his surprise.

Wamidh was never hotheaded. He always reflected, and he often cringed at words, ideas, or principles that seemed absolutist. He called the killing of the American contractors in Fallujah, their bodies burned and mutilated, "a human sorrow." But at the same time, he took pride in the resistance shown in Fallujah. A man steeped in honor and dignity, he, like most Iraqis, considered the fight legitimate, even heroic, and he shook his head at the toll he had witnessed. "They killed hundreds in Fallujah for the incident in which four people were killed. And I think up to now, they were unable to arrest the suspects." With grudging admiration, he was struck, too, by Sadr, a man he had long dismissed as too young and too brash to ever emerge as a truly national figure. "He gave very brave statements during the fighting," Wamidh told me.

As we sat in his living room, the doors and windows open to the Tigris outside, he leaned back in his chair. Dressed in a white dishdasha and leather sandals, he was unshaven as usual, his mustache melting into a two-day beard. A low thunder reverberated from the generator outside; the weather was getting warmer and electricity was still in short supply. Over coffee, we began talking about Karameh, and the power of myth in the Arab world. "The unity we witnessed was surprising even to an optimist like myself," Wamidh told me. He shook his head, in response, I thought, to the pace and immensity of those events in April. "I think it will be bigger than Karameh."

For all his pride, Wamidh worried about what might be on the horizon. I had visited him before the war, as the world he knew for decades was crumbling. I had visited him during the invasion, when the presence of foreign troops in his beloved city humiliated and bewildered him. And I saw him now, as his country's history was being written again. He was simply unsure of what that history would say. Sadr was still sectarian, and the armed opposition in places like Fallujah still lacked any political program. They knew what they opposed—namely, the Americans—but they had yet to elaborate what they supported. "I wonder if they will be able to achieve that," he said.

"Our experience has taught us not to be overoptimistic. Because whenever you are optimistic, you get hit with something else," he told me. "Our people make some awful mistakes and awful miscalculations. I never thought that Saddam, after eight years of war, and without sorting out the problems from that war, would provoke another war by invading Kuwait. That was the stupidest and most provocative act."

He dragged on his Dunhill cigarette. The remark that followed, I thought, was intentionally ambiguous. Wamidh might have been speaking about Saddam, the wars he launched that brutalized his country, the sanctions that followed and immiserated it. But probably not. He seemed to be giving me his own judgment. He spoke deeply, in a slow cadence, as was his custom.

"Wrong beginnings," he said, "tend to lead to wrong ends."

We both nodded and left it at that.

After leaving Wamidh's home, Karim and I drove through Adhimiya, where a street battle had erupted the night before. Wreckage was still strewn through the street. The burned remains of a Toyota Super Salon lay askew in the middle of the road. The car's insides had been disgorged, incinerated, and scattered around it like a pyre. A tree was uprooted in Antar Square, and a traffic light that had not worked in months was bent over like a clothespin. We passed two tanks and a Humvee with blue lights flashing at a checkpoint, soldiers peering at the few passing cars in streets that were largely deserted.

We drove through the somnolent city, passing a newspaper stand with an issue of *Shahid*, its cover a portrait of Sadr with his index finger pointing in the air. We saw the ubiquitous concrete barriers with rows of barbed wire, and a median crumbled in places, probably by a tank's driving over it. We passed airline offices shuttered since international sanctions were imposed in 1990. In a traffic circle on the way to the well-fortified Sheraton Hotel, where the *Post* had its bureau, we drove by a poster hung by the U.S. administration, the same one I had seen near Fuad's house in February. "Progress" and "Prosperity," it promised in white, over a green map of Iraq. A splash of black paint had blotted out half of each word. Underneath the poster was a trash dump, with a pile of rusted scrap metal at the side.

ON APRIL 9, 2004, THE FAMILY OF FIRAS ISMAIL STOOD ANXIOUSLY AROUND THE corner from Firdaus Square where Saddam's bronze statue had come crashing to the ground a year earlier. Almost in unison, they flailed their arms, shouting in desperation. "Go back!" they yelled to him. "Go back!"

Firas was trying to cross a street along the square. He was on his way home from work at a stationery store. But on this day, the anniversary of Saddam's fall, no one was allowed close to Firdaus Square. New rolls of glistening razor wire encircled the battered park, a precaution against attacks at nearby landmark hotels or potentially embarrassing protests. Tanks named *Beastly Boy* and *Bloodlust* waited vigilantly. Soldiers, edgy, had orders to shoot anyone with a weapon, and they fired in the air to warn Firas, who began to backtrack.

"It's like we're in a military base," his sixty-two-year-old father told me, as we stood on the sun-soaked street. "Look here," he grumbled, pointing down the block to towering concrete barriers. "Look there," he said, gesturing down another street where knots of soldiers stood guard. His friend Raad Fouad looked on. "We live in a city of ghosts," Fouad said. He paused, then repeated the phrase. "A city of ghosts."

A year after the toppling of Saddam's statue, that first lasting image of the American entry into one of the Arab world's greatest capitals, Firdaus Square had emerged as a symbol again—this time, of a city returned to the precipice.

"The people were oppressed for thirty-five years, and now this?" the father asked me, not expecting an answer. "It's gone from worse to even worse." Lines of worry furrowing his face, he offered me one of his Newport cigarettes and a glass of cold water. All of us were sweating as summer neared. "We were so happy with the fall of Saddam," he recalled, his white-and-orange T-shirt soaked with sweat. "We were all happy but we hoped it wouldn't become an occupation."

Fouad, a burly man with a walrus mustache who had lived in the neighborhood for thirty-four years, almost as long as the Baath Party had ruled, reflected on the day a year before as we spoke. He had stayed indoors then. The threat of more war was still keeping him inside these days. "You come home from work, you open the door, and you lock it," he said. "It's like we're in a prison now."

Fouad, a Christian, stood with Firas's father, a Shiite Muslim.

"Anything can happen now," Fouad said.

"We've seen everything," Firas's father added, "and this is the worst moment."

As they spoke, a Humvee drove down the street, its speakers blaring a message. "If we see anyone carrying a weapon, we'll fire on him. Please stay away from this area. Thank you." The message was repeated throughout the day, cutting through the soft strains of Quranic recitation and the call to prayer. At other times, the speakers switched to sounds more alien in Baghdad: "Heart of Glass" by Blondie, "Take It Easy" by the Eagles, "Sweet Child of Mine" by

Guns N' Roses, and "Ring of Fire" by Johnny Cash. Occasional bursts of gun-fire also broke the square's silence. In late afternoon, the thunder of a mortar round rolled over the street. Then another announcement, another vocabu-lary that never resonated, across a gulf that was never bridged: "To the people of Saadoun Street," the speaker declared, "if you feel angry because your shops are closed, be angry at the Mahdi Army. If you feel angry because you do not work, be angry at the Mahdi Army."

"This pressure," Fouad said, shaking his head. "What does this pressure give birth to? It creates hatred. Tomorrow, the day after tomorrow."

Early in the occupation, Iraqis often remarked to me that they wished they could have overthrown Saddam themselves. The sentiment inevitably came up in conversations about Saddam's relentless repression, ritual executions, and mass graves; as his final insult, he had brought an occupation that those who understood Iraq best knew could never succeed. "They got rid of Saddam for us. None of us could have done it," Firas's father said. "But they should have provided us with something better. Instead, we got something worse."

Fouad nodded. It was a question of respect, he said. "The example is in front of you," he said. "Someone enters the street and they shoot him. Is that respect?"

The anniversary of the statue's toppling fell on a Friday, the Muslim Sab-bath. The sermons that day were fierce, the messages bleak, pitting East against West, Muslims against others, Iraq and the Arab world against the United States and Israel. As I stood in the square that marked Iraq's liberation, I marveled at the fact that the first tentative signs of unity had arisen in detes-tation of the very military that had ended Saddam's apparatus of repression. However brief the unity might turn out to be, it was devastating in its judg-ment. I understood, too, the more sweeping folly of the endeavor. Like Wamidh, I suspected that occupation would probably never be tolerated. Iraq simply had too much history, too many wars and wounds; there were too many grievances in a city and country brutalized by sanctions and dictator-ship, few of them well understood by the U.S. administration.

"They came to overthrow Saddam," Samir Abed Wahid told me, looking out on an empty street, a few blocks from Firdaus Square. "Why are they fighting his victims?" Dressed in jeans and a yellow shirt, the thirty-two-year-old Wahid was the son of a Sunni father and a Shiite mother. A healthy street sense gave him a little swagger despite his slight build. He was frustrated by the bloodshed in Fallujah; he was angry about the crackdown on Sadr. In a sentiment I heard often in the Arab world, he was outraged at perceived injustice, but felt helpless to do anything about it. "We have no choice," he told me. "We're too weak. We have to listen. No, we have to obey. We're too weak to only listen."

Along the avenue before him were the tokens of Iraq's freedom. A Shiite banner commemorating Imam Hussein hung near the gas station. Drifting from a speaker inside were the chants of mourning to mark a Shiite holiday that would begin in a few days. Advertisements for satellite phones, which had been banned under Saddam, lined the streets. In the square itself, Saddam's initials had been erased from the cupolas, and the staircase destroyed by the Marine vehicle had been rebuilt. The remnants of his statue had long since disappeared, replaced by an unfinished modernist statue of a figure holding the sun and the moon, a work more of enthusiasm than art. A green religious banner fluttered overhead. (A few hours before I arrived, soldiers had found a ladder, climbed up the statue, and tore down a picture of Sadr, their new foe, pasted to its side.) Wahid paid no attention. "Saddam is gone and we'll have our freedom now. It's a big joke around here," he told me, his voice matter-of-fact. "A big joke."

It was dusk when I left. I walked back to the hotel along a circuitous route dictated by the concrete barricades, armored vehicles spaced one hundred yards apart, and American checkpoints with knots of alert soldiers. The streets were empty, and soon night would fall. When I entered the hotel, not a soul was left in the square.

Between the neighborhoods of Waziriya and Bab al-Moadhim is the British cemetery, built to bury the men who wrested Baghdad from the Ottoman Empire in World War I, then occupied it. They weathered a revolt that began on July 2, 1920, led by a segment of the population that had grown frustrated and resentful over the heavy-handedness of the foreign army. In the ensuing weeks, with a momentum that perpetuated itself, the rebellion spread through central and southern Iraq. The British army did not regain control for six months, until February 1921; the savage fighting killed an estimated six thousand Iraqis and roughly five hundred British and Indian soldiers, creating a fleeting moment of Sunni-Shiite unity and making the British project in Iraq exceedingly unpopular at home.

From then on, the driving logic of the British occupation was to find a way to end it and extricate themselves by granting Iraq independence, which ostensibly came in 1932 with Iraq's entry into the League of Nations. The prospect of a liberal, stable state in the swath of land long known as Mesopotamia was submerged in the calculus of political survival. The British, locked in the logic of empire, listening to the elite who spoke their language and, imbued with attitudes often prejudiced, never listened to the rumblings in a country around them. They were certain of the righteousness of their project and oblivious to the nascent nationalism they encountered. The country was set on a path that led, generations later, to Saddam's rule.

When I visited, the cemetery was overgrown and decrepit; the metal gate was closed with a rusted padlock. A worn dirt path led inside, through weeds a foot high and past towering palm trees whose dead branches hung down like a hula skirt. The once-grand plaza looked like an archaeological dig, with the detritus of a consumer culture: an empty soda bottle, a can of Ugarit Cola, and a pack of Pine Lights. A few pieces of blackened metal had been strewn across the courtyard by a car bomb that detonated across the street, near the Turkish Embassy. Beyond was row after row of simple tombstones—some upright, others knocked over or cloaked in weeds.

They carried the names of the forgotten, a foreign army in a foreign land. H. Martin, Royal Engineers, died 1918. B. W. Copping, Royal Field Artillery, died 1916. P. Riley, West Yorkshire Regiment, died 1917. F. F. Marshall, Norfolk Regiment, died 1917. J. A. Grant, Devonshire Regiment, died 1916. Some of the epitaphs were traditional: "Father, thy will be done." Others were more lyrical: "Until the day break and the shadows flee." Others, with a timeless quality, spoke of promises unfulfilled: "He died for freedom and honor."

At their center was the tomb of Major General Sir Stanley Maude. A man of sad eyes, lean face, and flowing mustache, he was the British soldier who commanded the Tigris Corps in World War I. In a series of battles in 1917 against the Ottoman army—Mohammed Abdul Hassan, Hai, Dahra, and Kut—he sliced through southern Iraq before approaching Baghdad in March 1917. In days, his enemy melted away, and the climactic battle for Baghdad never happened. In triumph and unopposed, his forces entered the city, where he was met with loud and raucous celebrations by the 140,000 inhabitants.

I had first heard his name as I sat with the artists at the Hawar Art Gallery on the eve of the U.S. invasion in March 2003, when another army was poised to march across the south on the way to the capital. They quoted something Maude said after his entry into Baghdad, an assertion that remains famous in the capital: "Our armies do not come into your cities and lands as conquerors or enemies, but as liberators." Maude's statement was part of a larger proclamation—a promise to an antique city whose past shamed its present, whose inhabitants stagnated under despotic rule, and whose expectations were always measured by its medieval glory. The general invoked Hulugu, the Mongol conqueror who made the Tigris run red with blood and black with the ink of culture when he sacked it in 1258, the symbolic end of the city's centuries-long flowering. And he ended with a pledge.

> Our military operations have as their object the defeat of the enemy, and the driving of him from these territories. In order to complete this task, I am charged with absolute and supreme control of all regions in which British troops operate; but our armies do not come into your cities and lands as conquerors or enemies, but as liberators. Since the days of Halaka [Hulugu] your city and your lands have been subject to the tyranny of strangers, your palaces have fallen into ruins, your gardens have sunk in desolation, and your forefathers and yourselves have groaned in bondage. Your sons have been carried off to wars not of your seeking, your wealth has been stripped from you by unjust men and squandered in distant places. . . . It is the wish not only of my King and his peoples, but it is also the wish of the great nations with whom he is in alliance, that you should prosper even as in the past, when your lands were fertile, when your ancestors gave to the world literature, science, and art, and when Baghdad city was one of the wonders of the world.

Now I gazed at his mausoleum, a stone shrine with two entrances, fifteen feet high, its roof buttressed by four columns. In block capitals, "Maude" was engraved on his sarcophagus. A plaque overhead, emblazoned with a cross, described his death: on November 18, 1917, nine months after his triumph, he fell victim to cholera. By legend, he drank bad milk. Underneath was a phrase by which to remember him: "He fought a good fight to keep the faith."

Hussein Abdel-Karim, the cemetery's tall, lanky guard, kicked a can that was tossed near the tomb, shrouded in years of dust. He was young, just eighteen, and dressed in street clothes—blue plastic sandals, black pants, and a cream T-shirt, untucked. "People in Iraq don't know much about him," he told me, trying to explain the ruin of the cemetery and Maude's tomb. Perhaps he was justifying his own ignorance. I quoted the remark for which Maude is famous and he finally nodded in recognition. He remembered the words, and he gave me his judgment. In a way, it was a critique of Maude's epitaph: faith, blind as it is, falls short. And, with a smile that hinted at irony, he seemed to conflate eras and experiences.

"How could they understand Iraq?" Abdel-Karim asked me. "It's impossible."

EPILOGUE

It's a long journey,
And in it, I'm a stranger.
And the night draws near,
And the day has ventured home.

The song "Sawah" by Abdel-Halim Hafez was playing in Karim's car, as we drove once again through Baghdad at the close of January 2005. From a scratchy cassette, smudged with months of dirty fingerprints and borne across hundreds of miles, I had listened to the music, almost every day since arriving in Baghdad before the invasion. Hafez's voice —resonant, sorrowful, and strangely soothing—would fill the car every few hours. Even a fleeting note of this song evoked the Baghdad I had come to know and everything I felt for this city of the past.

After a few months away, I had returned to Baghdad to cover the elections for an Iraqi parliament in January 2005, a moment expected to be a watershed for the troubled country, despite the uncertainty over what would follow. The trip back to the capital was a reunion, too—with Nasir, who with his wife and two children had fled the country a year earlier for neighboring Jordan.

Baghdad—a city that always chooses memory over the curse of its reality—passed before me once more. The elegant statues of Mohammed Ghani, artifacts of an ageless city, still graced their pedestals. Ghani's flying carpet fluttered into the boundless sky. Down the street was Shehrazad, with her flowing hair and dress, still perched over the Tigris like a lonesome sentry. A walk away was Kahramana, confidently pouring oil on the forty thieves in Ali Baba Square. Yet these reminders of the past paled against the sights of the present: the barbed wire and concrete barricades of the siege; other statues, once heroic, now dismantled; the buildings damaged in the looting that had gripped the city during those first anarchic days of freedom. The war's shadow still lay over Baghdad, and the threat of horrific violence never seemed to dissipate. Into the streets spilled rubble, the work of bombing during the U.S. invasion, while nests of steel rods, slabs of concrete, and twisted girders marked the sites of car bombs. The overall effect was one of devastation, despite the buoyant election hopes in some quarters. The city, unfolding before us, still rested on a precipice. As usual it felt like autumn in Baghdad, and the hour was always dusk.

Perhaps the soft light of the setting sun encourages *hanin*; in this city of memories, I returned to my own. One, in particular, will never leave me: in the neighborhood of Mansur, during Saddam's last days, I watched an uncle swaying as he stood, cradling his nephew's frail body. The child had been killed in the explosion of four 2,000-pound bombs dropped in an attempt to assassinate Saddam. A small moment of anguish on the vast stage of conflict, it always represented to me the inevitable divorce between war's aims and its reality. Another memory, from the uprisings I had covered the year before, was equally haunting. In Shuala, a poor Shiite neighborhood, furious men sauntered through the streets blackened by burning tires, their talk replete with the rage I had heard so often in Sunni towns like Khaldiya, Thuluyah, and Fallujah. Rifles in hand, militiamen with bandoliers directed traffic, and residents angrily gestured at the damage their photo shops and bakeries had sustained in an attack by the American military's Apache helicopters. In the street, eighteen-year-old Ali Kadhim, his brow sweaty, ran up to me. He gestured to a charred U.S. tank transport, still smoldering, deserted after an attack. "This is the future!" he yelled.

You have promised me,
You who bears witness for me.
You have promised me,
You who bears witness for me.

The future was being decided on January 30, 2005, when Iraqis voted in the country's first election in a half century. For weeks after my return, the city and other parts of Iraq had been silenced by terror; in Baghdad and its environs, citizens were reeling from constant violence that seemed to escalate in savagery with each new assault. Stretches of the country, particularly in the north and west, were only nominally under the government's control; in Baghdad itself, insurgents swaggered with their rifles down Haifa Street, a short way from the very headquarters of the Iraqi government and the U.S. Embassy. The violence was awful, even by Iraq's standards: brazen executions in the street, and beheadings so common they had become mundane. Hardly a day went by without a half-dozen bombs going off across the country, borne by cars and men. In the week before ballots were cast, still shadowy insurgents handed out leaflets that warned they would "wash the streets" with the blood of those who dared to vote.

On the day before the vote, the city crackling with the same anticipation I had remembered before the American invasion, I came across a man named Yahya Sadiq, a squat fellow with a mournful look. Just before our meeting, a car bomb had detonated along the street near where he sold firewood in Dora, a neighborhood so dangerous many Iraqis had long preferred to simply avoid it. The driver was killed in the bombing, as were four civilians. Four other people were wounded. The Interior Ministry had its verdict on the driver: "He went to hell, to what he deserves," said Colonel Adnan Abdul-Rahman, a ministry spokesman. The thirty-year-old Sadiq, looking down, had his: "Baghdad is not safe."

As we sat on a brisk afternoon, Sadiq stared out at the road, deserted but for uniformed policemen and plainclothes officers toting AK-47s, and an occasional U.S. Humvee speeding past a roadside denuded to deprive insurgents of cover. The risk was too great, Sadiq said quietly. He would stay at home on election day. There was a pause; we were both tense. "The fear and anxiety are greater than before the war," he told me finally, shaking his head.

Soon after, a blue Opel pulled down the street, parking a few feet away from us, in front of his shop. Sadiq glanced at the three men inside, and his face tightened: one could not know whom to fear. Abruptly, the conversation ended. We both walked away, glancing over our shoulders at the car behind us.

The next day, something startling happened. Fear, for a moment, receded. On the following morning, with U.S. forces largely in the background, tens of thousands of Iraqi police and soldiers fanned out over towns and cities throughout the country. For the first time since the war began nearly two years earlier, residents of Baghdad saw Iraqi armor in the streets—personnel carriers and Soviet-built T-55 tanks that were leftovers from the dissolved Iraqi army. Across the capital, roads, squares, and bridges were barricaded and manned by U.S. and Iraqi troops, a presence some residents ruefully noted would have probably stopped the looting after Saddam's fall. Police pickups, their sirens blaring, plied abandoned streets where children set up soccer goals with piles of shoes. Baghdad, overnight, was transformed: for the first time since the fall of Saddam in April 2003, the capital—and some other parts of Iraq—took on the air of a festival, as crowds danced, chanted, and strolled down streets made safe by the most thorough security crackdown in memory. Into those streets, from the Kurdish north to the largely Shiite south, voters ventured outdoors and, at thousands of polling stations, delivered a message: it was time to seize their future and reject a legacy of dictatorship and the bloodshed and hardship that had followed the American invasion.

In Baghdad, lines at polling stations started small in a tentative morning, then grew through the election's ten hours, sometimes dramatically, surprising even the Iraqis, who said they were emboldened by the crowds before them. Afterward, many triumphantly pointed their index fingers, stained with deep blue ink from the polls, and hardly flinched at the gunfire and explosions that interrupted the day. At one station, a woman showered election workers with handfuls of candy. At another, a veiled elderly woman kept repeating to grinning election workers, "God's blessings on you." Across town, three laughing Iraqi soldiers carried an elderly man, in his wheelchair, for two blocks to an elementary school and inside the polling station, where he voted.

"It's like a wedding. I swear to God, it's a wedding for all of Iraq," Mohammed Nuhair Rubaie told me. He was the director of a polling station in the largely Sunni neighborhood of Tunis, where after a slow start, hun-

dreds of voters gathered as the cloudless day progressed. When I saw him, he smiled almost ecstatically and gestured exuberantly. "No one has ever witnessed this before. For a half century, no one has seen anything like it," he insisted. "And we did it ourselves."

There was still the violence that had become the trademark of an increasingly desperate insurgency: suicide bombings, car bombings, and mortar attacks spaced, at one point in the morning, a few seconds apart. In Sunni regions of central and northern Iraq, where the insurgency had proved the most fierce, turnout was far worse than elsewhere, a sign of the guerrillas' strength and support in those areas and their ability to intimidate.

But across Baghdad, residents who had often given more credence to the threats of insurgents than to reassurances by the U.S. military and Iraqi security forces rejoiced at a death toll that, while dire, was far outdone by some of the capital's bloodiest days. The challenges that seemed so overwhelming before and after the election receded in a fleeting celebration of the moment, a time when Iraqis' voices were projected. To many, the election itself—the exercise of rights long denied—mattered more than the choice of any particular party or platform. Iraqis hoped that their participation might somehow create a momentum and finally begin to herald an improvement in their lives.

In some ways, the joy reminded me of those chaotic scenes during the release of prisoners at Abu Ghreib in 2002; the passion seemed even more urgent than after the fall of Saddam's statue at Firdaus Square. On this day, Iraqis—not their overlords, not foreigners—were the agents of change; they themselves were deciding their fate. Watching those jubilant streets, I realized that this was the first time since I had been in Iraq, through dictatorship, war, and occupation, that Iraqis themselves were claiming the right to make their voices heard. Their resilience, never extinguished through trauma after disaster, finally had a means of expression.

That afternoon, I met sixty-year-old Dhia Ali, a frumpy sort in a frayed sports jacket who lived in the same neighborhood of Tunis. He shuffled into the Aisha Elementary School, whose classrooms had been converted to polling stations. Clear plastic ballot boxes stood half full behind cardboard voting booths. I asked Ali whom he was voting for, and he shook his head. He had no idea; he said he only wanted to vote. Inside, the polling station director held his shaking hand as he randomly, with barely a thought, marked the tiny

party of the country's minority Turkmen. Minutes later, he thrust forward his stained finger, smiling. "We have to show the difference between what we had in the past and what we can have in the future," he said to me.

It was the same choice—what kind of future—that faced Mohammed Hayawi, the bookseller I had befriended on Mutanabi Street. I met him a few days after the election, in which he had participated despite his own expectations. He thought, wrongly, that "the roads would be flooded with blood up to our foreheads." He was friendly as always, although a little subdued. His exuberance had given way to reflection, and he shrugged.

"I thought about not voting, but I was embarrassed by the people around me," he told me, a little meekly. "It was like someone inviting me to lunch. I can't say no. If you say no, this is disrespectful. This is the explanation." We sat at his cluttered desk, over cups of tea, next to stacks of books sometimes ten high that were gathering dust.

"I knew that the paper I put in the ballot box was for America. I know I was being hypocritical. But there was no other choice," he said, waving his cigarette between his fingers. "The future of Iraq is a line that goes through the occupation. If you asked me why I was voting, it's because I want to find something to pull me out of this mud."

He looked at me for a moment. "Maybe this is the rope that will save us."

Oh moon, you who have forgotten me.
Show me the way to the lost one.

As those days ended, I thought about what was ahead, and I remembered what had passed since I first traveled to Iraq. It was difficult to separate the two. At one moment, I could see another future in Iraq, this country so long haunted by all it has suffered. At another, I feared that, despite the election and what it meant to Iraqis, too much had already happened; there was no turning back from the forces that had already been unleashed by dictatorship, then invasion and occupation. I thought back, too, to Nasir who, whatever happened, would never be able to reclaim what he had already lost.

In the days around the election, we were together again. But Nasir, his family left behind in Jordan, was glum. His stay in Iraq, his home since birth, was temporary. "You can't understand the feelings," Nasir told me, as we sat

together one night. "You have children, and you don't know what their future will hold for them." His emotions poured out. Again and again, he recounted the advice of Hazem, the fortune-teller, as if blaming himself for not heeding it. "You should not finish renovating your house," he recalled him saying. "You should leave it. You'll never be satisfied when it's done."

"It's my fault," Nasir told me. "I didn't listen to his warnings."

"*Safra tawila.*" It was a phrase Hazem had spoken to Nasir often. It can suggest death; it can mean taking a long trip. Hazem would never tell Nasir what he meant.

"Now we see that everything has come to the surface," Nasir said to me.

We shared drinks, trying to soften the edges of a bleak conversation. A mix of Arabic pop—with its infectious drums and synthesizers—was playing in the background. Rarely were there silences in our talks; this night, however, was different. A little self-consciously, I tried to remind Nasir of more light-hearted moments in our years of working together, his descriptions of army deserters, fucking assholes, and *abu al-arak*, Iraqi slang for a drunk. But sitting with him, I was shadowed with a sense of loneliness and loss—both his and mine. He was now a stranger, an exile in his own country, and I missed the company of the exuberant man through whose eyes I learned about Iraq. That man was gone. We both sensed this, and felt so many other things that were now missing.

"Onc hand cannot clap," Nasir said.

He thought for a moment, then added wistfully, "I can't ever come back."

Long before his departure, Nasir told me a story, a proverb invoked by the elderly to illustrate misfortune; it suggested the uncertainty I felt in those weeks after I returned. It is a tale of loss—the delusion of promise and the malice of truth. It is a story of Baghdad, a city where promise seems unending and loss keeps unfolding, as if dictated by its own momentum. As the story goes, a married woman is courted by a man named Ali. She is unhappy, in a loveless relationship, suffering from its years of misery. And there is the resplendent young Ali, full of charm and promise, the possibilities of their life together endless. She divorces her husband and embraces the unexpected, tantalized by her hope. And then, in that moment of promise, Ali unexpectedly dies. "She didn't keep her husband," the proverb goes, "nor did she get Mr. Ali."

Nasir was born in the 1970s, when Baghdad was experiencing a brief springtime and seemed poised for a better future. Oil brought confidence; with Saddam still in the shadows, the days ahead promised prosperity and well-being. But the days of hope were fleeting, and death in many incarnations would follow. Nasir lost his mother and then his best friends. His father would not speak to him. His country had changed, irrevocably, along a blood-soaked trail of broken spirits. And now—through war, fear, and dread—he had lost the city he, like so many, could never stop imagining. It would never again be his Baghdad. There was the promise of a much better capital, underlined vividly by the election, but who would see it, and when? And how many, like Nasir, would become lost in a brutal war that refused to end and in a struggle over identity that was beyond their control?

In the months after the election, many more would die, scores in just a few ensuing weeks. For a moment, the election had eclipsed the legacy of the occupation—those unintended consequences and unanticipated outcomes that were shaping what Iraq would be. But afterward, those forces of religious revival, growing militancy, and hardening sectarianism, underlined by grievance and a threat of even more strife, returned to the stage. Were they transient or permanent? I didn't know. I comprehend Baghdad less than I thought I did when I first encountered it, on those comparatively quiet days in 1998 at the Information Ministry, under the gaze of Saddam's statues, in a city of whispers. I think back to everything I have seen and felt: the frustration building in the lives of Faruq and Fuad, the bitterness of Yasmine, the lament of Mohammed Ghani, Amal's girlish handwriting, and the brief euphoria of election day, a moment filled with pride. I leave this place with thoughts of thwarted ambitions, of the failure of occupation, of a grim future inherited by men with guns and the culture they bring. But there is also a resilient hope among Iraqis, a tenacious refusal to surrender their country to the forces of violence and chaos. Their voice in the election was their verdict: they would still have a say in their destiny.

Through its storied history, Baghdad has had many names. Its medieval Abbasid rulers knew it as Medinat al-Salam, the City of Peace. The Baghdadis I met bestowed their own appellations over a weary two years of anticipation and, more often, disappointment: Baghdad is a city of lanterns amid the blackouts, a city of ghosts shadowed by fear, a city that is forsaken. The city I knew would always remain *ghamidha*.

SELECTED BIBLIOGRAPHY

Abrahamian, Ervand. *Iran: Between Two Revolutions*. Princeton: Princeton University Press, 1982.

——. *Khomeinism*. Berkeley: University of California Press, 1990.

Aburish, Said K. *Saddam Hussein: The Politics of Revenge*. London: Bloomsbury, 2000.

Aburish, Said K., et al. *Inside Iraq: The History, the People, and the Modern Conflicts of the World's Least Understood Land*. New York: Marlowe & Co., 2002.

Al-Amin, Hazem. "Moqtada Al-Sadr: Leader of Orphans," *Al-Ahram Weekly*, May 27–June 2, 2004.

Al-Ramli, Muhsin. *Scattered Crumbs*. Translated from the Arabic by Yasmeen S. Hanoosh. Fayetteville: University of Arkansas Press, 2003.

Al-Tabari. *The Early Abbasi Empire*. Translated by John Alden Williams. Cambridge, Eng.: Cambridge University Press, 1988.

Baram, Amazia. "Saddam Hussein: A Political Profile." *The Jerusalem Quarterly*, no. 17 (fall 1980).

Barrenechea, Ana Maria. *Borges: The Labyrinth Maker*. New York: New York University Press, 1965.

Batatu, Hanna. "Iraq's Underground Shi'a Movements: Characteristics, Causes and Prospects." *Middle East Journal* 35 (autumn 1981): 578–94.

——. *Old Social Classes and the Revolutionary Movements of Iraq.* Princeton: Princeton University Press, 1978.

Bengio, Ofra. *Saddam's World.* Oxford, Eng.: Oxford University Press, 1998.

Cockburn, Andrew, and Patrick Cockburn. *Out of the Ashes.* New York: Harper-Collins, 1999.

Coke, Richard. *Baghdad: The City of Peace.* London: Thornton Butterworth Ltd., 1927.

Coughlin, Con. *Saddam: King of Terror.* New York: HarperCollins, 2002.

Dodge, Toby. *Inventing Iraq: The Failure of Nation Building and a History Denied.* New York: Columbia University Press, 2003.

Dunn, Ross. *The Adventures of Ibn Battuta: A Muslim Traveler of the 14th Century.* Berkeley: University of California Press, 1986.

Esposito, John. *Islam and Politics.* Syracuse: Syracuse University Press, 1984.

Farouk-Sluglett, Marion, and Peter Sluglett. *Iran Since 1958: From Revolution to Dictatorship.* London and New York: KPI, 1987.

Francke, Rend Rahim, and Graham E. Fuller. *The Arab Shi'a: The Forgotten Muslims.* New York: St. Martin's Press, 1999.

Fromkin, David. *A Peace to End All Peace.* New York: André Deutsch, 1989.

Graham-Brown, Sarah. "Sanctioning Iraq: A Failed Policy," *Middle East Report* 215 (summer 2000): 8–13.

Hiro, Dilip. *Desert Shield to Desert Storm.* London: HarperCollins, 1992.

——. *The Longest War: The Iran-Iraq Military Conflict.* New York: Routledge, 1991.

Hourani, Albert. *A History of the Arab Peoples.* New York: Warner Books, 1991.

Ibn Battuta. *The Travels of Ibn Battuta.* Translated, with revisions and notes from the Arabic text, edited by C. Defremery and B. R. Sanguinetti. New York: Kraus (reprint), 1958.

——. *The Travels of Ibn Battuta.* Abridged, introduced, and annotated by Tim Mackintosh-Smith. London: Pan Macmillan, 2002.

"Iraq's Shiites Under Occupation," *International Crisis Group.* Baghdad/Brussels, September 9, 2003.

Jaber, Faleh A. "Shaykhs and Ideologues: Detribalization and Retribalization in Iraq, 1968–1998," *Middle East Report* 215 (summer 2000): 28–31.

——. *The Shi'ite Movement in Iraq.* London: Saqi, 2003.

——. "The Worldly Roots of Religiosity in Post-Saddam Iraq," *Middle East Report* 227 (summer 2003): 12–18.

Jaber, Hala. *Hezbollah: Born with a Vengeance.* New York: Columbia University Press, 1997.

Kaplan, Robert. *The Arabists: The Romance of an American Elite.* New York: Free Press, 1995.

Karsh, Efraim. *The Iran-Iraq War, 1980–88.* London: Osprey, 2002.

Karsh, Efraim, and Inari Rautsi. *Saddam Hussein: A Political Biography.* New York: Grove Press, 2003.

Kelly, Michael. *Martyr's Day: Chronicle of a Small War.* New York: Vintage Books, 1993.

Lassner, Jacob. *The Topography of Baghdad in the Early Middle Ages.* Detroit: Wayne State University Press, 1970.

Lewis, Bernard. *Islam from the Prophet Muhammad to the Capture of Constantinople.* New York: Harper & Row, 1974.

Makiya, Kanan. *The Monument: Art and Vulgarity in Saddam Hussein's Iraq.* London: I. B. Tauris, 2004.

———. *Republic of Fear: The Politics of Modern Iraq.* Berkeley: University of California Press, 1989.

Marr, Phebe. *The Modern History of Iraq.* Boulder, Colo.: Westview Press, 1985.

Mottahedeh, Roy. *The Mantle of the Prophet: Religion and Politics in Iran.* Oxford, Eng.: Oneworld Publications, 1985.

Rodenbeck, Max. "Bohemia in Baghdad," *New York Review of Books,* 3 July 2003.

———. "The Occupation," *New York Review of Books,* August 14, 2003.

Shadid, Anthony. *Legacy of the Prophet: Despots, Democrats and the New Politics of Islam.* Boulder, Colo.: Westview Press, 2001.

Tripp, Charles. *A History of Iraq.* Cambridge, Eng.: Cambridge University Press, 2000.

Watt, W. Montgomery. *Muhammad: Prophet and Statesman.* Oxford: Oxford University Press, 1961.

Wright, Richard. *Native Son.* New York: Harper & Brothers, 1940.

ACKNOWLEDGMENTS

Night Draws Near would have been impossible without the generosity, compassion, humor, and courage of my colleagues at the *Washington Post* in Baghdad. They are the spirit of this book. In a time of conflict and chaos, a group of Iraqis and Americans came together, enduring long moments of drudgery, stress, and uncertainty, interspersed with bursts of exhilaration. In a shattered country, we came to believe in one another.

I am especially indebted to Omar Fekeiki, Naseer Nouri, Bassam Sebti, Khalid Al-Saffar, Saad Sarhan, and Othman Mukhtar. I should also mention Ahmed Younis, Omar Asaad, Falah Hassan, Saif Naseer, Dhia Ahmed, Ghazwan Noel, Jawad Munshid, Rifaat Muhammed, Muhanned M. Salim, Sabah Fadhil, Muhammed Mahdi, Muayad Jabbar, Muhammed Munim, Fawziya Naji, Muna Jawad, and Naseer Fadhil.

Bringing them together was Rajiv Chandrasekaran, the indomitable bureau chief of the *Post*, who was an unparalleled colleague and a compassionate friend. He represented the spirit of the *Post*'s foreign staff, the most remarkable group of journalists with whom I have worked. All of them deserve mention, but I am especially indebted to Karl Vick and Daniel Williams, who repeatedly risked their life to tell the story of Iraq. I owe a special thanks to my editors at the *Post*. Phil Bennett and David Hoffman never lost sight of the events or the ambitions of our coverage, and their vision inspired the reporting. In many ways, it made the reporting possible. Through the war and its aftermath, they were friends as much as colleagues. I would say the same for my editors at the *Boston Globe*, Martin Baron and Jim Smith.

Loneliness can take its toll on correspondents who spend much of their time pursuing stories with no real end. Friendships are often the saving grace. Alissa Rubin of the *Los Angeles Times* was one of those rare colleagues whose compassion matched her talent, and I will always appreciate her support. I can never forget the ordeals that I endured with Hamza Hendawi of the Associated Press, who is one of the best that journalism has to offer. Sharing a room during the war, he was forced to endure the strain of bombing and the pettiness of my foibles, rarely losing his unparalleled humor and dignity. Hamza is a lifelong friend, in the true meaning of the word.

I am particularly indebted to Maria Ghanem Abousleiman, my intern at the Woodrow Wilson International Center for Scholars, where I wrote this book. Maria was tireless in seeing this project to the end. I won't forget her generosity, kindness, and keen eye. My thanks, too, go to the center, which provided the resources necessary to complete this book.

I would like to say a word about my editor at Henry Holt, George Hodgman, and my agent, Robert Shepard. Both men kept this book on track, despite my own pessimism. George was tireless in ensuring that the book came close to the vision that inspired it, and Robert was unflagging in his support to persevere through the attempts that fell short.

Looking back, it is my greatest hope that *Night Draws Near* somehow does justice to the long time I spent away from my beloved daughter, Laila. She had the misfortune of learning the word "Baghdad" far too early in life, and the good luck of being too young to know what it meant. My family was all too aware. My deepest regret as a foreign correspondent is the worry my work causes those I love. My father, my mother, and the rest of my family nevertheless supported my choices, and to them I owe my thanks and gratitude.

This book, of course, would have been impossible without the cooperation of the people I met in Iraq. Those individuals and families opened the doors of their homes to me, often at great risk to their own lives. They trusted me and shared with me their hopes and fears, their regrets and their ambitions. They often did so without hesitation.

Finally, a note about Nasir Mehdawi and Karim Saadoon. There is a saying in Iraqi Arabic. Loosely translated, it can be rendered something like this: "We're not from the same family, but we're still brothers." Nasir and Karim were my brothers in Iraq. We came together during a war and stayed together afterward. To this day, I have never met two men with more courage and loyalty. In true Iraqi fashion, each of them was a *seba'*, and month after month, story after story, we trusted one another with our lives, implicitly.

INDEX

Aani, Hashim Mohammed, 219–24, 227, 241
Aani, Omar, 296, 298
Aani, Riyadh, 223
Aani, Salman, 229
Aaraji, Hazem, 371
Abadi, Sheikh Kadhim al-, 179
Abbas, Abdel-Razaq, 202
Abbas, Imam, 177, 333, 342, 360
   shrine at Karbala, 162, 353, 354
Abbas, Sami, 166
Abbas, Shaker, 214
Abbas, Um, 69
Abbasid Empire, 19, 33, 42, 130, 160, 163
Abdel-Amin, Mohammed, 166
Abdel-Hussein, Mazin, 36
Abdel-Jabbar, Huda, 267
Abdel-Kadhim, Hussein, 78–80
Abdel-Karim, Hussein, 389
Abdel-Karim, Khairi, 231
Abdel-Rahman, Riad, 55–56
Abdel-Raziq, Faris, 71
Abdel-Rahim, Shaaban, 15–16

Abdel-Wahid, Hassan, 376, 377
Abdoun, Qahtan, 241–42
Abdullah, Abbas, 365
Abdullah, Ahmed, 202–3
Abdullah, Faris, 226
Abdullah, Khaled, 233
Abdullah, Majid, 111
Abdullah, Shafa, 269
Abdullah, Thamer, 269
Abdul-Rahman, Col. Adnan, 393
Abed, Dr. Abdullah, 82
Abed, Farhan, 237–38
Abed, Mohammed, 360–62
Abidin, Ali Zayn al- (fourth Shiite imam), 260
Aboud, Mohammed, 256
Aboud, Mohammed Kadhim, 4
Abu Bakr, caliph (A.D. 632–34), 160
Abu Ghreib prison, 2–5, 8, 132, 164, 183, 242, 395
Abzara, Wathiq, 122
Adhamiya neighborhood, 71, 144, 309, 378, 379, 381, 383

Afghanistan, 14, 114, 290
Afus, Aida, 78
Aghassi, Mahmoud Quul ("Abu Qaqaa"), 246–47, 291, 303–5, 307
Ahmed, Khaled, 310
Ahmed, Mohammed, 204–5
Ahmed, Mundhir, 268
Ahmed, Shlash, 235
Ahmed, Sultan Hashim, 181
Aidan, Ali, 166
Ajami, Mohammed, 296
Al-Arabiya (satellite network), 136, 263, 373
Albert, Dhikran, 119
Albright, Madeleine, 37
Albu Alwan village, 293, 297
Ali (cousin of Prophet), caliph (A.D. 656–61), 177, 178, 333, 342, 348, 360
  martyrdom of, 160–61, 163–67
  shrine of, at Najaf, 78, 161, 253–54, 351
Ali, Abbas, 122
Ali, Abdullah, 242–43, 310–11
Ali, Abed, 311
Ali, Ahmed, 268
Ali, Dhia, 395–96
Ali, Hussein, 71
Ali, Khudheir Mikhlif, 238, 241
Al-Iraqiya (TV network), 344
Al-Jazeera (satellite TV network), 41, 114, 136, 373
Allawi, Ayad, 173, 174, 380
Al-Mustaqbil (satellite TV network), 136
Alwiya Maternity Hospital, 140
Amin, Hassan, 111
amnesty of October 20, 2002, 1–8, 98, 132, 134, 183, 242, 395
Appelbaum, Sgt. Jennifer, 207
Arab-Israeli war of 1967, 39
Arab-Israeli war of 1973, 374
Arab world
  invasion and, 14–16
  myth and, 382
  nationalism, 45, 221, 273
  progress vs. weakness in, 41
  Sadr and, 365

Sunnis and, 227–28
symbolism of occupation and, 198, 214
U.S. and, 9, 39, 203, 212
Arasat neighborhood, 54, 90
Aristotle, 20
Asala, 97, 342
Ashura (religious holiday), 162, 347–48, 352–53
  bombings of 2004, 353–56
Assyrian civilization, 136
Aswad, Bassem, 352
Atraqji, Dr. Shahla Kadhim, 26–29, 313–15
Awad, Jamal, 280, 283–86
Ayyoub, Tareq, 114
Aziz, Tariq, 92, 129

Baath Party, 44, 86, 89, 98, 100, 119, 129, 158–59, 200, 202, 220, 223–25, 234, 262, 283, 312
  history of, 24–26, 34–36, 45–47
  militia, 13, 54, 69, 96, 106–7, 117
Babylon, 19, 51, 115–16, 136
Baghdad. *See also* Sadr City; *and other neighborhoods*
  anniversary of fall of Saddam in, 383–85
  architecture of past and, 318–19
  banned books in, 246–47
  bombing of, during invasion, 51–54, 61, 63, 68, 71–82, 85–86, 94, 96, 101–3, 110–13, 117
  culture of gun and, 43–44
  desire for progress in, and sense of deserving better, 39–43
  elections of January 2005, 391–92
  eve of invasion and, 13–14, 16–18, 21–22, 36, 43–44
  exodus from, as U.S. marches on, 67–69
  fall of, to British in 1917, 387–88
  fall of, to Mongols in 1258, 27, 62–63, 130, 163, 203
  fall of, to U.S., 105–9, 113–25
ghamidh ("mysterious" or "ambiguous"), 10

Ghani statues in, 136–37
Green Zone, 239
history of Sunni-Shiite feuds in, 162–63
insurgency of 2003–2004 and, 201,
    253, 274–76, 317–30, 343
invasion of, 51–72
Iran war and, 23, 25
looting and lawlessness of, after fall,
    117–18, 129–55
map of, 1
medieval history and founding of, 8,
    18–21
1970s as era of glory, 21, 40
occupation of, as humiliation, 203
occupation of, October 2003 optimism
    about, 245–46
postwar devastation and economic
    problems of, 147–48
Ramadan bombings of 2003 and,
    265–72
Saddam's martial style shapes, 34
Sadr movement and, 363, 368–69
shanashil as metaphor for, 318
uprisings of April 2004 and, 377–78
weather as sign of cataclysm in, 62
Baiji (town), 280–86
Basra, 29, 52, 97, 163, 170, 173, 175,
    363, 370
Bayaa neighborhood, 21–22, 268, 357
Bayati, Ahmed, 66
Beach, Specialist Ron, 207
Bidawi, Nawar, 294
blackouts, 70, 95, 105
    postwar, 134, 155, 210
Bremer, L. Paul, 134, 151–52, 204, 258,
    261, 271, 272, 279, 282, 307–8, 321,
    322, 328–29, 343, 359, 367–68,
    371–72, 374–76, 380
British Broadcasting Corporation (BBC),
    96, 108, 116
British colonial rule (1918–32), 17–18,
    136–38, 160, 387–89
    revolt of 1920 vs., 381, 386–87
    Sunni elite and, 88, 163
Bufarraj tribe, 226

Bujweri tribe, 226
Bush, George H. W. (senior), 90, 163
Bush, George W., 8, 14–15, 17, 68, 87,
    132–33, 141, 150, 214–15, 308, 313,
    322, 332, 339, 343, 375, 377, 381

Callan, Sgt. Michael, 203
Calvert, Capt. Michael, 240
Chalabi, Ahmad, 132, 173, 174
Challoub, Ibrahim, 213
Chandrasekaran, Rajiv, 252
chemical weapons, 26, 31
Christians, Iraqi, 88, 163, 180
civil war, 9, 329, 346, 378
Clinton, Bill, 37
Coalition Provisional Authority (CPA),
    184, 363, 367
Couso, Jose, 114
crime, 134, 329–31, 334, 344–45, 359.
    See also lawlessness, looting, and
    security problems
Crusaders, 142

Daham, Capt. Khalil, 238–39
Daif, Arkan, 73–75, 77–78, 80, 82
Damascus, 19, 144
Darraj, Ibrahim, 213
Darraji, Sheikh Hadi, 185, 264–65
Dawa Party, 351
de–Baathification program, 322
democracy and freedom, 386
    adil or justice vs., 15
    Amal's diary on, 338, 339
    economic distress and, 343
    Sadr uprising and, 377
    U.S. promise of, 72, 232
Dempsey, Maj. Gen. Martin, 371
Dhua, Mohammed Abu, 226
Din, Saif, 204, 205
Diwaniya (town), 363, 366
Doha (city), 246
Dora neighborhood, 71, 134, 393

economic devastation, 44–45, 141, 147,
    336–39, 341, 342, 344–45

education, 21, 37–38, 45
Egypt, 15–16, 18, 21, 42, 46–47, 246,
    265, 287, 291, 302
elections, 343
  of January 2005, 391–97
electricity shortages, 68, 70, 90, 95,
    104–5, 113, 134, 148, 151, 152, 175,
    204, 205, 210–11, 213, 214, 217,
    246, 261, 317, 321, 323, 327–29,
    331, 333–36, 343
Entezam, Abdollah, 260

Fadhil, Kadhim, 24–26
Fahdawi, Adel, 300
Fahdawi, Adnan Kamil Mahan, 240,
    288–92, 299–301, 303, 304, 311,
    357, 364, 371
Fahdawi, Khaled, 289
Fahdawi, Salah, 289–90, 299–301
Falaeh, Mohammed, 131
Falahat (village), 294, 295
Faleh, Hassan, 193
Fallujah, 27, 228, 291, 294, 297, 303,
    304
  attack of November 2004, 381
  protests of April 2003 in,
    233–38
  uprising of April 2004 in, 359,
    371–75, 377–82, 386
Fao Peninsula, 26, 52
Farag, Mohammed Abdel-Salam al-, 302,
    303
Fartousi, Sheikh Kadhim, 213–14
fatalism, 78–81
Fatima (daughter of Prophet
    Mohammed), 161
Fedayeen Saddam (paramilitary), 106,
    146, 225
Firdaus Square
  anniversary of Saddam's fall and,
    383–84
  statue of Saddam, 52, 120, 123–24, 326
Fleih, Hassan, 66
food rations, 147, 339, 343
Fouad, Raad, 384, 385

Fox News, 87, 89
fuel shortages, 141, 147, 343

Galen, 20
Garner, Lt. Gen. Jay M., 133–34, 224
Gaza, 187, 198
General Security Headquarters, 53
General Union of Iraqi Women, 129–30
Genghis Khan, 203
George, Shidrak, 125
George, Stefan Abu, 122
Germany (1918), 131
Ghaffour, Dr. Adel, 38–39, 274–76
ghamidh ("mysterious" or "ambiguous"),
  as mood of Baghdad, 10, 125, 205,
    305, 355, 398
Ghani, Mohammed, 40–43, 52, 135,
    136–40, 153–55, 392, 398
Girgis, Zuheir, 119
Golden Gate palace and green dome, 19,
    62
Green Zone ("Emerald City"), 239, 334,
    345, 363, 368–69, 374
  symbolism of, 260–62
Guantánamo Bay prisoners, 14
Gulf emirates, 42
Gulf War of 1991, 36, 37, 53, 55, 90,
    100, 133, 212, 217, 379
gun(s)
  availability of, 21–22, 84, 138, 181,
    210, 230, 241
  culture of, 43–44

Habbaniya (town), 295
Hadi, Hassan, 354
Haeri, Kadhim Husseini, 172
Hafez, Abdel-Halim, 13, 391
Haider, Um, 101, 335
Hakim, Abdel Aziz al-, 173, 363–64
Hakim, Ayatollah Mohammed Baqir al-,
    173, 174, 177, 191, 211, 351
  assassination of, 255-58, 262, 265, 356
Hakim, Grand Ayatollah Mohammed
    Saeed al-, 254–55
Halabja massacre, 144, 227

Halbousi, Saad, 235
Hallaj, al- (10th-century philosopher), 18
Hamas, 186, 187, 378
Hamdan, Hussein, 377
Hamed, Lt. Ahmed Khalaf, 238
Hamid, Kamel, 122
Hamid, Qahtan, 257
Hamid, Sayyid, 115
Hammadi, Ammar Ibrahim, 241
Hammoud, Rahim Hamid, 221–22,
    224–25
Hammoush, Mohammad, 225–26
Hanbal, Ibn, 163
Hanners, Lt. Noah, 295, 297
Hanoosh, Hussein, 122–23
Hanson, Pvt. Ian, 204
Harris, Specialist Stephen, 199, 205
Harvard University public health team
    report, 37
Hashemite monarchy, 45
Hassaan, Mohammed, 246
Hassan, Ahmed, 118, 355
Hassan, Azz el-Din, 166
Hassan, Faleh, 118, 119
Hassan, Rasmiya, 272
Hassan, Sabah, 74
Hatem, Raad, 112
Hattab, Mohsin, 82
Haumschild, Sgt. Nathaniel, 201
Hawar Art Gallery, 14, 16–18, 388
Hawza (Shiite religious leadership), 173,
    187, 190, 235, 258
Hayawi, Abdel-Rahman, 216
Hayawi, Mohammed, 215–18, 246–49,
    252, 265, 396
Hazem, Laith, 70, 71
Hazem, Luai, 70
Hazem (fortune-teller), 249–52, 358, 397
Heet (town), 228–31, 234, 236, 282
Heidar, Jamil Abu, 267
Hendawi, Hamza, 60, 61, 113, 121
Hezbollah, 186, 364–65
Hikma Mosque, 183, 185, 186, 190
Hippocrates, 20
Hollis, Sgt. Robert, 305–6

Horan, Hume, 180, 260–63, 362, 363, 368
hospitals
    invasion and, 85–86, 106, 115–16
    looting of, 129, 130, 134, 140
    occupation and, 334
Hulugu (Mongol leader), 130, 203, 388
humanitarian aid, lack of, 335, 337
Human Rights Watch, 233
Hume, Margaret Robinson, 260
Hunting Club, 26–27, 28, 313
Hussein, Ibrahim Ali, 223
Hussein, Imad, 75
Hussein, Dr. Mazin, 122–23
Hussein, Qusay, 110, 129, 144, 171,
    339–40
Hussein, Saddam
    amnesty of 2002 and, 1–7
    Baghdad bunker of, bombed, 51
    blamed for occupation, 306
    capture of, 307–14, 343
    fall of, 9, 119–20, 137–38
    fall of, unintended consequences of,
        232, 280
    hatred of, 45, 92, 94, 221, 326, 330
    history and legacy of, 8, 25, 28–29,
        33–35, 136
    invasion and, 13, 52, 96, 332
    Iran-Iraq war and, 23, 27, 28
    Iraqi attitudes toward, postwar,
        143–45, 268
    Iraqi military and, 146
    Kurds and, 88
    Mansur homes bombed, in effort to
        kill, 110–11
    Qassem assassination attempt and,
        46–47
    Reagan and, 92
    religion and, 36
    rumors about, after fall of Iraq, 181–82
    search for, 225
    Shiites and, 202, 158–59, 163–64,
        170–71, 214–15, 221, 351
    Sistani and, 189
    Sunni elite and, 88–89
    Sunnis and, 220, 223–24, 302

Hussein, Uday (Saddam's son), 110, 129, 141, 144, 339–40
Hussein, Uday (Sadr City resident), 214
Hussein (grandson of Prophet), 77, 161–62, 164–65, 167, 177, 333, 342, 351, 360
  Ashura and, 347–49
  martyrdom of, 56–57
  shrine of, 162
Husseini, Abu Ahmed, 355
Huzeimawi, Khalil, 291, 300

Ibn Haitham Hospital, 122
Ibrahim, Asad Abdel-Karim, 222, 224
Ibrahim, Mohammed, 199–200
ihtilal ("occupation"), symbolism of term, 198–99, 214, 221, 235, 236
infant mortality, 37
informers, 226, 227, 237, 241–42
infrastructure, failure to repair, 134, 217, 272, 323. *See also* electricity shortages; sewage and sanitation problems; water shortages
insurgency (guerrilla war), 345. *See also* Mahdi Army; Falluja; Heet; *and other specific uprisings*
  breaks out in Khaldiya, 236–37, 240–41
  complexities inherited from past and, 221
  disparate coalition behind, 286–87
  dissolving of army fuels, 152, 282
  effect of, on Iraqis sympathetic to U.S., 326–29
  elections of 2005 and, 393
  Fallujah and, 372–75
  gains strength in Sunni arc, 279–92
  Heet and, 228–31
  hit–and–run raids on military convoys, 201, 222, 282
  increasing organization and violence of, in fall of 2003, 253–54, 266–76, 282, 290
  as jihad vs. U.S., 288–92, 294

  police and, 236, 238–39, 240–41, 282–83
  political Islam and nationalism fuel, 232–33, 305–6, 287–307, 312–13
  rise of, with official beginning of occupation, 200–201, 206
  spreads in summer and fall of 2003, 245, 253–54
  Sunni Triangle and, 231–35
  threats of, believed by Iraqis, 272
  U.S. assessment of, 231–32, 282, 287
  U.S. raids during occupation fuel, 220–21, 225–31
interim government, 367
Internal Security headquarters, 53
International Committee of the Red Cross, 69–71
  headquarters bombed, 266
Internet, 41
Iran, 23, 40, 256
Iran-Iraq war, 8, 14, 34, 92, 118, 163, 249, 256, 274, 275, 289
  impact of, on Iraqis, 22–32
  prisoners of war, 24–25
Iraq
  ambiguities of, and amnesty of 2002, 5–8
  bombing of, during Gulf War, 37
  brutal rules of countryside and, 27–28
  collapse of armed forces in, 145–46
  confusion of, under occupation, 252–53
  culture, insurgency to defend, 279
  economic boom of 1970s, 21
  electricity, water, and sewage problems, post-Gulf War, 37
  eve of invasion and mood of, 16, 42–43, 47
  feeling of continuous war in, 274–75, 311–12
  imams buried in, 161
  invasion of, begun, 51–72
  lack of legitimate leaders in, 273

lost generation of, 24–25
map of, 1
Middle East opinion on eve of
    invasion of, 14–16
militarization of, in Iran-Iraq war, 23
Saddam seizure of power in, 22–23
two-dimensional portrait of, before
    invasion, 7–8
unforeseen consequences of U.S.
    invasion of, 8–9
U.S. bombing of civilians and, 74–81
U.S. invasion of, 51–72
Iraqi army
    disbanded by Bremer, 145–47, 152,
        201, 204, 284
Iraqi army, new
    recruited by US occupation, 236
    refuses to fight in Fallujah, 373
Iraqi Civil Defense Corps, 280–86, 236,
    379
Iraqi Communist Party, 65, 247
Iraqi exiles
    antipathy toward, 92, 273, 321–22
    leave during insurgency, 320–27, 358–
        59
    postwar plan and, 133
    Sadr and, 173
Iraqi Governing Council (IGC), 257–59,
    312, 321–22, 330, 346, 373, 380
Iraqi Islamic Party, 312
Iraqi Ministry of Higher Education, 131
Iraqi Ministry of Information, 5–6, 61,
    65, 107, 113, 152, 175
Iraqi Ministry of Interior, 393
Iraqi Ministry of Oil, 282
Iraqi National Accord, 174
Iraqi National Congress, 132, 174
Iraqi People's Court, 65
Iraqi police, 206–11, 228–31, 236–41,
    266–71, 281, 343, 370
"Iraqization," 281
Islamic law (Sharia), 190, 260, 309
Islamists, 280
Islam (Muslim). *See also* Shiite Muslims;
    Sunni Muslims

funeral rites, 74
Iraqi security forces labeled
    collaborators by, 283–84
Israeli-Palestinian conflict remade by,
    232
mystics, 249–50
new strain of, as ideology of
    insurgency, 9, 279–80, 287–93,
    297–307, 312–13
Saddam and, 36
shahada (central creed), 59
social work and, 186–87
Western decadence and,
    287
Ismail, Firas, 383–84
Ismail, Mahmoud, 240
Israel, 87, 215, 365
    messianic right wing in, 232
    U.S. support, 39, 212, 306
Israeli-Palestinian conflict, 14, 15, 198,
    232, 273, 287, 291, 303–4,
    373–74, 376. *See also* Palestine

Jaafari, Ibrahim, 173
Jabbar, Ahmed, 377
Jabbouri, Mehdi, 241
Jabbouri tribe, 241, 242
Jabbour tribe, 226
Jaber, Ahmed, 269–70
Jabouri, Mufid, 67
Jabr, Hassan, 76
Jabr, Mohammed, 75
Jackson, Lt. Col. Larry "Pepper,"
    281–82, 287
Jadriya neighborhood, 90
Jalal, Lieutenant, 30–31
Jalil, Rusul, 210
Jalil, Sgt. Sami, 209–10, 212
Jamal, Lava, 112
Jassim, Osama, 68–69
Jawad, Imam Mohammed Taqi, shrine,
    35
Jawhari, Aboud, 166
Jerusalem, 292
Jews, 163, 232. *See also* Israel

jihad
  concept of, 25
  insurgency as, 288–91, 303–7, 309
Jihad neighborhood, 83, 325, 379
Jimenez, Lt. Arthur, 219–20, 222
Jolie, Isabella, 207–8
Jordan, 15, 16
Jordanian Embassy bombing (2003), 253, 254, 356

Kaabi, Saad al-, 122–23
Kaczmarek, Sgt. Kenneth, 207–8, 210, 211
Kadhim, Ali, 392
Kadhim, Haider, 73, 75–77
Kadhim, Imam Musa, shrine, 35, 36
Kadhim, Raed, 69
Kadhim, Sadiq, 255
Kadhim, Ysuf Abed, 124
Kadhimiya neighborhood, 66, 257
  bombings, 353, 355–57, 362, 365
  Fallujah uprising and, 378, 379
Kadhimiya shrine, 35, 66, 165–67
Kahramana fountain, 136–37
Kamil, Saad, 297
Kaplow, Larry, 118, 119, 120
Karameh battle (1968), 373–74, 382
Karbala, 4, 29, 67, 69, 88, 164
  Ashura rituals at, 162, 167
  Ashura bombings (2004), 347–57, 362, 365
  battle of 680, 56–57, 162, 177
  pilgrimages to, 347–52
  Sadr and, 173, 186
  tombs of imams in, 161
  uprising of May 2004, 381
Karbalai, Bassam, 347
Karrada neighborhood, 53, 54, 56, 118
Kathir, Ibn, 62–63
Keeling, Pvt. Kasey, 202, 203
Kemal, Mustafa, 134
Khadhra neighborhood, 267
Khafaji, Sheikh Jaber al-, 172
Khalaf, Abdel-Latif, 293, 295, 296
Khalaf, Omar Ibrahim, 292–98

Khalaf, Qassim, 280, 286
Khalaf, Radwan, 293
Khaldiya, 228, 236–41, 270, 288–92, 299–303, 306, 357
Khaled, Mawaffaq, 297
Khaled, Mawlud, 294, 296, 297
Khalil, Ahmed, 81–82
Khalil, Ali, 81
Khalil, Aqeel, 81
Khalil, Laith, 291–92
Khalil, Shahida, 81–82
Khamenei, Ali, 351
Khartoum, Sudan, 246
Khazali, Sheikh Qais al-, 172
Khazraji tribe, 226
Kheiber, Faleh, 115
Khoie, Abdel-Majid, 191–92, 363, 369
Khoie, Grand Ayatollah Abul-Qassim, 169, 188
Khomeini, Ayatollah Ruhollah, 193, 212, 351
khoms (religious tax), 186, 191
Khorasan Gate, 19
Khusaf, Qassem, 264
Kimmitt, Brig. Gen. Mark, 372
Kindi Hospital, 115–17, 270
Kirtani, Abdullah, 303
Kirtani, Hamid, 291, 300, 303
Kirtani, Khaled, 300, 306–7
Kirtani, Ra'id, 291, 299, 300, 306
Kishk, Abdel-Hamid, 246, 304
Kubeisi, Abdel-Salaam, 312
Kuettner, Capt. Paul, 231
Kufa, 19, 161, 162
  uprising, 359, 361–63, 369–70, 374
Kufa Mosque, 192, 258, 361–62, 370, 374
Kurds, 25, 133, 174, 180, 312
  Iran-Iraq war and, 23, 27
  Saddam and, 144
  Shiite vs. Sunni, 88
Kut (town), 31, 363
Kuwait, 40, 246, 339
  invasion of 1990, 8, 14, 24, 32, 47, 94, 144, 382

Laden, Osama bin, 14–15, 246, 268, 272, 304, 355

Latifa, Ziyad, 242

lawlessness, looting, and security problems

  airport highway and, 200

  Ashura 2004 bombings, 355–57

  in Baghdad, and rising insurgency, 275, 314, 317, 320, 329–31, 336, 342–43, 345, 359

  in Baghdad, improvements in fall of 2003, 246, 247

  car bombings, 201, 266–70, 356, 393

  carjackings, 334

  drive-by shootings, 201

  elections of 2005, 393–95, 398

  fall of Baghdad and, 117–18, 129–35, 138–39, 140–41, 148–49, 150–53, 153–55, 181, 326

  foreseen by Iraqis before invasion, 18, 22, 56

  hopes that U.S. troops will stop, 200

  Iraqi civilians and, 205, 213, 217, 334, 339, 345

  Iraq subsumed in logic of violence and, 357

  Khaldiya looting and, 237

  kidnappings and, 141, 145, 151, 325, 327, 334, 344

  loss of respect for occupation and, 181, 197–98, 204, 210–11, 326–27

  Ramadan bombings of 2003, 271–76

  Shiite patrols quell, 157, 175

  Shiites criticize U.S. for, 174

League of Nations, 387

Lebanon, 9, 16, 21, 41, 287, 291, 364

  Israeli withdrawal of 2000, 374

legitimacy question (*sharaiyya*), 157, 235–36, 273

liberation, 9

  Amal's diary and, 338

  British colonialism and, 17–18, 203, 388

  as occupation, 198–99, 214–15

literacy, 37–38

Mahdi, Heidar, 355

Mahdi Army, 258–59, 264, 359, 361–71, 375–77, 379, 381, 385

Mahdi (Hidden or Twelfth Imam), 161, 258, 263

Majid, Ali Hassan al- "Chemical Ali," 144

Majid, Mustafa, 210–11

Ma'mun, al-, 20

Mansur, Abu Jaafar "Miqlas," second caliph of Abbasid Empire, 14, 19–20, 33, 62, 162–63

Mansur neighborhood, 26, 53, 93, 110, 154

Mareidy neighborhood, 148

martyrdom, 296, 299–301, 304–7, 375

Mashtal neighborhood, 206, 210

mass graves, 143, 316

Maude, Maj. Gen. Sir Stanley, 17, 387–89

Mawash, Khaled, 293

Mayah, Abdel-Latif, 273–74

medicine shortages, 343

Mehdawi, Ahmed, 175

Mehdawi, Akram, 65

Mehdawi, Col. Fadhil Abbas, 65

Mehdawi, Nasir, 65–67, 69, 79, 84, 96, 114, 175–76, 206, 249–52, 266, 267–69, 271, 285, 288, 309, 316, 343, 357–59, 391, 396–98

Mehdawi, Samah, 249

Mehdawi, Sariya, 65

Mehdawi, Yossi, 175

Mello, Sergio Vieira de, 253

Middle East

  Bush vision of, 8

  civilized propriety of, 9–10

  insurgency and, 288

  invasion and, 14–16

Midhas, Fadhil, 222–23

Mizhar, Ali, 117

Mohamed, Nabil Fadhil, 268

Mohamed, Um, 107

Mohammed (prophet), 160, 161, 168, 232

Mohammed, Abbas, 64
Mohammed, Adnan, 233
Mohammed, Ahmed, 234
Mohammed, Ali, 116
Mohammed, Amin, 320
Mohammed, Balsam, 317
Mohammed, Fadhil, 64
Mohammed, Firas, 93, 152, 317, 329
Mohammed, Dr. Fuad Musa, 93–96, 150–53, 316–19, 326, 328–31, 346, 398
Mohammed, Hala, 320
Mohammed, Hashim Ibrahim, 225
Mohammed, Hussein Hamoud, 223
Mohammed, Hussein (Yasmine's son), 320
Mohammed, Ibrahim, 267–68
Mohammed, Imad, 62, 64–65
Mohammed, Lubna, 317–19
Mohammed, Majid, 119, 120
Mohammed, Sara, 120
Mohammed, Shakir, 284–86
Mohammed, Suad, 93, 150–53, 317–18, 329, 330, 331
Mohammed, Yasmine, 150, 317, 320–22, 324, 328–30, 398
Mohammedi, Shihab, 233
Mohieddin, Khaled, 229
Mohsin, Hamid Abed, 272
Mongols, 62–63, 130, 163, 388
Mosul, 85, 97–98, 144, 146
Mubarak, Hosni, 15
Muhsin Mosque, 176, 178, 185, 264, 376
mujahideen (Islamic fighters), 270, 290, 345
Muljam, Ibn (assassin of Ali), 161
Musa, Yasmine, 90–93
Musawi, Sayyid Hassoun, 76
Muslim Brotherhood, 186, 287
Mustafa, Nazir, 123
Mustasim (caliph of Baghdad), 62
Mutanabi (10th-century sage), 247
Mutanabi (poet), 18

Naama, Ahmed, 354
Nadhme, Qudus, 274
Nadhme, Wamidh, 6–7, 44–47, 71, 180–82, 215, 272–74, 381–83, 385
Najaf, 4, 29, 67, 78, 97, 164, 166, 350–52
    assassination of Khoie at, 192
    assassination of Hakim at, 253–58, 265
    elder Sadr and, 170–71
    Horan vists, 262
    Muqtada Sadr and, 173–75, 185–86, 257–59
    religious leadership of, 88, 170, 173, 188
    tomb of Ali at, 161
    tombs of imams in, 161
    uprising, 359, 370
Nasiriya, 103, 158, 170, 175, 186
    Sadr movement and uprising, 359, 363, 365, 367, 370
Nasrallah, Hassan, 364–65
Nasser, Gamal Abdel, 45, 169, 302
nationalism, 9, 280, 283–84, 287–88, 375
National Library, 203
National Museum of Antiquities, 130, 203
natural gas plants, 201, 282
Nebuchadnezzar, King of Babylonia, 33
Negroponte, John D., 197
Nicephorus I, of Constantiople, 33
Noaman Hospital, 269
Nouri, Jaafar, 191
Nouri, Mohammed Ali, 191
Nouri, Sayyid Riyadh al-, 172, 189–91, 259, 362

Obeid, Hussein, 115–16
Obeid, Saad, 115
Obeid, Sheikh Tareq, 214
occupation (U.S. administration)
    alternative scenario of, 211–13
    anger at, in Fallujah, 233–235
    anger at, on anniversary of Saddam's fall, 384–86
    architecture of, in Baghdad, 319
    army dissolved by, 151–53

billboards in Baghdad by, 316–17, 383
blamed for insurgency, 265–73, 345, 355–57
blamed for lack of security and infrastructure problems, 210–11, 321–23, 326–28
chaos of, and Iraqi feeling of powerlessness, 334
collapse of, in uprisings of Falluja and Shiites, 359, 373–77
cooperators threatened, 312–13
disappointment in and pessimism about, 215–18, 328–31, 334–35
early resentment of, 138, 200–5, 210–11, 214–15
early resentment of Iraqis toward, 96
effect of, on Sunnis and Arab world, 228
electricity shortages and, 95
formal end of, 359
formal UN declaration of, 197–98
Green Zone as symbol of, 260–61
humanitarian aid not provided by, 338–39
incompetence of, 247, 317–21, 326, 329
Iraqis cry out vs., 333
Iraqis working for, targeted, 282
Iraqi term *ihtilal* for and symbolism of, 197–99, 217–18
Islam and meaning in Sunni triangle during, 232–33
Islamist jihad vs., 303–7
isolation of, from Iraqis and failure of, 259, 261–62
lack preparation for, 132–33
legitimacy and, 157
linked to Palestine, by Arab world, 228
looting, lawlessness, and disrepair allowed by, 132, 134, 140–41, 148–49, 151–53, 210
non-Muslim, of Muslim country, 235
official beginning of, 197–98
police recruited by, 236–40
promises broken by, 216–17, 272, 298, 339, 343, 346–47

Sadr calls for Sunni-Shiite uprising vs., 374–79
Sadr movement vs., 180, 258–63, 360–63, 367–71
seen through prism of Islam and perception of martyrs, 292–93
Shiite attitudes toward, 164, 174
Shiite politics and, 260–61
staff for, inexperienced, 260–61
Sunni regions feel besieged during, 239–45
Sunnis redefined by, 220–22, 224–25
surreal optimism of, in face of growing insurgency, 279
unintended consequences of, 280
Odeh, Ali, 353
Office of Reconstruction and Humanitarian Assistance, 133
oil, 21, 45
British colonial rule and, 17–18
invasion and, 47, 52, 200, 306
occupation and, 197
sabotage and, 201, 282, 236
Omar, Abu, 131
Omar, Ahmed, 55
Omar, caliph (634–44), 160
"Operation Iraqi Freedom," 87, 132, 332
"Operation Peninsula Strike," 220–24, 241
Order No. 2, 151–52
Ottoman Empire, 17, 88, 138, 160, 163, 180, 227, 386–88
Our Economy (Sadr), 246
Our Philosophy (Sadr), 246

Pachachi, Adnan, 373
Palestine, 122, 291. *See also* Israeli-Palestinian conflict
occupation of Iraq linked to, 228, 233, 303–4, 306, 376–77
Palestine Hotel, 60–61, 113–15
Palestinian refugee camps, 287
pan-Arabism, 45, 227
Persian Empire, fall of, 23, 34
Plato, 20

Pollard, Sgt. Charles, 205–9, 211, 212
postwar plan, lack of, 132–34
power plants, breakdowns and sabotage, 134, 201, 236, 282. *See also* electricity shortages
privacy, violations of Iraqi, 200
Protsyuk, Taras, 114
provisional government, plan to choose, 343
Ptolemy, 20
public health, 334
public transportation, 204

Qadisiya (battle of 637), 23, 27
Qassem, Gen. Abdel-Karim, 46, 65, 158
Qatar, 95, 339
Qawliya (Gypsy village), 366–67
Quds, Ammar Abu Nour, 309
Quds Army, 146

Radio Monte Carlo, 96, 97
Rahmaniya neighborhood, 74, 81
Rajoub, Dhiaa Din, 238–39, 240
Ramadan
    bombings, 265–72, 321, 343, 356, 373
    Iraqi security forces and, 283, 284
Ramadan, Taha Yassin, 113, 129
Rammadi, 237, 238, 240
Rashad police station, Baghdad, 207–11
Rashid, Abdel-Naser, 230
Rashid, Harun al- (caliph), 18, 33, 139, 304
Rathenau, Walter, 131
Ratledge, Specialist Seneca, 201, 205
Reagan, Ronald, 92, 134
reconstruction, 197, 248, 261, 282, 373
Red Zone, 239
Republican Guard, 106, 107, 146, 163–64, 171, 181, 225
Republican Palace
    barriers around, 319
    bombing of Baghdad and, 53
    captured by US troops, 107, 114
    occupation headquarters in, 151, 239
Ricks, Thomas E., 199, 201–3, 205, 206

rif (countryside), culture of, 27, 226
Rubaie, Muhammed Nuhair, 394–95
Rubaie, Muwafaq, 380
Rubaie, Sheikh Abbas, 171, 362, 363
Rudeini, Alaa, 202
Rumayadh, Jassim, 241
Rumsfeld, Donald, 92, 132, 133, 232

Saad, Mustafa, 265
Saadeddin, Faruq Ahmed, 55, 83–87, 89, 322–23, 325–29, 346, 379, 398
Saadeddin, Mona, 83–85, 89, 325–28
Saadeddin, Nadeen, 84–87, 323, 324
Saadeddin, Omar, 55, 83–87, 89, 322–25, 327
Saadeddin, Yasmine, 83–85
Saadi, Sheikh Nasser al-, 380
Saad Ibn Abi Waqqas (7th-century general), 34
Sabah (informer), 241–44, 251, 252
Sabar, Sheikh Aalam, 292
sabotage, 201, 282
Sabti, Abdel-Hakim, 235
Sadat, Anwar, 302
Saddam Art Center, 154
Saddam City, 18, 148, 156–57, 170
    renamed Sadr City, 158
Sadeq, Shihab, 269
Sadiq, Jaafar al- (sixth Shiite imam), 168
Sadiq, Yahya, 393–94
Sadr, Mohammed Baqir al-, 164, 177, 246, 351, 361
Sadr, Grand Ayatollah Mohammed Mohammed Sadiq al- (elder), 124, 167, 169–72, 177–78, 189–91, 361, 365
Sadr, Mouamil, 171
Sadr, Muqtada, 167–78, 180, 182–83, 185–88, 191–93, 211, 212, 214, 232, 235, 251. *See also* Mahdi Army
    calls for expulsion of U.S. from Najaf, 256–60
    funding of, 186
    Horan on, 262–63
    Khoie assassination and, 192

Shiite uprisings and, 351, 358–71, 374–82, 386
Sunni-Shiite unity and, 374–79
U.S. attempt to arrest, 363
Sadr, Mustafa, 171
Sadr City, 176, 183, 185, 261
protests over helicopter and flag in, 263–65, 362
Shiite patrols establish order in, 158–59, 175
uprising, 359, 370–71, 375–80
USAID clean-up effort in, 212–15
Safi, Adnan, 378–79
Saher, Kadhim al-, 28, 97
Sahhaf, Mohammed Saeed al-, 1, 113–14, 129
Saidi, Saad Hashem, 354–55
Saif, Abu, 105, 109
Saif, Um, 101
St. Rafael Hospital, 140
Salah, Abbas Ahmed, 25, 26
Saleh, Sheikh Abed, 290
Saleh, Thaer Abdullah, 238, 240
Salih, Awatif Faraj, 202
Salih, Rasul, 202
Salim, Jawad, 137
Salim, Mohammed, 217
Salman, Ali, 57–59, 97–100, 146–50, 335, 342, 344–46
Salman, Amal (Amal Hussein al-Shameri), 57, 98–109, 140–47, 149, 333–40, 344, 346, 347, 398
Salman, Duaa, 57, 99, 100, 103, 142, 149, 338, 340, 341
Salman, Fatima, 57–58, 98–100, 103, 148, 149, 335, 340, 344, 345
Salman, Hibba, 57, 99, 100, 103, 142, 149, 338, 340, 341, 347
Salman, Karima, 56–59, 97–102, 103, 104, 106, 108, 140, 147–50, 332–38, 340–49
Salman, Mahdi, 355
Salman, Mahmoud, 103, 149, 337–38, 344

Salman, Mohammed, 98, 99, 103, 141–42, 149, 335
Salman, Zainab, 57, 99, 100, 103, 145, 338, 340, 345
Salvadoran troops, 370
Samarai, Hashim, 268
Samarai, Maher, 17–18
Samarra, 89, 161, 237
Sanchez, Lt. Gen. Ricardo, 263, 309
sanctions, 8, 24, 37–41, 92, 164, 212, 272, 339
end of, 197
Sarraji, Alaa, 377
Sassanid Empire, 23
Saud, Ahmed, 230
Saud, Fawzi, 229–30
Saud, Taysir, 230
Saudi Arabia, 40, 339
Sayyib, Latif, 285
Sayyib, Wathban, 285
schools, 141, 335, 271
looting of, 140
Schroeder, Capt. Gerd, 201
security. *See* insurgency; lawlessness, looting, and security problems
Seif, Abu, 336, 358
Seminary, The (Sadr newspaper), 361
closed by CPA, 367–69
Senor, Dan, 375
September 11, 2001 attacks, 14–15, 47, 225, 252, 304
sewage and sanitation problems, 37, 38, 70, 134, 210, 214, 334
Shaabani, Ahmed, 300–301
Shaabani, Muthanna, 300
Shaabani, Omar, 291, 299–301
Shaab neighborhood, 79, 81, 266, 268–70
Shahid Sadr General Hospital, 376
Shahmani, Sheik Adnan, 186
Shaltak, Shoja, 209
Shameri, Amal Alwan Ameer al-, 337
Shawki, Ali, 156–59, 165, 175, 179, 183
Shields, Col. Guy, 231–32, 238

Shiite Marsh Arabs, 164
Shiite Muslims. *See also* Ashura;
      Karbala; Najaf; Sadr City; *and*
      specific clerics and leaders
   aid to Iraqis by, 212–14
   armed patrols establish order, 156–57
   books become available, 246
   clerics, 156–60, 212–14
   elections and, 343
   ethnic divisions and, 88
   fall of Baghdad and, 124
   Hakim assassination and, 254–58
   hierarchy of authority and, 301,
      302
   history of, 160–64
   Iraqi nation and, 25
   Kadhimiya shrine and, 35
   Karbala and, 162, 350–51
   Najaf and, 78, 253–54, 350–51
   religious identity and, 88
   religious taxes and, 186
   representatives of, 312
   resurgence of, 9, 157, 159–60, 164–67,
      180, 182, 232, 347–51
   sacred cities of, 29–30
   Saddam and, 4, 94, 221, 313–14
   Sadr movement, rise of, 173–93, 262
   shrines, Saddam and, 36
   Sunnis and, 91, 202
   Sunni schism with, 160–61
   uprising of 1991, 144, 163–64, 188,
      351, 379
   uprisings of 2005 after Karbala and
      Kadhimiya bombings, 359–71
Shinseki, Gen. Eric, 132
Shuala neighborhood, 75–77, 79, 81,
      112
Shukur, Nahad, 21–22
Shuweili, Sheikh Abdel-Rahman, 183–86
Sistani, Grand Ayatollah Ali, 177, 186,
      187–92, 211, 232, 235, 256, 257,
      262, 343, 363
Sistani, Mohammed Jawad, 189
Sistani, Mohammed Rida, 189–91
Sleikh neighborhood, 24

Special Republican Guard, 146
Sufian, Ahmed, 77
Sufis, 249
suicide bombings, 253, 353–55
Sumerian civilization, 136
Sunni Muslims (Arabs)
   Arab culture and, 227–28
   armed opposition of, unanticipated, 221
   diversity in, 88–89
   elite, 88–89
   hostility of, to U.S. troops, 200, 202–3
   insurgency and, 9, 201, 220–45, 253,
      235, 280–88, 298
   insurgency of, converges with Mahdi
      Army, 367, 378–80, 382
   Iraqi nation and, 25
   loss of power and humiliation of, 89,
      180, 221–22, 232
   Saddam and poor, 223
   Saddam's capture and, 309–13
   tribes, 144
   vacuum of authority in, and political
      Islam, 232–35, 301–3, 312–13
Sunni regions (Triangle), 201. *See also*
      specific towns
   anger of, at occupation, 220, 228–44
   insurgency of, in fall 2003, 252,
      280–88
   legitimacy issue and, 235–36
   rural traditions and Islamic identity of,
      283–84, 287–88
   U.S. raids into, 253
Sunni-Shiite relations
   history of schism, 160–63
   unity and revolt vs. British, 387
   unity, Sadr and, 262
Supreme Council for the Islamic
      Revolution in Iraq, 174, 256, 364
Syria, 40, 46, 85, 303

Tabatabai, Sayyid Mohammed, 172
Ta'i, Abu Zeid, 247
Taimiya, Ibn (14th-century scholar), 302
Talib, Hakim, 240
Talib, Jalal, 74

Tarek, Ziad, 209
Tarfi, Fuad, 368, 369
Tawil, Hussein, 366–67
telephone problems, 55, 70, 152, 153,
    204, 240
Thijil, Farhan, 352
Thousand and One Nights, A, 139, 148
Thuluyah (town), 27, 89, 219–28, 236,
    241–44, 251, 253, 282, 310, 312
Tigris river
    sewage and, 38
    symbolism of, 18, 19, 62
Tikrit, 27, 89, 144, 242, 307, 310
Touma, Raymond, 268
Tourism Board, 65, 250
Towfiq, Ehab, 342
tribal authority and law, 226–27, 230–31,
    241–43, 281, 285
tribes, 88
Tuama, Abdel-Rahman, 360–61
Tunis neighborhood, 394
Turkey, 40, 186–87, 287
Turkomans, 88

Ubaidi tribe, 226
unemployment, 135, 141, 147–50, 152,
    204, 283, 284, 328–29, 335–42
United Nations, 208, 343
    headquarters bombed, 253, 254, 271,
        356
    Security Council, 24, 37–38, 197,
        200
United States. *See also* occupation seen
    as infidel, 235, 236, 292, 298, 304,
        305, 316
U.S. Agency for International
    Development, 212, 213, 340
U.S. Army, 78, 208, 370
    1st Armored Division, 199–206, 371
    3rd Armored Cavalry Regiment, 231,
        294
    4th Infantry Division, 222–23, 242,
        307
    43rd Combat Engineering Company,
        294

82nd Airborne Division, 233, 371
307th Military Police Company,
    206
entry Baghdad, 105–9, 113–25
U.S. Central Command, 110, 120
U.S. Congress, 132
U.S. Defense Department (Pentagon),
    132, 133
U.S. Marines, 1st Expeditionary Force,
    371–73, 381
U.S. military
    attacks on, by insurgents, 206, 237–38,
        282, 294–300, 305–6
    early occupation of Baghdad and, 138,
        199–211
    enter Baghdad, 120–25
    Fallujah protesters killed by, 233
    Iraqi perception of, 142, 199–205,
        212–15, 218
    Iraqis insulted by behavior of, 138,
        142, 204, 234, 311, 327
    maps of Baghdad, 200
    morale of, 206–11
    occupation staff vs., 261
    Palestine Hotel attacked by, 114–15
    restrictions on reporters' conversations
        with, 206
    Sunni insurgency and raids, 219–20,
        223, 225–26, 228–31, 237–38, 253,
        294
    troop rotation, in 2004, 367
    troop strength and, 132–33
    unprepared for occupation, 132–34
U.S. National Security Presidential
    Directive No. 24, 133
U.S. Special Forces, 213, 284–85, 369
U.S. State Department, 92
    Bureau of Near Eastern Affairs, 133
Upton, Capt. Stewart, 110
Ur, 51
Uthman, caliph (A.D. 644–56), 160

vendettas, 226–27, 242–43, 281
Vidal, Maj. Arthur P., III, 213–14
Vrozina, Gayle, 38, 274–76

Wahhabis, 262, 355
Wahid, Samir Abed, 385–86
Wala'a General Humanitarian
    Organization, 212–13
water shortages, 37, 55, 68, 70, 105, 147,
    148, 175, 205, 210, 213, 323,
    333–35, 343
Watson, Capt. Andrew, 231
weapons of mass destruction, 8, 215, 272
Witness to the Fall (Salim), 217
Wolfowitz, Paul, 132
women, 204, 229, 230
    rights, 21, 135
    veil and, 36, 185

Yaacoubi, Sayyid Mustafa al-, 172,
    362–63, 369–70

Yarmuk Hospital, 105, 130
Yarmuk neighborhood, 200–205
Yassin, Sheikh Ahmed, 378
Yazid, 164, 347, 348
Yazidis, 88
Yusuf, Atef, 112
Yusuf, Hamid, 280, 281, 283–86
Yusuf, Nizar, 254–55

Zafraniya neighborhood, 130
Zaidan, Dr. Asad, 3, 4
Zarqawi, Abu Musab al-, 287, 355
Zayir, Sadiq, 348
Zeinal, Emad, 29–32
Zinni, Gen. Anthony C., 120
Zionism, 265
Zubeidi, Mohammed Arsan, 270

ABOUT THE AUTHOR

Anthony Shadid is the Islamic affairs correspondent for the *Washington Post*. Since September 11, 2001, he has reported from Egypt, Lebanon, Iraq, the Persian Gulf, Europe, Afghanistan, Pakistan, and Israel and Palestine, where he was wounded in the back while covering the fighting in the West Bank. In March 2003, weeks before the U.S. invasion, he traveled to Iraq, his third visit to the country. He remained in Baghdad during the invasion, the fall of Saddam Hussein, and the war's aftermath. He left in June 2004, then returned later that year.

Shadid previously worked for the *Boston Globe* in Washington, covering diplomacy and the State Department. He began his career at the Associated Press in Milwaukee, New York, Los Angeles, and Cairo, where he was a Middle East correspondent from 1995 to 1999. He is a native of Oklahoma City, where his grandparents emigrated from Lebanon, and a graduate of the University of Wisconsin–Madison.

Shadid was awarded the Pulitzer Prize for International Reporting in 2004 for his dispatches from Iraq. That year, he was also the recipient of the American Society of Newspaper Editors' award for deadline writing and the Overseas Press Club's Hal Boyle Award for best newspaper or wire service reporting from abroad. In 2003, Shadid was awarded the George Polk Award for foreign reporting for a series of dispatches from the Middle East while at the *Boston Globe*. In 1997, he was awarded a citation by the Overseas Press Club for his work on "Islam's Challenge." That four-part series, published by the AP in December 1996, formed the basis of his book *Legacy of the Prophet: Despots, Democrats and the New Politics of Islam*, published by Westview Press in December 2000.